Osceola's Legacy

Fire Ant Books

A Dan Josselyn Memorial Publication

Osceola's Legacy

Revised Edition

PATRICIA RILES WICKMAN

THE UNIVERSITY OF ALABAMA PRESS
Tuscaloosa

Typeface: Sabon

∞

The paper on which this book is printed meets the minimum requirements of American National Standard for Information Sciences-Permanence of Paper for Printed Library Materials, ANSI Z39.48–1984.

Library of Congress Cataloging-in-Publication Data

Wickman, Patricia R. (Patricia Riles)
Osceola's legacy / Patricia Riles Wickman.— Rev. ed.
p. cm. — (Fire ant book)
Includes bibliographical references and index.
ISBN-13: 978-0-8173-5332-2 (pbk. : alk. paper)
ISBN-10: 0-8173-5332-1
1. Osceola, Seminole chief, 1804–1838. 2. Osceola, Seminole chief,
1804–1838—Death and burial. 3. Osceola, Seminole chief, 1804–1838—Portraits.
4. Seminole Indians—Kings and rulers—Biography. 5. Seminole Indians—History.
I. Title. II. Series. III. Fire ant books.
E99.S28O88 2006
975.9004'973859092—dc22

2005034156

To Genie Price and Sam Proctor, who believed . . . and, above all, to the Seminole people, who survived!

Contents

List of Illustrations / ix

Acknowledgments / xi

Preface to the Revised Edition / xv

Introduction / 1

1. A Short Life / 5

2. Family Matters / 30

3. Man versus Myth: Setting the Record Straight / 67

4. Through the Eyes of Those Who Saw Him / 107

5. A Lonely Grave / 134

6. The Forensic Report / 153

7. The Search for Osceola's Head / 163

8. The Weedon Family / 200

9. The Weedon Artifacts / 211

10. Osceola's Hair / 223

11. Descendents East and West / 229

12. Pitcairn Morrison's Mementos / 257

13. A Far-Flung Legacy / 265

Epilogue: Two Very Expensive Alleged Osceola Artifacts / 282

Appendix A: Summary of Osceola Artifacts / 291

Appendix B: Graphic Representations of Osceola / 297

Notes / 305

Bibliography / 343

Index / 363

Illustrations

1. Earliest image of Osceola (William Keenan, 1836) / 109

2. First image drawn from life (pencil sketch by
John Rogers Vinton, 1837) / 110

3. Robert John Curtis portrait (oil, 1838) / 117

4. George Catlin (oil, no. 301, 1838) / 118

5. George Catlin (oil, no. 308, 1838) / 120

6. Osceola, two wives, and child (George Catlin,
watercolor, 1849) / 132

7. Frederick Weedon, diary entry, 29 January 1838 / 145

8. Osceola's grave, Fort Moultrie, Sullivan's Island
(Charleston, South Carolina) / 152

9. Osceola, mold from the death cast, 1838 / 176

10. Valentine Mott, M.D., 1857 / 191

11. Home of Valentine Mott, West End, New York City / 194

12. Frederick Weedon, M.D. / 204

13. Mary Wells Thompson Weedon (Mrs. Frederick) / 205

14. Osceola's brass pipe (collected by Weedon) / 216

15. Osceola's silver concho (collected by Weedon) / 217

16. Osceola's silver earrings (collected by Weedon) / 219

17. Osceola's garter (collected by Weedon) / 221

18. Plaited lock of Osceola's hair (collected by Weedon) / 224

19. Young wife of Billy Bowlegs, 1858 / 238

20. Fixico hadjo chupco or "Long Jack" / 239

21. Oceola Nikkanochee / 241

22. John Douglas Bemo / 253

23. Osceola's beaded belt (collected by Webster) / 278

Acknowledgments

Reviewing the original text of these acknowledgments only emphasizes the time that has elapsed since I first undertook this research. Far too many of the individuals who were integral to it then are now deceased, and I treasure their participation and their memory, even as I mourn their loss to the academic community and to all of us who respect our collective past. An entirely new group of individuals has joined in the search, however, and they must be offered the gratitude that they so richly deserve.

As I pointed out originally, no researcher works completely alone. Research advances because the academic community at large chooses to support the enhancement of our total body of knowledge. But the ever-widening circle of interest and support does not include only the members of the academic community. In the case of Osceola, his descendents in blood and in spirit, the Indian people of the lower Southeast, have tremendous personal interest in his story. In every way, his story is also theirs, and they have supported and encouraged this research in ways that I could never fully describe. They are his first family of interest, and they were completely unrepresented when I conducted the original research. I am humbled now, from this vantage point, by my amazingly limited amount of cultural understanding, and I offer them my deepest respect and gratitude for their wisdom, patience, and great humor.

Above all, I thank James E. Billie, chairman of the Tribal Council (1979–2003) of the Seminole Tribe of Florida, for giving me carte blanche, in Florida and Oklahoma, to pursue this research. His commitment to his culture and history is as passionate as was Osceola's, and his wars against the U.S. government continue to this day, changed in form but hardly lessened in intensity. In particular, I also wish to acknowledge Florida tribal citizens Geneva Shore, Maryjene Cypress Coppedge, LaVonne Kippenberger, and Henry John Billie (now deceased) for their long and unwavering support of their cultural and linguistic heritage and for their patience with my incessant questions. In Oklahoma, Seminole Nation citizens Lewis and Louise Carpitche, Ted Underwood, and Seminole County supervisor of elections Joe Cully (deceased) were warmhearted and helpful in critical ways. These were the principal people who provided the "ground truthing" (as the archaeologists say) for the entire research.

Research as complex and far-ranging as that described here could never have been undertaken, much less brought to any semblance of fruition, without the help of a large number of my academic colleagues as well. They made their own expertise, as well as the resources of their organizations, available time and again over a period of many years. I gladly—and gratefully—share with them the joy of the completion of this new phase of the research. I myself, however, am completely responsible for the misuse of any information they have so graciously shared. Samuel Proctor (also deceased), distinguished service professor of history at the University of Florida, Gainesville, and long-time editor of the *Florida Historical Quarterly,* offered critical advice and support during the first phase of the research. Jerald T. Milanich, past professor of anthropology at the Florida Museum of Natural History/University of Florida, and John Mahon (now deceased), professor emeritus of history, University of Florida, critiqued the work and enthusiastically provided contacts and suggested avenues of investigation.

The resources of the Museum of Florida History and the Division of Historical Resources, Tallahassee, were invaluable to the original research. Among sources for the materials, Mary Weedon Keen (now deceased) repeatedly made her documents, artifacts, memories, and even her home available for this research. She was a staunch protector of her family's heritage and an intrepid avocational researcher. Mr. and Mrs. C. M. Howell and Gregg Weedon Howell also were most generous in their willingness to share important family papers. John Griffin (also deceased), formerly chief archaeologist for the southeast region of the Department of the Interior/National Park Service, had a long-standing personal interest in this subject and shared his work most generously. His work at Osceola's grave at Charleston provided the touchstone for important segments of this research.

It was not only fortunate but also vital that numerous good researchers were just a telephone call or a short drive away. Their knowledge and willingness to share were superseded only by their patience. Curators Robert Cason and Robert Bradley, Alabama state archaeologist Greg Waselkov, and curator of education Alice Knierim of the Alabama Department of Archives and History took personal interest in ferreting out artifacts, documents, and sources that were critical to making sense out of some very obscure shreds of evidence. Michael Carrigan, assistant director of the National Museum of American History, Smithsonian Institution (SI), graciously made important sources available. Jim Hutchins, historian of the Dwight D. Eisenhower Institute for Historical Research/SI, generously shared his personal research and even volunteered to investigate National Archives files. Edward Garner, in charge of the physical anthropology collections at the National Museum of Natural History/SI, patiently withstood esoteric questions, even before his first cup of morning coffee.

The list goes on. Helen Purdy and Esperanza Varona of the Otto G. Richter Library, University of Miami, Coral Gables, guided me through the myriad documents of the Mark F. Boyd Collection and personally provided many additional details. Director Page Edwards and librarian Jacqueline Fretwell (both now deceased) of the St. Augustine Historical Society always had time to discuss esoteric points and offer helpful information. Forensic anthropologist William Maples (also deceased), C. A. Pound Human Identification Laboratory, Florida Museum of Natural History/University of Florida, Gainesville, clarified scientific material that was integral to the research. John Mulrennan, director of the Department of Entomology, Department of Health and Rehabilitative Services, Jacksonville, even volunteered to bring his own microscope to assist with the project.

Despite the geographic range of the project, the brunt of the work regularly fell upon my close colleagues, the staff of the State Library of Florida (SLF), in Tallahassee. Joan Morris, founder of the Florida Photographic Collection, Florida State Archives/SLF, enthusiastically cooperated in locating 150 years' worth of images of Osceola. Dr. Dorothy Dodd (also deceased), one of the undisputed deans of Florida history, had an insatiable thirst for knowledge and an indefatigable sense of humor. Receiving her enthusiastic assistance and patient interest will long remain an honor to me. Furthermore, no members of the circulation, reference, documents, and genealogy sections were safe from my continuing search.

Last, but far from least, I must thank all of the museums listed throughout this document whose artifacts and graphics were the core of the original research. Caring staff members combed files, attics, and storerooms for bits of information, sometimes long disused, that might finally make sense in the light of current research. More important, they reaffirmed the quality of the professionals who work in museums around the world.

Preface to the Revised Edition

First and foremost, I want to express my appreciation to the thousands of readers who have bought and enjoyed the first edition of this book. At the same time, however, it has been your kind compliments that have impelled me to revise it. In my original research, I focused on the material culture that had survived Osceola—his legacy to all of us. That research was undertaken on the premise that his material culture legacy was the only part of his story that remained insufficiently explored. So much had been written about the man that the documentary element of the search seemed complete. But this did not prove to be the case.

Even the initial publication of the book did not mark the end of my researches into the life and subsequent story of Osceola. Our relationship (his and mine) has continued unabated for more than twenty years now, since I first began to write the book. Even now, I continue to be amazed at the amount of interest that his name and story have generated, and at their durability. The year 2004 marked two complete centuries since his birth. A lesser individual would long since have slipped away into obscurity. And yet, just a couple of years ago, I completed an entry in his name for the *Oxford Companion to American Military History*.[1] Only this past summer, a friend brought home to me a souvenir porcelain statuette of Osceola, fairly accurate in its detail, made in Italy and sold in a tourist shop in Belgium! The Discovery Channel has featured him and his people in its award-winning series *How the West Was Lost*. I am still contacted regularly by individuals who are named after him and want more information about their namesake and by non-Natives who are sure that they are somehow related to him.

To be sure, a main objective of my researches since the initial publication of the book has been to gain a fuller understanding of the cultural, social, and historical context of the man and to locate his missing head. This latter aspect of his story has a high cultural and spiritual value to the Seminole people, and especially the Florida Seminoles, with whom I lived and worked for all the years that the first edition of this book was in publication. It is, consequently, they who have my deepest appreciation for their willingness to share of themselves and of their rich and fascinating universe. It is their belief that the spirit of a deceased person passes out of the physical body through the head in order to make its journey westward, across the Milky Way, to the realm of all the spirits. If the head does not remain connected to the corpus, therefore, the confused spirit may remain too close to the living and can become malevolent, at worst, or a wanderer, at least.

It is indisputable that Osceola's last wish was that his body should be returned to Florida, and this directive is recorded in the pages of Dr. Frederick Weedon's diary as I have printed them here, in chapter 5. It is also indisputable that this wish was ignored by the U.S. military establishment that buried him at Fort Moultrie. Nevertheless, they did bury the famous warrior in a visible and documented location although it is only now, almost 170 years later, that this action has value in the Indian world. Maskókî (Creek) and Seminole tradition would have taken him to a distant and secluded spot where he probably never would have been found again. Consistent with the traditions of his ancestors, however, it is only the members of his own clan who should have the right to make decisions regarding his remains today. Because his clan affiliation appears clear today, the right to speak for him devolves on that clan and the larger people, his tribe. (In chapters 3 and 11, I have added a discussion of Osceola's clan affiliation.) Even this fact presents difficulties, however, because historical U.S. government pressures and disregard for traditions have pushed the core Maskókî—known as the "Muscogee (Creek) Nation"—and Seminole peoples (the "Seminole Nation of Oklahoma") together in Oklahoma in nontraditional living patterns. As a result, Osceola's people fairly may be judged to be in two states and among three tribes today.

Unfortunately, these aspects of Osceola's story—the whereabouts of his head and the disposition of his physical remains—also attract a great deal of interest outside of the tribes, and this interest runs the gamut from academic to New Age spiritual to sensationalist—from the sublime to the ridiculous, as it were. My academic colleagues have provided, and continue to provide, some very sound research leads on this and other parts of the story, for which I am very grateful. On the other hand, however, not so long ago I was contacted by a county commissioner in Florida who offered to call the host of the national television program *America's Most Wanted* and have the search publicized there or, alternatively, to take the fight for possession of the remains to the Florida legislature. Obviously, she did not know of the political battles that had already raged in the early twentieth century between Florida and South Carolina, which I have mentioned in chapter 6. Nor did she realize that the era when non-Indian politicians could choose unilaterally to make decisions regarding federally recognized American Indian tribes is in rapid decline as well. Then, for more than a year, I was besieged by an avocational psychic in Texas to whom Osceola supposedly appeared on full-moon nights, giving her directions on how to find his head at the now-submerged site of a log cabin that had collapsed into a river. Apparently, Osceola never saw fit to mention to that individual how and when he had gotten to Texas in the first place. And an Internet Web site hyping worldwide oddities included the search for Osceola's head among its list of unsolved gory mysteries.

Fortunately, beyond the bizarre facets of the story, there have been numerous legitimate research avenues to explore, involving the people, Indian and non-Indian, whose lives paralleled or crossed Osceola's, and I have been able to add fullness to a number of them. In all fairness, the phenomenal boom in genealogical research that has occurred over the past decade had made the search significantly easier. As but one example, numerous documents that were buried in obscure and seemingly unconnected record groups in the National Archives and Records Administration in Washington, D.C., Fort Worth, Texas, and Atlanta, Georgia, are now available online, from the comfort of one's home. Even relatively esoteric documents such as parish registers of seventeenth-century Scotland are available there for the asking. I am firmly convinced, nevertheless, that no amount of information available online will ever replace the accumulated wisdom of professional archivists, for whom locating esoteric bits of our common past remains a supreme joy.

Above all, however, my own privileged experiences among the Seminole people, both in Florida and with the removed Seminoles in Oklahoma, have tremendously expanded my understanding of the cultural matrix of Osceola's life story. I want to share some of these insights with all of you, my readers, and offer you a fuller glimpse inside of Osceola's world. Even now, however, it has not been possible to put "paid" to the story and, so, the search continues.

Osceola's Legacy

Introduction

The year 2004 marked the two hundredth anniversary of the birth of Osceola, the "Seminole" Indian. The public fascination with the story of Osceola, an intense and passionate warrior who gained a brief period of national notoriety in the 1830s, has extended far beyond the relatively short span of his life (ca. 1804–1838), as well as beyond the relatively limited geographic area where he lived and died. His birth and the obscure period of this youth took place in Alabama and close by the borders of Florida. The conflict with whites that catapulted him into public prominence occurred entirely in Florida, and the final chapter of his life passed, under duress, on a tiny island in the harbor of the South Carolina city of Charleston. During and since that time, however, whites have reported, recorded, discussed, disputed, and rerecorded his alleged exploits.

Herein lies the paradox of the Osceola story, that the primary vehicle for his continued visibility should be the recordings of whites, the specific group most culturally antithetical to an understanding of the man and all of the values for which he fought. For, although a tradition of Osceola has persisted among Florida's latter-day Indian groups, as well as among their relocated cultural kin in Oklahoma, this portion of the story has survived only as oral tradition, thereby precluding the critical element of large-scale dissemination. Moreover, the Indians' own cultural defensiveness has, except in limited individual instances, made them reluctant to discuss these traditions and to share their information with non-Indians.

In a further irony, even as whites have interested themselves in this Indian figure, the attitudes with which they have approached their subject have varied radically. From American expansionist antagonisms of the early nineteenth century, to the white-supremacist disdain of the Darwinian period, through the romantic, the thoughtful, the intellectually curious, and the sensationalists—Osceola's story has provided fertile ground for any and all; tiny would-be truths have been used, discarded, and reshaped to accommodate the point of view of the reporter. The result is that, after all these years, the clues in this fascinating detective story may not be totally lost, but they most definitely are obscured—frequently by individuals attempting to image the man according to cultural traditions not his own. Making chronological and cultural sense out of many of them has been analogous to unraveling a skein of tangled black wool in a very dark room.

Interestingly, one potentially invaluable source of information about Osceola has been almost totally overlooked, and it is the one that was the original impetus for this research: the personal information to be gained from an examination of the artifacts and types of artifacts that were the possessions of the man himself. These artifacts, considered "mementos" or "scientific specimens," were important enough to the whites who were Osceola's contemporaries that they were separated from him, recorded, preserved, cited, and, in the case of at least one, investigated. Thereafter, they were largely ignored for about a century. Only with the rise of the New History in the mid-twentieth century was their investigation broached again, and only in a relatively cursory manner.[1]

Thomas J. Schlereth, in his fine work *Artifacts and the American Past,* observed that "artifacts are cultural statements" and that "the historian's primary function in using artifacts is always to interpret them in their cultural history context."[2] In the case of the current investigations, the search for Osceola's possessions has become, in itself, a doorway to an investigation of the larger, cultural setting that formed the man so well known and so little understood.

I had not originally intended to provide a definitive restatement of Osceola's life story although, throughout the earliest research, this larger story continually revealed itself in a manner that could not be ignored and, over the years, has subsumed the original material culture research. I sought, first, to use one specific class of historical materials, the artifacts, as a point of investigation in order to provide a comprehensive basis for reassessing the entire story. To accomplish this goal, I needed to reconstruct, as fully as possible, the movement of these pieces over the past century and a half. This facet of the research quickly assumed critical proportions for two reasons: by this it was deemed possible to establish an acceptable provenance for artifacts that, at the outset of the project, were believed to exist, and there was the chance of discovering, as well as providing provenance for, other artifacts that had been undisclosed formerly. As it turned out, both possibilities were realized. Given a basic understanding of the historical setting of Osceola's story and the preparation of a comprehensive bibliography, it would have been very easy, however, at the outset of the research, to assume that few undocumented portions of the picture remained. This premise proved to be thoroughly inaccurate. It quickly became apparent that many existing sources had not been tapped, many known and examined sources had not been fully integrated into the larger picture, and certain new ones had become available that were important to a reevaluation of the entire story.

A mail survey of the reported holders of artifacts, as well as numerous other public and private institutions, artifact dealers, and individual collectors who, for geographic, cultural, or professional reasons, might have artifacts or information regarding artifacts, elicited much useful information. In addition, another line of research that developed from the literature and mail survey was a file of graphic images representing Osceola from all periods. Emphasis was given, of course, to contemporary images painted from life, but the entire range of images was useful in establishing the breadth and strength of interest in the Osceola story. As it turned out, this facet of the research became even more important because the graphic images provided visual evidence of the evolution of the complex Osceola story. Some of these "first generation" images are reproduced in this volume. Current economic considerations have limited the overall number of images in this revised edition severely, however. Other images have been elided to make room for some of the images that have come to light since the original publication, which can broaden our understanding of the larger story. Appendix B, however, lists this first generation of graphic representations of Osceola along with their current locations.

As for the artifacts, I was able to examine many of them personally. They were measured, described, and evaluated in the light of current research. In some instances, the artifact images are reproduced in this volume, along with their current locations, when known. Appendix A provides a checklist of Osceola artifacts, including a synopsis of the provenance for cited and located items.

The synthetic phase of the project was, of course, the most complex, the most exciting, the most rewarding, and the least orderly. Hundreds of hours of telephone calls yielded information that had to be checked against known bits of the story, corroborated by any documentation that could be tracked down, pieced together into a coherent whole, and then examined in the light of current historiography. The product (certainly not the *final* product, as I now know), has taken shape like a beautiful tree and has continued to grow since its planting. All of the lines of questioning have been productive, to greater or lesser degrees. Many have borne fruit. Others have been stunted in their growth—they could not survive for 170 years. Osceola, the root, continues to flourish, however. The passion engendered, in his heart as well as in the hearts of his opponents, by his emotional attachment to his Indian heritage and his Florida home, will keep his story fresh and vigorous for many more generations to come.

1 / A Short Life

The man known to the world at large as "Osceola" previously was known to many English speakers of the Southeast as the boy Billy Powell.[1] To his cultural world, the insular world of his mother's Indian clan and her town and her people, his earlier "boy name," the name he received after surviving for his first four months, will never be known to us. Even inside that most personal of worlds, only his closest relatives and the medicine people of his clan and his tribe would have been privy to that name.

He was born in the Maskókî, or "Creek," town of Tallassee, near present-day Tuskegee, Alabama, in or about 1804.[2] He was the child of Polly Copinger, a Tallassee woman, and an English trader named William Powell. He was not Polly's only child, either by William Powell or by other fathers, as we shall soon learn. His later fame became so great that it obscured many family details, but there are sufficient references in later documents as to make it a certainty that he was not an only child. The Powells' nuclear family also included William's two daughters by a previous marriage with an Indian woman, possibly the clan sister of Polly Copinger. The possibility that Billy Powell's mother and William Powell's earlier wife were clan sisters proceeds from the fact that the daughters remained with William and Polly after the girls' mother passed out of the picture, in whatever manner. If the girls' mother had been of a different clan, she would have taken the girls with her. If she had died, her mother and her clan would have taken the girls nonetheless. These are only possibilities, not certainties, but they are consistent with Maskôkî and Seminole traditions that persist in many instances to the present day.[3]

Billy Powell's first nine years were fairly stable. His maternal great-grandfather, a Scotsman named James McQueen, was highly influential among the Tallassee people. James was reputed to have been the first white man to have gone among the Tallassees, and the Tallassees gave him one of their daughters for a wife. His own daughter, Ann, called Nancy, married a man whose surname was Copinger, about whom little can be known, but more can be conjectured (see chapter 2).

By the time of Billy's birth, many of the Tallassee townspeople were mixed-blood Indian/English/Scottish, and some few may have had African blood as well. Billy himself may have been all of these. By the time of his birth, the English language was becoming ubiquitous in the Creek territories, as the Spanish language had been up until only fifty or so years before. Billy had a facility for languages—a valuable attribute in the world of his day. He almost certainly heard, understood, and, probably, spoke English in addition to core Maskôkî or Creek, his native tongue, although, for political and cultural reasons, he obscured this facility from both Indians and whites. He undoubtedly heard, and may have been functional in, Hitchiti (now called *Mikísuúkî,* or "Miccosukee"), or other dialects of the core language, Maskôkî. By the end of his relatively short life, or perhaps long before, he spoke Spanish as well.

It is obvious that, by the genetic standards imposed upon Indians in the United States today, Billy Powell was barely an Indian. His maternal grandmother, Nancy, was a "half blood." His mother's blood quantum was one-quarter. His own quantum, therefore, would have been only one-eighth—enough for citizenship in the (removed) Seminole Nation of Oklahoma, but less than the minimum required for citizenship by the Seminole Tribe of Florida; and enough to be listed on the Tribal Roll, but not enough to hold office in the (removed) Muscogee (Creek) Nation of Oklahoma, all of which tribes are homes to his descendents to this day. It is instructive to consider this reality, if only in order to understand the limits of its value. Of all the Indians of the Southeast over time, perhaps none stands in higher relief than the heroic and tragic figure of the warrior Osceola, whom Billy Powell will become. Certainly no one would question his "Indianness," his commitment to an Indian identity, or the passion of his resistance to the forced removal of his people from their ancient homeland. Yet, judged artificially—that is, by genetic standards alone—he was hardly an Indian at all.

At the same time, however, his family background was not unique among his generation. It was, more accurately, his generation that seems to have been unique in the history of the Creek tribes. Billy Powell was born into an era when Anglo-Americans—"whites"—were making not strictly speaking their first but certainly their most significant genetic and cultural impact upon the Indian people of the lower Southeast. As a result, he grew up between two cultures. Many of his day—and of his own family—rebelled earlier and more violently and renounced the white culture entirely. Throughout his short adult life, Osceola attempted to walk a peaceful line between the two. But the white people and their times would not permit him the luxury of peace.

Within a few short years of his birth, Billy Powell's world began to destabilize. In 1811, his great-grandfather died. Power passed to James McQueen's son, Peter McQueen, the most politically active of the four known children and clan grandfather (great-uncle) to young Billy. In that same year, the clouds of war began to gather over his home. Tecumseh, the great Shawanóe (Shawnee) orator and disciple of his brother, Tensquátowah (the Open Door), called a prophet by whites, came among the southeastern Creek tribes. He spoke to a council of the Creeks in the town center of Billy's own town and preached war and destruction as the only means of ridding all of the Indians of the evils brought by the whites.

Peter McQueen "took his talk" and was among the Creek warriors and medicine people (frequently all called prophets by whites) who returned with Tecumseh to his people in the north to learn more. When the Creek men returned to their own homes almost a year later, they brought the seeds of war. They abjured the northerly tribes around them and the more southerly, or "lower" tribes to rise up against the whites and kill them or, at the least, push them out. Benjamin Hawkins, the powerful U.S. Indian agent, was able to influence many of the lower tribes not to rise up. The unfortunate result of their decision not to go to war, however, was the instigation of a civil struggle, known in Euroamerican history as the Creek War of 1813–1814. It pitted the anti-white faction of the more northerly ("upper") Creek towns (those whose leaders had taken the red sticks that signified their bellicose intentions) against the more southerly ("lower") towns that wanted to remain on friendly terms with the whites.

This condition of civil warfare would have been enough to destroy the peace, even if Andrew Jackson had not chosen to enter into the fray. He saw an opportunity to settle the old "Indian problem," gain military preferment, and position himself in the national spotlight all at the same time. The results were disastrous for the family, the town, the people, and the world of Billy Powell.[4] For Jackson and the United States, however, the results were highly favorable. The concluding Treaty of Fort Jackson, forced upon the Creeks, broke their military control of the territory and, of even more profound consequence to the Indian people, effectively ended their cultural dominance over the lower Southeast.[5]

The larger war of this same period, the U.S.-British War of 1812, ended in 1814 also, with the signing of the Treaty of Ghent. The British, in an attempt to reward the bravery of the Creek warriors who had fought with them against the United States, negotiated as Article Nine of that treaty the requirement that the United States restore to the Creeks all of the lands they had occupied in 1811, that is, prior to the war. The United States, however, for political and cultural reasons, chose to ignore this article, and the Creek tribes—those that had been loyal to the United States as well as those that had fought against it—were coldly dispossessed of their ancestral homes. Thus began the southeastern "Trail of Tears" that propelled many of the southeastern Maskókî tribes westward, across the Mississippi, in an attempt to avoid the trajectory of white settlement.

Many of the warriors and their families who had survived these horrendous events, however, migrated southward, across the international frontier between the U.S. territory that would become Alabama and the still-Spanish province of Florida. Among them were Peter McQueen and his nuclear family, although Peter's sister and brothers seem to have remained in or near their old town, about six miles south of present-day Tuskegee, in Macon County, Alabama. William Powell and Polly Copinger went along with Peter, as well as Billy Powell (who was now about nine years of age) and William's daughters by his first marriage, who would have been about fourteen and eighteen years old. Soon after their departure, however, if not immediately upon it, William and his elder daughters (who certainly accompanied him by their own choice), turned eastward and remained near the Chattahoochee River until at least 1836–1838, when they emigrated farther still, to Indian Territory in the West. Billy and his mother, and probably other clan relatives as well, moved into Florida with Peter McQueen and his warriors.

At this point the story of the family divides yet again. Peter McQueen and his warriors kept up their resistance to U.S. authority, skirmishing with U.S. troops and moving continually down and across the Florida peninsula. His wife, Betsy Durant, and their four children went with him. Peter died in late 1818 or early 1819 at Cape Florida, his camp on the Atlantic Ocean side of the peninsula. Betsy and the children returned to the Tallassee area, where she remarried one of Peter's brother's sons, Willy, and had four or five more children.

Throughout those same five or six years, while Peter and his warriors were fighting farther and farther down the peninsula, Billy and his mother and the clan lived a seminomadic life in the region between the St. Marks and the Suwannee rivers in northern Florida. The ongoing conflicts between Andrew Jackson's U.S. forces and the Indians would not permit them to reestablish peace and stability. Nor would the next stages of the United States' eastern Wars of Indian Removal permit them to find a lasting peace ever again in their lives.

Shortly after 1818, with the end of Jackson's military campaign in Spanish Florida, Billy and his mother, who had taken another husband and probably had had at least two more male children, moved farther southward, into central Florida. Here they entered a short period of less transience, but one nonetheless tenuous, due partly to the vacillating attitude of the U.S. government toward the future of all the Florida Indians and partly to a period of severe climatic conditions that prevented the Indians from producing sufficient crops to sustain themselves adequately. It was undoubtedly during their stay in this area, however, when young Billy gained his ceremonial name—the one by which he would be known forever after. (For a discussion of this event, see chapter 3.) In addition, in the course of a traditional life, at some point during the ten years following his passage into manhood, the young adult Osceola would have entered into an arranged marriage and begun to have children. The fact that we have no documentary evidence regarding this facet of his personal life does not preclude its probability.

In preparation for his role as a warrior, he also was apprenticed to one of the most powerful medicine practitioners of his day, Abéca. In fact, this facet of Osceola's warrior training might have begun even before he completed his right of passage into manhood. Most consistent with tradition was the probability that Abéca chose him, rather than the opposite.

Already old in his years and in his power, Abéca was the holder of more than three hundred years of tradition, medicine, and power incorporated in a single name, which echoes even to the present day among his Florida descendents. As early as the sixteenth century, the Spaniards had documented a town identified by that name (in current north-central Alabama) as one of the "mother" towns of the Maskókî (Creek) people.[6] Consistent with its position as a founding town or, more accurately, as a town of founding people, the word signified in Maskókî, "he goes ahead, he goes out in front." The name was passed down from clan father (maternal uncle) to son/nephew and, therefore, inside the same clan, along with the esoteric traditions of making the most powerful of war medicines. Dislodged from his ancient seat and forced southward by the same encroachments of whites that ultimately dislodged Billy Powell's family, the clan father of Abéca from whom he had obtained the succession had reached Florida at least by the mid-1700s. He was already an old and venerable man and was known to whites as their implacable foe by the time of the British treaty council with the Indians held on the Alachua savanna in 1765.[7]

His name and the name of the town, being the same, and passed down through the generations specifically because of its power, accrued even greater power with the passing of the years and the cumulative knowledge and skills of its holders. By 1837, he resided at the village of Okahumke, in central Florida.[8] Variant spellings of his name abound, and this has created some confusion in the historical record. Hitchiti speakers (today's "Miccosukees") know him as *Abiákî,* although the meaning remains the same. English speakers have transliterated the name as Arbeka, Arpieka, Arapieka, and Arpiuki, inserting the intrusive English "r" sound.[9] Most often, it was by the Hitchiti word Abiákî that he was known during the nineteenth-century Wars of Removal in Florida. He was a *tastenákî thlocco:* big *(thlocco)* because of his skill at making medicines that would protect him as a warrior *(tasakía tanákî[t]* or *tas'tenákî).* The Indians recall that he taught Osceola to find and make the medicines that would give him military prowess and protect him in war. Thus, even in his too short military career, Osceola also became a tastenákî thlocco. Ultimately, this knowledge of plants and their uses, and the chants that gave them power, would protect him against the mortal damages of white man's bullets, but not against the civilian illnesses to which we all are prey.

By the Treaty of Moultrie Creek, signed in 1823, the U.S. government sought to move most of the Florida Indians—both the survivors of the original Florida tribes, known in English as "Seminolies" or "Seminoles" since the arrival of English speakers in Florida, and the Maskókî Creeks who had migrated southward following the Creek War—on to a four-million-acre tract of central Florida wilderness. The governmental mechanisms for accomplishing the move were slow and unreliable, however, and the Indians were loathe to be pushed together in such a vulnerable and nontraditional manner. Furthermore, white settlers encroached all too frequently on the Indian-assigned area to settle or to trade illegally, especially in liquor, with the Indians. They stole the Indians' cattle, pigs, and horses and thereby increased the level of animosity that already existed between Indians and whites. For their part, the Indians, anxious for food, ammunition, and too often for liquor, provoked and attacked whites, and antagonisms only escalated further over time.

Throughout the 1820s and early 1830s, local and national sentiment for the complete removal of the Florida Indians grew. To complicate matters further, the parallel but separate subject of African slaves, who had been escaping to Spanish Florida for more than a century irrespective of the Indians, began to intrude upon the Indian issue, as the Indians were pressured by the U.S. government to give up slaves they had bought legally or captured or were harboring. At one point, in 1828, the treaty annuity promised to the Indians was withheld in order to increase pressure on them to turn over slaves.[10] The result was, indeed, to exacerbate the hunger of the Indians, but their core resolve to resist removal, and to resist removal of their slaves, was only strengthened. In no manner, however, does this appear to have been an act of solidarity with the slaves. The Indians were fighting a white enemy who wanted to take away everything they were and had. Their slaves were one of many things the white men were not going to take away.

National sentiment in favor of removal was ultimately codified in the Indian Removal Act, which passed Congress in 1830 almost immediately upon the elevation of Andrew Jackson to the U.S. presidency. Osceola witnessed the increasing antagonisms between Indians and whites, and this only increased his own personal commitment to the anti-emigration fight of the Creek warriors, a fight that had been begun partly by his own family. Several cultural factors, however, both positive and negative, influenced the manner in which his attitudes and abilities would be exercised among the Indians.

It is critical to an understanding of Osceola's short but brilliant public career to realize, first and foremost, that he was never an official leader of any group of Indians other than those clan members and the few African slaves who chose, later, to follow him. He was never, in white man's terms, a "chief."[11] He was, however, intelligent, passionate, and committed to the cause of Creek and Seminole resistance to removal. In addition, he had heredity on his side, but only to a limited extent. In today's English social terms, we might say that he came from a "good" family. That is, his people were respected and imaged as having had a long history of dignity and military prowess and were connected by marriage to other high-visibility families (see chapter 2 for a discussion of these connections). His clan grandfather, Peter McQueen, had taken the talk of Tecumseh and become a leader of the "red stick" (war) faction. The young boy, Billy Powell, had spent several of his most formative years among the *hilíswa haya* or *hilis'haya,* the "keepers of the light" or medicine people whom whites called the "prophets"—the spiritual keepers of the Native revivalist flame. Thus, the young man, Osceola, was a known entity among his Creek kin who had moved southward after 1813–1814, as well as among his Seminole kin in Florida.

In addition, he also had several important personal traits that gave him visibility among the Indians and, therefore, notoriety among the whites. For example, he had the ability to speak persuasively, a talent that had long been highly valued among the Maskókî people all across the lower Southeast. He also had passion in his beliefs and in his speech, another highly valued personal characteristic, as they bespoke a caring for the people that was the *sine qua non* of Maskókî trust, itself the core value of Maskókî leadership. These qualities were coupled with an honesty and dependability that conferred on him a powerful degree of influence. But these were all only *in*direct forms of power.

Beyond these qualities, he was a handsome man, about five feet ten inches tall, and slender. He was delicate in his features and elegant in his manner of dress. He was given to finery, within the range of those symbols permitted to a warrior of his age and limited experience. He liked collecting unique items of personal adornment as well and wearing them in his own unique manner. Both Indians and whites took note of his forceful ego—he apparently did not much restrain it, but he did temper it with a respect for the traditions to which he was committed, both by birth and by personal inclination.

Despite all of these unique personal characteristics, however, he came from a people whose traditions of warfare did not include the concept of large-scale, unified action under the leadership of a single individual.[12] Warriors followed individual big warriors, in a social pattern based upon clan and town affiliations that were, in turn, based upon heredity. Moreover, as regards leadership, Osceola's own youth mitigated against him. In terms of knowledge he was growing rapidly, and in terms of visibility, great things might be expected of a warrior of his family, but he had to build his reputation and earn the people's regard, just as did all the other warriors. This would begin to happen rapidly in late 1835 and throughout 1836 and most of 1837, as the Second Seminole War of Removal opened and progressed, but not before, and by then it happened too late.

In Florida, old squabbles among the numerous Maskókî tribes—cultural kin who fought among themselves, as members of any family fight—were superseded by the need to unite in the face of mounting white pressures from growing numbers of white settlers, from the government of a brand new territory of the United States seeking growth and development (Spain had ceded Florida to the United States in 1821), and from the U.S. government, furthering its own expansionist aims. None of the Florida lands were unknown to the Indians. The Seminoles, whose ancestors had lived across these lands for thousands of years, had been joined by their Maskókî clan, "brothers" and "sisters" from Alabama and Georgia, whose families had hunted the Florida lands for thousands of years also.

Nevertheless, the relationship of the Indians to their ancient lands in

Florida and, indeed, the entire Southeast, was irrelevant to the aims of the U.S. government. Consistent with the stated policy of the Indian Removal Act, the United States concluded a treaty in 1832, at Payne's Landing on the St. John's River south of St. Augustine, by which its Indian signers agreed to remove to the West within two years. Soon repudiated by the Indians and compromised by the United States, this treaty never completely accomplished its purpose.

By 1834 Osceola was living in central Florida in the Big Swamp, near Fort King (present-day Ocala). He became a familiar face to the soldiers, and he watched their maneuvers closely, following the actions of his mentor, Abiákî. Abiákî entered military compounds under the pretext of selling fish to the garrisons, a ruse that led the white soldiers to dub him "Sam Jones" (after a parody on a popular poem of the day featuring "Sam Jones the Fisherman of Sandy Hook"). At the Fort King council in October 1834, Osceola's vehement determination to remain in Florida and to exhort others to resist removal first became obvious to whites. Subsequently, U.S. Indian agent "General" Wiley Thompson (formerly a Georgia militia leader) singled him out as influential and spent the next ten months trying to flatter and placate him with gifts, among them a silver-mounted rifle (of which more later). This is the beginning of the brilliant, public phase of Osceola's life, a short period of only three years and three months. Near the end of his life, Osceola would speak privately and sadly of the hardness of his fate and of the great things that he might have done if he could have united his people and could have been obeyed. He was charismatic. He was the right man—but at the wrong time.

During the first half of the 1830s, however, his star was still on the ascent. It may have been during the spring or fall of 1834, during a council meeting at Fort King, that Osceola's vehement recalcitrance (in the eyes of whites) became all too clear, and his later public image was set—by rumors of an incident that probably never took place. Lt. John T. Sprague, U.S. Army, reported that General Thompson, "while communicating to the chiefs in council" the president's intention to enforce removal, was constantly interrupted by derogatory remarks.[13] Osceola sat beside Micanopy (mikkó anópî[t], a Mikisuúkî leader of leaders, a big leader by hereditary right) and whispered to him, putting words in his mouth, as it were. Micanopy was known for his lack of decision-making ability, and although it appears that the young warrior had gained a degree of influence with him, Micanopy already may have been leaning toward accepting removal. In this decision Micanopy was heavily influenced by his black confidante, Abram (Abraham), who was also in the employ of the U.S. military. By the time of

Osceola's capture, the Indian resistance faction would have put a price on Abram's head.[14] Perhaps as early as this moment, in 1834, Osceola and the others already had begun to suspect his double-dealing.

Sprague reports that finally, in great anger, Osceola spoke out: "The only treaty I will execute is with this!" and he drove his knife into a table. This entire event probably is apocryphal (see chapter 3 for a discussion of its merits). It certainly is not consistent with the Seminole axiom, "A good warrior never lets his enemy see his anger," but Osceola's mentor, Abiákî, was present at the council and also refused to cooperate with Thompson's demands; moreover, Osceola's anger was barely concealed in other, better-documented, circumstances. Regardless of its validity, the impact of the report was the same as if the act had, indeed, taken place. The light of public attention was turned on Osceola, and it has continued to shine through almost two centuries.

When agent Thompson finally admitted to himself that no number of gifts would induce the young man to accept removal, he quickly reached the end of his patience with what he saw as Osceola's inflammatory attitude. Following a personal confrontation between the two men in June of 1835, Thompson publicly shamed the young warrior by having him put in irons and jailed. Agent Thompson knew exactly what he was doing, too. Just a few weeks later in June, there would be a small clash between Indians and white settlers as a result of which Thompson would counsel Captain S. V. Walker concerning the Indians he might capture: "And I think it will have a good effect to lodge them in gaol. The Idea of a gaol carries terror to the Indian mind."[15]

In his official report of the altercation with Osceola, Thompson wrote to Gen. George Gibson, the commissary general of subsistence, in Washington, D.C.

Sir

A few days ago, Powell, one of the most bold & aspiring & intrepid Chiefs of this Nation, and one that has been more hostile to emigration, and has thrown more embarrassments in my way than any other, came to my office and insulted me by some insolent remarks. He had done so before, and I then apprised him of the consequences, should he venture to do so again. He apologized & I forgave—on this occasion I confined him in Irons, as I was fully satisfied the crisis had arrived when it became indispensable to make an example of him. On the next day after he was arrested he sent to me a proposition to sign the acknowledgment of the validity of the Treaty, & begged that I would release him. I informed him that without satisfactory security

that he would behave better & prove faithfull in future he must remain in confinement. I &c sent for some of the friendly Chiefs and
begged them to intercede for him. They done so. I then informed him
that I would put his sincerity to the test, by releasing him and relying
on his word to come in five days, meet those friendly Chiefs and in
Council subscribe to the acknowledgment of the Treaty. He replied
that he would not only do it himself, but that he would bring others
with him for that having been brought to proper reflection he was perfectly satisfied that the course which he had been persuing was well
calculated to [win] him and his people. True to his professions, he this
day appeared with seventy-nine of his people Men, Women & children
(including some who joined since his conversion) and redeemed his
promise. He told me that many of his friends were out hunting, whom
he could & would bring over on their return. I now have no doubt of
his sincerity and as little that the greatest difficulty is surmounted.

Most respectfully,
Your Obt Sevt
Wiley Thompson[16]

Thompson was premature, to say the least, in his optimism. Furthermore, it was a moment that sealed the fate of both men. For Osceola, the
degradation was too much, and his brash taunts turned to cunning resolve
in what shortly would be a series of calculated and daring moves orches-
trated by the elders of the war council and carried out by the eager young
warrior, Osceola, among others.

First, however, in the next month, it appears that Osceola took it upon
himself (undoubtedly with the permission of his elders) to arrange a traditional Indian ball game at Fort King. This he surely promulgated for symbolic reasons, as a medicine man might, to remind the Indians of their common cultural heritage, to confirm them in their commitment to tradition,
and to unify them in their resolve to resistance. As a public incentive, he
used the game to secure ammunition, under the guise of a prize, from the
game's white military hosts. After this event, he and his people retreated to
the dense refuge of their hidden camp, on the Cove of the Withlacoochee
River.

It was just a few months later, in November of 1835, that the first plans
of the Indians' war council were put into effect. Just as they had in Alabama
during the earlier Creek War, the war council, composed of medicine men
and big warriors from the various clans, had decreed that any Indians who
agreed to succumb to the offers to sell their cattle and hogs to the white
government and move to the West would die for their weakness. Charley

Emathla had been in the party that had gone to Indian Territory in 1832 to inspect lands proffered to the Florida Indians by the Treaty of Payne's Landing, and he had recently sold out his livestock and agreed to depart. Thus, it was Osceola who was sent out with a small party to execute Charley Emathla, thereby confirming the decree of the war council and, at the same time, removing a vocal and visible member of the pro-emigration faction. It was also Osceola who said, reportedly, that the white man's gold that Charley was carrying, wrapped in his neckerchief, was made of red men's blood. And, forbidding any of the others to touch it (because of the bad medicine it carried), he "threw it in every direction."[17] Once again, we have Agent Thompson reporting to General Gibson on the event, never knowing that his own life would be forfeited in a similar manner within a few short weeks. "On the 26th inst. Charley Emathla the most intelligent active & enterprising Chief in this part of the Nation friendly to the Removal, was murdered by those opposed to the Removal. This murder was effected through the treachery of a Sub-Chief (Powell) who proposed to be, and was considered friendly. The consequences resulting from the murder leaves no doubt that actual force must be resorted to for the purpose of effecting the Removal, as it has produced a general defection among those Indians now in the Nation who were pledged to Remove voluntarily."[18]

Next, in his first experience as a field commander, Osceola was sent out to lead an ambush on a U.S. military baggage train, on 18 December 1835, near the Alachua savanna. This hit-and-run style of warfare was thoroughly consistent with the Indians' traditions and would remain the strategy of choice for them in Florida until warfare permanently ended, in 1858. In this 1835 encounter, known in white man's military history as the Battle of Black Point (on the north-central Kanapaha Prairie), Osceola and about eighty warriors captured military baggage wagons en route from Jacksonville, Florida, to Wetumpka, Alabama, with the troops. A newly raised militia was patrolling the area, and thirty horsemen galloped up just as the Indians were securing their prize. But the army horsemen failed to respond to their officer's order to charge, and retreated instead, with casualties. U.S. scouts located the Indians' temporary camp a few days later and recovered some of the papers and items of military equipage, some of the troops waist deep in water as they fought the warriors. It was, as historian John K. Mahon noted, "the first of an almost unending series of desperate fights to be waged under cruelly adverse conditions"[19]—cruelly adverse for the white soldiers, that is.

The next step in the war council's strategy surely satisfied Osceola. It decreed the elimination of Wiley Thompson, at the time the most visible official symbol of the white government's determination to remove the Indians. Osceola himself was sent out with a small party of warriors to accomplish the mission. This also was consistent with Maskókî tradition, which assigns the right of redress to the aggrieved clan. In the early evening of 28 December 1835, Osceola accomplished his mission (of this, more later). Literally at the same time, a larger party of warriors was achieving another objective, which had military as well as symbolic significance. Under more experienced leadership, the Indians were attacking a column of white soldiers under the command of Maj. Francis Dade, marching from Fort Brooke (Tampa) to Fort King. Rather than a European-style pitched battle, this was a Maskókî-style unilateral attack—and so successful was it that whites viewed it as a massacre.[20]

From the rapidity and success of these swift encounters, it seems quite clear that the Indians were attempting to send a message to the U.S. government. First and foremost, they were demonstrating their determination and their ability to resist, with power, the attempts to separate them from their homelands. Many of the Indians in Florida had been in the Creek War in Alabama. Consequently, this was merely the latest episode in their ongoing fight against the white men, and it was nothing new. But the core of the resistance was composed of the people whose ancestors had always been in Florida, and those ancestors had fought the Europeans, literally ever since the Europeans' arrival in the sixteenth century. Their descendents recall, to this day, the admonition of their grandfathers' grandfathers. Even more than a "simple" act of resistance, they had been told, often and long, that this land, which the Hitchiti speakers knew as *ichî bomet,* the nose of the deer, and the Maskókî (Creek) speakers called *ékon fuskéi(t),* the sharp or pointed land, would be their final refuge.[21] They would make their stand here, at last, and nowhere else. Perhaps the war council truly believed that a significant show of strength would convince the United States that the Indians should be left alone. If so, in the short run their strategy was successful. In the long run success came at a terrible price.

Three days after the execution of Thompson and the destruction of Dade's column, U.S. forces moved to surprise the Indians in their strongholds on the Withlacoochee River. On 31 December 1835, a pitched battle took place, the third salvo and the first full battle in what would become a seven-year-long conflict to be known as the Second Seminole War. The outcome of this "First Battle of the Withlacoochee" was indecisive, partly because of poor communication among the U.S. troops and partly because of conflicts in command, both problems that would plague the U.S. military throughout the war. With this battle, however, Osceola already reached the zenith of his too-short military career. He led perhaps 220 warriors at this event, plus 30 blacks, the greatest number he would ever lead, and may have received a slight wound, although his growing notoriety increased the rumors of this event from a single slight wound, to two wounds, to his reported death.[22] Already he had reached the peak of his power, and both his following and his own physical strength would begin to wane over the year following this encounter.

Throughout the year 1836, Osceola continued to play a visible part in the military encounters, and the newspapers continued to report his exploits. Several times he and other Indians attempted to parley with the army officials to express their weariness with the fighting and their willingness to negotiate compromise boundaries for the Indians' territories, but to no avail. Neither side really trusted the other any longer (if trust ever really could have been an effective issue), and the Anglo-Americans were determined that the only permanent solution to the "Indian problem" was to remove them, either peaceably or by military force.

In January of 1836, an unfounded rumor circulated that the army had marched to "Powell's Town" and burned it.[23] Osceola is reported to have sent word to the commander of Florida troops, Gen. Duncan L. Clinch, pledging his determination to fight to the last drop of his blood.[24] Myer Cohen, a Charleston, South Carolina, volunteer and certainly a nexus, if not the origin, of a large part of the gossip mill in Florida, reported that Osceola boasted that he would "breakfast at Picolata and dine in Augustine," meaning that the Indians would attack and overcome the whites in two of their strongholds: at the Picolata fortification on the St. John's River, which was the western "door" to St. Augustine, and on into the city itself.[25] Late in February, the Indians pinned down army troops, again on the Withlacoochee River. For days they besieged the white soldiers, who were under the command of Gen. Edmund P. Gaines. On the sixth of March, in a moment of calm, an impromptu parley took place between Gaines and the Indians. The war leaders Jumper, Alligator, and Osceola would not leave their home, they said. But they would accept the Withlacoochee River as a boundary between Indians and whites. Some of the troops thought that the talk was, in reality, a treacherous attempt on Osceola's part to reconnoiter the soldiers' camp in order to plan another massacre.[26] Regardless, in the midst of the parley a relief party with supplies for the starving white soldiers arrived and began to shoot before asking questions. The parley ended precipitously.[27]

All through the summer of 1836, the Indians operated at the head of the Florida peninsula, especially pressing the white soldiers at the tiny settlement that whites called after the Indian leader, Micanopy. Osceola is reported to have been one of the war leaders, and he certainly should have been involved.[28] As his notoriety compounded into fame, however, he was assumed to have been either a leader or a powerful participant in almost everything that occurred. Newspaper accounts and letters home, fed by a rumor mill that functioned constantly in an era when official communication lines were too slow to keep pace with the public desire for news, began to include his name regularly. And the war was hard on everyone that summer, too. It was "an uncommonly sickly season."[29] Fortifications on the interior of the territory were gradually abandoned as the Indians aggressed them beyond the capacity of the sick soldiers and their officers to defend. Fort Drane, about ten miles distant from Fort Defiance, near Micanopy, had a full third of its complement unfit for duty. The fort was closed, and soldiers and equipment were headed for Defiance when Osceola and a force of about two hundred Indians attacked them on 19 July. Recorded as the Battle of Welika Pond, the incident already had become tiresomely repetitious in its inconclusiveness. The soldiers fought their way back behind stockade walls. The Indians melted back into the thick Florida piney woods from whence they had come.

The toll on the white soldiers fighting what was, to all intents and purposes, a three-front war—against the terrain and the climate as well as the Indians—was enormous. The drain on the Indians' resources, both material and physical, was profound as well. It appears that sometime in July or August, Osceola himself may have become ill, contracting malaria at the abandoned army post of Fort Drane, and the recurring nature of this illness would have diminished his physical capacity significantly. In addition, the critical scarcity of food supplies made it necessary for the Indians to roam farther afield and in smaller parties than previously. The army was probing deeper and deeper into their strongholds, and it was no longer always safe to retreat and regroup there. In October the army almost reached Powell's Town, Osceola's hidden base camp on the Cove of the Withlacoochee.

Indeed, only a failure in leadership kept the soldiers from reaching Osceola's stronghold during the Battle of the Wahoo Swamp (across the Withlacoochee from the Cove) in November. Osceola was not in the thick of the fighting, having been sent to a slightly distant position where the Indians erroneously thought that the white soldiers would cross. Many of the army's efforts had come to focus on locating and destroying Osceola's camp. It appears that, as the army's frustrations at being unable to find and dislodge their enemies had grown, and as Osceola's centrality in the minds of white Americans had risen, his hidden camp had become a symbol of that frustration. In December, the new commander of Florida forces, Gen. Thomas S. Jesup, absolutely opposed any plan that would take the soldiers away from the Withlacoochee, "where he strongly expected Powell with his warriors would be found."[30]

Meanwhile, the soldiers continued to destroy any other Indian towns and crops that they could find, and the Indians' situation was becoming desperate. Within the year, they were living on *cóntikî(t)*, or "coontie," as English speakers heard it (the starchy tuber of the Red Zamia plant, a member of the Cycad family), and beef without salt. Reports indicated that Osceola, or Powell as he was still frequently called, had powder but no longer had men. His force had dwindled to only about eight warriors. He also was reported to be sick, which would partially explain his decline in status among the Indians. His diminished capacity to provide vigorous leadership would have prompted the warriors to look elsewhere for a leader, even though his status and visibility among whites remained strong and was growing stronger.

As 1836 wore on into 1837, reports of Osceola's being ill still continued to circulate. In January, the "negro, Primus" reported that Osceola's warriors had been dispersed, that he had only three warriors and his family with him, but that he could collect about a hundred warriors if he wanted to.[31] On 6 March, after several failed attempts at calling the Indians together, General Jesup succeeded in gaining the signatures of a few headmen on a "capitulation" that, among other provisions, bound the Indians to assemble at a point south of the Hillsborough River for removal to the western Indian Territory. All throughout the spring of the year, Lt. Col. William Harney, headquartered at Fort Mellon (present-day Sanford) would report to General Jesup hopefully on rumors and promises that various Indian groups were headed for Tampa Bay to turn themselves in to await emigration.

Reports and rumors concerning the health of Osceola continued to circulate, and such items had a direct impact on the prosecution of the war. In March of 1837, Lt. Henry Prince heard from Ansel, "a negro who travels with the unit," the account that Osceola had given him of a harrowing incident during the "battle of the spotted lake." Powell told Ansel that

> he had been stunned by the wind of a cannon ball passing near him. He was carried off & did not recover for several days—the ball passed through the hollow cypress at which he had posted himself and "cut his breath"—it went through the tree just as if it were fired close by! He said too that he was very glad the Gen. did not come on further— he was glad to see him go back again—for he would have been obliged, had the troops advanced further, to "move his house" [i.e., his secret camp might have been discovered]—but—"when he saw [the soldiers] go back from the creek to the pine ridge he went & staid at his old place."[32]

Four days later, the white troops would, indeed, locate Powell's "house," and he would be forced into a life of even greater movement. Most immediately, Osceola made his encampment about fifteen miles away from Fort Mellon—except for the night of 7 May, when he accepted the hospitality of none other than Col. William Harney, the camp commander, and slept in the colonel's own tent. He spoke reassuringly to the colonel, but it was only a ruse. By the closing days of May 1837, Harney had lost his optimism in regard to the Indians' willingness to turn themselves in, and he had become bitter. To Jesup he confided, "I am more mortified and distressed about the positive assurances which I gave you of the sincerity of the Indians than I can possibly express." He blamed "Powell" specifically for this state of affairs, believing that he had negatively influenced those Indians who had been willing to emigrate: "That double rascal Powell is the whole cause of the change. I never knew or heard of an Indian carrying deception so far as this scoundrel has done—to come and eat, drink, sleep and smoke with me and saying everything that I could wish and with such an open candid manner. I would have staked my life on his sincerity, and so would any person else, if they had been here and *seen* and *heard* them & *him.* I have changed my opinion of being able to get the Chiefs in. [A black informer] says that Powell said that he would never come here again except to fight—but if he *should* come, I will never let him return, but will send him off immediately, unless I find that I can make good use of him."[33] Obviously, Harney never saw the irony in his own insincerity.

General Jesup also reported to Secretary of War Joel Poinsett that at the earlier Fort Mellon meeting, Osceola had received subsistence to take his group to Tampa, that is, to Fort Brooke and the point of embarkation established by the army, where Indians already were being collected. Then, "in violation of his plighted faith," Osceola did not go and, moreover, prevented Coe Hadjo, who was cooperating with Harney and had agreed to emigrate, "by force and threats" from going also. Osceola even attempted to kill Yaholo hajo, Jesup's unarmed messenger to Coe Hadjo and Nocose Yaholo.[34]

Jesup, who ultimately would become the architect of Osceola's ignominious capture, would store all of these instances away as defenses of his later actions. He built up a veritable storehouse of beliefs that Osceola had acted dishonorably by giving his word and then disregarding it and, consequently, forfeiting his right to be trusted or treated as trustworthy. Here is a glimpse straight into the heart of war: that individuals should convince themselves that the "other" is incapable of seeing the righteousness of whatever cause impels the aggression and, therefore, is acting outside of the bounds of the aggressors' expectations. This unilateral imaging, which can afford to admit absolutely no understanding of the cultural values that impel the other, is the *sine qua non* of war. It destroys the brotherhood of humanity by melding individual human beings into faceless hordes and thereby dissociating the horrors of fratricide.

Earlier in May, in a desperate attempt to reinvigorate the struggle and perhaps yet again as a reaffirmation of the Indians' heritage, as well as an attempt to reconsolidate his own diminished leadership, Osceola, with Coe hadjo, organized another ball game (as Osceola had previously, at Fort King, in the summer of 1835). This time the game was played at Fort Mellon, and the stated purpose to the white authorities was to bring in Indians who would agree to emigrate. Many attended, but, not surprisingly, none agreed to emigrate.[35] Unfortunately, this ball game would have unintended consequences for Osceola. Harney told Jesup, "I am told that Powell has hurt his foot in a ball play & will not come down [to turn himself in]."[36] There may have been truth in this, or it may have been a convenient cover for his true plans. On 2 June, Harney wrote to Jesup again, reporting: "Powell sent word that he was lonesome to see me but that his foot was too sore to ride—*hanging* it down made it swell and very painful."[37]

Even as Harney was reporting on Osceola's incapacity, literally on that same night, when Micanopy and several hundred Indians had gathered, or been gathered—the effect was the same—in captivity at Fort Brooke, Osceola and his mentor, Abiákî, were miles away, leading a party of about two hundred warriors and quietly cleaning out the camp.[38] Neither the war council, nor Osceola, nor any of the other resistance leaders were ready to permit this forced emigration. This action, however, and the psychological impetus of the Indians who left the camp that night, embodied feelings that reverberate to this day among the removed Seminoles and Creeks of Oklahoma in relation to the Seminoles who fought and remained in Florida. Many of the Indians who left the camp that night later averred that they had been forced to leave. This may, indeed, have been so, but it should not be taken to indicate that any of the Indians assembled there had been ready to leave Florida voluntarily. They were leaving under profound duress. They had seen their homes destroyed, and their emotional reserves had been worn down completely, leading them to conclude that their lives had been destroyed. As a result, they imagined no other recourse than to capitulate to the white man's demands. Their descendents would pay for their decisions to leave Florida with a degree of guilt that would remain, unabated, down the ensuing generations. Because of their actions, their clan kin who managed to remain in Florida would internalize a degree of betrayal so deep that it would continue, as well, down the generations. The resulting sense of estrangement that distances the people who have re-formed as two separate tribes today may never abate or be lost.

Harney continued to hatch hopeful plans, but privately he confided to Jesup four days after the escape of the Indian prisoners, "I fear somewhat that Powell and Jones are too smart for me."[39] A week or so later, Harney asked Wildcat to send a messenger to Osceola and other leaders to ask, yet again, whether they intended to turn themselves in. On 16 June, he reported to Jesup, "The man whom the Wild Cat sent with my message to the Chiefs has just arrived and states that Powell told him that they would get through their medicine & dancing and would be sure to come down within the time I appointed—*but it is all a lie*!"[40] In addition to showing us Harney's state of mind, this comment provides two other pieces of information. First, even in the midst of the war, the Indians had not ceased to gather for the powerfully significant Green Corn Ceremony. Second, the fact that they were, indeed, celebrating this busk, or fasting time, provides a possible insight into Jesup's loss of his prisoners at Tampa Bay. Undoubtedly many, if not all, left willingly so that they might participate in the central ritual of the Creek and Seminole belief system.

Beyond its effect upon the Indians and Harney, the effect of the release of the prisoners upon Jesup was profound as well. He considered that the campaign to force the Indians to emigrate had "entirely failed." He now advocated for complete extermination as the only recourse. He was so depressed that he asked to be relieved of his command, although rebound anger impelled him to stay.[41] Two months later, his anger had only grown, and he wrote explicitly to a subordinate commander: "The Comdg. Genl. [referring to himself in the third person] is utterly indifferent whether the Seminoles determine for peace or war—but if they are so infatuated as still to resist the fulfillment of their treaties, his Indians [those "friendlies" who fought as U.S. allies] will sweep them from the face of the earth—their mode of warfare is to kill all the males & to make slaves of the women & children of their enemies. No restriction will be placed upon them in the next campaign." This extremist position, and Jesup's subsequent actions based on it, however, would cost the commander dearly. For the rest of his life, memories of his actions would dog him publicly, nipping at his heels, clouding his military legacy, and destroying his personal peace. No one on either side would escape from this war unscathed in some way.

It is clear from his subsequent words and actions that Osceola himself also realized the import of his actions and the larger historical moment that they created. The war council denied any further power to Micanopy, who had caved in to white pressure and had been ready to emigrate. Instead, they gave war power to Abiákî, the intractable foe of whites and of removal. Separately, but at the same ill-starred moment, a number of the blacks who had thrown in their lot with the Indians, either voluntarily or involuntarily, began to tire of the war, life on the run in the Florida "scrub," and their maltreatment at the hands of the Indians and began to turn themselves in to Jesup's U.S. forces.[42] Lt. R. H. Peyton was encamped one night when he was hailed from the darkness of a lake by a voice speaking English. The voice turned out to be that of one Rufus, and the canoe in which he was traveling contained "12 negroes who were delighted to deliver themselves up to white people again." They all had been captured by the Indians more than a year since and "were anxious to be delivered up, for they complained of very severe treatment from the Indians. . . . The Indians (Rufus continued) will not allow any of the negroes to go towards our camp[,] they threaten all who attempt to escape with death or some very severe punishment and as an instance says that a man was found going towards Fort Mellon by some Indians[,] they beat him with sticks until he was nearly dead."[43] This, of course, highlights the severity of the position in which Osceola and the resisters were functioning. They were, in reality, fighting a multifront war—not only against the whites but also against those of their own people and those blacks who had lost the will to resist.

Then, on 9 September, soldiers captured the camp of Philip, the Spanish brother-in-law of Micanopy, who was allied by marriage to the family of Cowkeeper, Payne, and the first Bowlegs and was, therefore, among the most significant of the remaining war leaders.[44] Taken to imprisonment at Fort Marion (originally the Spaniards' Castillo de San Marcos, in St. Augustine), Philip was permitted to send for his son, Coacoochee (cowácuchî[t], little cat or Bob Cat, usually translated into English as Wildcat). With other captures at about the same time, the number of prisoners being assembled in Fort Marion was rising steadily.

It was at this pivotal moment when Jesup, obviously frustrated beyond his personal limits with the desperate—in his mind, duplicitous—tactics of the Indians and criticism of his conduct by fellow officers, all of which was exacerbated by internal squabbles over command in Florida, took an action that he considered necessary to bring the war in Florida to a close. When Coacoochee and a fellow warrior, Blue Snake, responded later in the month to Philip's call and went in under a white flag of truce to speak with Jesup, the general betrayed this universal symbol and took them prisoners. It was a decision considered by whites and Indians to be thoroughly inconsistent with the honorable rules of the conduct of war, but it worked—and Jesup was about to use it again, to his everlasting detriment.

On 20 October, Osceola, Coe Hadjo, and the rest of his family and followers were encamped about eight miles south of St. Augustine, about a mile below the tiny stockade designated as Fort Peyton, on the south side of Moultrie Creek. Osceola sent Juan Caballo (Cowaya/Cavalo, John Horse, an active black resistance fighter) to Gen. Joseph Hernández at St. Augustine, to ask for a parley.[45] Jesup instructed Hernández that Osceola should not be permitted to leave the conference freely. Osceola was sick—in body and in spirit. Many Seminoles to this day recall that Osceola knew that he was sick and that it was his time to quit the fight. His support base among the Indians had never been as large or sustained as he had hoped, and it was now far smaller than he needed to continue his personal involvement in the struggle. He knew that the acts he had committed against the whites were such that they would not let him out of their grasp again.

On 21 October 1837, General Hernández and his U.S. troops moved toward the Indians' encampment, an open spot in the Florida piney woods where Osceola and Coe Hadjo awaited them. This time, Jesup stayed out of sight, inside the stockade of Fort Peyton. Once again, the Indians flew a white flag of truce, but Osceola, for one, knew better than to trust in its protection. He was right. Soon after the parley commenced, a prearranged signal was given (an officer lifted his hat), and the troops closed in on the Indians and made them prisoners. They were marched eight miles north to imprisonment within Fort Marion.

Meanwhile, General Jesup wrote to Col. (later, U.S. president) Zachary Taylor, who was commanding the infantry at Fort Brooke on Tampa Bay, in a manner that confirms the duplicitousness of Abraham, Micanopy's black confidante, and sheds light on Micanopy's disposition toward removal. Jesup placed Taylor in command of troops and posts south of the "We-thlocco-chee" (the Withlacoochee), north of Charlotte Harbor and west of Kissimmee. He instructed Taylor to build a storage depot (among other activities) and act on his own authority to seek out Indians in his area. Furthermore, he commanded, "Abraham, Murray, and William [will] be taken as guides and interpreters—they are acquainted with the trail, and with the country. The Indians have threatened to kill Abraham; and I have ascertained from the prisoners recently taken, that they have actually appointed twenty warriors to kill him. I desire that he be informed of their intention. It will ensure his fidelity; and convince him that nothing short of the intire submission of the Indians can secure him from the danger which [threatens] him." Later Jesup reiterates this point and adds, "Assure Abraham that his family will be free, and Murray that he and his wife Katy will be free if they be true to us. Abraham is very much attached to Micanopy—I have heard from that Chief, and he only waits a favourable opportunity to join us."[46]

During their confinement, on Tuesday, 14 November 1837, the Indian prisoners were visited in Fort Marion by a delegation of Cherokee Indians who approached them on a peace mission from the president of the United States, "in the character of mediators between the United States and the Seminoles; And to bear to them [the president's] talk of friendship and peace." The head of the delegation, Cherokee leader and pro-emigration apologist John Ross, reported to the president on the mission and reasons for its ultimate failure, most of which he laid at the feet of General Jesup and his active sabotage of the peace process. Just before reaching St. Augustine the delegation had met with General Jesup at Picolata, the old Spanish guard post on the St. John's River west of the city, and "in conversation with him, he strongly opposed our mission, because it was taking affairs of Florida out of his controle; And [he] said many things to discourage and operate upon our fears as we thought." Nevertheless, the Cherokees, old enemies of the Creeks, were received amicably by the prisoners and took them gifts of pipes and tobacco. Later, as the group sought to visit other Seminoles who were still in the field, Jesup detained the Cherokees with equivocations and empty promises of help. He told the Cherokees that he "had no *confidence* in anything the Indians said, that they had *deceived him too often to be trusted.*" To the secretary of war, Jesup explained, rather, that he had withheld their talk as far as possible because the "condition of Emigration" was "not insisted upon as a primary article."[47] John Ross, nevertheless, saw through Jesup's rationalizations and concluded that Jesup "was determined, it would seem, from the bitterness of his feelings to frustrate every [peace] plan [and] to capture his [Indian enemies] no matter in what way it should be attempted to be effected, whether under the waving banner of peace or in open battle field."[48] With his words, Ross put the human face on the feelings that sealed Osceola's fate.

Meanwhile, the *New York Evening Star* reported, on 5 January 1838 that "the Cherokee (Indian) Ambassadors or mediators have returned to Charleston in the steamer *Santee* from Florida. Sam Jones at his last interview with them, said, 'Gen. Jesup may catch me if he can, I have no faith in him after the Oceola affair.' Sam and his Seminoles should remember that they have none of them been distinguished for their remarkable sincerity or faith to treaties and pledges."[49] Sam Jones, of course, had had no faith in whites before the "Oceola affair" either, and the Indians were far beyond trusting the U.S. government on the subject of treaties or any other subjects.

Osceola was allowed to send out a runner to call in his family, and a party of about fifty Indians and blacks eventually came in. The party included one of Osceola's clan (half) sisters, his two wives (probably his only wives at the time), and two children, and they turned themselves in to the soldiers at Fort Mellon on 30 November. (These events will be discussed in greater detail in later chapters.) They were sent on to Fort Marion as well. In all, about 237 Indian prisoners were assembled there in the close confines of the fort, and conditions were not healthy for them.

During the approximate ten weeks of their stay at St. Augustine, Osceola's health declined still further. His health was the primary reason he gave the Indians for not choosing to escape with Coacoochee and eighteen others in November. Then a measles outbreak further weakened the group, killing fifteen in early December. There is no evidence that Osceola contracted the illness, but there is evidence that he was sick, and there is evidence that he—and, undoubtedly, many others as well—were victims of a lice infestation and its detrimental effects that were another result of the crowded and unsanitary conditions under which they were being held.

It was during this imprisonment at St. Augustine that Osceola met and came to know Dr. and Mrs. Frederick Weedon. It was Dr. Weedon, at this time a contract surgeon to the U.S. Army, who would become the next unwitting instrument of the immortality of the young Indian war leader. Weedon was the white medical doctor who would minister to Osceola in his final illness and death. It was Weedon who would remove all of his clothing and his personal possessions and would keep a few of them for himself. It was Weedon who would, in what came to be viewed by the white citizens who had lately ennobled him as the final act of ignominy, remove from him even his head.

Considering the escape, the illnesses, and the difficulty of securing the location sufficiently, Capt. Pitcairn Morrison, in charge of the Indian prisoners, decided to move them from St. Augustine, Florida, to Fort Moultrie, on tiny Sullivan's Island in the harbor of Charleston, South Carolina. Accordingly, the remaining Indian prisoners arrived there on New Year's Day 1838, among them Osceola. His life had entered its final phase. *The St. Augustine Florida Herald* described the scene and the circumstances.

The Indian prisoners lately confined in the Fort, embarked in the steamer *Poinsett,* for Sullivan's Island. When they were told to prepare for their departure, they manifested much opposition to it, and some difficulty was anticipated. However, the presence of a strong guard, convinced them that all opposition would be unavailing, and they were marched on board with little trouble. The following officers accompany them:
PITCAIRN MORRISON, Capt, and Chief Superintendent Seminole emigration.
DR. WEEDON, Act. Asst Surgeon U.S.A.

Lieut. WHARTON, 6th Infantry commanding guard.
The whole under the command of Capt. Morrison.
INDIAN CHIEFS—MICANOPY, Principal Chief Seminole Nation.
COAHAJO, LITTLE CLOUD, KING PHILIP, OSCEOLA, and one hundred
and sixteen warriors together with eighty two women and children.

Within a few months, most of the prisoners (official U.S. documents invariably refer to them as "emigrating Indians," thus obscuring the horrendous events that had placed them in that position), including Osceola's sister, wives, children, and possibly his mother and one or more of her other children, would be sent on to Indian Territory in the West. Osceola, however, never left Fort Moultrie. He entered a final, brief period of celebrity there. He was viewed there by curious and interested Charlestonions, among whom undoubtedly were members of the families of men whom he had fought in Florida. He sat for artists there, always pleased to be the center of attention, and met the famous George Catlin, the last white man with whom he would form a friendly relationship. On 30 January 1838, Osceola died at Fort Moultrie and was buried on the fort grounds.

What can we say, then, about this unique individual whose life and passions struck such a responsive chord with his friends and his enemies alike that he continues to occupy a place in their living memory so long afterward? He was, above all, just a man. He laughed, talked, hurt, made love, cared about his family and his people, and needed friends, no matter what the color of their skins. He was not a murderer, acting out of blind, irrational anger. He was, more accurately, an avenger operating out of a cultural code that was radically different from that of his white contemporaries and, tragically, antipathetic to their objectives.

Osceola had a strong pride, born of passionate beliefs, and he enjoyed proclaiming his own individuality in every area, from his mode of dress to his actions. He was a man who purposely lived in two worlds and was considered complex by the standards of both. He obviously admired, or at least saw the value of, many facets of white culture and seems to have felt that he would have been capable of moving in that other world if circumstances had permitted. His personal frame of reference, however, was overwhelmingly Maskókî Indian. His qualities of personal leadership and his charisma were recognized by Indians and whites alike. His fame and lasting memory have not been the result, merely, of the circumstances of his capture and death—that is, of events outside himself. Osceola, as a person, also left an indelible stamp upon his times.

Of the myriad words that have been written about Osceola, three paragraphs stand out as the most balanced assessment of all. Neither too critical, too supercilious, too romantic, nor too condescending, they leave us with a better understanding of a fellow human being and his special place in our collective and individual worlds. In a final irony, the summation was written, once again, by a white man, Thomas W. Storrow, as the coda of his 1844 *Knickerbocker Magazine* article. Storrow had never met his subject, but perhaps because of his distance from the man rather than his proximity, he was able to temper white recollections with dispassion and, despite a degree of cultural chauvinism, to provide all of us with his own small legacy of better understanding. He wrote:

> Sufficient may be gathered from these pages to prove that Osceola was not an ordinary man; neither perhaps will it be admitted that he was a hero. Yet it certainly will be seen that he had within him many of the elements that heroes are composed of, with perhaps more merit to the title than is possessed by many educated persons who figure in the temple of fame.
>
> He evidently possessed strong good sense, with the capacity to apply it aptly; and it is equally clear that to this alone was he indebted for the commanding influence he acquired over his countrymen at a very early period of his life. He was an ardent lover of his country, and a warrior skillful beyond his opportunities. He possessed, even in the savage state, abilities his race does not lay claim to or covet, and which in the civilized world go to humanize and adorn private life. He was not filled with the stoicism so much prized by the savage, which makes him alike indifferent to sorrow or joy, but alternately exhibited the emotions of anger or pity, as circumstances called forth the exercise of these passions. He seems to have been adapted to the quiet of retired life, yet when once the warlike spirit, dormant within him, was aroused, he laid aside peaceful habits, acted his part with intelligence and vigor, and at last, although a captive in a strange land, died a warrior in his paint. In his narrow sphere he displayed many heroic virtues; his life was engaged in a nobler cause than that which incites the actions of many whom the world calls great; and in his last moments he displayed the workings of a lofty spirit, which commands our admiration.
>
> If those who have devastated the earth to gratify their selfish ambition or thirst of conquest, have historians to record their deeds, and poets to sing their praise, let us not withhold a token of applause to one who committed fewer wrongs, and during his life was a brave defender of his country.[50]

2 / Family Matters

Sources regarding the early private life of the man whom non-Native history would remember as Osceola are so limited that probably no definitive account ever will be assembled.[1] Nevertheless, a great deal of peripheral information is available from which we may draw inferences with a high degree of probability. His birth and early years coincide with the opening of a period of major upheaval and dislocation among the Maskókî peoples of the lower Southeast, known to the non-Native world as "Creeks." In fact, it is only shortly after the epithet "Creeks" first came into common English usage that Osceola's family history first enters the historical record.

Since 1510 at least, the Spaniards alone had had direct and continuous interactions with the culturally related Maskókî tribes, whose camps, villages, towns, and cities ranged across the southeastern area that today comprises all of Florida, Alabama, Georgia, South Carolina, and Mississippi, as well as some eastern portions of Louisiana, Tennessee, and Kentucky.[2] Only a century and a half later, in 1670, did the determination of the English to obtain a foothold in Spanish-occupied territory finally result in the establishment of a permanent settlement, at Charles Town, in the English colony of the Carolinas. Despite their relatively late start, within twenty years—the span of a single generation—English traders searching for raw materials to feed the burgeoning English mercantile system had stumbled upon the old and densely populated Native settlements in the areas that its people

referred to as *ogichî* and *oconî*, situated around the confluence of two powerful creeks in today's southern central Georgia.[3]

The traders informed the lords proprietor of the colony that the area and
the waterways, which they transliterated into English as the "Oconee and
Ogeechee Creeks," was a potentially lucrative trade zone. Within another
decade, however, they had tired of repeating "Oconee" and "Ogeechee"
and had begun to refer to both the area and the tribes generically as the
"Creeks." The simple name stuck, among English speakers.[4] As English
traders pushed their routes of commerce inward from the Atlantic seaboard
and across the territories historically dominated by the Maskókî tribes,
English military, political, and commercial reporters spread the use of the
generic "Creek" to denote the peoples they found along their ways.

Long before the coming of the Europeans, however, Shawanóe speakers
(today's Shawnee Indians), who seem to have been permitted to roam across
their territories, called the people of the lower Southeast the Maskókî—in
reference, it may be, to their preference for building their towns and cities
along watercourses.[5] The Tchlokî(t) people, the old enemies of the Maskókî
peoples, whose territories lay to the north and east, continued to call them
"Coça people," after the principal town of their rich and powerful central
province, which had existed since well prior to the sixteenth century and
the documentation of Europeans, as a founding or "mother" town of the
Maskókî people.[6] In turn, the Maskókî speakers referred to these old enemies to the north and east as Tchlókî(t), or "foreign speakers"—that is,
people who do not speak "our" language. English speakers transliterated
this word as "Cherokee" and, thereby, partially obscured the realities of
both of the groups whose power had long dominated the entire Southeast
at the time of the first coming of the Europeans.[7]

It is not long after the entry of the English into the lower Southeast that
the earliest information concerning Osceola's family history comes to light.
It appears that his first non-Indian ancestor, his maternal great-grandfather,
was the Scotsman named James McQueen, who reached the old Coça province, in what is now eastern central Alabama, by 1716 and was permitted
by the Indians to "sit down" in the Maskókî town of Tallassee.[8] In many
ways, McQueen was the archetype of so many English speakers who would
move into the Maskókî lands of Alabama and Georgia during the eighteenth century. Their numbers would reach a crescendo during the period
of relative calm that punctuated the tumult of the American Revolutionary
War and its finale, the War of 1812.

It was Thomas Woodward, another white man who spent much of his
life among the Maskókî people, who later recalled that McQueen had been
serving on a British ship anchored "at" Spanish St. Augustine when he

struck an officer and, wisely, decided to leave the ship rapidly and permanently. He was, by his own later account, thirty-three years old at the time.[9] As is so often the case, we find no information concerning the Tallassee woman he would be permitted to take as his wife or the tremendously long genealogy of her family in the town. Our only imaging comes obliquely, as in a distant mirror, from the powerful families and persons to whom her family subsequently would be connected in marriage and leadership and the visibility they would obtain in the coming wars.

Benjamin Hawkins (1717–1816), the influential U.S. Indian agent mentioned in the previous chapter, also lived among the Maskókî people. His entry into the region predated that of Woodward, and he presented an alternate scenario. "In 1797," he wrote, "the traders were James McQueen, the oldest white man in the Creek nation, who had come to Georgia as a soldier under [General James] Oglethorpe in 1733, and William Powell."[10] This latter gentleman is certainly the William Powell who will have James McQueen's granddaughter, Polly, as a wife shortly. Hawkins is saying that these two men were the only two traders in that area and at that time. Hawkins spoke of Powell as a man of little property and apparently unambitious. At another time, he also mentioned having visited William "Pound" at Tallassee in 1796, who is certainly the same man. At that time Powell had already resided for four years in the nation and had a pretty little Indian woman and one child.[11]

We will return later to the matter of William Powell and his family as it existed in 1796, but, first, several considerations need to be weighed in assessing these two alternate scenarios as they relate to personal information concerning McQueen. Hawkins entered Maskókî territory earlier than Woodward and, for the most part, had a direct, positive, and influential relationship with those Indian people who came into contact with him. His information should be reliable. Woodward, however, rode with the warriors and led them in battle. He visited them in their towns, had at least one Indian wife, and lived directly among them for many years, and has proved himself a cogent observer time and again. He seems to have known, particularly, many of the people directly connected to the life of Osceola.

As regards Hawkins's assertion that James McQueen entered the English colony of Georgia with its founder, James Oglethorpe, in 1733, the first shipload, ninety-one passengers, were mustered on board the *Ann* at Grave's End, England. There were no McQueens among them.[12] By September of 1738, however, there was a James McQueen serving as a private in Oglethorpe's Regiment in Georgia. In the following year, James McQueen signed the 1739 Creek treaty as the son of James McQueen of Corebrough, Invernesshire, Scotland.[13] If we accept the premise that the James McQueen who was Osceola's great-grandfather was, indeed, in Tallassee by 1716, then Oglethorpe's soldier is not the same person. There is a James Mac-queen [*sic*], a quartermaster in an English regiment who was taken pris-oner by the Spaniards during the battle at Fort Mose (Gracia Real de Santa Teresa de Mose), just north of Spanish St. Augustine, in June 1740.[14] So far, however, there is no reason to believe that this individual and the James McQueen who had been in Tallassee since 1716 were related in any way.

Furthermore, Woodward went so far as to state in print that James McQueen had himself told Hawkins directly that he (McQueen) reached the Creek nation as an English naval deserter.[15] Hawkins undoubtedly con-fused Osceola's great-grandfather with another McQueen.

Thomas ("Tom") Simpson Woodward, whose information is so central to our understanding of the life of Osceola, was a native of Elbert County, Georgia, and a woodsman and soldier who spent most of his life among Indians by choice. Woodward was born on 22 February 1794 (or 1797; he had no way of ascertaining for certain). During Andrew Jackson's cam-paigns against the Creeks in 1817–1818 in Florida, Georgia, and Alabama, he was a major general in command of a force of pro-American Indians ("friendlies"). His *Reminiscences,* first published as letters to the editor of the *Montgomery Mail,* were assembled into book form in 1859. Even writ-ing some forty-plus years after many of the events he was describing, his lucidity and recall of details were prodigious. He wrote with an ease of style and familiarity of description that could only have been born of personal association with the people and events that he recounted. From his narra-tives, then, we will assemble much of the genealogical and cultural matrix that influenced the character of the mixed-blood boy who would become one of the best-known figures in American Indian history.

In regard to the information that Woodward related, it has not yet been possible to pinpoint the name of a ship on which McQueen might have reached the Atlantic coast or the exact date when it arrived. There are, however, several reasons why it might have been in Spanish-claimed and Spanish-defended waters, although none is definitive. During the entire sev-enteenth century, Scots were levied to serve in the English navy. Conse-quently, a Scotsman might well have been aboard any English vessel that was able to enter Spanish waters. Scottish merchant vessels also were trad-ing to the southern Caribbean through much of the seventeenth century and, after 1707, had unlimited access to English colonial ports.

Jamaica was a busy trade center for Spanish-English trade, and its com-mercial network included Spanish Florida (which included the later English colony of Georgia). Robert Christie, a merchant from Culross in Fife, Scot-land, wrote home from Spanish Florida in 1667, indicating that he intended to move on to Mexico. His entrée to the Spanish provinces may have been Roman Catholicism, feigned or real, but the fact remains that he was there. By the Spanish-English Treaty of Utrecht in 1713, the English obtained a royal *asiento* (official assent or license), valid for thirty years, to sell four thousand slaves per year in the Caribbean, giving them easy legal access to Spanish ports.[16] Finally, beginning in 1716, various McQueens, Jacobite prisoners of war, were transported to Carolina plantations. Thus far, however, no James McQueen has been identified as having been among any of these Scots.[17]

We cannot even be sure that McQueen left a ship in the same year in which he reached Tallassee. Indeed, it is more likely that he did not. As Woodward tells us later, McQueen named one of his daughters after the queen of England: "Ann [sic] . . . whose service he quit when he came into the Nation." This intimate detail may offer an important insight into the mind and actions of James McQueen. Anne, of the Scottish Catholic House of Stuart, ascended the throne of England in 1702, at the age of thirty-seven, without heir—the last of her seventeen children having died in 1701. The Act of Succession, signed in the following year, forbade the ascension of any more Roman Catholics to the throne of England. In 1707, during her reign, the Act of Union was promulgated, which joined England and Scotland as Great Britain. Queen Anne's War, or the War of Spanish Succession, began in 1704 and wore on for six years, ending with the Treaty of Utrecht in 1713. The reign of Queen Anne of England ended a short year later with her death, and she was succeeded by a widely unpopular monarch, George I (George Louis of Brunswick-Luneburg), the first of the Hanoverian line of British rulers.

The year 1714, therefore, would have been an appropriate moment for a young Scottish, and probably Catholic, lad to have quit a long series of civil wars between his homeland and the English, wars that had consumed all the years of his short life and had finally ended with the death of his "own" Scottish queen and the advent of an unpopular foreign ruler. It would have been typical for him to have moved from settlement to settlement over a period of a year or two years until he finally chose a place to stop or, more probably, until he finally found an Indian community that would permit him to stop. Woodward tells us that, since at least as early as the time of the Spanish explorer Hernando de Soto (in 1540), Tallassee town had been situated in what is today a part of Talladega, Alabama. In 1725, the town was reported to have 40 men (adults, warriors) and 110 women and children.[18]

By 1756, after forty years among them, James McQueen had acquired sufficient influence among his wife's people to be able to induce them to move their town southward to the Tallapoosa River area in Montgomery

County, "near where Walter Lucas once had a stand, at the crossing of Line Creek."[19] We do not know why McQueen saw the move as advantageous— it may have been for environmental reasons or for political ones—but McQueen certainly wielded no unilateral power; the tribe had to agree to the move. Furthermore, he also convinced a body of "Netches" (now "Natchez") Indians to fill their vacant seat, along with a Hollander named William Moniac. (Incidentally, Woodward makes a point of saying that "Moniac," a famous surname and one that also intersects the life of Osceola, is the correct spelling of the surname and that he is not a Scot. These points continue to be controversial to the present day.)[20]

McQueen lived among the Tallassees until his death in 1811, at which time he would have been 128 years old by his own reckoning. A search of the Old Parochial Register of Births, Deaths, and Marriages of Scotland, however, turns up no James McQueen born in 1683 and fewer McQueens, generally, than one might expect. Admittedly, this is not definitive either, because many births in this period were either not recorded or their records were later lost or destroyed. There is, however, a christening entry for Friday, 18 October 1695, in the Parish of Edinburgh for a James McQueen, son of Rebecca Inglis and John McQueen. Witnesses for the christening were [Abel] Robertson, a "taylor"; Spencer James Watson, a painter; Thomas Watson, taylor; and [J_____] Van der Plank, wright. John McQueen was indicated as an ensign in a colors regiment. Rebecca herself was the daughter of Anna Turner and Robert Inglis and had been christened in Edinburgh District on 17 December 1671.[21]

Therefore, the mother would have been twenty-four years old at the birth of a son, James, and the father of indeterminate age but, presumably, close to that of the mother. So, if this information does indeed document our James McQueen, then he was between fifteen and twenty years of age when he reached Tallassee, rather than thirty-three. Such youth gives him an edge in physical survival. In addition, it is still consistent with, and possibly more typical of, his service on a naval ship and makes his death age, now 116, slightly more plausible. None of this information, of course, explains why James McQueen would have represented himself as older than he was when he reached Tallassee, unless he truly did not know or unless it reflects the Maskókî preference for age as equating with adulthood. Traditionally, men and women took life partners in their late twenties, and the counsel of men first began to gain value as they entered their late twenties and early thirties.[22]

↩

The relocated Tallassee town of James McQueen and his Tallassee wife, and the one into which Osceola would be born about 1804, therefore, came to be near the later city of Tuskegee, Alabama, which was founded by Thomas Woodward. "[Osceola's birth place] was in an old field between the Nufaupba (what is now called Ufaupee), and a little creek that the Indians called Catsa Bogah, which mouths just below where the rail road crosses Nufaupba." The term Nufaupba/Ufaupee may be the core Maskókî designator for thick, deep woods, especially deep woods where a stream or creek flows. "Catsa Bogah" is the vernacular contraction of *gatsa abókita* or *gats'abókita*, "the place where the Panther people [*gatsa*] live [*abókita*]." This place and an understanding of its intrinsic meaning will become useful in a later chapter as we examine the possibilities concerning the clan into which little Billy Powell was born. Tom remembered the large cedar tree that had shaded the place—he had moved five small cedars from beneath its branches to his own property. He recalled, furthermore, that "the rail road from Montgomery to West Point runs within five feet, if not over the place, where the cabin stood in which Billy Powell, or Ussa Yaholo, was born."[23]

Woodward's use of the word "cabin" in his description is instructive. Throughout his writing, Tom Woodward proves himself to be a man aware of details. His choice of this word implies that Osceola passed his early years in a stable, at least semipermanent, structure, built after the white man's style. This also correlates positively with the observation of a contemporary "gentleman of the [Florida] province," who cited the towns of the Seminoles as being "built of pine logs."[24] But Osceola's world shortly would go up in flames. None of his family or his extended cultural kin would escape the dislocations of the United States' Wars of Removal that would consume more than half of the entire nineteenth century: the War of 1812 between the English and the young United States; the Creek War of 1813–1814; the First Seminole War in Florida (1817–1818); the Second Seminole War (1835–1842), which would end his career and his life; the Creek War in Georgia (1836); and the Third (and final) Seminole War in Florida (1857–1858). As these war years dragged on, the Indians would revert to earlier structural styles, using only four corner poles and a gabled roof of palm thatch. Simple, free, and barely visible in times of necessary hiding, this *chokó* (in core Maskókî or Creek) or *chikî(t)* (in Hitchiti) would continue in use to the present day and come to be known among English speakers as a "chikee."

Benjamin Hawkins's report does not conflict with Woodward's regarding the town or the people. The Tallassees and their neighbors across the river, the Tuckabatchys, were "both original Musqua and Muscogees." About the year 1800, Hawkins wrote, the town was situated "in the fork of Eu-fau-be on the left bank of the Tal-la-poo-sa [River]. . . . The land on it is poor for some miles up, then rich flats, bordered with pine lands with reedy branches, a fine range for cattle and horses. The Indians have mostly left the town and settled up the creek, or on its waters, for twenty miles. . . . The Indians who have settled out on the margins and branches of the creek have, several of them, cattle, hogs, and horses and begin to be attentive to them. The head warrior of the town, Peter McQueen, is a snug trader, has a valuable property in negroes and stock and begins to know their value."[25]

Thomas L. McKenney, U.S. superintendent of Indian affairs from 1816 to 1830, later offered a description of men such as McQueen.

A considerable number of persons who have risen to distinction among the southern Indians, within the last quarter of a century, have been the descendents of adventurers from Europe or the United States, who, having married Indian women, and adopted the savage life, obtained the confidence of the tribes, and availed themselves of that advantage to accumulate property. They were at first traders, who carried to the Indians such goods as they needed, and bought their peltries. . . . They lived in a state of semi-civilization, engrafting a portion of the thrift and comfort of husbandry upon the habits of the savage life, having an abundance of everything that the soil, or the herd, or the chase, could yield, practicing a rude but profuse hospitality, yet knowing little of any thing which we should class under the names of luxury or refinement. Their descendants form a class which, in spite of the professed equality that prevails among the Indians, came insensibly into the quiet possession of a kind of rank.[26]

James McQueen was "said to be, by those who knew him well, very intelligent, and [took] great pains to make himself acquainted with the history of the Creeks." Woodward wisely surmises, "From the early day in which he came among them, and they knowing at that time but little of the Whites, their traditions, were, no doubt, much more reliable than anything that can now be obtained from them."[27] Woodward gives us this personal account of Mr. and Mrs. McQueen's family.

I knew several of the children—that is, his sons Bob, Fullunny, and Peter. Bob was a very old man when I first knew him. He and Fullunny had Indian wives. Peter, the youngest son, married Betsy Durant [a woman of mixed blood]. They raised one son, James, and three daughters, Milly, Nancy and Tallassee. Yargee, the son of Big Warrior [Menawa], had the three sisters for wives at the same time, and would have taken more half sisters. After Peter McQueen died, his widow returned from Florida and married Willy McQueen, the nephew of Peter, and raised two daughters, Sophia and Muscogee, and some two or three boys. Old James McQueen had a daughter named Ann, commonly called Nancy. He called her after the Queen of England, whose service he quit when he came into the Nation. Of late years it was hard to find a young Tallassee without some of the McQueen blood in his veins. This daughter, Ann, raised a daughter by one Copinger and called her Polly. She was the mother of Ussa Yaholo, or Black Drink—but better known of late as Oceola.[28]

This is a dense body of information, and we will examine it closely, piece by piece. As for James McQueen, he continued to exert personal, familial, and political power over the Tallassees, possibly for as long as ninety-five years. Through his personal influence, the Tallassees and the Natchez never took up arms against the colonies during the American Revolutionary War. Old James McQueen finally died in 1811—by his own count, as noted earlier, at the age of 128 years. His great-grandson, still known as Billy Powell except to his closest family, would have been about seven years of age at the time—old enough to have known this powerful and respected man personally, to have felt the influence of his large family, and to have been imprinted with his leadership capabilities. Great-grandfather McQueen was buried on the west (Montgomery) side of Nufaupba Creek, on property later owned by "a Mr. Vaugh," about a mile from the birthplace of Osceola.[29]

Woodward tells us that he knew only "several" of James McQueen's children, and he names them. In other words, there were other and unspecified children whose names we do not have. However, they are nonetheless members of Billy Powell's family. If they were sisters, they and their children would have been part of his clan. Brothers would have married women from other clans, and their offspring would have been members of their mothers' clans. Benjamin Hawkins offered a clue to this part of the family history also, however, when he first described McQueen in 1797, saying: "He is healthy and active; has had a numerous family, but has outlived most of them."[30] This could have included more than a single wife as well.

Then, Woodward indicates that Bob was "very old" when he first met him, which may mean that Bob was the eldest, or the eldest surviving, child, and he surely had a family as well. As for the unusual name "Fullunny," it is easily and interestingly explained. It is a transliteration of the Maskókî (Creek) words *cá laní*, or "yellow hair." It would appear that James McQueen was a blond or redhead, which certainly would have been consistent with his Scottish genealogy, and one of his children (probably only one in the first generation, since only one is known to have carried the "yellow hair" designator) received this genetic inheritance. The fact, although certainly an anomaly in its time, must have become commonplace later because Woodward did not find it sufficiently interesting as to comment upon it. In fact, he commented on just the opposite: "Of late years it is hard to find a young Tallassee without some of the McQueen blood in his veins," he observed. Perhaps Woodward was acknowledging a growing number of blondes in the area also.

Thus, we recognize that the intrinsic dynamic of the white settlement frontier as it pressed upon Indian country in this period comprised, to a great extent, the enigmatic identity of the non-Indian frontiersmen and the ephemeral nature of sociosexual relations. In this regard, certainly, one of the most enigmatic members of Osceola's family tree is the husband (or, simply, partner) of James McQueen's daughter Ann, or Nancy, and, therefore, Osceola's maternal grandfather. Woodward tells us only that he was named "Copinger," without indicating a forename or an ethnicity, and he mentions him dismissively, making it appear that he was not a particularly visible or well-known actor in the Creek world of the period. There are several possibilities here, two of which are very intriguing, and one of which might be corroborated by memories of the Seminole people themselves.[31] One possibility is that he was a black escaped slave or freedman, and another is that he was—even if only nominally—a Spaniard. These two possibilities, interestingly, are bound up together in the surname "Copinger," one that would have centrality and visibility in the history of the lower Southeast, in the only circumstances found thus far that coincide with all of the other information.

When Col. José María Coppinger y López de Gamarra (1773–1844) became the last Spanish governor of East Florida in January of 1816, he was forty-three years old. He had traveled to St. Augustine from Cuba, where his family had lived for only a short generation and a half, but very prosperously. His paternal grandparents were Henry Coppinger of Ballyvolane, County Cork, Ireland, and Hellen O'Brien, daughter of Conor (Cornelius) O'Brien of Kilcor. The family was staunchly Roman Catholic and had paid highly for it. Henry's own father, Henry, and his three brothers had been attainted for high treason and suffered outlawry for their loyalty to James II, ill-fated king of England and Scotland. Joseph's father, Cornelius (Cornelio) Coppinger, according to the family tradition, had had to flee Ireland for the treasonous offense of having hidden a Roman Catholic priest. It seems possible that the fate of James McQueen and that of the Coppinger family may have been caught up in the same historical currents over time, with a fascinating intersection in the American Southeast.

Cornelius, whose Irish forbears were significant property owners, successful merchants, military officers, and civic officials, must have had much of the fabled Irish charm as well. Cornelius reached Havana in 1763, when the Treaty of Paris, which capped the Seven Years' War, returned captured Havana to the Spanish crown and ceded erstwhile Spanish Florida to the victorious British. In 1767 he was naturalized a Spanish citizen, by which act he gained commercial entrée to the Spanish Southeast. He managed to meet and marry Maria de los Delores López de Gamarra y Hernández Arturo, a daughter of Francisco López de Gamarra y Ayala, a magistrate of the Real Audiencia, Spain's supreme court in Havana, and accountant of the Royal Treasury. They were married in Madrid, Spain, and returned to Havana, where Cornelio *"tenía una casa de contratacíon de esclavos."*[32] Cornelius Coppinger made his money selling slaves.

The Joseph or José who would become Governor Coppinger of East Florida was the second son of Cornelius and Delores. He was baptized a Roman Catholic in Cuba on 19 April 1773. During his seventy-one years, he "gallantly distinguished himself on various occasions, especially at St Juan d'Alloa, in Mexico, and in the Floridas."[33] His would be the responsibility for governing East Florida for the Spanish crown from January 1816 until his relinquishment of Spain's dominion, for the last time, in 1821, as East and West Florida became a single territory of the United States. He was described by those who dealt with him as "kindly, accessible to even the lowest of his fellow citizens, and of a particularly just nature."[34]

He came to Florida *un soltero,* a bachelor, and in St. Augustine he met his first wife, María Josefa Saravia y Villegas.[35] José and María married in Cuba on 11 July 1797. When the Adams-Onis Treaty was ratified and the flag of Spain was lowered for the last time on 10 July 1821, Governor Coppinger and most of the Peninsulares and Flordanos returned to Cuba to continue their lives there. There is no reason to believe, however, that José Coppinger never saw Florida again. Nor, more important, is there any reason to believe that José Coppinger had been seeing Florida for the first time when he entered as governor in January of 1816. The Coppingers were a merchant family, and Florida and the Southeast were well-known markets for slaves and for all manufactured wares.

Although the Coppinger surname appears, from the American Revolutionary War period onward, in the northeastern United States, there are only two documented presences in the lower Southeast. The earliest is Benjamin Hawkins's own list of traders in the Creek country in 1797. "Copinger"—no first name—is indicated as the trader at Ecunhutkee in September of that year.[36] Ecunhutkee was a small village on the Tallapoosa River, southeastward from Montgomery. Relatively speaking, it was not a hard ride from Tallassee. Coppinger had not been indicated on the two previous lists, those of December 1796 and May 1797.[37] Nor is he listed later. The year 1797 is too late for him to have become the sexual partner of Ann/Nancy McQueen and the father of Polly Copinger. But the fact that a member of the Cuban Coppinger family—either José or his father, Cornelius—may have been there in 1797 is tantalizing and raises the prospect that the Coppinger men may well have gone among the Maskókî tribes earlier and often. The year 1797 simply marks the first time that they obtained a trading license from the agent Hawkins, who had just been sent among the Indians partly for that purpose.

In 1820 we will find documentation of yet another generation of the family doing business in the lower Southeast. A Joseph Coppinger, eighteen years old and of Spanish nationality, reached the port of Charleston, South Carolina, on the schooner *Margaret*. Surely, this is the son of our East Florida governor José. He is too young to be considered the father of Polly Copinger, but his presence certainly indicates the family's continuing connection to the area.[38]

The children and children's children of José and María Josefa continued to make their primary residence in Cuba for another century and a half, until the upheavals of the modern Cuban revolution, the overthrow of Fulgencio Bautista, and the rise to power of Fidel Castro in the mid-twentieth century. As a result of these events, many Coppinger family members returned to Florida—in their eyes still a Spanish land and always close to the history and fortunes of Cuba. As one modern Coppinger family descendent in Florida put it: "We Cubans, whose forefathers were born in Spanish Florida more than six generations ago, look upon this land as a familiar place and . . . neither the laws, wars, revolutions or atheism will take it from our family traditions."[39]

Consequently, there are at least two principal routes by which the surname Copinger may have reached from the island of Cuba to the center of Maskókî Creek country. The most obvious possibility is that Cornelius Coppinger and, soon, his son, José, traveled in and out of the lower Southeast to trade with the Maskókî tribes and, in at least one instance, obtained a trader's license. Also, in at least one instance, the traveler stopped in or near the village of Tallassee. He and James McQueen certainly would have had felicitous associations. It is highly possible that he and Nancy McQueen did also.

The other, but more distant, possibility is that the Havana Coppingers sold a slave in St. Augustine or in Pensacola and that that individual chose to seek freedom among the Indians, taking the slave-seller's name with him. One bit of information that has become available only in recent times concerns the skeletal remains of Osceola that rest at Fort Moultrie, South Carolina. A 1968 report by Drs. T. Dale Stewart and Erik Reed posited that Osceola had had a black ancestor; this possibility was based upon the unique formation of one of the long bones (more of this in chapter 6). Although this type of physical evidence has since been challenged by other forensic anthropologists, it is not inconsistent with the possibility that Osceola's maternal grandfather, Polly Copinger's father, may have been a black man.

Then there are several other intriguing bits of information to consider that are provided by the Seminoles and Maskókî Creeks themselves. Many of them, both in Florida and in Oklahoma, remember Osceola as "a Spanish man."[40] Cornelius Coppinger and his son, José, certainly were fluent in Spanish. Any slave sold by them may well have had facility in Spanish as well. From 1784 until 1821, the Spaniards still held sway over much of the Maskókî territory, as they had for most of the three centuries up to that moment. All of the tribes had numerous and regular interactions with the Spaniards. But, imaging Osceola as a Spanish man indicates an even more intense and personal interaction and may be one more of the reasons why, as a young warrior, he would have such cachet. From a historical standpoint, it certainly is intriguing to think that one of the most famous Indian warriors in U.S. history may also have been the grandson of the last Spanish governor of East Florida.

As a result of all these considerations, we are left with the probability that Osceola's mother's father reached Tallassee sometime between 1770 and 1783 (in order to satisfy the age requirements of all the other concerned parties) and married, or at least had a physical relationship with, Ann (Nancy) McQueen. By 1804, Polly Copinger, born of this union, had reached childbearing age herself and had had at least one child, Billy Powell and, more probably, as we will see, one or two daughters as well. Within another short decade, the Creek War would destroy their lives and their lands, and a number of the warriors and allied families who had survived the war would migrate southward, into Spanish Florida, where Andrew Jackson would pursue them, and war and rumors of war would become their lifelong companions.

↬

Four days after Christmas in 1796, Benjamin Hawkins was traveling through Creek country on his way to take up his station. Only a scant five weeks earlier, he had arrived at Hopewell, on the Koowee River in South Carolina, and noted in his journal that he was on his way "to the Creeks as principal temporary agent for Indian affairs south of the Ohio." On Thursday, 29 December, he noted:

I sat out for the lower Creeks, took the path up the Eufaube, thro' the Tallassee. I called at the house of James Moore, who accompanyed us, continued on 8 miles to James McQueens, an old trader, he was from home [i.e., not at home]. I was very desirous of seeing this old man, he being the oldest white man in the nation, and trader, he has accumulated a considerable property. Continue on 2 miles farther and cross the creek, 30 feet wide, at Baskets one of the grandchildren of Mr. McQueen. The Indians are settled upon the banks of this creek, many of them prettily situated and fenced. The huts neat and cleanly, the last one particularly so, the family remarkable industrious, the field large and fenced. Continue on half a mile and call at the house of William Pound [Powell], here I dined; he has been four years in the nation, has a pretty little Indian woman, and one child. I saw a great number of fowls, and they gave me stewed fowls and pork. I continue on 2 miles farther and encamp.[41]

As for William Powell and his family as Hawkins encountered them here for the first time, one researcher has speculated whether the "one child" might have been Billy Powell, the later Osceola. He concludes not.[42] The weight of the evidence discounts this possibility as well. Furthermore, evidence also indicates that the "pretty little Indian woman" whom Hawkins saw was not the mother of Billy Powell either.

The William Powell whom Hawkins met in 1796, and whom he would mention in the following year as "of little property and not desirous to accumulate much," is yet another of the indistinct actors in Osceola's life drama. The surname Powell was not unknown in the Southeast in this period. Indeed, the surname abounds, and the problem is to differentiate among the various families that are associated with Indians.

One large Powell family, for example, already had settled, illegally, in Cherokee territory. Hawkins described this community as "an extensive settlement west of Clinch and south of Campbell's line, without any pretext to cover their intrusions."[43] It appears that it is this same Powell family, of Virginia and Orange County, North Carolina, however, that provides information that, interestingly enough, does not conflict in its main elements with any of the documented story and may add a dimension.

According to family genealogy, William Powell, the Indian trader, was the eldest son of James Powell (Sr., ca. 1733–1790) and Alse (maiden name unknown) Powell (deceased prior to 1756), who had moved from Brunswick County, Virginia, to Orange County, North Carolina, prior to 1772. By 1799 James (Jr., d. 1830), the son of James and brother of William, was residing or at least had property in Glynn County, Georgia.[44] The family records name male ancestors for three generations prior to the birth of James (Sr.) but give a birthplace only for James's father, Thomas. He was born in Isle of Wight County, Virginia, and died in Brunswick County, Virginia, in 1757. William Powell was the second of eight children, seven brothers and one sister. The only birth date known for the siblings is that of the youngest, a brother, born 7 January 1783. Therefore, William must have been born no later than 1775. Family tradition offers the following information, unsubstantiated by any documents. "*William,* the eldest son, was an Indian trader. He married a Creek Indian Princess, the daughter of an Indian Chief, and they lived in what is now Seminole County, Georgia, on the Chattahoochee River. They had one son, *Osceola,* the famous Indian of the Florida War, and two daughters, one named Maurnee. For some reason, Osceola's mother fled with him to the Seminoles in Florida. . . . Later, William Powell moved with his two daughters to the *West.* This tradition has been handed down to each succeeding generation of this family."[45]

This family tradition does not take into account the degree of movement required of many traders among the Indian settlements. Nor does it include the probability of multiple relationships. But its main story line does not conflict with those elements of Osceola's story that can be confirmed. If William Powell had more than one Indian partner in his lifetime, it certainly is possible that he had more than two. In fact, the documents may indicate that there was a fourth as well. If he was the eldest son of a father born in 1733, then William may have been born circa 1775 and, therefore, about seven years of age when the family moved to North Carolina. That would mean that he could have begun trading at a young age (possibly as an agent for his father), traveled into Indian Country and established himself at or near Tallassee by 1792. If that was the case, then he had taken an Indian wife (probably his first) and had one child, probably a daughter, who was between one and four years of age when Benjamin Hawkins saw the family in 1796. Hawkins described them as having "a child," rather than an infant, so the inference is that the child was closer to four than to one. If this child was a daughter, and if Powell and this first wife had one more daughter soon after Hawkins met them, this would agree with later census records (below). Within a couple of years, Powell's first wife died and was succeeded by Polly. By 1804, Polly had at least two daughters (her own biological daughters, in addition to the two clan daughters William had had by his previous wife) and one son, Billy. How many other children she might have had between 1804 and 1814 we cannot say, but the probability is that she had others.

To this Powell genealogy, then, we must next add the fascinating information provided much later by William Orrie Tuggle, a native Georgian and legal counsel to the Creek Indians in Oklahoma during 1879–1882. Tuggle earned the respect of many of the Oklahoma Creek leaders and recorded a sizeable number of their traditional stories, which John R. Swanton later subsumed into his own researches. Tuggle recounts an introduction to an Indian woman whose name he recorded as "Hepsy Homarty" and described as a sister of Osceola. "Hepsy was stout, had a pleasant face, hazel eyes, somewhat resembling the picture of her brother. She was fourteen years old when her people left Alabama. . . . She said that her father was a White man named Powell, who was also the father of Osceola, but their mothers were not the same; that she remembered some of the incidents [in] the war of 1836, and was now a widow. She did not know her age."[46] Neither did Hepsy speak English.

Tuggle's comments actually appear in two sources. The first is a notebook containing just that—fragmentary notes that he recorded on his first visit to the western Indian Territory in 1879. Later, between 1880 and 1882, Tuggle also wrote sketches of Indian life and personalities that he intended to publish as a book. There are inconsistencies in some of the notes and later sketches that require reconciliation. Tuggle's notes and later sketch of Hepsy Homarty are among such instances, but a close reading makes them reconcilable. The quotation above is from the later sketches. In his early notebook, Tuggle recorded the following.

Met sister of Osceola. Powell was the father of Osceola—a white man by an Indian woman. Hepsy Leeder, or "Hamarty" is her name. Was 14 when she left Ga in 1838—55 yrs old—Black eyes, black hair tinged with gray, large good looking very pleasant face—

She is a widow—Col Sam Chicola married her sister, another sister of Osceola. Her mother was not Osceola's mother—1/2 sister.

Jim McHenry [Major McHenry, a Methodist minister] introduced me to Hepsy—She had just come into Turner & Harrison's store to trade. Came [in] a Studebaker wagon drawn by two ponies—followed by a colt—

Saw her buy 3 lbs of cotton padding in rolls or sheets at 16 2/3 cts per lb—(or shilling a pound as Sanger said) 3 lbs at 50 cts for a quilt—

She was born in Ga—Remembered West Point. I talked to her through Jim McHenry as interpreter. When I used words "West Point. Chattahoochee" she would smile & chuckle—She was pleased when I asked her how old she was. She did not know—Knew she was 14 in 1838.[47]

The "Homarty" is, according to the Maskókî-speaking Seminoles in Florida, an English transliteration of *emathlî* (var. Emathla, Emarthla, Emarthi, Emarthlee, and so on). The Maskókî honorific, emathlî, was a man's civic title, indicating an individual who had been singled out for the respect of the community, much in the way of Cherokee "Beloved" men and women. It was one of many titles and single words that wound up being transliterated into English as surnames by English-speaking officials in the West. It does not exist as a surname in Florida, although it does continue to be passed down to the present day as an Indian man name in certain clans. Hepsy would have been in her late seventies when the U.S. Commission to the Five Civilized Tribes, more commonly known as the Dawes Commission, compiled its "Dawes Rolls" if, indeed, she had not died by then. Variants of "Homarty" occur on the Dawes Roll of the Muscogee (Creek) Nation of Oklahoma (enrolled 1899–1906), and several variants of "Emathla" are shown, although none appears to indicate our Hepsy. The surname "Leader," obviously a variant of "Leeder," occurs there and on the Dawes Roll of the Seminole Nation of Oklahoma and on the Dawes Rolls of the Chickasaws as well.[48]

Given Tuggle's lack of knowledge of the Maskókî language, the "Col Sam Chicola" who had her sister as wife could have been Col. Sam Checote, who had been principal chief of the Muscogee (Creek) Nation in Oklahoma for several terms when Tuggle reached Indian Territory. Possible descendants of these families will be examined further in chapter 11.

If Hepsy was fourteen years old in 1838 and had lived in West Point, Georgia, then that explains why she remembered some of the events of the "war of 1836," by which she refers to the Creek War of 1836 in Georgia. Therefore, she was born around 1824. Whether the sister she indicated was older or younger, they were daughters by the same mother, and, either way, William Powell could have been their father if they were the products of a union that occurred during the time after Powell and Polly Copinger split up in 1814 and Powell went into Georgia before migrating to the West. If Powell reached West Point in 1814, he was then only thirty-nine years old—young enough to have lived a long life yet and to have had any number of other children.

West Point was a relatively short distance northeast from Tallassee, just on the Georgia side of the Chattahoochee River and, therefore, well placed relative to transportation and trading routes. If Powell turned eastward as soon as the family left Tallassee, he could have stopped in West Point very soon. By 1832, however, he was living in the large Creek town of Coweta, on the Chattahoochee just south of West Point. The 1832 Creek census, known as the Parsons-Abbott census, lists the following as separate heads of households:

45. William Powell (alias Cho fe-harjo)	01[males]	03[females]	00 [slaves]	04[total]
46. Lucy Powell (alias Lucy Had ke)	01	01	00	02
47. Martha Powell (alias Lucy Lar, nee)	00	02	00	02[49]

Without names and ages for the unnamed members of the households indicated here, it is difficult to state anything with certainty, but there are two women who appear to be adult daughters of William Powell living next "door" to him. These should be the two daughters whom he had with his first Indian wife, the one who preceded Polly Copinger, and each of them would be in her forties by now. Lucy "Had ke" obviously is Lucy *hútkî* or "white Lucy," but we have no way of knowing why she might be known as such. It could be something as simple as an ability to speak English or a penchant for white man's clothing that has earned her this epithet, or it could be that she looked white, like her father. Whatever the basis for the nickname, she has a male living in her household, and he is probably a son, because she is indicated as the head of household. Martha Powell is known as Lucy "Lar, nee" or *lanî*, probably because she has blond hair that must have come to her from her Powell ancestors. She has only another female in her household, probably a daughter by a husband or partner now gone. William Powell (aka *Chufî hadjo*, mad or drunk rabbit) already has three other females in his household. One of these certainly could be a third wife. Another certainly is Hepsy, the daughter who would have been eight years old in 1832 and fifty-five when she met Orrie Tuggle in Oklahoma. The third could be yet another daughter, Hepsy's sister and the future Mrs. Sam Checote.

One other undocumented but strong probability deserves to be mentioned in regard to William Powell and his Indian wives. When Powell's first wife was removed from the family and Polly entered the picture, it appears that the Powell children remained with their father and Polly. Indeed, they appear to have remained with Powell even after Polly went her own way with her biological son and daughters. They were still living next door when Powell took a third wife, and one of the children by the third wife, Hepsy, referred to herself as Osceola's sister. Tuggle explained that she and Osceola had not had the same mother, but he did not yet understand clan kinship as opposed to white man's kinship patterns. When the Creek War of 1813-1814 caused the breakup of the Powells, it was not only a single family that was dislodged. It almost certainly was an entire clan camp and, more probably, an entire town, and Powell appears to have remained with part of the clan family. Indeed, the white man William Powell was so firmly embedded in the Indian world that he even had an Indian nickname, Chufî hadjo. Therefore, it is highly probable that all three of William Powell's wives were of the same clan, that is, they were clan sisters. That would explain why Powell's daughters would image themselves as Osceola's sisters. That would explain the entire process of the "splits" as they occurred and much that transpired later in their lives.

Irrespective of this, John Sprague was right. Myer Cohen was right. A "split" had indeed occurred within the Powell family. There is no reason, however, to believe that the split came about in anger or for any cause other than the pressures of war, personal choice, and the differing social customs of the Indian and white worlds. Certainly, these were enough. The story of Polly Copinger and her son, Billy Powell, had veered off on its own course, independent of William Powell and his story, as early as 1814. We will pick up the Powell family story again later, in Oklahoma. For now, we must return to the broader McQueen family genealogy and then follow Polly, her daughters, and little Billy Powell into Florida.

∽

Tom Woodward gives us yet another informative comment concerning James McQueen's family when he mentions that Yargee (iakít, the "r" is an English intrusive), one of the sons of Menawa, aka Big Warrior, the powerful headman of the important town of Tuckabatchee, took three sisters — the three daughters of Peter McQueen and Betsy Durant McQueen — as wives and would have taken more "half" sisters. This is a European kinship term that has no validity in the Creek world. Woodward is probably referring to Sophia and Muscogee, the later daughters of Betsy Durant McQueen by Peter McQueen's nephew, Willy. The five girls would have been full sisters in Maskókî terms because they had the same mother and, therefore, were of the same clan, but half sisters in white man's terms because they had different fathers, and their ages could have been at least five or ten years apart. If Yargee was so inclined, however, the girls were not. Sophia McQueen (ca. 1821-1900), at least, emigrated to the West and married Robert W. Stewart, a white man. Their descendents are living in Oklahoma today (see chapter 11 for further information).

Peter McQueen, the youngest son of James McQueen and his Tallassee wife, gained notoriety in his own right as a principal leader of the Native revivalist movement that became the Creek War of 1813-1814. He was one of the Creeks who heard Tecumseh speak in 1811 and took his talk and returned with him to hear also the talk of his brother, Tensquátowah. Peter's role should not be construed as chieftainship or formal leadership in the white American sense any more than it should be later in the case of Osceola and his influence among the Florida Indians (as discussed in the preceding chapter). This point is frequently misconstrued by whites, whose own concept of power is set in a strongly vertical framework, and a misunderstanding of this reality has led to much confusion and many errors concerning the true nature of the warrior Osceola's power base among the Indians during the ensuing war years.

The woman whom Peter had as wife, Betsy Durant, was one of the five children (four girls and one boy) of Benjamin Durant (a non-Indian of French descent) and Sophia McGillivray, herself the daughter of the wealthy and influential Lachlan McGillivray, a Scotsman, and Sehoy Marchand (II). Sehoy (II) was the half-blood daughter of Sehoy Marchand (I), a full-blood Maskókî woman of the powerful Wind Clan, and a Captain Marchand, commander of the French Fort Toulouse from 1714 until his death there in 1722. Sophia was as well the sister of the famous and famously ambitious Alexander McGillivray (1746–1793). Betsy's sisters and brothers were Lachlan, Sophia, Polly, Rachel, John, and Sandy.[50] The marriage could have been a brilliant connection if Peter had been interested in gaining power in the white man's world. In fact, prior to 1811, it appeared that he was doing so in terms of property, as Benjamin Hawkins noted (above). But he cannot have been content in his relationships with whites. Peter took the talk of Tecumseh and rose up against the whites in lower Alabama not merely as a warrior but as a visible and determined war leader.

During the last decade of his relatively short life, Betsy Durant's maternal uncle, Alexander McGillivray, had tried determinedly to direct Creek political policies in a single direction, away from the United States, and had succeeded in establishing himself as a guiding political force among the antiAmerican faction of the Creeks, at least for a short time. By allying himself with the family, Peter McQueen was allying himself with the anti-U.S. faction. McGillivray's overarching theme was consolidated power, but among a people whose traditional power structure did not include a vertical power hierarchy or universal self-imaging. His personal ambitions, together with his attempts to wield the power of alliances with the British and the Spaniards, were viewed with suspicion by many who saw them as blatant empire building. After his untimely death, no other Indian leader attempted to create a national policy among the Creeks or to exercise a leadership role in any national sense.

The person who is generally considered to have succeeded McGillivray as a dominant force among the Creeks, Benjamin Hawkins, was not only a white man but also a representative of the U.S. government. Hawkins was appointed agent to the Creeks three years after the death of McGillivray, and his greatest aim was to persuade the Indians to adopt a "civilized"— that is, white American—style of life. In so doing, he tacitly or overtly fostered a radical increase in internecine strife that would have dire consequences for the Creeks. An increasingly intense split developed between the more northerly or upper towns and the lower towns over issues such as power in the Hawkins-promulgated "National Council," competition over the site of council meetings, dissention over the distribution of the annuities, and attachment to Hawkins and his political and agricultural programs. Too quickly, the balance of power across the upper and lower towns began to shift in a nontraditional manner, toward those lower towns that were closer to Hawkins and the agency, and soon schism was growing among the towns.[51]

By 1811 the situation was a powder keg, for which the spark was provided by the visit to the Creeks from the great Shawanóe leader, Tecumseh. His mother is recalled by the Creeks as having been a Creek woman, and Tecumseh himself may have been born in her town, in which case he honored her by returning to her people. He preached a Nativist doctrine first promulgated by his brother. Tensquátowah, the Open Door, that called for revolt against white encroachments into the Indian world. A party of men from the upper towns around Tallassee and Tuckabatchee went north with Tecumseh to hear the word of his brother and returned in 1812, ready to put the teachings into action. Foremost among the firebrands were Peter McQueen of Tallassee; Josiah Francis or Hilis' Hadjo, a medicine man later called by whites the Prophet Francis, who was from Autauga, a Koasati town; and Cusseta Tustunugee or High Head Jim or Jim Boy and Paddy Walsh, both Alabamas. Through preaching and prophecy they gained a substantial following and declared the old Tallassee Mikkó as their leader. In the name of their cause, they declared a scorched-earth policy: cattle and hogs were slaughtered, stored grain was confiscated or destroyed, and few crops were planted in 1813.

Late in July 1813, "at the crossing of Burnt Corn Creek on the Pensacola Road, a motley collection of White settlers . . . and mixed-blood Creek planters from the Little River area above Pensacola attacked a pack train of gunpowder led by Peter McQueen and High Head Jim." The aggressors were forced to take refuge in a makeshift fort that had been constructed around the homestead of an old Georgia trader, Samuel Mims, and "what began as an attack ended as the infamous slaughter of Fort Mims. Instead of acting to ameliorate the situation, Hawkins exacerbated it when he intervened militarily and the might of the U.S. became involved." The antagonists, who answered the call of McQueen and the other Nativists, were called "Red Sticks" because they had voted by choosing red sticks in council, signifying their decision in favor of war. They quickly were pitted against their own Indian kin, those who sided with Hawkins and wanted peace with the whites. The situation escalated radically when Andrew Jackson saw a nexus of the uprising and his own personal ambitions for military leadership, and "seeing the chance to pick up much rich, free land after an easy contest, Tennessee, Georgia, and Mississippi Territory rushed armies into the Nation" at his call. "After a bitter fight that involved the Choctaws, Cherokees, and many nonNativist Creeks as allies of the Whites, the Red Sticks succumbed. . . . Peace left much of the . . . country a scarred and smoking ruin."[52]

This Nativist uprising, which turned into the Creek War of 1813–1814, was, in every sense of the term, a civil war among the Creeks of Alabama. Towns—and even clans—split and reformed as military alliances. Hereditary lineages were neither forgotten nor forsaken, but military expediency would create fictitious alliances—at least in times of war—for many years to come. If politics creates strange bedfellows, as the old axiom admonishes, warfare can be even more confusing.

When the Nativist prophets began their preaching, James McQueen was no longer alive to counsel his family. Localized disturbances rapidly escalated into regional warfare, exacerbated by the opportunistic entry into the fray of Andrew Jackson and his troops. The treaty of capitulation finally forced upon the Creeks by Jackson on 9 August 1814 required that they cede to the U.S. government two-thirds of their remaining lands in Alabama and Georgia—which included property occupied by Indians who had sided with the Americans as well as those who had opposed them.[53] "Sharp Knife," as the Indian friendlies called Jackson, rationalized his way into this profound betrayal of his Indian "friends" because, he said, the Creeks had failed to stop Tecumseh when he first began his preaching. They should have taken him prisoner immediately and handed him over to U.S. authorities, Jackson declared—or they should "have cut his throat."[54]

Regarding this horrendous treaty and its effects upon the Tallassee people, Woodward recalls that by the time Jackson, "Jacksa Chula Harjo" or "Old Mad Jackson" (*chula*: old; and *hadjo*: drunk, crazy, mad) as the Indian Nativists called him, reached "Franca Choka Chula, or the old French trading house, as it was called by the Indians" (that is, Fort Toulouse, soon to be Fort Jackson), a group of Creek dissidents gathered up their followers and left their homes. These included Sowanoka or Savannah Jack, whose name would seem to indicate that he was a Shawanóe or Shawnee Indian, and Hossa Yaholo, whom Woodward tells us was sometimes confused with Osceola but was a grown man with an established reputation, while Osceola was still a child. They joined Peter McQueen and Betsy Durant, along with her father and her mother, Sophia. "The boy, Billy Powell, who was the grandson of one of Peter McQueen's sisters [Ann, called Nancy], was then a little boy, and was with this party. They all put out for Florida, and on their route they split among themselves."[55]

Woodward advances no reason for the split. The modern Seminoles recall only that the father did not want to go to Florida, which was sufficient, and so he turned aside, and we now know that along with him went both of his daughters by his first wife, who were old enough to make their own choices to accompany him.[56] Indeed, as we see now, they may not have been solely accompanying him but, rather, remaining with a larger portion of their clan. John T. Sprague, a U.S. army officer who provided a written account of the later Second Seminole War in Florida (1835–1842), offers information on Osceola's family as well. Although questionable on several points, the account indicates that, at the breakup of the Powell family, two daughters went away with the father, and the son remained with his mother.[57] This scenario has been questioned by researchers—not the split itself but, rather, the method of dividing the custody of the children. Nevertheless, in view of the later statement of Hepsy "Homarty," information from the 1832 census, and in the light of Maskókî (Creek) tradition, this would have been the traditional way of dividing the family if the two daughters were the issue of Powell by his previous marriage to the "pretty little Indian woman" and were old enough to decide for themselves and if Billy Powell was still a child whose life was tied to that of his biological mother.

This scenario holds true also if the two wives were clan sisters as well, because of the ages of the offspring. Hawkins reminds us that "marriage gives no right of the husband over the property of his wife; and when they part she keeps the children and the property belonging to them."[58] Moreover, the story also fits with Hawkins's observation if the child he saw was Osceola's clan (half) sister because she would be one of the adult daughters by his first wife, and there are two Powell women living next door to him in Coweta. The white Powell family tradition that Osceola's family lived on the Chattahoochee River coincides with Sprague's allegation also. Sprague also reports that William Powell remained in Georgia until he migrated to Arkansas in 1836.[59] This would account for the fact that Hepsy, a child of Powell's third family, recalled events of the "1836 war." The white family tradition, however, would seem to have compressed events to exclude the northern Alabama "prologue" to the story. At the same time, nevertheless, the family history does include the detail regarding William Powell's subsequent move to the West.

Those refugees who had followed Peter McQueen into Florida found succor, for a few years at least, among the British and the other Creeks who had migrated from the upper towns into the erstwhile Apalachee territory of West Florida. Shortly after their arrival, Hawkins reported to Governor Early of Georgia that the Prophet Francis and Peter McQueen had been seen wearing British uniforms at an outpost newly established by the British on the Apalachicola River.[60] Agents for the British crown, operating from what was still Spanish-held territory, were attempting to finesse the support of the Creeks against the Americans by promising the return of lands that the Indians had been forced to cede to the United States by Jackson's 1814 treaty.[61] The war leader, Hilis' Hadjo (i.e., the Prophet Francis), and a delegation of Indians, pleased with the British courtship, left Florida in 1815 for a trip to England.

Sowanoka Jack and his people turned westward. Peter McQueen and many of his family, along with many of the erstwhile war leaders, moved southward into their old and familiar hunting grounds in Spanish Florida. The family split, and Peter McQueen, whose chosen course kept him in the forefront of the resistance to removal, obviously traveled farther and faster than Polly Copinger Powell and her son, Billy Powell. Peter, closely aided by his brothers-in-law, John and Sandy Durant, fought on. In November of 1816 Woodward saw McQueen at Fort Hawkins, where the Indians had gone to trade.[62] A few months later, on 17 March 1817, Alexander Arbuthnot, a British agent (later hanged by Jackson), wrote to Fort Gaines from Ocklockonee Sound complaining that "Negroes" had been stolen from Peter McQueen.[63]

Later that year, on 30 November, a group of Apalachicola Creeks, apparently including some of McQueen's followers if not McQueen himself, attacked a boat party transporting army stores from Mobile Point up the Apalachicola River to Fort Scott in Early County, Georgia. All were killed except two soldiers who escaped and a white woman named Mrs. Stuart, the wife of a sergeant, who was abducted by the Indians. General McIntosh, Maj. Tom Woodward, and a Capt. Isaac Brown, in command of the body of Indian friendlies accompanying Jackson's troops into Florida in the early spring of 1818, pursued McQueen's warriors, whom they knew to have the captured woman. "While marching on between St. Marks, and Sewannee Town, distance about one hundred miles, on Sunday, the 12th day of April, we discovered fresh signs of Indians."[64] Woodward, in the best position to tell us what actually happened, says that during the fight the women and children were purposely cut off from the warriors in order to capture them and the white woman who was calling for help. He and his Indian friendlies overtook and captured a part of the group, consisting of ninety-seven women and children, including Mrs. Stuart. "This was at Osilla [the Aucilla River, about ten miles east of St. Marks], and was known as the McIntosh fight." Woodward specifically mentions that among the prisoners taken that day was Billy Powell, or Osceola. Woodward knew Osceola well. He recalls, "Capt. Isaac Brown and myself, with a party of friendly Creeks and Uchees, made him a prisoner . . . and he was then but a lad."[65]

After the capture of the Indians, General Jackson was "sought out" by an old Indian woman, to whose people Jackson offered amnesty in return for the surrender of Peter McQueen to the commandant at St. Marks. Jackson's report of this affair, naturally favorable to himself, says that only the old woman was let go, with a letter to the commandant of St. Marks concerning the agreement. But, together with later known movements of McQueen's group, the inference is that the women and children were set free to convey the offer to McQueen, although McQueen chose not to avail himself of the proffered clemency of the Americans—if the offer ever even reached him.[66] During the next year, Peter and his people moved down the Florida peninsula to Tampa Bay, later the site of the U.S. army post, Fort Brooke. There, Sandy Durant died, and his brother, John, left Florida for Nassau, New Providence, in the Bahamas.

Such independent movement of groups is also consistent with Maskókî tradition. Benjamin Hawkins avers that, prior to his own attempts to impose Euroamerican-style organization upon the Creeks, they had no national government or law. By this he could only have meant to imply that they had no *unified national* government, in Euroamerican terms. This reality is thoroughly consistent, however, with their traditional horizontal power structure. Of course, he disregards the Spaniards' long interactions with the tribes and Spanish attempts to impose their own European style of government, but his assessment of the traditional horizontal power structure of the Maskókî world is nonetheless accurate. The term "Creek Confederation," used too often and too flagrantly in later historical accounts, was purely a situational forum for consensus decision making at a large-scale level. Each Creek town had its own *mikkó* (core Maskókî) *or mikkî(t)* (old Hítchitî; today's Miccosukee), "there being several so called in every town, from custom, the origin of which is unknown" and a number of specialized counselors.[67]

Hawkins may not have known the origins of the word, today written as "Micco," but its antecedents seem eminently clear from the perspective of modern researches, and its historical function—albeit slightly altered in form—remains to the present day. Florida Seminole tribal elders define the term as "I give it to you; you give it to me"—a clear statement of the reciprocity that is expected of town leaders in all their actions, because all their actions are expected to be done on behalf of the people.[68] A Micco superintended all public and domestic concerns, received all public characters, heard their talks, laid these talks before the town, and delivered the talks of his town to other towns. He oversaw, above all, the physical well-being of the town's residents, directing the collective labor of the town's fields that created the communal reserves, which were, in turn, distributed by the Micco. This was particularly necessary during the depths of winter, during periods of drought or famine, and for the ritual mourning period following a war, when many women temporarily were without husbands to hunt and provide food for them. As early as the sixteenth century, the reciprocal nature of the position is demonstrated in Spanish documents and in the earliest images of North American Natives by the French Huguenot Jacques le Moyne de Morgues in his depiction of transporting foodstuffs to the public granary.[69] In other words, the Miccos acted as spokesmen for the collective will of the people, deriving their power from the respect and collective consent of the people and the confidence reposed in them to place the needs of the people above all personal considerations. So, the people gave to them, and they gave to the people, and, in so doing, they kept the local world in balance.

Warriors were also prominent in town affairs because of their prowess in battle, which was to say, their ability to protect the physical well-being of the people. Young men could be appointed leaders in various situations if they distinguished themselves in "warlike enterprises" and, through repeated successes, could rise in the estimation of the people. There was no such thing, however, as an "automatic" rank or even a permanent one. Power could be gained and kept, or squandered and withdrawn. The will of the people was paramount. In the case of Peter McQueen, as in the case of other prominent war leaders later in the Seminole Wars, their leadership positions were a combination of heredity, skill, and the continuing confidence of the people who followed them. Osceola himself would prove an obvious example of this process. When heredity no longer served, however, or skill became attenuated by poor health or changing situations, their followers sought out other leaders, and the old leader stepped aside for the good of all concerned.

Ultimately, Peter McQueen's travels in Florida carried him as far south as the Atlantic side of the lower peninsula, near Cape Florida. There he died "on a little barren island," probably in late 1818 or 1819. This date and place seem most likely on the basis of Woodward's comments, military documents, and information from collateral descendents, citizens of the Seminole Nation in Oklahoma. By 1821, his widow, Betsy Durant, had already returned to Alabama, remarried (to Willy McQueen), and had at least one more child, the daughter whom she named Sophia after her own mother.[70] Unfortunately, no information found thus far specifies which of Peter's brothers was the father of Willy McQueen. The descendents of Betsy's daughter Sophia are discussed in chapter 11.

In late 1821 Andrew Jackson sent a report to the secretary of war that included a list of twenty-two Indian villages in Florida as known to old Neamathla (*hinéha emathlî* or respected warrior), the Hitchiti leader of the Fowltown, which had been Jackson's early target in the First Seminole War. Number 7 on Neamathla's list was "Peter McQueen's village, the other side of Tampa Bay."[71] Two other towns, numbers 6 and 10, also contained McQueen's people. Number 10, Old Suwannee Town (Old Town, Suwannee Old Town), had been burned in 1818, however. Number 6, "Sow-walla village," had no indication of location but may have also been an older village. Regardless, Osceola and his mother may have joined the group on "the other side" of Tampa Bay. This possibility also fits with other reported events.

The period 1818–1821 marks a cultural as well as a politicomilitary watershed in the life of young Osceola specifically, the lives of the Indians in Florida generally, and the Indians' place in state and national history. Osceola had left his home, his hometown, and many of his clan kin in Alabama at around ten years of age. He had been living a seminomadic life for almost four years—four of his critical, formative, adolescent years. During this time, the mixed-blood culture and minimal tolerance for whites that had dominated his worldview were forcibly shifted by the polarizations of warfare against a predominantly white enemy. The enemy, however, was not British or Spanish, or even American per se. This enemy was the United States government rather than each individual white American citizen. We shall have ample proof throughout Osceola's life that he was capable of making this distinction.

As regards the larger world of the Maskókî people of Florida, Alabama, and Georgia, it was during this short four-year period also when a social amalgam began to take place among the citizens of various culturally related tribes: those who had been dislocated by the Creek War in Alabama as well as those whose lives were permanently altered by Jackson's international incursions into their original homelands in Spanish Florida. As a result of the events outlined here and precipitated by the pressures of the U.S. government, the amalgamation took place inside of the political area now known as Florida. The Creeks who had fled the previous war were undoubtedly represented by a disproportionate number of noncombatant women and children. The continuing pressures of warfare inside Florida would inevitably blur original tribal lines as intermarriages and procreation began to reshape alliances. The lowest common denominator of Maskókî life had been, and continued to be, the clan. It was the core of village, town, and city life. The clans, therefore, would provide affinity bases for displaced cultural kinfolk, providing them with an already well-established formula for social reorganization. The clans would continue to provide cultural and social continuity throughout the horrors of the coming four decades, until the white soldiers finally left the most determined Indians in a semblance of peace, in their last retreat, deep in the fastnesses of the Florida interior in 1858.

By the last quarter of the eighteenth century, and partly as a result of the brief British dominion in Florida, the indigenous people who had survived the Spanish pressures to assimilate had become known generically as "Siminolies" or "Seminoles." These were remnants of various earlier Maskókî tribes that had amalgamated principally at the head of the Florida peninsula, on the Alachua savanna, and westward along the Suwannee River. In their own eyes, they were *yatî siminolî(t)* or *yat'siminolî(t)* — "free people," in the old Hitchiti dialect of the mother language, Maskokî.[72] The Miccosukees, the Miccosukee Seminoles, and Creeks use these terms to the present day. In core Maskókî or Creek, the same term is *istî siminolî(t)*, both *yatî* and *istî* in this case indicating "people," the plural of "person." Not every English speaker cocooned the various tribes in this generic term; many close observers realized that the Indians knew the fine distinctions of their own unique heritages as Hitchiti, Euchee, and so forth.

Tom Woodward, who stands out even among such close observers, explained it thusly. "The Seminoles is a mixed race of almost all the [Maskókî] tribes . . . but mostly Hitchetas and Creeks. The Hitchetas have by the whites been looked upon as being originally Muscogees, but they were not. They had an entirely different language of their own, and were in the country when the Creeks first entered it."[73] What Woodward did not have sufficient information as to realize, of course, was that the two languages he cites had been a single language in the distant past and had become mutually exclusive only over time. Over the coming two centuries of war and amalgamation, these two would be the dominant, ergo the survivor, languages. Furthermore, they were older inhabitants of the country than he could have realized, but they were, indeed, already in the "Florida" country when their more northerly "Creek" cousins entered it. Possibly five to six thousand "Seminole" men, women, and children lived in Spanish-controlled Florida at the opening of the First Seminole War.[74]

It was during this same period, 1818–1821, when young Billy Powell grew to become Asse yahola (or Ussa yaholo, as Woodward spelled it), the singer of the wolf's song, or Black Drink Singer (as will be discussed further in chapter 3). These years constitute the period when the boy would have passed through his fifteenth to seventeenth years and when his town (or, at least, the core people of his clan family) would have been settled once again, long enough to plant, harvest, and celebrate the Green Corn Ceremony, the major annual busk. It appears that by the time Osceola went through his passage into manhood, his mother had taken another husband. Sprague says that all three "removed to a hammock near Fort King."[75] His presence at and around Fort King as a young man was noted by other white military reporters as well. The stage was being set for the next, and more public, phase of Osceola's life.

Regarding the story of Osceola's extended family at this time, Lt. John Sprague mentions in passing that Osceola had as a wife a Creek woman named "Che-cho-ter (the Morning Dew) . . . [and] by her he had four children."[76] He gives no time frame for this union, nor do any other sources corroborate this detail. The possibility, however, does not conflict with any other known information. The *American Anti-Slavery Almanac* of 1839 also would promulgate the story that Osceola had been married to the daughter of a former slave and an Indian chief.[77] The unnamed wife allegedly was seized by slave hunters in 1835 as Osceola and a daughter watched. This event was supposedly the basis for the later argument between Osceola and the Indian agent Wiley Thompson, although, as we have learned (in chapter 1), Thompson did not mention this point of contention in his report of the incident. Joshua Giddings, an ardent abolitionist, repeated this story in 1858, as did Myer Cohen, the gossipy Charleston lawyer who was the first to publish a book about his experiences in the Second Seminole War.[78] Although the idea that Osceola may have had a part-black wife is not implausible, the chronology of the story is unlikely, the association of the event with Thompson is questionable, and the sources are suspect. As a consequence, the reference is considered unreliable.[79]

The fact that Osceola did at a later point have two wives and probably two and, possibly, three children is well established. The documentation all centers on late 1837 and early 1838, the time of his capture and death. We even have available to us today one graphic image of the two wives with one of the children. Dr. Robert Lebby, Dr. Frederick Weedon, the artist George Catlin, and Lt. John Pickell, U.S. Army, all of whom spoke from their own observations, mentioned that Osceola had two wives at the time of his capture. The list of family members who turned themselves in at Fort Mellon at a summons from Osceola following his capture indicates that there were two wives and that each wife had one child. In a drawing created some years after Osceola's death for inclusion in one of his *Albums Unique*, George Catlin sketched two wives and one child (see figure 6 in chapter 4).

From a negative copy of a document in the collections of the St. Augustine (Florida) Historical Society, we obtain the list of Indian prisoners held in Fort Marion during the period of October–December 1837.[80] Captured Indians and escaped slaves were being assembled there for transportation to the West or return to their owners. Among them are the names Ui-chee and Ah-lik-chen, who are listed as Powell's wives, and each has one child, unnamed. They are among the Indians who arrived at Fort Mellon on 30 November 1837. "Ui-chee" may have been the adult woman's nickname, or it may indicate that she was a Euchee woman. The sister of Ui-chee was with her, as well as a sister of Osceola, but the document does not indicate which they were. This information was reported by Lieutenant Pickell.

There is a "Polly" listed among the women who had turned themselves in previously at Fort Mellon, but no indication of any relationship that she might have had with Powell/Osceola. Nevertheless, Fort Mellon was the military outpost nearest to the place where Osceola and his followers were encamped prior to his capture. It was the place where his people turned themselves in in response to his message for them to do so, and there is only one adult "Polly" on the entire list. She is listed as having a child, her own, with her. The child was called Se-ma-to. This is not definitive, but it is indicative. In 1837, Polly probably was upward of sixty-seven years old. If this is Osceola's mother, as it appears to be, then the child may have been a grandson of a deceased daughter. In addition, there is a separate notation on the list for "Powell's People," and there are fifteen names in this group, all of them warriors except for the name of one daughter of a warrior. The people on the list are grouped according to the warrior with whom they turned themselves in or were captured or according to the date on which they fell into the hands of the soldiers. That is, there was no impetus at this moment for their white captors to attempt to discover family relationships any broader than those of nuclear families.

⸏

In his publication *The Five Civilized Tribes*, Grant Foreman quotes a letter from the Reverend Orson Douglas to the U.S. commissioner of Indian affairs written on 15 August 1843 regarding a man who was also a member of Osceola's extended family.

John Douglas Bemo was a Seminole Indian with an interesting history, who distinguished himself in the service of his people. The son of a chief, he was also the nephew of . . . Osceola. In 1834, when he was about ten years old, he was carried away from his home in

Florida. One of his abductors was a man named Jean Bemeau from whom the boy received his name. He was taken to sea . . . for eight years. . . . In 1842 his ship made the port of Philadelphia and while there he visited the [Presbyterian] Mariner's Church and met the pastor, Rev. Orson Douglas. The minister said that Bemo was one of the most extraordinary characters he had ever met; he was greatly concerned about the persecution of the Seminole tribe at the hands of the government, and expressed a strong desire to return to and serve his unhappy people.

Bemo was received into the church and plans were made to fit him to teach and preach to the Seminole people in their western home. Mr. Douglas in September 1842 "put him into the best schools our city affords, so that all the instruction needful to prepare him to be a blessing to his people had been furnished. He is so desirous to do them good that his mind is bent on returning" to them in the fall of 1843, "to live or die with them & for them." It seems to us a singular providence, that, while they are so prejudiced against the whites, one of their number should be raised up of God for their welfare. When Osceola died at the fort near Charleston, John was present and sent word by the warriors that so soon as they ceased fighting he would return & be their chief. It is the Rev. Orson Douglas who is writing . . . for assistance in sending John Bemo to the Seminole Nation in the West; he offers to take the Indian to Washington for the commissioner to interview him.[81]

We will follow John Bemo to Indian Territory in chapter 11. He certainly could have been the nephew of Osceola if his mother was Polly's daughter, an older sister of Osceola, and was the wife of Yaha hadjo, a contemporary and war leader. After Osceola was taken prisoner in October 1837, it was Yaha hadjo whom Osceola asked to have sent for, to take a message to his (Osceola's) family to turn themselves in. In a letter to Lt. James Chambers, Col. A. G. W. Fanning instructed him: "The letter herewith inclosed was sent to me by Capt. Lowd. It is from Paddy Carr [a half-blood Creek and strong supporter of removal] and I have caused its contents to be interpreted to Philip and Powell. They have requested me to send this letter to Coahajo—Further, they request Coahajo to send them a messenger and wish that this messenger might be Tom, the brother in law of Powell, called Yahajo."[82]

Ya'hadjo (the Maskókî contraction of Yaha hadjo, "drunk or crazy/mad wolf") had been one of the signers of the Treaty of Payne's Landing (Florida) in 1832. In addition, he had been among the Indian representatives who had traveled to view the western Indian Territory in 1832–1833 and had signed the infamous Treaty of Fort Gibson, both of which treaties Jesup was attempting to enforce. Even more interesting at this particular moment, however, is the fact that Yaha hadjo had been reported killed during the several skirmishes that took place during March of 1836.[83] Inaccurate death reports were not unusual in the excitement of the war. Either these two were different individuals, or, more likely, the report of the death of Yaha hadjo was in error. Nevertheless, a warrior called Yaha hadjo had as a wife a sister of Osceola. Osceola would not have considered him a brother-in-law if the wife had been a half sister by a mother not of Osceola's own clan. Therefore, we have further confirmation that Polly Copinger had at least a second daughter. Further evidence concerning the other daughter comes to us from another source, and an interesting source in himself.

James Andrew Welch, M.D. (1797–1852), was a member of the Royal College of Surgeons of England.[84] He reached St. Augustine about 1822 or 1824 and, during his sojourn of twenty years or so in the United States, was a man of some mystery as concerned his English family and his finances. He was a bit of an opportunist and, unfortunately, given to much hyperbole in his writings. St. Augustine mayor J. B. Gould labeled him "self-centered" and "ruthless."[85] Despite all of this, his narrative of a young Indian boy whom he said was named Nikkanochee, whom he took as a ward and identified as a nephew of the war leader Osceola, contains much accurate cultural information concerning the southeastern tribes. The accuracy of his cultural information, in turn, lends verisimilitude to his story of the younger "Oceola Nikkanochee," as Welch called him (see figure 21 in chapter 11).

This boy was, he wrote, the son of Osceola's sister by Econchatti Micco (the *mikkó* of *ekun chattî* or red ground) and had been born while they were living in the Chattahoochee River area.[86] In his 1955 examination, Mark Boyd discounted this story.[87] Nevertheless, as in so many other instances in the life of the famous warrior Osceola, the fascinating story has a ring of truth.

Econchatti was a tribal town that, prior to the Creek War of 1813–1814, was socially and politically allied with the Abéca people and had been situated on part of the site now occupied by Montgomery, Alabama.[88] Its Micco, a respected and powerful man who was not interested in fighting, moved his town southward in the displacement of war. He and five other powerful leaders, including Neamathla (*hinéja emathlî*, respected warrior), were given permanent reserves on the Apalachicola River by the terms of the Treaty of Moultrie Creek (1823) for their long support of peaceful relations with the United States. But as Indian-white aggressions escalated,

Welch reports accurately when he says that the town was attacked and raided by whites who stole or destroyed the Indians' property. By 1836, Econchatti Micco and his people were in the woods on the Apalachicola River and starving. About the same time, Richard Keith Call reported that Econchatti Micco and some of his people had moved southward down the Florida peninsula to seek the protection of the U.S. Army at Fort Brooke (Tampa) following the execution of Charley Emathla (on 25 November 1835). By July of 1836, however, Econchatti Micco seems to have returned to the Apalachicola/Chattahoochee area. Archibald Smith, Jr., a white settler who had known the Indian leader for fifteen years, wrote twice to Gen. George Gibson, commissary general of subsistence, from Gadsden County, Florida, pleading for beeves and corn for their supply.[89]

The Indian child Nikkanochee, only five or six years old at the time, was captured by white soldiers as he and his family scattered and ran from them on 26 August 1836. The exact place of his capture is not cited by Welch, but the nearest army post, to which he was taken, was Newnansville in central Florida, about thirty miles west of present-day Gainesville and a significant distance from either the Apalachicola town or Fort Brooke. Col. John Warren, the military officer who received the captives, took pity on the little boy and took him to the Warren home at Jacksonville, where he remained until October of the following year. Colonel Warren, "being on the point of making an important change in his own family,"[90] then gave custody of the child to Welch, who had expressed much interest in him. It was some time, however, before the child was willing to share with the white family the details of his early life.

Econchatti Micco's wife (possibly only one of his wives), the mother of Nikkanochee and sister of Osceola by Polly, must have given birth to the child in 1830 or 1831 while they were still on the Apalachicola. Econchatti Micco's town, which Welch places on the Chattahoochee River, was just below the area where the Flint and Chattahoochee rivers at their confluence change names and become the single Apalachicola River. Smith describes Econchatti Micco's town as about sixty miles south of there, on an island in the Apalachicola River. The confluence of these three rivers also marks the geographic point where Alabama, Georgia, and Florida meet, their modern political frontiers only having been established in the first decade of the nineteenth century. The child's memories of his mother were sad ones. It appears that she was sick over a long period of time, as her son had "no recollection of her in health," and she succumbed to her illness "before the war began," according to his only frame of reference.[91] His relationship with his father was close, however, and he shared with Welch his memories of their playing together and sleeping wrapped in the same bear skin. He recalled his father's having visited his mother and sitting beside her lovingly during her illness. At the moment of her death, however, Nikkanochee was her only attendant.

Nikkanochee would be captured by soldiers not once but twice during the first eight months of the coming year, that is, 1836, the first year of the war. The first time, he was traveling through a pine forest with the women and children "in the charge of a woman who had been taking care of him since his mother's death," the warriors having separated themselves two or three days earlier, when they were overtaken by soldiers.[92] Over the next few days, he managed, along with two women and a little girl, to escape during an unguarded moment. By August, however, he was captured once again, and this time, for his own reasons, chose not to make another escape.

Nikkanochee did not make any point of telling Colonel Warren or Dr. Welch about other members of his family or his relationship to Osceola. It came out one day in conversation, quite some time later, after he had begun to attend the white man's school. The teacher whipped him for some infraction, and the doctor asked him if he had ever been whipped before. He replied, yes, that his uncle, Osceola, had whipped him once with small switches to make him walk faster (the inference being that they were in danger or being pursued by soldiers). Welch reports that he did not at first understand the relationship between the child and the warrior, but it was explained to him by Capt. John Graham during a dinner party at the St. Augustine home of Judge (later Florida governor) Robert Reid on 1 August 1838. Welch also adds that this information later was confirmed by Dr. William Simmons, who knew both Graham and Osceola personally.

The child's mention of his clan uncle, Osceola, adds value to our understanding of the story. First, it indicates that the group with which Nikkanochee was traveling at a time when the group was running, that is, during that first war year, was Osceola's family group. Then, we have a passing mention from Lt. John Pickell, U.S. Army. Pickell was stationed at Fort Mellon when Osceola's family arrived there in response to Osceola's message to them to turn themselves in following his own capture in October of 1837. Pickell said that among the group was a sister of Osceola.[93] He does not name her, however, and she is not identified as such on the list of prisoners, compiled shortly afterward at Fort Marion (St. Augustine). Nevertheless, she was most likely Osceola's full sister (by clan and blood) who was the wife of Yaha hadjo.

All of this certainly is consistent with tradition. Osceola and his mother and other clan members had traveled southward out of Alabama with their clan uncle, Peter McQueen. Polly and Billy had lived, at least for a few years, in "a hammock near Fort King." It is always possible that this hammock was the same site that just a few years later would be Osceola's secret camp on the Cove of the Withlacoochee, the one that would not be located by the white soldiers until April of 1837. In choosing it, Osceola was returning to a site that he knew well. Polly's elder daughter had gone with the Econchatti Micco earlier or by that time. Alternatively, when Osceola's clan sister became the consort of Econchatti Micco, her mother, sister, and other women of the clan could also have chosen to take refuge for a while in his village on the Apalachicola. Now, however, at least six years later, we see the adult Osceola, a warrior in his own right and, as we know, rapidly rising toward the zenith of his own personal power and influence. When Osceola's sister, the mother of Nikkanochee, died, care of the child would have reverted to her own clan sister. Polly, a second husband, and other members of Polly and Osceola's clan would have followed the rising young warrior, Osceola.

Yaha hadjo, husband of a sister who already would have been in Osceola's entourage, would have accompanied the rising young warrior also if they had not been together already. Children fathered by him would have, therefore, remained with their mother, her mother, and other clan members in this manner. At some point, late in 1835 or in the first days of 1836, Osceola, a sister, a nephew, possibly his mother, his wives, the warriors of his clan, any other Indians who chose to follow them, and a few ex-slaves were traveling and operating independently. Nikkanochee, the child of Osceola's deceased sister, would be captured from this group two times by August of 1836.

All of Dr. Welch's associations and events are completely plausible, and he speaks with the authority of personal knowledge about people and places that are well documented in Florida history. On the other hand, the doctor rarely permits his lack of personal knowledge to stop him from speaking with an assumed authority on any topic, and, consequently, it is left to us, his readers, to exercise caution. In this story, however, there is nothing obviously contradictory. We will follow Osceola Nikkanochee's later life, as least as far as we can know it, in chapter 11.

In addition to his story of Osceola's nephew, Welch also gives us his version of the story of Capt. John Graham's personal relationship with Osceola—a story that was told by several contemporaries, but in several versions. In the Welch version, Graham establishes a physical relationship with Osceola's niece, "Nathleocee," who may have been about seventeen years old when she and Graham met. The girl's father, whom Welch (not surprisingly) dubs a "King," has been killed in battle. She is an orphan, Welch says, although he tells us nothing of her mother, who would have to have been another of Osceola's sisters. All we know is that she has been raised by Osceola, although this may have been a slight exaggeration also, because it was the girl's female clan relatives who would have cared for her even if they were traveling and living in Osceola's entourage and, therefore, under his protection and that of his warriors. She meets Graham, who "became enamoured of her extraordinary sylvan charms," and, over the course of their relationship, she has three children.[94] The coming war destroys their symbiosis, however, and Graham is required to resume his personal life within his own culture. Graham and Osceola retain the memory of their close friendship, however, and it serves to protect Graham, at least during the early war years. Nathleocee and her children are captured, according to Welch, and confined in Fort Marion with the other Indian prisoners while Graham is on leave visiting friends in New York. Subsequently, she and the children are transported to Indian Territory in the West with the rest of Osceola's family. There are certainly possible realities in this account, but there are also sufficient questions raised by the other accounts as to make it worthy of further examination. Consequently, it will be examined separately in chapter 3.

By the summer of 1837, a year after the capture of Nikkanochee, it appears that Osceola no longer had a separate group of his own. Illnesses, which have been discussed earlier, may have been part of the cause of his having combined forces with those of another, more powerful leader. In April, however, the white soldiers finally had managed to locate his long-hidden camp on the Cove of the Withlacoochee River, so he and his people no longer had the protection of its isolation.[95] Furthermore, it was during the summer of 1837 when the resistance forces replaced Micanopy's leadership with that of Abiákî, or Sam Jones. Micanopy was known as a weak leader who favored emigration. Abiákî was the most implacable foe the whites had in Florida and a man who possessed strong war medicine. Indeed, he was the *hilíswa haya* or medicine man who was Osceola's mentor. In July 1837, Lt. John C. Casey sent to General Jesup a list of the various Indian "bands" currently in the field, as supplied to him by Abram (Abraham), the black double-agent.[96] There was no individual listing for a group headed by Osceola. There was, however, a listing for a group headed by "Apai-akkee," and it was the largest of all the groups listed, with 280 members. This group also included Philip, an important leader, and, although it is not explicitly indicated, Osceola's people probably also were included.

By the end of the summer of 1837, however, Osceola's star already was on the descendent. That rainy season was a particularly unhealthy one, and he may have contracted malaria. Although the war would drag on for another five years, Osceola's role in it would last barely another three months, and his life itself would be over in another six. Several, and probably many, of his clan and nuclear family members would be captured and transported to Indian Territory (Oklahoma) to be inundated in a veritable sea of dispossessed southeastern Indians. Every detail of their lives that we can find, however, sheds more light on his life and on the processes of their survival, as individuals and as a people, to this moment. We will continue this story throughout the coming chapters.

3 / Man versus Myth

Setting the Record Straight

"I will here try and account to you for an error that many have fallen into, about Billy Powell or Osceola," Tom Woodward wrote.[1] From the basic question of the names by which Osceola should be known, to his birth date, the language or languages he spoke, and even the most basic statistics of his life, Tom Woodward probably would be fascinated to learn how far into error his readers have fallen over the last century and a half. At the same time, perhaps Woodward also would be pleased to learn that, after a century and a half, enough interest in this remarkable man still remains as to have perpetuated both errors and controversies. Here we will examine several of the more prominent controversies, and possibly in the doing, we may reendow this larger-than-life human with a bit more of his own humanity.

Rise to Prominence

Woodward continued, "Besides, I know that Osceola, as he is called, was not a chief, nor ever was known to the Tallassees as such, until after the killing of Gen. Thompson. You see that it is generally the half-breeds and mixed-bloods that speak our language, that the whites get acquainted with; and if, as in the case of a little war or anything of the sort, one of those that the whites know, go off among the hostiles, he is by the whites dubbed a chief. The Indians soon learn whom the whites look upon as being their leaders, and not being as ambitious of distinction as the whites generally are, when any talking or compromising is to be done, those persons are *put forward*."[2]

Although Woodward digresses after this statement to discuss Indians other than Osceola, several points are inescapable in his commentary. First, we see Osceola identified as a mixed-blood, and, indeed, from all of the evidence presented in chapter 2, this is undeniable. Second, his lack of hereditary right to leadership, and the subsequent conferring of the honorific "chief" by whites rather than by the Indians, is confirmed. The word "chief" is a white man's word, built on a European concept of power as a vertical hierarchy. White Americans have only a limited frame of reference for the force of the horizontal power structure that exists in the Maskókî world. Capt. John Rogers Vinton explained it very well when he wrote to Gen. Jesup that "Powell,—or Uscin-Yahola as the Chiefs pronounce his name is certainly a man of high consideration. Whatever may be said of his subordinate grade in the list of Seminole Chiefs his power and influence is obviously acknowledged by them. He is unremitting in his attention to the wants and interests of his men, and in return, receives from them an unqualified personal devotion. I doubt if the commands of Micconopy or his council, could invalidate his authority over the tribe of which he is the leader. This adhesion is, therefore, his own individual act,—and I believe is determinedly fixed by the dictates of his own mature judgment and sound sense."[3]

In other words, although Osceola did not have the critical requisite for official leadership—heredity—he did exercise a form of power and influence built upon the critical twin elements of adherence to tradition and reciprocal caring. These were the same qualities that the people looked for in a Micco—a person who would preserve the old ways and keep the world in balance by taking care of them even as they took care of him.[4]

As we take this opportunity for a further glimpse inside of Osceola's world, it is also important to view the negative side of his image. Just as many Indians respected and followed him, many others saw him as a serious problem—a tiresome impediment to ending the conflict. Coe hadjo, who had determined to emigrate, and who was constantly trying to position himself as a sort of power broker between the Indian resistance leaders and the U.S. military establishment, told one of Colonel Harney's officers that "Powell was a very bad man, that he did not mind the *talks*, that he went his own way & does pretty much as he pleases, &c, but that he would come in before long some way or other."[5] Indeed, it would be Coe hadjo who would be walking beside Osceola as he met Gen. Joseph Hernández and his troops just six months later, in late October 1837.

Woodward further tells us that Osceola's status would not begin to rise significantly among the Indians until after he killed the U.S. Indian agent Wiley Thompson on 28 December 1835. He may be correct in this claim, because he had spent most of his adult life in a position to understand the Indians and their attitudes toward status. Among the whites, however, it seems clear from the documented references that Osceola had been gaining recognition for at least a year previous to that event. Once again, as so often happens in history, what we seem to be seeing is two major currents—the times and the man—moving together independently, but inexorably, to place an individual in the limelight. After the United States acquired the territory of Florida in 1821, the government's means of dealing with the Indians there passed through three major, overlapping stages by late 1835.

1. Treaties and councils: through 1835
2. Voluntary removal: from early 1825
3. Removal by offensive military force: from 1835

Concomitantly, the types and amounts of cultural stress, either directly or indirectly, real or perceived, that were brought to bear upon the Florida Indians rose steadily during that same period. The factors of this stress overlapped somewhat and fluctuated in relative significance from event to event. Generally, however, we can identify four kinds.

1. *Physical*: containment, boundaries, military presence, continual relocation (transience), confrontations, distance and communications problems
2. *Economic*: inadequate rationing and supply systems, altered subsistence patterns, limited fertility of soils, compensation for livestock ownership, undependable trade systems, unlicensed traders
3. *Ideological*: internecine warfare, slave ownership and compensation, reclamation, removal, external and internal influence
4. *Cultural*: white encroachment, fragmentation of some cultural patterns, alcoholism, language barriers, imposition of nontraditional patterns and requirements (e.g., regarding leadership and decision making)

The long-range causes of the outbreak of physical violence between Florida's Indians and the whites were simply the territorial imperative and the fear of the cultural other. The immediate causes, beyond those outlined above, were stalemated negotiations regarding removal and logistics as well as the factionalization of intransigents on both sides in a situation constantly exacerbated by emotion. The result was bloody—and inescapable.

The Treaty of Moultrie Creek, signed 18 September 1823, was the first in a long series of attempts by the United States government to negotiate away the problem of two very disparate cultures attempting to occupy the same lands at the same time. By 1834—eleven years, three treaties, and numerous councils and talks afterward—the situation had only worsened considerably.

Andrew Jackson, the nation's leading advocate of Indian removal, also became its most powerful proponent with his election to the U.S. presidency in 1828. Gad Humphreys, Indian agent in Florida for eight years and known among the Indians as sympathetic to their plight, was removed in 1830. His replacement, Maj. John Phagan, was, as one historian described him, "the willing instrument of the new administration's policies."[6] It seems an inescapable conclusion that Phagan coerced or duped representatives of the Florida Indians into signing a removal agreement at Fort Gibson, Arkansas, on 29 March 1833. Why the document was signed or by whom was not the crux of the problem as far as the more vocal element of the Indians was concerned, however. This group contended that the party that had traveled to view proffered reservation lands was empowered to do nothing more than look. That is, the delegation had no authority to commit to any agreement binding on the whole, and this attitude certainly is consistent with Maskókî tradition.

Phagan, who was understandably unpopular among all the Indians, was dismissed in August of 1833 and was succeeded by Gen. Wiley Thompson, a native of Georgia.[7] Woodburne Potter, a staff officer under Gen. Edmund Gaines in the early days of the Second Seminole War, says of Thompson's tenure, "In the administration of General Thompson, (no doubt through a mistaken zeal for the Indian), various acts of injustice were practised which have materially affected the cause of Removal."[8] Potter, an officer and a gentleman, is definitely giving Thompson the benefit of the doubt. Agent Thompson's first critical (and delicate) assignment came in 1834, the year after the Treaties of Fort Gibson (1833) and its predecessor, Payne's Landing (1832), were ratified by the United States Congress. He was instructed to convene a general council of the Seminole "chiefs" in order to announce to them the imminent enforcement of the emigration provisions of the treaties and to secure their decisions regarding specific arrangements. This council was set first for 21 October 1834, but when several important Indians failed to arrive on time, the council was postponed for two days. Accordingly, the talks finally began at eleven o'clock in the morning on Thursday, 23 October. With his opening message, Agent Thompson made it clear that, in his own mind as in that of the president, removal was a foregone conclusion. The question for the council was not whether to go but only when and how.

The Indians' response to this pronouncement was to resort to their traditional process of consensus decision making. Unfortunately, in the face of a nontraditional, united opposition from the whites, the Indian system began to lose some of its effectiveness. This sociocultural scenario would be replayed time and again throughout the period of conflict: the Indians would fall back upon the cultural court of last resort of a horizontal society—the conclave—which would be countered by the steadfast, philosophical unanimity of a white, vertical society uniting more and more behind the determination to back its demands with force. Each time the stress became too great for the Indians, they would resort, singly or in limited common-interest groups, to violence—which would be countered with violence. Following this posturing, further attempts would then be made to resolve the differences through "talking," and the cycle would repeat itself.

It was during this point in the white/Indian negotiations that the young adult Osceola first came to the official attention of the white hierarchy. Micanopy, known among whites as "the governor," was senior in status at this conference but, despite his hereditary claims to power, was considered a weak leader by the Indians. Osceola appeared, to Indians and whites alike, as a strong voice. His power to persuade was observed by the whites, who quickly gave him more status than had his cultural peers. The *St. Augustine Florida Herald* described Osceola in 1836 as *"The Indian Chief Powell*—The character of this chief is but little known, and not sufficiently appreciated. He is represented to be a savage of great tact, energy of character, and bold daring."[9] Woodburne Potter, whose reports are generally thoughtful and evenhanded, attempted to portray him from both the Indian and white points of view. "It will be seen that the standing of Assiola, (Powell,) was, prior to the war, much inferior to a number of the other chiefs, and although his influence was seemingly great, it was still less than that of Miconopy, Jumper, Holata Mico, Coa Hajo, Abiákî/Sam Jones, Abraham, and several others; but he was with the mass of warriors who were the anti-Removal party, and themselves possessing as much influence as their chiefs; so that the marvellous reports of him, and the influence it is supposed that he exerts over the Indians is very much exaggerated, and have their origin only in the bold, desperate and reckless murders which have been perpetrated by the band of Micosukees, of which he is a sub-chief."[10]

Jacob Rhett Motte, a young army surgeon, offered a description more in line with the romanticized image that newspaper sensationalists promulgated and that would so capture the imagination of the public. "Oceola was always represented as an upstart in the nation; a novus homo. . . . Although not an hereditary chief, he was a ruling spirit among these wretches and exercised with autocratic power the sway he had acquired by his superior shrewdness and sagacity over their stern minds, and exacted from them the homage of vassals and dependents. Exercising more influence over these disorganized bands than their hereditary chiefs possessed, these latter through jealousy had always denounced his power in the nation. If only half that has been said of this indomitable warrior be true, he was a most remarkable man."[11]

Clan

The clan, the core unit of society in Osceola's world, was (and is) composed of blood relatives who were related through their mothers. Men only marry into a clan other than their own and never gain membership in any clan other than the one into which they were born. The strength of clan frontiers is very great in the Maskôkî world. Preference for the mother's clan and differentiation between it and the clan of the biological father is buttressed, for but one example, by an entirely separate set of kinship terms for the less important, paternal relatives. Furthermore, although transgressions do sometimes occur, there is an absolute injunction against marrying within one's own clan (that is, the clan of one's mother). No such injunction exists, however, to prohibit marriage into the clan of one's father. In fact, in certain circumstances, such intermarriage is preferable.

In the 1955 "Osceola Number" of the *Florida Historical Quarterly*, William Sturtevant surveyed then-current opinions from a few Florida Seminoles on the topic of Osceola's clan and concluded that there was no consensus.[12] Tribal citizens cited Alligator, *aktayáhca:Lî*, and Eagle clans. Alligator and Eagle clans no longer exist in Florida, and Snake Clan is very small, although these facts have no bearing on the reality of Osceola's life.

The simplest and most obvious answer to this question comes from a piece of information that Sturtevant also discarded. Among the Florida Seminoles, Fos'yaholi or Charlie Osceola (ca. 1823–1898) was considered by tribal elders to have been the brother of Osceola by Polly Copinger. That is, they had the same mother and, therefore, the same clan. The clan of Fos'yaholi was cited as Bird. Consequently, Osceola would also have been a member of Bird Clan. Fos'yaholi had as his wife a woman called Nancy (ca. 1815–ca. 1898), later known as Old Nancy. The couple were the first (in Florida or Indian Territory) to take "Osceola" as a surname—in honor of a brother famous among Indians and non-Indians alike. As such, they became the progenitors of a numerous family still bearing the Osceola surname to this day.

They and their descendents are discussed further in chapter 11, but there is no reason not to accept this Florida Seminole tradition. There is nothing in this scenario that conflicts, socially or chronologically, with other information, either. Moreover, a few other pieces of historical information tend to support it.

The first is an ambiguous indication from Thomas Woodward that the village where Osceola was born was just across the river from "Catsa Bogah" or, more accurately in Maskókî, *gatsa abóketa*, "the place where the Panther People [Clan] live." This would seem to indicate that Osceola's people were not Panthers. Their juxtaposition to the Panther Clan camp may have meant that they were, rather, members of one of the two other high-status clans in the Maskókî world, Wind and Bird. Because the three clans of Wind, Panther, and Bird constitute a power triad in the Maskókî world, and a traditional social preference existed for reciprocal marriages between certain status-linked clans (although not between certain socially linked clans), we might expect Osceola to have been born into Wind Clan or Bird Clan.

There is also much evidence that Wind Clan was powerful in the area near Tallassee, and a strong piece of evidence narrows those two alternatives further. Osceola's powerful clan uncle, Peter McQueen, took as a partner Betsy Durant, the daughter of Benjamin Durant and a sister of Alexander McGillivray. The mother of Alexander McGillivray is documented, and her clan is documented also. She was a member of the elite Wind Clan. Consequently, her daughter would have been Wind also. It would have been social and political death for Peter McQueen to have married into his own clan, and his subsequent high visibility in the warrior world of the Maskókalkî evidences a high positive social regard for him. To this day, the Mikísuukî speakers call people who have sexual relations with members of their own clans *if'athî* or "dog people." Because it was Peter McQueen's sister, Ann or Nancy, whose clan was passed to Osceola through Nancy's daughter and his own mother, Polly, then we must rule out Wind as Osceola's clan.

There is also the indirect evidence provided by the documentary mention that one of Osceola's sisters was the wife of Yaha hadjo. This brother-in-law's title ("name") seems to indicate that he was a member of Wolf Clan. If so, and if the wife was Osceola's biological sister (born of the same mother), or his clan sister, then Osceola must not have been a Wolf or a Bear (a socially linked clan), or his sister would not have married into that clan.

Another piece of inferential information is the fact that, in late June of

1837, when Abraham listed the Indian camps in Florida (see chapter 2), the camps of Philip and Abiákî were combined, and Osceola was not listed as having a separate camp. He had had one, but it had been discovered by the white soldiers just a short two months earlier. He and his family needed either to make another separate camp (of which Abraham was not permitted to know) or to meld their people with an affinity group. Despite the known strength of his medicine or, perhaps, because of it, the clan of Abiákî is not known, although his status as a maker of medicine would seem to place him in Panther Clan, the premier medicine clan. The clan of Philip can be deduced, however, from the clan of his relatives and descendents, many of whom remain in Florida today (see chapter 11). They are Panthers. Abiákî is recalled by Seminoles in Florida and Oklahoma as having been Osceola's mentor—which could mean that they were of the same clan. But it could just as well mean that Osceola was Bird Clan, the other elite clan, because Osceola's home was across the river from the Panthers. Bird Clan people are lawgivers and law enforcers, and this certainly is consistent with Osceola's public image among both whites and Indians.

In addition to the collateral line of Fos'yaholi, two other Florida families may well be associated with Osceola. We will review these in chapter 11.

Name

The topic of names is complicated initially by the fact that the Creeks and Seminoles have had no written language. Thus, any spelling assigned to the subject of our discussions will, necessarily, be an arbitrary one. Then, the "naming" system used by the Maskókî people traditionally is not analogous to the European naming system, which assigns to a single individual a single name that remains with the individual throughout life (marriage notwithstanding). We have already discussed the fact that the boy called Billy Powell and the man known as Osceola also had an Indian "baby name" that we most probably will never know. Furthermore, we have examined and accepted the fact that "Osceola" was not actually a personal name but, rather, a ceremonial or busk title.

The traditional rite of passage into manhood for young Creek males occurred (and continues to occur) somewhere between their fourteenth and eighteenth years. The particular age had no importance; indeed, traditional Seminoles and Creeks neither recall nor celebrate "birthdays" to this day. The critical element in the transition to manhood concerns that moment when the young man becomes physically and psychologically ready to sustain the four days of fasting necessary for participating fully in the principal *búsketau,* or "busk," known as the Green Corn Ceremony. This ceremony, an annual cycle of ritual fasting, dancing, feasting, and solemn communal events, marks the time when the boy name is superseded by a ceremonial title conferred when the young man participates in the rituals for the first time.

In the case of Billy Powell, he was given a position of centrality. His role was to carry the powerful liquid *iäpún* ("it is mixed" in Maskókî and Hitchiti; in transliterated English, "yaupon"), the main ingredients of which were *ásse* (in Maskókî; in Hitchiti, *pásse*; in English, button snake root, also known as rattlesnake master) and *Ilex vomitoria* (a species of Florida holly), to the medicine man and his assistants at the height of the ceremonies. A chant or song accompanied the presentation, and it was *yáhola*—that is, it mimicked the cry of the *yaha*, or wolf, and was "sung" (chanted) to infuse the "medicine" with power. Consequently, the ceremonial title of the individual given this role was *Asse yahola*, which the vernacular Maskókî language contracted into Asse'ola. By English speakers, this would be transliterated variantly as "Asseola," "Oceola," "Ussa Yahola" (a spelling by which he is too frequently confused with another warrior with the same title who lived farther eastward, in Georgia), and "Osceola."[13] One anthropologist writes the title as *así:yaholí*.[14] The simplified translation generally, then as now, was "Black Drink Singer."

Woodburne Potter explained "Osceola" thusly: "[Assiola] is the correct orthography of his name, which he has distinctly pronounced more than one hundred times in the presence of the gentleman alluded to." Although we are never given the identity of "the gentleman alluded to," we are informed in Potter's note "To the Public" that "the names of the principal Chiefs and Sub-Chiefs were furnished by a gentleman who was, until the war, intimately associated with them. [Might this gentleman have been John Graham? He does fit the description.] The author is well aware that the names are not literal translations, but their own assumed *fancy* names; as they were furnished, so he gives them. The orthography of their pronunciation in the Seminole language is correct."[15] Thus, through Potter, we "hear" the name of our subject pronounced as if it were spelled as he spells it, "Assiola," rather than as it was more commonly spelled, "Osceola."

Throughout his narrative, Potter shows himself to be a critical, lucid reporter who is consciously attempting to separate reality from rumor, even in the face of the strong prevailing emotional climate that constantly attempts to distort the picture. With his terse statements, he confirms for us two important items. First, as previously stated, he offers the most acceptable English orthography of the name. Second, he reminds us that this name is only an "assumed *fancy* name," by which he confirms that it was, indeed, a busk name. This insight, in turn, corroborates two other conclusions that are also borne out by previous information. The first is that Osceola's cultural milieu, undoubtedly because of the changes in Indian society occasioned by their dispossession and relocation, was such that he had not yet had the opportunity to obtain further or other Indian names through the traditional systems of warfare, civic service, and honoring. This process occurred over time, and time was compressing the lives of the Indians at this moment. This conclusion might also explain some of what whites perceived in him as belligerence and ambition.

Second, then, we may also be seeing an excellent example of Thomas Woodward's assertion that the Indians' traditional patterns changed in direct and immediate relation to white perceptions. Osceola first came to white notoriety while his busk title was still new, and it was at that moment when whites began to recognize him and identify him by that title. They used that title as if it were a name and permanently attached to the individual to identify him to both other whites and Indians alike, and even after he had begun to distinguish himself among his Indian peers in acts of warfare (after December 1835), he continued to be known, among both whites *and* Indians, by that "name."

In the course of a long and traditional life, this title would not have been used as an everyday "name." It would have been reserved for use annually at the Green Corn Ceremonies. In the course of a long and traditional life, the holder of the title would have been given a nickname for everyday use, and he would have acquired other clan, military, and civic titles by which he might also have been known. But, although "Osceola's" was a traditional life, unquestionably, it was not a long one. Because of the tutelage he received from Abiákî, learning war medicine to protect himself, he did obtain sufficient prowess in battle to be viewed as a *tastenáki thlocco,* a "big warrior," among his peers, but this and any other titles he might have received were generally unknown to English speakers, from whom they were kept, purposely, by his Indian contemporaries.

Language

Once again, it is Thomas Woodward who offers the earliest bit of information on the topic of the languages spoken by Osceola. In the comments quoted earlier, he writes: "You see that it is generally the half-breeds and mixed-bloods that speak our language, that the whites get acquainted with." In using this phrase to describe Osceola, he seems to be letting us know that Osceola spoke at least some English. Nevertheless, Osceola's linguistic ability has been framed as a continuing question over the years. Certainly, there can be no argument that his base language, the language of his home and town, was Maskókî (called Creek), and he undoubtedly acquired facility in this language long before the dislocation of war occurred.

In addition, however, his great-grandfather James McQueen, who was alive until Billy Powell was at least seven years old, spoke English as his base language and probably communicated much of that language to his family. Certainly, he used it around the child in the presence of government agents and traders who were moving into the area. Furthermore, the boy's grandfather Copinger may have spoken Spanish, English, or both. His father, William Powell, absolutely spoke English, and by the time of his arrival in the lives of Osceola and his family, English was becoming a prevalent language in the entire area. Therefore, living as he did in a multilingual society, and being the particularly intelligent person whom we know him to have been, from his accomplishments if nothing else, it would be more logical to discuss the number of languages he knew ultimately, rather than limiting ourselves to a discussion of English.

Nevertheless, we will begin with a discussion of the English language, simply because various documentary mentions seem to answer the question. Although this list is not exhaustive, it does illustrate the range of problems associated with making a definitive judgment. For a variety of reasons, however, usually having to do with the cultural restraints of the man himself or the cultural imperatives of the writers, the statements are equivocal. Even those that suggest that he did not speak English, however, are ambiguous at best.

1. Woodburne Potter quotes Indian agent General Thompson regarding Osceola's whispering to Micanopy during the Fort King council of 24–25 October 1834. Thompson says, "The interpreter informed me . . . that Powel . . . "[16] This council was an official function at which it certainly would have been to the advantage of the Indians to speak among themselves in their own tongue, regardless of their individual abilities to do otherwise.
2. Later, discussing the Second Battle of the Withlacoochee, Potter says directly, "Assiola, or Powel, does not speak the English language."[17] Most of Potter's information is very reliable.
3. Dr. Robert Lebby, Fort Johnson, South Carolina, wrote to Dr. Johnson, Charleston, South Carolina, 21 June 1844, "I think this man's name was Coa Hadjo—of this I am not so certain—but he was the individual who addressed the Indians and communicated all instructions to them."[18] Lebby, a fairly reliable observer, nevertheless took events at face value. This statement is not definitive in that he may or may not have been including Osceola in this statement.

4. Further on in his letter, Dr. Lebby also says that Osceola "would speak with the Dr. [Weedon] thro' the Interpreter but never in English."[19] Again, Lebby is reporting what he saw, not making a statement of possibility. In order to have observed it, he would have to have been present, constituting an intrusion.

5. Dr. Benjamin Strobel attempted to treat Osceola, in extremis, at Fort Moultrie and reported, "I requested his permission, through the interpreter."[20] Undoubtedly, regardless of whether Osceola could speak English, this would have been the simplest approach for the white doctor, a stranger, in treating a "foreign" patient who was already having physical difficulty in speaking.

6. George Catlin, with whom Osceola conversed long into the nights that Catlin spent at Fort Moultrie, observed later, "All his conversation is entirely in his own tongue."[21] This statement has a great deal of credibility. It is firsthand information from an otherwise reliable observer who had a significant opportunity to form an opinion on the subject. Catlin, however, may have been perceived by Osceola as a vehicle for conveying his political views to the official white world. Therefore, using the services of an interpreter would have ensured that Osceola's opinions would have been more fully and accurately transmitted. We also have no indication that Catlin ever obtained a totally private interview with Osceola, and the two had too short a time together to form a truly intimate association.

7. Myer Cohen, in discussing Osceola's friendship with Lt. John Graham, says, "Osceola's motive in sparing Lieut. G. was gratitude for attention to his child, which he also endeavored to repay by teaching the Lieut. the English language, for he speaks a little English, and is very intelligent."[22] Cohen has confused himself (and his readers as well) with this statement. It has been interpreted to mean that Graham was teaching Osceola the English language. This interpretation, however, would require us to believe that Cohen convoluted an entire phrase and, as a result, the entire thought. It seems more reasonable to conclude that Cohen (or his printer) confused only one word, "English," in the second phrase of the sentence. If we read "teaching the Lieut. the Indian language," then all the rest of the sentence still makes sense. In that case, Cohen is saying that Osceola does speak "a little" English.

8. Joshua Giddings describes the interview between Osceola and Gen. Joseph Hernández that culminated in the capture of the former. General Hernández read to Osceola questions prepared by General Jesup. Osceola "exhibited the most perfect astonishment at hearing these. . . . He appeared, however, instantly to comprehend the situation. Turning

to Coe Hadjo, he said to him in his own dialect, 'You must answer; I am choked.' "[23] This report would seem to imply that Osceola at least understood English. However, even if Giddings were a reliable reporter (he is not), this event would have the same qualifications as number 1 above.

9. In his account of the murder of Thompson, Potter cites information supplied by a female black cook who was hiding in the kitchen and overheard Osceola and quoted him.[24] This detail is unique among the accounts. Potter arrived at the site of the murder a few weeks after the event. Did the black cook speak the Indians' language? Did Osceola use English here? The statement is ambiguous.

The evidence from all these citations is still inconclusive. The positive statement in number 7, however, is now backed by the evidence of one other very important source that has come to light only in recent times. Together with other, circumstantial evidence we thus may form a tentative conclusion. The new source is an entry from Dr. Weedon's own diary, written at Fort Marion, in which he seems to quote Osceola directly in what can only be interpreted as the broken English of a non-English narrator. (See quotation in chapter 5.) In what is almost (in the twenty-first century) a stereotypical Indian dialect, he offers direct quotations—but then, as easily, says that it is untrue that Osceola has had the advantage of speaking the English language. Certainly, we should be able to accept the word of this observer—but which word? With the possible exception of John Graham, Frederick Weedon probably knew Osceola as well as any white person had for many years. Elsewhere in the meager diary accounts that are extant, Weedon offers another quotation from a member of the Indian prisoners' group in the same sort of broken-English notation. In neither instance does he indicate that an interpreter was present. Judging from the myriad interpreted Indian statements quoted by whites elsewhere in contemporary accounts, one would expect an interpreted quotation to have been noted in restructured English. Certainly we may believe that there were sufficient interpreters available in and around Fort Marion and Fort Moultrie. Weedon's position and duties, however, should have made his interactions with the Indians less official, more frequent, more private, and, therefore, more comfortable.

Other bits of information can now be considered that also may bear on this topic. Billy Powell was raised in a home with a white father who undoubtedly could speak English. The frequency of its use in the household may have been limited, but certainly it was not completely absent. Osceola's maternal grandfather may well have spoken English, or even

Spanish, and his maternal great-grandfather definitely spoke English. The fact that Osceola's mother and grandmother both bore English as well as Indian names may be viewed as prima facie evidence that the English linguistic matrix was not forgotten in the family. From these points we may conclude that, for at least the first fourteen years of his life, years when languages are assimilated with least difficulty, Osceola had sufficient opportunity to learn and use English.

Following their relocation in 1814, Osceola's group is known to have associated with the British at Fort Gadsden. Certainly he would have heard English spoken and, given his acknowledged intelligence, would have found advantages to be gained from at least an understanding of the conversations around him. After this short period of transition, however, events allowed the Indians to restructure their cultural patterns in more isolated circumstances, in central and southern Florida. This fact, together with his rapidly increasing cultural alienation from things white, may have produced a long period of separation from, and disuse of, the English language. Much later (in 1834 and early 1835), we are told that Osceola spent a good deal of time around the military post of Fort King, where he was liked and trusted, interacted freely and regularly with whites, and even formed acquaintances and friendships. Here he certainly had another excellent opportunity to refresh his English, especially in the context of his close friendship with a white soldier (see the following section regarding Osceola's friendship with John Graham).

Finally, we must consider one other point that may well bear upon this topic. Several observers have noted that Osceola was characteristically quiet, somewhat shy, and generally reticent to present his personal feelings except with those who had gained his confidence—exactly the characteristic of so many individuals who also maintain an outward display of bravado. Despite the seemingly contradictory nature of all the statements, then, in the light of this information it becomes less difficult to reach a conclusion on this subject. Osceola had obtained a working knowledge of the English language, although he probably understood more than he spoke. His inability to use the language fluently might easily have led a man of pride to reserve its use for only nonofficial, comfortable, private circumstances—exactly the settings least likely to have been observed by the majority of his contemporary reporters. More important, however, is the effect that his using English might have had on his Indian peers and followers. We will see that, even as he lay dying, Osceola refused the ministrations of white doctors, the inference being that he was loathe to have the other Indians believe that he had any confidence in, or friendship with, whites, which would have been perceived as evidence of divided loyalties. This would have provided a major impetus for Osceola to have hidden his facility with English. As for the statement from Dr. Weedon that Osceola had not had the advantages of the English language, we are possibly seeing here a glimpse of the doctor's own mind-set: Osceola was an Indian who had not had any formal (white) education and had not learned fluent (cultural) English, ergo he could not "speak" English. The final conclusion on this point is, then, that in the strictest sense of the term, Osceola *could* speak English.

Although the questions concerning Osceola's linguistic ability have focused on whether he spoke English in addition to his native tongue, the subject has never been expanded to include a discussion of Spanish as an additional language. Interestingly enough, this heretofore undiscussed language facility is the one facet of the controversy that can be settled.

Among both the Florida Seminoles and the removed Seminoles of Oklahoma are many clans, the members of which have passed along memories of Osceola. In numerous instances, in response to the question, "What did your grandmother tell you about him?" they have responded, "Well, all my grandmother told me was that *he was a Spanish man*" (emphasis added).[25] This does not necessarily have to mean that Osceola's parents were Spaniards, although the genetic implications of this imaging have been examined previously, or that he was born in some place other than in Indian Country. Within the sociolinguistic usages of the Seminole people, it could simply indicate that he was a Spanish speaker, and, indeed, we now know that he was. We have an eyewitness account of a Spanish *criollo* from St. Augustine, Venancio Sánchez, who, as a young man, witnessed Osceola's capture. We will review his comments shortly.

Obviously, the fact that Osceola spoke Spanish when he was thirty-eight years old does not mean that he learned Spanish as a boy growing up. It is important to recall also, however, that the Florida of the late eighteenth and early nineteenth centuries still sprawled across the frontiers of several of the states as we know them today and that, when Osceola was born, *La Florida* still was Spanish-claimed and Spanish-occupied territory. When Osceola's family was dislocated by the Creek War, Florida was still Spanish territory and would remain so for another seven years. In fact, it will be the year 2108 before Florida will have been a part of the United States for as long as it was a part of the Spanish colonial empire. Even after the final cession of Florida to the United States in 1821, many Spaniards remained in Florida to occupy and protect lands granted to them previously by the king of Spain. Young Billy Powell had many opportunities to meet, interact with, and learn the language of Spaniards and to meet and interact with many Indians of the Florida peninsula who had long interacted with Spaniards also. His clan great-uncle, Peter McQueen, had frequently traded with the

Spaniards at Pensacola. In all probability, McQueen also spoke Spanish. This fact may, indeed, have contributed to the Indians' traditional imaging of Osceola as "a Spanish man."

In addition, Florida's old sister colony, Cuba, would remain within the domain of Spain throughout the nineteenth century, and Cubans would continue to view Florida as a social and commercial extension of their own sphere of interest. The statement of Governor Coppinger's descendent Mrs. L. Vianello, quoted in chapter 2, certainly embodies this close association. It is obvious from their many comments on the subject that members of the U.S. military were also cognizant of this close association between Cuba and Florida. The main reason for the construction and location of Fort Brooke on the shores of Tampa Bay was the army's fear that Cubans, already using the area for commercial fishing camps, would use it also to import arms for the Indians. The association of the Cubans and the Indians was particularly close there. In June of 1837, even at the height of the war years, Lt. John Casey wrote from Tampa Bay to inform General Jesup that he had learned that "the Spaniards at the Rancho will cross all their Indian women to the main land to remain with the hostiles. They prefer this to Arkansas."[26] The relationship of the Indians and the Cubans was a very long and close one indeed.

Our final evidence of Osceola's ability to speak Spanish is provided by the recollections of the Spanish gentleman of St. Augustine mentioned earlier. In his youth, Vanancio Sánchez (1809–1899), was employed in New Smyrna in an uncle's store that was frequented by the Indians. There, he said, he came to know Osceola well. In October of 1837, the young Mr. Sánchez was in St. Augustine visiting with family when he heard that General Hernández, with several companies of soldiers, was going to Fort Peyton "on an eminence south of Moultrie Creek, to have a talk with Osceola and his followers." Sánchez mounted his horse and rode out in advance of the troops to watch the encounter. He was, he recalled many years later for a St. Augustine newspaper, "near enough to hear the conversation, but not near enough to understand its import." He saw and understood the lifting of an officer's hat, signaling the troops to close in and capture the Indians. He described Osceola as "a handsome, brave speaking Spanish, which he learned from the Cuban traders on the west coast."[27] Young Mr. Sánchez may not have been accurate about the source of Osceola's Spanish, but he certainly knew Spanish when he heard it.

Finally, then, we must also consider the number of Maskókî dialects Osceola may have spoken. Although there is no specific evidence on this topic, there is no reason to disregard it either and every reason to believe that he spoke or at least understood more than one. His own base language was core Maskókî, or Creek, which was the mother language among the lower southeastern tribes. At the time of the southeastern Wars of Removal, Hitchiti, Euchee, Yamássee, and others still were prevalent. We will never know with which or how many of these Osceola obtained facility. It is only for us to cease limiting an individual whose intellect obviously was not limited by his culture.

Friendship with John Graham

Accounts of the life of Osceola have generally discounted rumors of his friendship with a white army officer, but the evidence indicates that such was in fact the case. John Graham (1814–1841), a native of Pennsylvania, graduated from the United States Military Academy at West Point on 1 July 1834. He was immediately breveted a second lieutenant in the Fourth Infantry Regiment and sent to join his regiment, one company of which was already in garrison at Fort King, Florida, under the command of Capt. William Montrose Graham (no kin). By the spring of 1835, when a council took place at the fort, Graham and Osceola had struck up a close personal friendship, which endured throughout the remaining three years of Osceola's life. This friendship is an excellent example of Osceola's personal ability to compartmentalize his emotions—separating his personal affinity for an individual from his conceptual antipathy to the cause represented by that individual.

John Bemrose, a young English hospital steward who was stationed there during this period, mentioned that the two were inseparable at Fort King: "They were seen daily together."[28] Myer Cohen was the first to elaborate, in print, on the basis for the friendship. "It seems that Powell has a little daughter, to whom Lt. G. was kind, and had presented with frocks, in which the young girl, who grew very fond of him, always insisted on being dressed, whenever she perceived Lt. G. (for whom she often looked out) coming to visit her."[29] In another citation, a St. Augustine newspaper account published in July 1837 mentioned concerning the character of Osceola, "Toward Lt. Graham he entertained the kindliest feelings of friendship, not to be broken by the unhappy war which exists between this nation, and the white man. During his visit at Fort Mellon, he took occasion to present Lt. G. with a handsome plume of white crane feathers to be worn as a badge of protection in the battle field. This is a remarkable instance of friendship and may it not be taken as an evidence of his authority? There is something which smacks of romance in the friendship between Lt. Graham and Osceola."[30]

Andrew Welch, whom we have met earlier, was the next to publicize the bond that existed between the two men.[31] His details are sensationalized to create maximum sympathy in his readers—and would cause us to discount the entire episode were it not for the other strong evidence that is available to corroborate at least the central element of the story. According to Welch, Graham spent six years in Florida before the war began—three before he struck up the friendship with Osceola and three more as partner to Osceola's niece (not daughter), Nathleocee, and alleged father of their three children. When the war commenced, Osceola himself drove Graham from his Indian home back to his own white people, never more to be reunited with a grieving Indian family. Welch knew Graham personally or at least met him at dinner at the home of Judge Robert Reid in St. Augustine in August of 1838. Welch also cited Dr. William Simmons in confirmation of the story. Irrespective of the verisimilitude of Welch's account, however, certain elements of his story are contradicted by documentary evidence.

Thomas Storrow, writing the story of Osceola in 1844 from the collected accounts of many who were personally associated with the events, repeats the Cohen scenario with slight embellishments.[32] Although his source is not named, the direct correlation between the two accounts, as well as the lack of confirmation of this story by other writers, points to Cohen as the narrator. Both Cohen and Welch include a child in the narrative as a vehicle for the endurance of the connection between the Indian warrior and the white soldier. Welch's assertion that Graham had spent six years in Florida before the opening of the Second Seminole War and had established a blood kinship with Osceola, however, does not correlate with the military record of the only John Graham (there were several of the same name who served in Florida during this time) who seems the most obvious choice to be the man in question.

Nevertheless, John Bemrose and Myer Cohen both also recount the point that, after the First Battle of the Withlacoochee, Osceola inquired most anxiously after the health of Graham. The Englishman Bemrose, acerbic but astute, tended the wounds of the soldiers who returned from this battle. He said: "Company D were lucky in possessing a Lieut. John Graham in their midst for everywhere he was stationed the balls flew less thickly. This was owing to Graham's former friendship with the savage chief Osceola. Afterward in communication with the Indians we learned that Osceola had given his warriors [orders] not to fire upon Graham who was a good mark, being a very big man, so he protected him in battle."[33]

Woodburne Potter confuses this account chronologically by ascribing it to the Battle of Camp Izard in March 1836. He refers to it as a "manufacture" that has appeared in "a late publication" and dissects it completely, finally saying that he has been informed that the story "grew out of a little jest of the Lieutenant [Graham]."[34] The "late publication" was probably that of Myer Cohen, whose book was the only one to report this detail and came out in the same year as Smith's. Perhaps Lieutenant Graham did jokingly brag of a talisman created by his friendship with Osceola. We do not know enough about the personality of John Graham to make any judgment about the way he viewed his association with an Indian. Nevertheless, neither embarrassment at the possible derision of his cultural peers nor the nervous jest of a young officer who had just seen comrades fall around him in battle for the first time negates the possibility of the earlier association. This is especially plausible when it is considered together with two other pieces of information.

The first, although tenuous, is interesting because it illustrates the manner in which shreds of historical information may survive over time. William Sturtevant, writing in 1955, related some oral traditions that existed among the twentieth-century Seminoles concerning Osceola. One is an account of the capture of Osceola that was told to Sturtevant in English by a Miccosukee Seminole. Many of the recorded events were compressed in the oral tradition. Some of the then current attitudes, as Sturtevant mentioned, were heavily influenced by white traditions. One tiny detail of the Indian's account is unique, however. He says that at an interview between Osceola and the soldiers at Fort Peyton in 1837, "Captain Johnny (*kapíncá:nî:*) talked to *asonyaholî:*, while his people listened."[35] Sturtevant remarks that he does not understand this reference because the talk was conducted by Gen. Joseph Hernández. It makes much sense, however, if one considers the military record of John Graham. United States Army surgeon Nathan Jarvis tells us that General Hernández took with him to the meeting near Fort Peyton two companies of mounted volunteers and all of the Second Dragoons Regiment.[36] On 1 October 1837 John Graham was promoted to captain of the Second Dragoons and, from September through 6 November 1837, served as aide-de-camp to Gen. Joseph Hernández.

Outside of a short tour of duty in garrison at Baton Rouge, Louisiana, in mid-1836, Graham saw action in Florida in the Battle of Camp Monroe (Fort Mellon) and was stationed there at the same time that Osceola and his band were encamped nearby during the armistice of 1837. Graham also participated in the surprise attack on the Indian camps that resulted in the capture of Philip in September 1837.

John Graham resigned his commission on 28 January 1838 but remained in Florida. He served as adjutant general of the state of Florida and inspector general of Florida troops from 14 January 1840 until his death (during a yellow fever epidemic) on 30 July 1841. Graham resided at Blackwood Plantation, Tallahassee, with his wife, the daughter of Florida's governor

Robert Raymond Reid (1839–1841). This Reid was the same Judge Reid at whose home Graham and Welch had dined, at least once, in 1838. Judge Reid's daughter may have been dining with them, and a romance may have been blossoming already between the two young people. Graham felt comfortable enough to discuss Osceola and the boy, Nikkanochee, but certainly not comfortable enough to discuss any physical relationship he may have had with a niece of Osceola. That would have been extremely indelicate.

The second and most substantial piece of information that ties together the Indian and white warrior is a letter addressed to Florida's secretary of state dated 10 February 1939 from John Tharpe Lawrence of Delavan, Minnesota. Lawrence was the paternal great-nephew of Capt. John Graham, who had been, he wrote, "very intimate with Osceola." Mr. Lawrence continued: "As a boy I often heard my grandmother, Elizabeth Graham Lawrence, tell tales from the Captain's letters, about Osceola and what a great chief he was. From what I remember it seems that the captain went through some kind of ceremony that made him what was called a blood brother of Osceola."[37] Although such a ceremony was probably an embellishment of the story, the fact remains that John Graham's family also knew of his close association with Osceola. The letter even goes on to discuss several personal artifacts that Osceola gave as gifts to Graham and reiterates the tradition of the high regard for Osceola that has remained with the Graham/Lawrence family throughout the years. The artifacts and their subsequent disposition will be discussed further in chapter 13.

What may we conclude, then, concerning this confusing story? Bemrose and Cohen present the more likely scenario. Graham and Osceola liked each other. Graham gave a small gift, or gifts, to a child who could have been either a niece or daughter to Osceola; the war leader had both in his entourage by the time Graham arrived. Welch may even have been given her name, Nathleocee. Could a white soldier, involved in a war already under way, have achieved any degree of intimacy with an enemy war leader and his family? Yes. Osceola later would demonstrate his ability to compartmentalize his own belligerency, with Colonel Harney, with Dr. Weedon, and with the artist Catlin, at least. In fact, in reviewing these accounts, one gains the impression that Osceola was much more capable of ignoring cultural barriers to friendship than were the white men.

Setting the Stage

One of the critical misconceptions held by the military and civilians alike throughout 1834 and most of 1835 concerned the ability and commitment of their enemy. This also appears to have been a critical period for

Osceola in particular and the antiremoval faction of the Indians in general. Throughout the first half of 1835, many Indians moved to the vicinity of Fort King in order to collect their annuities from the Indian agency that was close by. A statement by John Bemrose articulates well the opinions of several others in regard to this point. He says: "But where I stood amongst a group of [the Indians] watching our men at target practice, I could not help but see that they knew and felt their own superiority. Also, when the [white] men were drilling in the woods at Indian fighting, [the Indians'] faces would express to each other a sense of the ridiculous, intuitively conveying to me their knowledge of our inferiority if opposed to them in the native wilds. And I cannot help thinking that during these five peaceful moons they saw too much and formed their plans accordingly. How common it is for civilized and trained combatants to teach themselves to despise these wild men, thereby entailing upon themselves defeat and disaster! The true policy is never to despise an enemy."[38]

Osceola, in particular, watched. His basic desire to live in peace with the whites, geographically and philosophically, is amply proved in this year, 1835. His own personal sense of honor, however, based upon an Indian, rather than a white, societal imperative is also clearly indicated in the brilliant and violent climax of his life, the events that took place beginning in the second half of 1835. The twenty months following, until his philosophical capitulation (his "capture" in October 1837), would be dénouement; his imprisonment and death, the finale. This climactic phase encompassed a series of four events: a confrontation with the white government agent Wiley Thompson in the summer of 1835, the ritualistic execution of Charley Emathla in November of that year, the symbolic slaying of Thompson in the following month, and the first full display of Indian force—his first test of leadership in warfare, at the First Battle of the Withlacoochee, on 31 December 1835.

Osceola and Thompson

Numerous explanations have been offered for the impasse that developed between Wiley Thompson and Osceola. All the accounts, of course, have been offered by white peers of the agent and, to greater or lesser degrees, constitute an apologia for his actions. Despite all protestations of his true interest in the welfare of his charges (which may well have been accurate, from a strictly paternalistic viewpoint), we are still left, however, with a picture of a man of obdurate nature, used to the exercise of command, and either possessing little diplomatic skill or superciliously oblivious of the need for its use with persons perceived to be of inferior cultural status.

Osceola, it appears, was not interested in permanently playing the role assigned by this white man. Osceola, Bemrose noted, was "much noticed by the agent, who made him many handsome presents, no doubt supposing he would assist in bringing over the refractory portion of the nation."[39] This distribution of gifts to the Indians as lures of "friendship" was not at all unusual. Despite several specific citations concerning Thompson's beneficence to Osceola, including the presentation to him of a silver-mounted rifle, there is no reason to conclude that Thompson's motives in gift giving were any beyond those noted by Bemrose.

As for the most plausible details of the confrontation that sealed Thompson's fate, we have already reviewed Thompson's own report of the affair. But we also have the report of an eyewitness to substantiate that account. It comes from an unidentified soldier who was present at the time of Osceola's capture and imprisonment. He was writing to the editors of the *National Intelligencer* on 23 February 1838 in rebuttal to an item that had appeared almost a month earlier, just before Osceola's death at Fort Moultrie. Our author took exception to statements by a Mr. Wise to the effect that Thompson's motives in securing Osceola were to force him to consent to removal. The author then continues:

> It is much to be regretted that Mr. Wise had not drawn his information from a more correct source. . . . The writer of these remarks was stationed at Fort King when the transaction alluded to took place. Osceola was not arrested by General Thompson to compel him to bring in his Indians to give their assent to the treaty, but from a totally different cause. It was some time during the summer of 1835, the officers were in their mess-room at dinner; General Thompson came in much agitated, and said he wanted their advice on a delicate subject; that Osceola had come to his office in a very bad humor, and had used violent and insulting language to him; that on several previous occasions he had been guilty of the same impropriety, and had been warned if he ever repeated it he should be punished, that amongst other things he said that he, General Thompson, was an intruder on the Indian lands; that he despised his authority and would make him leave them.
>
> The General argued that he could not consistently with his duty to himself or to the Government consent to have his authority thus publicly questioned and contemned; that his influence over the Indians must be maintained; and if this conduct on the part of Powell was again overlooked, it would only increase his arrogance, and lower

him, the agent, in the estimation of the whole tribe, especially the friendly Indians.

We fully concurred with him, and Powell was arrested handcuffed, and put in the guard house, there to remain until he came to his senses and made a suitable apology. For the first day or two he refused to eat and exhibited all the vindictive fury of the savage; he gradually, however, assumed a milder mood and at the expiration of a few days, sent for General Thompson to come and see him. He told the General he had been reflecting on his conduct, and acknowledged he had been a fool, that if he would release him, he would sign the treaty, and be a friend to the whites. The General replied, that he had often promised to behave himself, and had as often deceived him; that he put no faith in his promises; but that if he could get any of the friendly chiefs to become responsible for his future good conduct, he would set him at liberty, as he felt no desire to punish him.

Powell then desired that Charley Amathla and Coahajo, the two most prominent friendly chiefs, should be sent for; they arrived the next day, or the day succeeding, and, after a long interview with Powell, came to General Thompson and pledged themselves as his sureties, stating they were satisfied with the sincerity of his protestations, and that he would be a valuable acquisition to the emigrating cause. He then returned with them to the guard house, when Powell reiterated his promises, and said he was ready to sign the treaty. General Thompson told him he should not sign it whilst in confinement, lest it should be said that advantage was taken of his situation to coerce him to an act which, of his own accord, he was unwilling to perform, but that he should go home, talk with his people, and, if he was sincere, return with them in ten days and sign the treaty. He was liberated, and punctually, on the tenth day, returned, with about twenty-five of his followers, and signed the treaty.

These are the main facts connected with the arrest of Powell. Could any agent have acted with more forbearance, more discretion or more propriety, than General Thompson. From the day of signing the treaty, Powell became to all appearance an altered man. He was on the most familiar terms with the garrison; visited us in the most social and friendly manner; invited us to his town, and performed many little acts of kindness, which could not be forgotten. He enjoyed the full confidence of the agent and was employed by him, on several delicate and important trusts. Did an Indian commit any depredation upon a frontier settlement, Powell was deputed to find out the aggressor, and he never failed to bring him to punishment; he acted always with good faith, and so well pleased was the agent with him, that, as a reward for his good conduct and valuable service, he presented him with a handsome rifle.

Nor was the confidence reposed in him by the friendly chiefs less marked. He was admitted to a seat in their councils, both public and private; took an active part in their deliberations, and vied with the best of them in their efforts to reconcile their brethren to emigration. How did he requite their confidence? His first victim was Charley Amathla, the very man who offered himself as surety for his good behavior, when released from prison. With a party of his men he waylaid him and his family as they were collecting their cattle, preparatory to driving them to the place appointed for valuation, and shot him with his own hand. This was the beginning of the war. His second victim was Wiley Thompson, and he shot him a few weeks after, with the very rifle he had presented him as a pledge of peace.

Thompson did not die then, the "day after" Powell's release [as had been stated in the earlier article], but several months after.

This account, it is hoped, will satisfy Mr. Wise, that the statement contained in the above extract from his speech is not sustained by the evidence in the case. Should more be required, reference may be made to an officer now in the Office of the Commissary General of Subsistence, who commanded the guard that took Powell into custody.

[signed] A.[40]

In a note published at the end of this article, the editors of the *National Intelligencer* indicated that the writer of the article was a gentleman in whom they had implicit confidence. Only one source, John Bemrose, offers an actual date for the argument, 3 June 1835.[41] Because Bemrose also tells us that his unit had left Fort King and that he only received this information several weeks after the event, we need not be concerned, however, that his report slightly condenses the subsequent events.

"A" offers us, for his account, the corroboration of an officer then stationed in the newly created office of the Commissary General of Subsistence in Washington. Such an officer was indeed there at the time. As a matter of fact, three of the six officers in the department would eventually be associated with the Osceola story. Maj. J. H. Hook, officer commanding, would, just a few weeks after this article, receive a gift of Osceola's personal possessions from a former fellow officer of the Fourth Infantry, Capt. Pitcairn Morrison.[42] (See chapter 12.) One of Major Hook's assistants in the Subsistence Department, Capt. John C. Casey, would obtain the artifacts after

Hook's death in 1841. A third member of the department, Capt. Thomas W. Lendrum, however, was probably the man to whom "A" was referring, or he may have been "A" himself. Lendrum had been on duty at Fort King in April 1835 with the Third Artillery and had witnessed the Indian council held then and remained there until the fort was evacuated in mid-1836.[43] As of 7 July 1838, Lendrum was appointed a commissary of subsistence with the rank of quartermaster.[44] Unfortunately, Lendrum has left us no known personal account of his duty in Florida.

This entire scenario of Osceola's altercation with Thompson and its interpretation by "A" is further confirmed by another eyewitness, who sent his account to the *Army and Navy Chronicle* and signed himself only "WARTULA." In conclusion he says, "With regard to the effect which the confinement of Powell may have had on the war, I would give the opinion of many, whom I consider competent judges, as they were acquainted with all the circumstances; they think that the mistake was in *releasing* and not in confining, this truly great warrior; to which opinion your correspondent fully subscribes."[45]

The Execution of Charley Emathla

There seems to be universal agreement that a group led by Osceola carried out the sentence of execution prescribed for Charley Emathla on 26 November 1835. Once again, we have read Agent Thompson's report of the event (in Chapter 1), which leaves us with no doubt that Osceola led the execution party. Several other accounts would seem to favor the view that the murder occurred strictly out of bloodthirstiness on the part of Osceola. John Bemrose, however, mitigates this point most rationally by saying, "It appeared that the act was deliberately determined upon by the chief of the nation owing to a law previously stated: that any Indian who should leave his people to aid the whites forfeits his life."[46] Sprague reiterates this mandate, making it clear that the death sentence was a fact well known not only among the Indians but also among the white troops. Sprague calls the execution of Charley Emathla a "cowardly, revengeful, and atrocious act" but, nevertheless, states clearly that in this act, Osceola "acted as the voluntary agent of the nation, of the hostile chiefs."[47] Sprague certainly did not understand that Osceola had been chosen and directed by the war council but undoubtedly was not an unwilling actor in the drama.

In fact, Osceola was so determined in his resistance and, as a consequence, so controversial among the Florida Indians that the longer he fought, the more precarious his existence became among both the Indians and the whites. Lt. R. H. Peyton (for whom the small fortification south of St. Augustine would be named), in a moment of prescience, wrote to a fellow officer: "I expect if the truth was known Powell is afraid of being killed should he emigrate by some Indian who has a grudge against him."[48] In addition, we also now have the report of Dr. Robert Lebby, who later recalled: "[Osceola] manifested considerable reluctance to go to the West without his people, for he said, he knew that the family of Charley O'Mathla, (whom he shot) would kill him—This he told Dr. Wheedon several times—and I think communicated the same to Capt. Morrison."[49] Osceola did indeed tell Dr. Frederick Weedon this specific fear. The doctor recorded it in a diary entry on 29 January 1838 (see chapter 5).[50]

The conclusion here is that Osceola did personally carry out a sentence of death prescribed by his superiors in the antiremoval faction not out of a personal vendetta but, rather, out of commitment to the will of his first loyalty, the Indians who were fighting to remain in their homelands. Nevertheless, the right of a clan to seek redress for the loss of one of its members remained, and Osceola certainly could have been subject to the right of Charley Emathla's clan to restore balance to the larger Creek world if he had reached Indian Territory. Although they were not of the same clan, Tee-wa-sah-he-yay, the forty-one-year-old wife of Charley Emathla, two daughters, Ick-ko-ho-lay or Betsy and Li-yo or Nannie (twenty-three and seventeen years old, respectively), and a seven-year-old son, Toney, turned themselves in at Fort Brooke on 8 March 1837.[51] There they joined other Indians awaiting transportation to Indian Territory in the West. No indication is given in the same list of emigrating Indians whether any members of Charley Emathla's clan were emigrating at the same time, although they undoubtedly were. Their descendents remain in Oklahoma today, except for one male descendent who has, ironically, returned to Florida and married a Florida Seminole woman of the Big Town Clan.

The Death of Thompson

Neither is there any doubt that indeed Osceola led the attack in which Wiley Thompson was killed on 28 December 1835. Late on that afternoon, about three or four o'clock, Thompson and a dinner companion, Lt. Constantine Smith, decided to take an after-dinner stroll outside the gates of Fort King. There they were surprised and killed by a party of Indians led by Osceola. The body of Thompson was riddled with balls and was scalped. At the same time, another segment of the Indian party also attacked and killed the sutler Erastus Rogers and his two clerks as they sat at their meal in the sutler's cabin nearby. The commanding officer of the fort heard the shots and immediately ordered the gates of the stockade closed, not realizing that the agent was outside. Consequently, some time elapsed before he reopened the gates to investigate.

Dr. Weedon, in a diary entry for 29 January 1838, quoted Osceola as saying, however, that he "had done nothing except killing Gen. Thompson."[52] This may appear to conflict with another of Osceola's statements (above) in which he expressed his concern over the probable vengeance of Charley Emathla's family in Indian Territory. More probably, it illuminates Osceola's own imaging of his actions in the Indian and white worlds as entirely separate. Two accounts also quote an eyewitness, the black cook in the household of Mr. Rogers, as having seen and heard Osceola during the event.[53] A third, official account indicates that Osceola's "shrill peculiar war-whoop" was recognized by interpreters and one or two friendly Indians at the fort.[54] With this redress of personal grievance, an important balance was restored to Osceola's world. At the same time, a profound and critical blow was struck at the power of the white government. Undoubtedly, the war council had considered this in deciding upon the act.

The First Battle of the Withlacoochee

The First Battle of the Withlacoochee, which took place on the Withlacoochee River only three days after the raid at Fort King ended the life of Wiley Thompson, was the first major confrontation between official forces of the two antagonists: the antiremoval Indians and the white soldiers. Each had used the pacific encounters of the preceding year to "take the measure" of the other. Each side was confident of its superiority and its ability to bring the conflict to a psychological climax with this show of strength. The result of the conflict was that each side was rather badly disabused of its unrealistic notions.

There seems to be majority agreement on two points as regards Osceola and this engagement. First, he was "leading" the Indians—although his ability to control their actions was less than Richard Keith Call's control of the white volunteer forces. Again, we recall the southeastern Indians' traditional attitudes toward leadership: heredity or prowess conferred status and deference, but not absolute authority. Osceola's position in the forefront of this battle would have been ordained by the war council, and the warriors who fought in it were under the command of their own individual leaders.

Second, numerous reports agree that Osceola was injured in this battle, and all place the injury in an arm or hand. John Sprague gets his information from Alligator.[55] W. W. Smith, the "Lieutenant of the Left Wing," tells us that rumors circulated following the event to the effect that Osceola had been severely wounded, but more accurate information soon confined the wound to the hand.[56] Lt. Henry Prince quotes an express from Tallahassee as saying that "Powel received two shots and is recovering."[57] Although these reports may well have been no more than wishful thinking, the forensic evidence indicates that any such wound must have been slight because there was no indication of major trauma to most of the bones of the hands and arms. (See chapter 6.)

On one further point, W. W. Smith offers the information that Osceola was observed to be wearing a "uniform coat of our army," a point that Mark Boyd attempts to invest with added significance because this encounter took place three days after the destruction of Major Dade's command.[58] It was the blacks and not the Indians, however, who looted the bodies of Dade's men. We also know that Osceola had spent almost a year and a half in a position to obtain United States Army uniforms and accoutrements; Thompson may even have presented one to him as a gift. Osceola's motive in wearing the coat now was almost certainly as a display of contempt, power over an enemy, protective coloration, a facet of war medicine, or all of these.

Knifing of a Treaty

In his *Florida Historical Quarterly* article in 1955, Mark Boyd reviewed some of the evidence regarding a legend of Osceola's having stabbed a knife into a treaty, but neglected several points.[59] Only one direct eyewitness account exists of Osceola's having drawn or brandished a knife in anger. Four such reports are documented, but one is totally unconnected with any treaty signing, a second is ambiguous, the third says that a table was stabbed, not a treaty, and the fourth is recounted by an unreliable narrator.

John Bemrose cited a report that reached him after he had left Fort King concerning Osceola's argument with Thompson on 3 June 1835. The report indicated that Osceola "broke out with ungovernable rage, drawing his knife, which he brandished in a threatening manner."[60] This notation was made only in his private papers at the time, however, not in any publication.

An article signed only "Viator" and reprinted from the *New Bern* (N.C.) *Spectator* of 26 February 1836 appeared in the *Army and Navy Chronicle* on 31 March 1836. The author, in the only eyewitness account, said:

> I recollect once to have seen him [Osceola] on the piazza of the officers' quarters [at Fort King], whilst Micanope, the ostensible Chief of the nation, was closeted with General Clinch, in his office, which opened upon the stoop. Micanope . . . is ever a stupid fool, when not replenished by his "sense-bearer," (as he calls him) Abraham, who

was on the present occasion absent. Oceola well knew this . . . [and] betrayed . . . anxiety . . . to be near Micanope, to give him the proper cue for a non-commitment. He would stand in the door apparently in the attention of an eaves-dropper; then he would be peeping into this and then into that window; ever assuming that peculiar air of curiosity, discernible only in the Indian. Becoming more and more impatient of his exclusion from the conference, he suddenly stalked across the stoop, jerked out his knife, and flourished it around his head with the most savage vehemence. Never have I seen a more striking figure than he presented at that time.[61]

This incident may well be the source of the event that was convoluted into legend by later writers. It was contemporary, reported by a firsthand observer, and contained all the elements—military official, Indian chief, talk regarding emigration, Osceola, anger, a knife—that would remain in the legend. Andrew Welch apparently was the first to print the convoluted story, which he did in 1841. In his account, however, the event takes place in December 1835, and the force of Osceola's knife not only pinions the treaty paper but continues through the table beneath. Welch had a penchant for sensationalism.[62]

The story next appeared in Thomas Storrow's article of 1844.[63] In this account, Osceola drove the knife into the "midst" of the "paper," but Storrow's rhetoric is such that we are left to wonder whether the knife was planted in the middle of one paper or in among (that is, in the midst of) several papers. Storrow did not identify his source, but his account has all the earmarks of John Sprague's story, which Sprague published in his own work four years later.[64] In Sprague's account, Osceola drove his knife "into the table," not into a treaty at all. Because Sprague was not a witness to many of the events that he recounted, it is highly possible that he had read the *Chronicle* article or even that he knew "Viator" and simply confused the exciting old story.

Capitulation

Osceola, the young Indian mixed-blood warrior, spent at least the last year and a half of his life, from January 1836 through mid-1837, trying to prove to whites that he would not, under any circumstances, be forced out of the home that he claimed in Florida and, at the same time, trying to show that he could live in peace with whites. Despite the seemingly contradictory nature of these two points, it seems clear that Osceola's attitude of armed defiance was not aimed at white individuals or settlers per se but at the concept of forced dispossession. At the encounter dubbed the Battle of Camp Izard in late February and early March 1836, for example, Osceola offered to accept a new boundary line between whites and Indians if peace could be arranged. At this parley, he even recognized a soldier whom he had met while confined at Fort King, and he spoke to him cordially.[65] Dr. Robert Lebby of Charleston also recalled an exchange with a white visitor on this point. "A gentleman said to him, Osceola, if you were at home, and I visited you at your Wigwam, would you treat me with the kindship [i.e., kindness] that has been bestowed upon you? He promptly replied, if he came with the same spirit and intention as he did there, he would treat him in like manner, but if he came as the pale faces generally did, he would give him his knife— (at the same time showing this weapon)."[66]

We do not have sufficient information to understand just exactly when Osceola's staunch determination began to yield to the reality of defeat, although the pressures on him to do so had been constant and immense. A man of lesser determination and passion would have given up earlier, as so many did. In January 1837 the ex-slave Primus reported that soldiers had dispersed most of Powell's warriors; he had only three left with him, in addition to his family. Furthermore, Primus said, Osceola was sick.[67] Lt. Henry Prince, Fourth Infantry, recorded in his diary the comments of a female Indian prisoner: "21st [January 1837] . . . Talked with the prisoners about the war. Their conversation is very amusing. An intelligent one says . . . Powell is a good warrior and a *gentlemanly indian* 'the most gentlemanly indian in the nation—he don't take white folk's things he never has even got a horse'—he would be a good chief if he had men."[68]

General Jesup managed a diplomatic coup in March 1837, after several weeks of negotiations. Several of Micanopy's representatives signed a capitulation (of a sort), binding the chief and others to emigration with their blacks—a point that was also a capitulation (of a sort) for the United States government. Those Indians from the central and southern part of Florida who were finally resigned to emigration began to congregate near Fort Brooke to receive much-needed subsistence. Among many Indians who remained along the St. Johns River, Osceola gathered his people at a camp site on the St. Augustine Trail, about fifteen miles from Fort Mellon (formerly Camp Monroe). Once again, Osceola cooperated with the military, offering to arrange a ball game to gather Indians who wanted to emigrate.[69] On the night of 7 May 1837 he even shared the hospitality of Col. William Harney's tent. Once again, however, in early June, in what may have been a last, passionate effort to spur the Indians to maintain their resistance, Osceola helped to liberate the camp of Indians held for emigration at

Tampa and returned to his current base of operations near Fort Mellon (see chapter 1).

Living conditions during this time of year were not conducive to good health for any of the combatants. They were not healthy for the white soldiers, who were withdrawn from Fort Mellon for the summer due to the possibility of malaria and other illnesses. Conditions certainly were not healthy for the Indians whose principal subsistence base had been lost by flight from gardens and homes at the Cove of the Withlacoochee some months prior. The Indians, however, tired of constant vigilance and flight, stayed at their camp near the unhealthy fort throughout the summer. United States troops scored sizable psychological victories in early September with the surprise captures of King Philip, Uchee Billy, his brother Jack, Blue Snake, and Philip's son Coacoochee. The leadership of the antiremoval faction was seriously diminished. General Jesup decided to press this advantage in a decidedly ungentlemanly manner: he determined to press the Indians into compliance by force. Waiting for them to remove of their own volition had proved to be a frustrating and tiresome task. Their unwillingness to leave Florida was irrelevant. Their reasons for staying were irrelevant. Jesup was angry and determined, and, for a few pieces of white cloth, he acted rashly and tainted his own reputation forever. Osceola became the icon of his dishonor.

On the afternoon of 21 October 1837, Jesup sent Gen. Joseph Hernández, commanding troops east of the St. John's River, and a company of soldiers to meet Osceola, who came bearing a white flag of truce, and take him prisoner. For his actions, Jesup was widely excoriated and called to justify his conduct before the United States Congress.[70] This single act certainly did more to solidify the image of Osceola as a hero in the minds of the American public than anything that the man had previously accomplished on his own. Jesup was called upon, time and again over the following years, to justify his "treachery and fraud."[71]

In 1858, almost twenty years after the event, Jesup was still explaining to the public. Almost half a century later, in 1880, his defenders were *still* explaining.[72] In a *New York Times* article dated 25 October 1858, Jesup repeated his rationalizations of some of the critical points in rather interesting ways, however, and this rationalization he clung to for the rest of his life. He said, "A matter has recently been brought into discussion with which my name was connected some twenty years ago, and, though explained at the time, seems not even now to be understood." He began by attempting to undermine Osceola's image with a weak non sequitur. Jesup contended that, although history had called Osceola the victor of the Battle of the Withlacoochee, there was "some doubt whether Osceola was in that battle at all." Furthermore, Osceola had murdered General Thompson, violated his parole, killed Jesup's messenger during the time of truce, and had, by his repeated violations of the usages of war, "forfeited his life, particularly in his attempt to use a flag for hostile purposes, at St. Augustine."[73]

Jesup declared that he had "known" beforehand that, at the Fort Peyton parley, Osceola had intended only to reconnoiter the whites' troop strength preparatory to forcing the release of Philip. "I had become acquainted with their designs through [the] negroes some of whom remained with the Indians and possessed the contract pay [that is, they were under contract to the army as spies], and I received from them information of all that took place, or was about to take place, among [the Indians]."[74] In ascribing this motive to Osceola, Jesup seems to have been deluding himself, irrespective of what he had or had not heard from the blacks whom he paid. Moreover, he averred that the other chiefs had earlier "expressed some apprehension that, in coming in to me, they might be attacked by my scouting parties, and their people be scattered. To enable them to join me without danger of attack from these parties, I provided them with a quantity of white cotton cloth, to be used as flags in communicating with any of those parties they might fall in with on my outposts; but the flags were to be used for no other purpose. And the chiefs were distinctly and positively told that none of them nor their people must attempt to come in again, but to remain."[75] Jesup's white piece of cloth seems to have served him as a flag of all circumstances.

Documentary evidence proves, however, the manner in which Jesup manipulated memory to his own advantage. The Indians did have reason to believe that they might be attacked by scouting parties on their way to legitimate meetings. Army communication systems were not sufficiently rapid across the Florida peninsula, despite the fact that messengers were constantly on the move. But what seemed "distinctly" clear to Jesup about the understanding of the Indians did not necessarily seem distinct, clear, or positive to the Indians, and we know now that Jesup's subordinate, Gen. Joseph Hernández, had made it very clear to him that the Indians did *not* share his interpretation.

Three letters penned by Hernández and addressed to Jesup reveal the essence of the "white-flag situation." In the first, written on 29 September 1837, Hernández is confirming a personal discussion that he and Jesup had just completed at Bulow (a residence and sugar mill near present-day Daytona that had been burned down by the Indians in the opening days of the war). Upon his recent capture, Philip had asked Gen. Hernández to send out a messenger to his son Coacoochee and his family to "come in to him." Philip had asked to have an Indian called Tomoka John sent out with his message, and Hernández had agreed. (Jesup later wrote that it was Coacoochee who took the message, but it was *to* Coacoochee that the message was sent.) Tomoka John, however, had failed to wait for explicit instructions from Hernández or even to wait to hear what Philip's message might be and had delivered his own message instead.

Hernández had, however, managed to give Tomoka John a piece of white cloth to be torn into pieces and carried by any Indian parties wishing to come in. Hernández believed that it would be made clear to the Indians that, by "coming in" they were *turning themselves in*—permanently—for emigration. Jesup asserted in his report that he had told the Indians in a recent meeting that they should come in only to give themselves up. Tomoka John told them, nevertheless, that *Hernández* was inviting them to come in; that he had a "*good talk*" for them; that he wished to put an end to the war; and that he "would assign to them a portion of the country to live in."[76] In other words, they had every right to expect that they would be free to "come in" only to hear the talk and then *go out again,* freely.

When Hernández realized the misunderstanding, if not the ambiguity of Jesup's earlier statement, he confronted the messenger. As explanation of his willful deceptions, Tomoka John "excused himself by saying, that he was obliged to resort to them, to induce any of the Indians to listen to the proposition of coming to St. Augustine."[77] Jesup had, nevertheless, captured those who "came in," and Hernández wanted to send back at least one of them to keep other Indians from believing that the army was acting in bad faith. Clearly, Hernández was loathe to disregard the Indians' perception of their own freedom, and he made the Indians' point of view perfectly clear to Jesup in a personal conversation and in writing.

In the second letter, written just eighteen days later, Hernández states that one of Philip's brothers and two of his sons, including Coacoochee, had reached St. Augustine and had informed Hernández that Powell and about one hundred Indians were also on their way toward the town. It was Hernández's decision that they should all meet at Moultrie, about seven miles south of St. Augustine, near Fort Peyton. However, Hernández informed Jesup: "So far as their views can be learned from the little communication which has been had with Coacoochee, they have come in under the belief, that they are to be at perfect liberty, and in the expectation of a further understanding."[78] Hernández informed Jesup that he would do nothing to disabuse them of this notion until he heard from Jesup. He advised Jesup quite clearly, however, that there were only two alternatives. No "middle course," he said, could "be pursued with any safety." Either they must be left to come and go as they would, or they must be taken prisoners.

Obviously extremely anxious about the entire situation, Hernández wrote, yet again, the same afternoon to say that Coacoochee did not wish to remain in St. Augustine awaiting the others because he believed the area to be too confined and potentially sickly. He believed they (the Indians) would all die if they stayed there. Hernández wanted more troops to wait in readiness at Moccasin Branch (south and west of the city). Jesup responded: "Let the Chiefs and warriors know that we have been deceived by them long enough and that we do not intend to be deceived by them again." Although this statement could have been perceived as just as ambiguous as the last, Jesup's instructions to Hernández were not: "Order the whole party directly to town. You have force sufficient to compel obedience."[79] This appears to have been what Hernández was waiting for. He obviously did not want to violate the flag of truce solely on his own authority. He wanted his superior officer to take the responsibility. He knew how poorly the Indians would view such an action; perhaps he sensed how poorly the American public would view it also. He was right. Both the authority and the responsibility lay with Jesup, and with Jesup—not Hernández—would lay the blame.

Osceola and his people did not go into the town, however. They stopped about eight miles or so below St. Augustine and made camp. Obviously, Jesup received this information just a few minutes or hours after sending the note to Hernández—it could have been no more—and devised an alternate plan of capture for Osceola's group. He sent Hernández southward to meet Osceola on the road. As events transpired, they met about a mile below Fort Peyton (which was seven miles south of St. Augustine, on the south side of Moultrie Creek).

Osceola was well aware that, no matter what the pretext, his meeting with Jesup's forces at Fort Peyton could be final. He went to the meeting with his gun unloaded as a sign of good faith to "hear the white man's talk and see if it was good."[80] Coe hadjo, a long-time advocate of removal, went with him. The Indians suspected that Coe hadjo, formerly respected, had become an ally of the U.S. military, which was in fact the case, and the resistance fighters had ceased to trust him.[81] So Osceola knew that Coe hadjo was in league with the white soldiers. Dr. Robert Lebby later recounted Osceola's conversation with Coe hadjo, which he must have gotten from one of the people who was with them:

> The Indian that accompanied Oceola, when he surrendered to Genl. Jesup, was at Fort Moultrie, with him, a very intelligent man, and I think was the Counselor or Lawyer of the nation—He said repeatedly that Osceola, surrendered himself, knowing and believing

that he would not be permitted to leave the Camp again,—and he repeated a conversation that occurred between himself and the Chief a day or two before they got to the Genl's Camp—I think this man's name was Coa Hadjo.... In the conversation referred to, he said when Oceola met him—he asked if he was going into the Genl:—Hadjo's reply,—yes for he was satisfied that his people could do nothing more—they were worn down by sickness, and starvation, and he was going in—Oceola's reply—that he would go with him that—he was now done—and asked Hadjo, if it was likely the Genl would let him come out again to gather his people—Hadjo said, that he was certain Genl. Jesup would not let him go—if he ever went in, and if he wished to gather his people, he had better do so before he surrendered,—for he had done a great deal against the whites, and they would not permit him to go out again.[82]

Coe hadjo was correct. The white flag did nothing to protect Osceola and the warriors who went with him. Jesup captured them regardless. About a month later, Lt. John Pickell, on duty at Fort Mellon, noted in his journal:

Thursday [November] 30th.... Several days ago an Indian runner was sent out at the request of Osceola who is a captive in St. Augustine, to bring in his family, Their arrival has been expected for the last three days, but did not arrive until 4 o'clk this afternoon. They came with a white flag, hoisted upon a staff or pole 8 feet high and presented altogether a pitiable sight. The bearer of the train was a fine looking young warrior and at the head of the train, which was composed of about 50 souls.... The negro part of the train was a wretched picture of squalid misery.... They have been on their way a number of days and were much fatigued when they arrived; they brought two miserable looking Indian ponies with them. From the voraciousness of their appetites when they were supplied with food, they seem to have been nearly starved.[83]

Escape from Fort Marion

The escape from Fort Marion involved Osceola only tangentially, by virtue of his omission rather than commission. Yet it illuminates further his state of mind, along with the reality of the human relationships that existed irrespective of the official state of belligerence existing between Indians and whites.

The prison to which Osceola and those captured with him were taken, and in which Philip, Coacoochee, and their people were held, was and remains the oldest and largest masonry fortification in the nation. El Castillo de San Marcos, guarding the mouth of St. Augustine harbor, was constructed for the Spaniards by Indian levy laborers from 1672 until its substantial completion in 1695. The Americans renamed it Fort Marion in honor of Francis Marion, the "Swamp Fox" of American Revolutionary War fame. It is a classic Vauban-style fortification, with crenelated walls, bastions, a gun deck, vaulted bombproofs, a sally port gate and drawbridge spanning a moat, a demilune, and a covert way, all surrounded by a glacis—a field of at least a musket-shot's distance denuded of trees to preclude any stealthy approach by an enemy. The fort has seen warfare, and in every instance it has repulsed attack. The fort is not isolated. This tenth and last of the Spanish forts to guard St. Augustine was built as an integral part of the community, and even in 1837 it lay—almost literally—nestled in the arms of the townsfolk.

From a military point of view, the Indian captives were in an excellent place nonetheless. Within the fort, on the quadrangle, and even from the gun deck, there was little need for close guarding because the structure itself was the guard. There was only one way in and one way out (ostensibly)—through the sally port—and it was guarded day and night. The walls were thirty feet high, and the drop was precipitous. Curious townspeople came and went to see the Indians whom they had feared for so long. The Indians' muskets and rifles were unloaded and stacked, standing in tent fashion, in the quadrangle. Officers, messengers (white and Indian), and soldiers came and went.

Coacoochee was extremely displeased with his surroundings. He had never expected to become a prisoner, and he was chafing for freedom from the first moment. He had already told Hernández that he feared the town was unhealthy. Normally, the town was known for just the opposite condition. In the latter years of the nineteenth century it would become the refuge of "consumptives" and other northerners recuperating from various illnesses. Inside the thick, porous walls of the fort in winter, however, the seaport's damp, cold, and changeable weather could be deadly. As it turned out, it was a measles epidemic, begun farther down the peninsula several months earlier, that brought death inside the walls of Fort Marion. Philip's people had succumbed to it as early as August of that year, well prior to their capture. But once they were confined in unnaturally close quarters inside the old fort, fourteen Indian prisoners died between 1 November and 12 December, and at that time, two more were not expected to live.[84] Without a doubt, all of these considerations, together with his own passion and natural ambition, led Coacoochee to decide upon escape, and late on the night of 29 November he and a group of determined followers left the fort.

The fact of their going is not disputed. Their number and the manner of their going are. The numbers cited in the reports, both by the military and the newspapers, range from eleven to twenty.[85] The official report indicates that the escapees were Coacoochee, John Co-wai-yie (Caballo), sixteen other warriors, and two "squaws." A contemporary list of the escapees resides in the files of the St. Augustine Historical Society and lists the individuals.[86] They were as follows:

Coa-co-chee (Philip's son)
Is-po-Ko-Kay
Ok-tai-a-chee
Ta-co-sa-Tustenukke (Philip's brother)
Hal-pah-tah-Hajo
Apäi-ah-Kee-Micco-chee
No-cose-Hajo
Holata-Tustennukke
Hotulkee-Haja
John Ca-wai-yie
Hoke-pissee-Emathla-chee   } Philip's
Nea-he-thloth-Kee-Emathlee } sons

                              Micca-Su-Kees
Emathla-Tustennukke
Holat-Tustennukke   (his sister Nok-op-ho-yay)
Holata-Tustennukke
Ah-ha-Micco-chee
Ah-ha-lak-Ha-chee
Echo-Emathla   }   Woman A-pee-e-ay

Apparently, this source was not available when Kenneth W. Porter was investigating the story of John Caballo (John Ca-wai-yie, above), but he reasoned that his subject must have been with Coacoochee, and he was correct. The list of prisoners still in custody that accompanies this list of escapees divides the Indians into "Philip's People," "Powell's People," "Seminole Slaves," "Micca-su-Kees," "Coe Hadjo's People," "Tallahassees," and "Uchees."

Among the prisoners who remained in custody were Osceola; his two wives, Ui-chee and Ah-lik-chen; and his two children, one child belonging to each wife. As-la-täi-kee, a sister of Ui-chee, was in their group also. Between Jesup's report on this escape to Secretary of War Joel Poinsett and two newspaper articles, some confusion has continued to the present day concerning this aspect of Osceola's family. The list clarifies the matter, however. It does not appear that the two wives of Osceola were sisters (although the custom of sororate polygyny, taking multiple sisters as wives, certainly existed among the Creeks and Seminoles in Osceola's day and continued long into the twentieth century). There were two sisters with Osceola, but they were not both his wives. One was his wife, and the other was *her* sister. There is a woman named Polly who appears on the list as having arrived prior to 30 November, and she is neither specifically associated with Osceola nor indicated as an "old woman," as others are. Neither of these facts is definitive, however. The list of "Powell's People" includes the following:

1	Assee-n-yahola (Powell)
Tusten=	{Ya-ha Hajo
nukkees	{Holatea Emathla (Died 11th Decr 1837)
4	E-con-chattee Emathla {daughter Chok-ful-ai-kay
6	Ta-co-sa Fixico
7	Ho-kee-illis-sa Hajo
8	No-cha-kee-ay
9	Sit-ho-keé
10	Talope Hajo
11	Ah-mee-chäi-kee
12	Micco-läi-kee
13	Tustennuk-ho-päi-o-chee
14	Nee-täi-ee

Capt. Harvey Brown transmitted the military response to the escape to Capt. Lucien B. Webster, in command of Fort Marion. He reported:

> You will put the whole of Philip's people now remaining prisoners here, in irons, and so keep them until further orders. You will please explain to them that this course is adopted as a consequence of the late escape which the Commanding General thinks should have been stopped by Philip and the elders of the tribes.
>
> You will also explain to the other Chiefs that they will be held responsible for any further attempts which are made to escape, and the moment that any are discovered no matter of what party, the whole will be placed in irons, to be dealt with in the severest manner.

No citisens will be permitted to enter the Fort, and an officer will, as heretofore, be kept on duty there constantly and any person who you may suspect of attempting to escape, you will immediately put in irons.[87]

A board of officers, which comprised Captain Gould of the Florida Volunteers (and erstwhile mayor of St. Augustine), Lieutenant Dunn of the Fourth Artillery, and Lieutenant Capron of the First Artillery, reported that the Indians had made their escape from the room in which they were being held by means of "an aperture in the wall, about eight inches wide and five feet long, and situated about fifteen feet from the floor. One of the iron bars which formerly closed the aperture, was Removed and the Indians descended into the ditch by means of a line fastened to the remaining bar."[88] In reality, the aperture was a gunner's loophole, extremely narrow and tall on the inside of the thick wall and splaying to the outside where there was only a sheer thirty-foot drop to the moat. Even removing a bar would have left an opening too small for an adult human to pass through. And the question of the "line" that was used to descend to the ground remains also. Perhaps they did cut up blankets and the muslin that may have covered straw mattresses but, if so, with what? Surely they had not been allowed to keep knives, even though later, in Charleston, they seem to have been permitted access to their guns.

It was Coacoochee, so fond of making up stories to amuse people, who gave out the version that would be most often cited as the true story of the escape. Little of it rings true either, however. Coacoochee begins by saying that Talmus Hadjo was the only one who escaped with him. But this individual is not even on the list of prisoners. What about the other nineteen persons, including two women, who were found to be missing the next morning? His account of getting up to the loophole makes the task more difficult than it would be in reality, and, again, the opening is hardly wide enough for an adult to pass through. The military report admits that that corner of the fort was not well guarded, and Captain Brown's orders, quoted above, seem to indicate that only a single officer was on guard duty at night.

Two main versions of this episode remain among the Seminoles and Creeks of Florida and Oklahoma. One version says that the Indians made medicine to make themselves very small. A medicine man among them told them to watch the ants, and they saw the ants passing into a crack in the wall. With the aid of the medicine, they followed the ants through the wall and down to safety outside.[89] Of course, Coacoochee eventually went to Oklahoma, and his version of events, including the taking of medicine to reduce himself in size, went with him. The making and taking of medicine may have been accurate. We know that the Indians, before their imprisonment, were concerned lest the soldiers refuse them permission to gather the plants they needed to make medicines for themselves. At least one newspaper article mentioned that, during their imprisonment, the Indians made four trips outside the fort walls to gather herbs. Obviously, the reporter did not understand the significance of the number "four" to the preparation of powerful medicine.[90]

The other version of the escape, which remains among the Florida descendents, says that Osceola helped the escapees to make war medicine. That was, after all, his forte, his knowledge having been acquired over years of study with the most proficient medicine man in Florida, Abiákî. The medicine made water, standing in puddles in the quadrangle, rise up as steam and obscure the escapees from the sight of the guards and thus permitted them to walk out through the sally port.

The most likely scenario, however, is that all three versions contain elements of the truth. There was a guard; he was asleep by the guardroom fire, or possibly even drunk. Other guards may have been in the guardroom in front of the fire as well, rather than out in the cold and windy sally port. There may have been some sympathy for the Indians among one or several of the white soldiers. The soldiers may well have believed that the size and strength of the fort made it a sufficiently safe prison that they did not need to be especially vigilant. The escapees may well have passed the soldiers without being seen—right through the sally port gate and out across the drawbridge to freedom. Such a scenario would have been rather embarrassing to report, however, and would have been a permanent black mark on the military record of the fort's commander.

On the morning following the escape, when Capt. Pitcairn Morrison, in charge of the prisoners, discovered what had transpired, Osceola sent word through him to Jesup that he (Osceola) and his people could have left also but had declined to do so. Osceola's time for fighting was over. Richard Fields, a member of the Cherokee delegation that had visited the prisoners while they were in Fort Marion, reported on the visit to Cherokee chief John Ross, saying: "When Wild Cat made his escape from the Fort Osceola refused to escape with them: this man is the great spirit of Florida. The utmost confidence is placed in his ability by all the Seminoles, and Micanopi paid him a high compliment yesterday by asking for his release and demanding his presence here whenever the chiefs meet to deliberate again upon their affairs, he said that he was a man of business, and whatever he said he would do and that all the people depended upon his judgment and wanted him to be there."[91]

4 / Through the Eyes of Those Who Saw Him

The fame of George Catlin and that of Osceola have become inextricably linked over the years since the death of the latter because of the widely circulated, striking, and colorful portrait that Catlin executed at Fort Moultrie. George Catlin, however, was not the first to paint a portrait of Osceola, nor was his necessarily the best, from the standpoint of likeness.[1] He certainly was not the first to capture an image of Osceola on paper either. He did undoubtedly produce more images of this celebrity than any other artist, and these images certainly have gained wider circulation and notoriety than any others.

Once again, however, as with all the other facets of this complex and convoluted story, we must start at the beginning and try to place all the verifiable facts in chronological sequence. This will accomplish two objectives. First, it will add yet another dimension to our social and historical portraits of Osceola as a human being. Second, it will clarify the artistic record.

The images of Osceola produced since the 1830s fall loosely into two categories, or generations. The first generation is composed of those works, in whatever medium, that were executed during Osceola's lifetime and afterward, up to the period of the American Civil War. Even among these were a number of direct copies from much better known originals and, undoubtedly, some obscure works. We shall deal with the most germane, and the directly related, members of this first generation here.

During the decade of the 1860s, Americans were distracted from the problems of territorial expansion and Indian conflicts by the horrendous problems of civil war. American attention would not fully return to the Indians until the end of Reconstruction and the next major wave of westward settlement. By that time Osceola had passed out of the living memory of most Americans. Images of him produced during the next century would run the entire gamut from accuracy to pure fiction. The members of this second generation, too far removed temporally to be considered as possible primary documentation, will not be considered here.

Keenan, 1836

The earliest image of Osceola seems to be a full-length steel engraving by William Keenan (see figure 1) that was produced specifically to accompany Myer Cohen's book of personal experiences of the Florida war.[2] Cohen and Woodburne Potter were the first of a number of officers who took part in the war to put their experiences in print, both volumes appearing at the booksellers in 1836.[3] Cohen literally rushed his publication into print, however—he reached Charleston, his home, only on 18 May, and by 16 August the *Charleston Courier* was announcing the publication of *Notices of Florida and the Campaigns, by M. M. Cohen, accompanied with a Map and a portrait of Osceola, engraved by Keenan.*

The plate in Cohen's book also contains the information that the image was "Drawn, Engraved, and Printed by W. Keenan."[4] William Keenan was one of Charleston's local artists who had been advertising himself as early as 1828 as "Historical, Portrait, Landscape and General Engraver."[5] This was not the only portrait of Osceola that Keenan produced, although technically it should not be considered a likeness, because there seems no reason to believe that Keenan had either some depiction of his subject or personal experience upon which to base the piece. The Keenan engraving bears no relationship whatsoever to reality, nor is it even well executed artistically. Myer Cohen's acceptance of this fantasy art as worthy of his publication does not speak well for the credibility of a book also suspect in its text.

Vinton, 1837

The next image of Osceola, chronologically, was produced indirectly from life and has served as one of the seminal images of its subject (see figure 2). This work was only a small pencil sketch, a right-profile bust, executed by

Figure 1. Engraving of Osceola by William Keenan. Published in M. M. Cohen, *Notices of Florida and the Campaigns* (1836).

A correct likeness of Oceola the Seminole Chief engaged in the Florida war 1835, and taken prisoner by me under orders of Gen.ʸ Jessup, in October 1837.

Figure 2. Pencil sketch of Osceola by John Rogers Vinton, 1837. (Courtesy of the Heye Museum of the American Indian, Smithsonian Institution, New York City.)

John Rogers Vinton on 4 May 1837, but it seems to have gained wide popularity. Captain Vinton was almost of an age with his subject, having been born in 1801. He was a Rhode Islander and West Point graduate who had been in active service in the army for twenty years before he and Osceola met at Fort Mellon, in peace, during the armistice of 1837.[6]

Vinton had several points in his favor as regards his ability to draw, but his later efforts were hampered by an ambiguous attitude regarding historical accuracy. By 1837 John Vinton had spent several years of his military career doing topographical duty, thereby developing his artistic talent.[7] He also had traveled in Georgia and Florida off and on over a ten-year period and developed a keen eye for landscape (which seems to have become his forté) and military detail.[8] Throughout his subsequent works, the topographical features retain a draftsmanlike quality, even as they increase in facility and general quality of execution. The human figures, at the same time, retain an obvious naiveté, which lends to the whole a certain charming romanticism, if not professionalism.

The original 4 May bust sketch survives today in the collections of the Museum of the American Indian, Heye Foundation, New York City, neg. no. 26048. A photoduplicate of a two-page handwritten document in the WPA files held by the Florida Historical Society, however, contains the information that partially explains the sketch. The note describes a "Pencil sketch of Oseola on paper 3 1/8 in × 3 1/4 in an old frame 8 1/8 × 5 1/4 under glass. On slip of paper pasted below sketch is written in ink 'A correct likeness of Oseola the Seminole Chief engaged in the Florida war 1835, and taken prisoner by me under order of Genl Jessup in October 1837.'" Below this is pasted another slip of paper bearing the signature of "Joseph M. Hernández, Brigadr. Genl. Comndg. E. F. [Terr.]." On the original wood backing of the frame is written in lead pencil (perhaps ink faded) "Os-se-he-hola" (the remainder of the two lines unclear). Below is pasted a slip of paper on which is written in ink "[torn] se-he-hola, known to the whites as [torn] seola, the Florida chief, a Seminole in the war of 1837. Taken prisoner under Genl Jessup's orders, in October of that year, by Genl Hernández. Died in prison—sketch from life by Capt Vinton USA." On the back of the frame is also written in lead pencil (perhaps ink) "~~Sketch by~~ Oseola by Capt Vinton USA, 4 May 1837, in St. Augustine."[9]

Three very important bits of information are provided by this document, beyond its fixing the date of execution. First, nowhere does this legend indicate that this sketch was given to General Hernández, as has been assumed by other researchers.[10] It appears to be, rather, a simple testament to the credibility of the likeness, such as was provided frequently in this period by artists or their agents as an added inducement to public purchase and acceptance.

Second, this information states that the sketch was produced in St. Augustine, not at Fort Mellon. Undoubtedly, Vinton saw Osceola at Fort Mellon before and after 4 May 1837. Given the young officer's artistic bent as evidenced by other known sketches, it would not have been difficult for him to have filled any number of sketchbook pages with studies of the Indians on which later compositions might be based. This was George Catlin's technique as well. On 4 May, while he was in St. Augustine, it would have been an easy task to produce the simple little sketch for the edification of the public.

Finally, from the events and attributions mentioned in the various notations on the frame, we learn that the sketch, although executed on 4 May, was not authenticated by Hernández until some time after 21 October 1837, the date on which Osceola was taken prisoner. This information, in turn, brings into question other heretofore accepted details concerning Vinton's sketch. The *St. Augustine Florida Herald* of 7 July 1837 notified the public: "OSEOLA. We have been presented with a well executed likeness of this celebrated chief. . . . It was drawn from life by Capt. J. R. Vinton of the Army, at Fort Mellon, on the 4th of May last. . . . It is considered a nearly correct likeness."[11]

Nothing is known of the whereabouts of this *Herald* sketch—if indeed it was a separate piece. It is highly possible that the 4 May sketch mentioned by the *Herald* publisher, James M. Gould, and the one authenticated later by Hernández (the one that now resides in the Heye Foundation's collections) were the same. Vinton certainly made other of his sketches public intentionally. As we shall see, this same image was being (or about to be) publicized as an illustration for John Lee Williams's book on Florida, a book that was being published in New York and embellished with lithographs prepared there. A further reproduction from the same image, as an accompaniment to John Sprague's book, was prepared by a New York engraving firm, and the image finally passed into the collections of a New York museum, as we shall discuss shortly.

In light of these circumstances, it becomes reasonable to believe that John Rogers Vinton did not give a sketch to the *Herald* at all. Gould said, "We have been *presented* . . . " (emphasis added). Rather than a report of a gift, what we are reading here is, more probably, a nineteenth-century press release. Subsequent researchers have been interpreting Gould's phrase as "we have been given" when it should be interpreted as "we have been shown" or "it has been presented to us." All we have to believe is that Gould heard the information accompanying the sketch that was "presented" to him merely for information purposes. Then, courteously acceding to the desire of the artist to make his work public and the correlative desire of the public for up-to-the-minute information, he reported the event. If he condensed its salient points to strengthen a narrative that he knew to be substantially true by saying that the sketch was drawn at Fort Mellon rather than produced from studies drawn at Fort Mellon, he would be following a common practice among newspaper reporters of the day.

Williams, 1837

Sometime in 1837, then, John Lee Williams published his laboriously prepared *Territory of Florida,* containing the lithograph that could only have been produced from the Vinton bust sketch. Williams's illustration bears no attribution. The other illustrations that appear in his book are also stone lithographs, however, bearing no artist's name but signed "Greene & McGowran's Lithography, 30, Wall Street, New York."[12] Stone lithography was still considered a new and exciting artistic technique in this period. Sometimes the original artist was also the lithographer, sometimes not. In this instance, the lithographers may have taken several works by Vinton submitted by Williams and prepared the stones for printing. The two genre scenes bear resemblance stylistically to Vinton's work. No other Vinton drawings of Osceola were made public in 1837.

The rest of the year proved to be eventful, and doleful, for Osceola. In late October he was made a captive of the military forces and, after a short stay in Fort Marion at St. Augustine, was transferred to Fort Moultrie at Charleston, South Carolina. In Charleston the prisoners, and in particular the Indian whose colorful and romanticized exploits had been reported regularly to South Carolinians, gained immediate celebrity. By this time, however, Osceola's countenance had begun to change somewhat as a result of his physical debility and depression.

One visitor to the fort described him thus:

Today being Saturday I took leave of the city about 11 o'clock, embarked in a Packet Boat for Sullivan's Island, arrived there at 1/4 past 12, visited Fort Moultrie, saw Mickanopy, Oseola, Allegator, Jumper, Cloud, Billy Hix and about two hundred more Seminole Indians— Oseola was the one I was most curious to see. He is about 35 years old, large sized, about 6 feet high, well formed, has every appearance of the Indian, does not speak English, has an intellectual countenance, with a sad expression. He is now in rather bad health. . . . It is a mistake about Osceolas being an educated man. He is no doubt a good indian warrior and nothing more. . . . I can assure you that I have not been so well pleased with any excursion for some time as this today.[13]

This observer, of course, was viewing the Indians at their physical and emotional nadir. His comments stand in marked contrast to the way Osceola is remembered and described earlier. Two points in particular are common among descriptions by those who came in contact with him earlier: the delicacy of his features, almost to the point of effeminacy, and the expressiveness of those features—the animation of his eyes and mouth in ardent discourse. This, then, highlights the main informational difference between Vinton's sketches and the better-known 1838 images: Vinton depicted (although naively) the "old" Osceola—the confident and still optimistic war leader—whereas Curtis and Catlin would be left to capture (even though much more professionally) the infinite sadness of a passionate man defeated.

Catlin, Laning, and Curtis, 1838

Not only was the general public anxious to see Osceola, but also artists were enthusiastic to paint his portrait. When George Catlin, a preeminent painter of American Indians, learned in late December 1837 of the imprisonment, he closed his Indian Gallery in New York and ended his lecture series, determined to go to Charleston.[14] The War Department, learning of his disposition, commissioned him to obtain portraits of the five principal Indian leaders.[15]

Catlin arrived in Charleston aboard the steam packet *New York* on 17 January 1838.[16] He found that he was only one of the artists who were at the fort for the same purpose, and arrangements had to be made to accommodate them. Some years later, Thomas Storrow described the circumstances of Osceola's portraiture from the memory of individuals who witnessed it.

When the wishes of these gentlemen were made known to Osceola, he readily consented to sit; and to prepare himself to be drawn in a costume that he thought becoming, he devoted all the early part of a day to arraying himself in a manner which, in his eyes, was best calculated to set off his person to advantage. This was not done after the usual way of Indian warriors, with all the implements of war upon him, his body disfigured with dirt, his face made hideous with paint of many colors; but there was a marked display of what we should call taste, in the arrangement of his whole attire. His face was presented in its natural teint, but his person was arrayed in his best garments, covered with many ornaments, and on his head was a cap adorned with plumes which fell behind with studied grace. In short, if he had not presented a figure to command respect, one might say that he was somewhat of an Indian elegant, who desired to attract the gaze of the multitude.

For the convenience of the painters, it was agreed that two should work at the same time in one room, one at each end, while Osceola occupied a seat in the centre, or moved about when he wished to be relieved from restraint. Beside being a relaxation to him, the plan was of great advantage to the artists, by exhibiting his features while undergoing the alternate expressions of action and repose. The room was generally well filled with visitors, who came to see the progress of the work, more probably for the purpose of seizing this favorable occasion of beholding the original; and as the chief moved back and forth in a placid mood, became animated by conversation, or excited by the wondering audience, the artists were able to catch every lineament of his countenance with an accuracy which many of our most celebrated painters often fail to obtain. Osceola was much pleased with the portraits, and often regarded them with marks of evident satisfaction.[17]

On 27 January, when Osceola's illness became serious, Dr. Weedon blamed his condition on the Indian's good nature, saying, "His afflictions I am confident have been produced from his disposition to oblige everyone—he has for 6 or 7 days been secured up in a warm room for Lemners Who wished to take his Likeness."[18]

Besides that of George Catlin, the names of only two other of the artists who painted Osceola at this time are known to us. One was an artist of limited ability named W. M. Laning, who worked in Charleston in December 1837 and possibly in early 1838. If the limited and slightly conflicting information available on this artist is correct, then his portrait of Osceola may have been completed earlier than those of either Curtis or Catlin. Its seniority, however, could not compensate for its dearth of quality.

The painting, titled *Osceola, Chief of the Seminoles,* is now in the collections of the Chrysler Museum, Norfolk, Virginia. This stylized genre piece contains a number of elements that are analogous to those depicted by Curtis and Catlin. Osceola stands in the foreground of a semitropical scene, while an adult male Indian is posed in the center ground, and an Indian youth with bow and arrow and other Indian figures recede into the misty vanishing point. Osceola's characteristic flintlock longarm, leggings with buttons up the front, garters, belt, beaded sash, gorgets, choker, earrings, and ostrich plumes are all recognizable. The pose is tranquil, but the body is disproportionate, and the face appears stark, to the point of emaciation.

Both the *Charleston Courier* and the *Charleston Mercury* reported that a "William L." was painting in the city in December 1837. Two finished works were mentioned, neither of which was the Osceola portrait.[19] The artist was later mentioned as working in Charleston in 1838, but no other information was given concerning an Osceola painting.[20]

The third artist who is known to have painted Osceola at this time was Robert John Curtis of Charleston. Notices concerning Curtis and his work had been appearing in the Charleston newspapers since 1833. He was a "native talent" who had "just finished his course of study under Neagle of Philadelphia." Unfortunately, it appears that Curtis was never very successful in his work, and by 1842 his portraits were being advertised for half price.[21]

In early 1838, however, his portrait of Osceola was well accepted (see figure 3). On 23 January the *Mercury* reported that he had produced "a very striking portrait of Osceola" that "showed with great fidelity the intelligent and melancholy countenance which distinguishes this chief."[22] Interestingly enough, for an artist who was sitting in the same room as George Catlin and painting the same subject, Robert John Curtis also managed to capture on his canvas an entirely unique image, including several pieces of Osceola's clothing.

Part of this uniqueness may be explained by the fact that Curtis finished his portrait before Catlin completed his work, as evidenced by the news report. Of course, too, Curtis produced only one painting, whereas Catlin, in about seven days, nearly or completely finished all the commissioned portraits as well as a second, full-length painting of Osceola and numerous sketches of these and other Indian subjects. There are, nevertheless, major differences between the images, as well as the items of attire, depicted in the two formal portraits of Osceola (those of Curtis and Catlin), whereas Catlin's full-length painting contains ornamental elements common to both.

The items of personal adornment shown in the Curtis portrait are of everyday Creek-Seminole dress, namely, the hunting shirt, the geometric-patterned sash and belt, the simple neckerchief, and the colorful shawl tied across the shoulder. When he sat for George Catlin, however, Osceola (the Indian elegant, as Storrow later dubbed him), chose several of the unique items for which he seems to have had such a penchant. These included an elaborate sash with beaded motives, which mark it as being of "foreign" (that is, non-southeastern Indian) manufacture. Over the cloth neckerchief he added several strands of beads: one choker, probably of brass (although it was presumptuously described as "gold" in the lithograph documents), and two or three longer strands of colorful glass trade beads (see figure 4).

For Catlin's other, full-length, work, Osceola wore the necklaces, but not

Figure 3. *Osceola,* oil painting by Robert John Curtis, 1838. (Courtesy of the Charleston Museum, Charleston, South Carolina.)

the elaborate sash. He put on his hide hunting pouch and powder horn and took up his gun. The difference between the darker hunting shirt and the lighter, sprigged long shirt (elements that are highly stylized in Catlin's portrait) is now made obvious. Tied silver wristbands, a warrior's accoutrement of status, also are obvious in this version, and finally, Osceola's characteris-

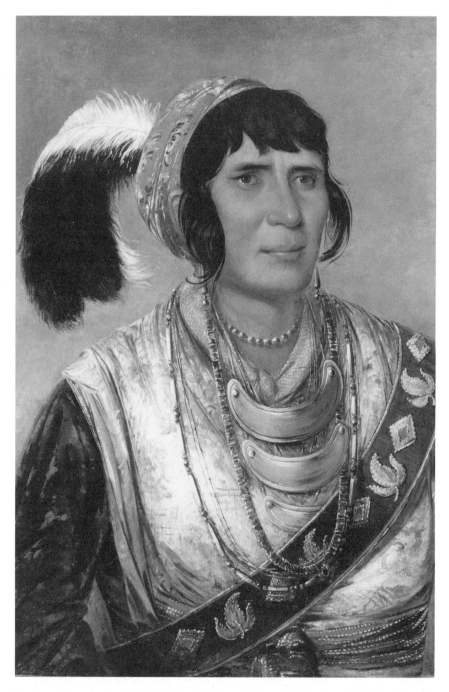

Figure 4. *Osceola, the Black Drink, a Warrior of Great Distinction,* oil painting by George Catlin, 1838 (no. 301). (Courtesy of the Smithsonian American Art Museum. Gift of Mrs. Joseph Harrison, Jr.)

tic leggings with the buttons up the front of the legs, rather than up the outsides, are shown.

It finally can be documented now, however, that the occasion for this full-length painting occurred spontaneously, precipitated by Osceola himself rather than by any request from Catlin. Dr. Robert Lebby of Charleston explained the scene: "He [Osceola] was extremely sensitive about Florida, and anxious to hear any news from that territory—I am under the impression that when his likeness was taken by Mr. Catlin, he was told of one [of] the engagements, in which the Indians were represented to have been successful—The effect was electrical—The whole man was changed instantly—He grasped the rifle in his right hand, and while in that position, Mr. Catlin succeeded in taking his picture.—When completed he was pleased with it, but insisted that while he held the rifle in one hand the White Flag should be represented in the other—This request could not be complied with, as he did not surrender himself under a Flag."[23] On this last point, of course, as well as on one other, Lebby also is mistaken. Catlin's standing Osceola holds his rifle in his left hand, a thoroughly natural stance for a left-handed man (see figure 5).

Beyond the individual elements, one other major factor marks the difference between the paintings produced by the famous George Catlin and the portrait by the relatively unknown Robert John Curtis. Catlin's works are clean and dramatic, whereas the Curtis portrait is decidedly softer—and much more human. In the portrait depiction by Catlin, Osceola's features are finer, his skin is more taut, and his entire bearing is more formal than in Curtis's work. Curtis, on the other hand, seems to have depicted for his viewers Osceola's humanity, including his sadness. Only the intensity of the eyes and the thoughtfulness of the knitted brow—features that many other observers remarked upon—have been captured by both artists. In all these regards, then, the full-length Catlin is much less formal than the portrait, and its facial expressions, now explained, are definitely brighter but still more conventionalized than Curtis's depiction. Both men undoubtedly intended to capitalize on the celebrity of their subject. Curtis advertised immediately that he would produce copies of his portrait for all interested buyers. The original Curtis portrait survives today in the collections of the Charleston Museum, acc. no. AZ-76.

Keenan and Catlin, 1838

Within a month, William Keenan, the Charleston engraver who had manufactured one (albeit imaginative) image of Osceola, had produced another, this time "lithographed . . . from the portrait painted recently by R. J. Cur-

Figure 5. *The Black Drink,* oil painting by George Catlin (no. 308). (Courtesy of the American Museum of Natural History, New York City.)

tis, Esq."[24] Two Keenan prints of this Osceola image are extant, in the collections of the South Caroliniana Library, University of South Carolina, Columbia. On a rock in the lower right foreground is the legend "O.CE.O.LA OBT. JANY. 30. 1838." The attribution reads: OCEOLA. (Powell). The Celebrated Seminole Chief who died at Fort Moultrie 30th January, 1838. (Landscape Fort Moultrie Sullivan's Island) From the Portrait Painted by R. J. Curtis, Esq. Pub. by W. Keenan, Engr. 51 Broad St. Charleston, S.C."

This piece, however, raises some questions even as it answers others. First, it is an engraving, not a lithograph, but this discrepancy may simply reflect confusion on the part of the newspaper reporter. Keenan advertised himself as an engraver, not a lithographer, and his earlier image of Osceola is an engraving. If, however, the newspaper report was accurate, then he may have produced an engraving *and* a lithograph, only one of which is extant.

Second, the Curtis portrait was bust length, and the Keenan engraving is full length. This opens the possibility that Curtis also produced a full-length image, unknown today, from which the engraver worked. The Keenan piece incorporates a background of the beach and Fort Moultrie, which Keenan could have added, however, from his own observations. The torso and legs of the figure, nevertheless, exhibit correct details of clothing that Keenan had already proved himself incapable of supplying from his own imagination.

A particularly intriguing detail of the Keenan engraving is its depiction of Osceola as wearing spurs. Only one printed account mentions his wearing spurs, and that is Thomas Storrow's article for the *Knickerbocker Magazine* printed much later, in 1844. Osceola is first quoted as saying, "I wore . . . these spurs when I drove back General Clinch." Later, as death approached, he is described as wearing "silver spurs on his heels." Storrow does not identify his informant for either of these scenes, but the unique detail of the spurs opens the possibility that the visitor who entered Osceola's death chamber (as described by Storrow) and, consequently, the observer who supplied Storrow with his personal account was either Curtis or Keenan.[25]

Consequently, there is also the possibility that either William Keenan was one of the unnamed artists who visited Fort Moultrie and made his own sketches or else Robert John Curtis also prepared a full-length drawing of Osceola—or both. It is interesting to note the visibility of Keenan's artistic limitations, as evidenced in the 1836 and 1838 works. In both instances, the upper halves of the bodies are handled in much more acceptable proportions than the lower extremities. William Keenan's strength appears to have been more in the engraving process than in his art.

As for the famous George Catlin, according to biographer William Truettner, he "intended, no doubt, to use the public sympathy generated by Osceola's death to call attention to the severe Indian policy of the Jackson administration. But he also knew that the controversy, and the addition of the unique Seminole portraits [to his existing Indian gallery], would make his collection more valuable." Catlin departed Charleston on 26 January

1838 and returned immediately to New York, where he placed his Indian portraits on exhibition at the Stuyvesant Institute.[26] He also prepared a stone lithograph of the full-length painting of Osceola, the hand-colored prints of which he sold at the exhibition. The lithograph was subsequently copyrighted on 27 February 1838.

Both the portrait and the full-length painting survive. The portrait, no. 301 in Catlin's catalog, is titled *Osceola, the Black Drink, a Warrior of Great Distinction* and is held by the Smithsonian American Art Museum Smithsonian Institution, as cat. no. 1985.66.301. The full-length work, no. 308, is in the American Museum of Natural History. We have no idea exactly how many of its lithographed images were produced. Several are extant, at least four of them in Florida. One is held by the St. Augustine Historical Society, a second by the Museum of Florida History, Tallahassee, a third by the State Library of Florida, Dorothy Dodd Florida Collection, Tallahassee, and the fourth in a most appropriate location—by the descendents of General Joseph Hernández, in St. Augustine.

Curtis, after 1838

Both the Curtis and the Catlin paintings, as we have already begun to see, spawned their own "families" of Osceola images. Although Curtis advertised that he would paint copies of his portrait, only two images survive today (in addition to the original) that are attributed to Curtis, and neither of those attributions has been firmly established. The first is currently among the collections of Flagler College, St. Augustine, where it may have been a part of the Kenan-Flagler collection. It is a portrait in the small, which bears some artistic resemblance to the authenticated Curtis.

The other was obtained in Paris, France, by Elmerside, Inc., New York and London art dealers. No acceptable provenance is available for this work, and artistically and technically it has little in its favor. The style is markedly different from that of the original Curtis. Moreover, the treatment of portions of the clothing and ornaments makes it obvious that this artist had never painted his subject from life.

Neagle, between 1838 and 1865

Another portrait of Osceola, a direct copy of the Curtis work, was painted by John Neagle, Curtis's mentor and a well-known American portraitist of the period, sometime between 1838 and 1865. The portrait appeared in 1941 in a catalogue raisonné of art objects from the collection of William Randolph Hearst. It was exhibited by Hammer Galleries in New York as no. 1189-4, "*Osceola, the Great Seminole Chief,* by John Neagle (1799–1865), American. A lively portrait of one of the most romantic Indian figures in American history. Formerly in the Michaelson Collection."[27] Unfortunately, Hammer Galleries is unable to locate the records pertinent to this exhibition, and so details concerning the Michaelson Collection and the provenance and eventual disposition of the work are unknown. It is no longer, however, in the Hearst collections, and it has not become part of the collections of American Indian portraits held by the Smithsonian Institution.[28]

Bufford/Currier, 1838

During the year 1838, following Osceola's death, two more images of him were made available to the public, both in the popular new lithographed form, and both were produced by the same lithographic printer, although obviously taken from two very different sources. There is no indication which appeared first, but one was a single sheet published for individual sales by William W. Hooper, New York. It bore the legend, "Sketched from life at Lake Monroe, Florida, while he was on parole at that post in May 1837 by Capt J. R. Vinton of the United States Army." The delineator (lithographic artist) was "J[ohn] H. Bufford of N[athaniel] Currier's Litho" (lithographic printing company). Bufford worked in New York from 1835 until 1839, when he moved to Boston. In 1845 he finally opened his own firm, which was still in business in 1871.[29] The topographic elements of the piece are typical Vinton, but the image of Osceola has been noticeably stylized; for example, the lower half of the hunting shirt has become a gathered skirt, the belt is carefully arranged, the moccasins have almost become shoes, and the skin-tight leggings (with buttons up the outsides) are secured with garters tied in bows at the ankles and calves. The face and head, however, taken in profile, are unmistakably Vinton's work. Regarding the original sketch from which the lithograph was prepared, we have no information.

Pierce/Currier, 1838

The other 1838 lithograph is also a full-length image, without background, and bears only the legend, "Os.ce.o.la." The delineator was F. Pierce, another lithographic artist with Nathaniel Currier's lithographic print shop in New York. The image was printed as the frontispiece for *Osceola; or, Fact and Fiction* by James Birchett Ransom ("A Southerner"), published by Harper and Brothers, New York. The fascinating part about this little print is that it appears to have been taken directly from William Keenan's engraving of the Curtis portrait of Osceola.

Ransom was in Charleston while Osceola was at Fort Moultrie. He could have been aware of both the Curtis portrait and the Keenan lithograph. His book was not published until at least four months after the appearance of both.[30] He probably purchased a print of the Keenan work and sent it to his publisher in New York, who commissioned a New York job press lithographer (Nathaniel Currier) to prepare the stone and the necessary prints. Furthermore, out of the myriad images of Osceola, only this vignette and the Keenan lithograph depict Osceola's spurs.

McKenney-Hall, 1838–1875

The little 1838 Pierce/Currier lithograph and its antecedent, the 1838 Keenan engraving, also may offer insights into another of the Osceola mysteries, that of the so-called McKenney-Hall portrait. Thomas Loraine McKenney served as superintendent of Indian affairs for the United States government under Presidents Madison, Monroe, Adams, and Jackson from 1816 until 1830. "For sixteen years, as he liked to boast, he controlled the destinies of more Indian nations on the American continent than any one man."[31] Even though he had conceived of the idea several years earlier, it was in the winter of 1821–1822 that McKenney first persuaded the federal government to commission the well-known American portraitist Charles Bird King to begin making portraits of the prominent Indians who were being brought to Washington by the government. The paintings were paid for out of government funds and were the property of the United States government. They were hung in McKenney's offices on the second floor of the War Department in Washington, D.C.

By the time President Andrew Jackson took office in 1829, the Indian gallery contained more than one hundred paintings, among them several portraits of Florida Seminoles that had been painted during delegations' visits to Washington in 1825 and 1826.[32] Osceola did not accompany these delegations, and no evidence indicates that his portrait was in the collection in 1829. All of the paintings in the collection were either the original works of Charles Bird King or portraits by King based on the watercolor sketches of the frontier artist John Otto Lewis and a few other known artists.[33]

As early as 1825, however, McKenney had responded to a request from Florida's territorial governor William P. DuVal, informing him that he was to be allowed "one hundred dollars for the purpose of procuring for the [War] Department the likenesses of a few of your most distinguished Indian Chiefs, which should be taken in the costume of the respective Tribes who may be represented by them—The dimensions of the likenesses will be 17½ inches by 14, to match those which have already been taken of Chiefs in Washington."[34] Apparently McKenney's Indian Office had been allocating comparable funds to other superintendents, but the Territorial Papers do not give any indication of whether, when, or in what manner the Florida government complied with this request. Nor do we have any reason to believe that, if portraits were sent, Osceola's would have been among them. At about twenty-one years of age, he was not yet prominent among Florida Indians or whites.

Thomas McKenney's political fortunes waned radically after President Jackson took office. Jackson and his subordinate did not agree on Indian policy, and McKenney was dismissed from his position in 1830. Mr. and Mrs. McKenney moved to Philadelphia, but the Indian gallery remained in Washington. Nevertheless, McKenney forged ahead with earlier plans to publish a portfolio of plates of the Indian portraits and notes on the history of the tribes. In the spring of 1832 he commissioned young Henry Inman, artist and later a founder of the American Academy of Design, to make copies of the Indian portraits. "Because of Jackson's lack of principle," McKenney said, he was forced to remove the portraits from Washington surreptitiously, several at a time, so that Inman could copy them in his Philadelphia studio and they could be prepared for the lithographer.[35]

In 1836 McKenney published an introductory *Catalogue of One Hundred and Fifteen Indian Portraits* to announce the forthcoming three-volume edition of the prints.[36] The portraits, copies of the King works by Inman, were then on exhibition in Masonic Hall in Philadelphia, and 101 of them were numbered and described in the *Catalogue*. Fifteen of these pictures were Creeks and Seminoles, and although Osceola is mentioned (erroneously) in the commentary on the first portrait, that of "Tuko-see Mathia, or Hicks," his portrait is not included in the catalogue.

Also in 1836 the services of a prominent jurist and writer of popular Western history, James Hall, were secured. The first volume of plates, with commentary prepared from notes that McKenney had been collecting from various sources for many years, was published in Philadelphia in 1836. It was reissued the following year in Philadelphia and London and again in 1838 in Philadelphia, along with volume 2. It is in the first edition of volume 2 that the Osceola plate first appears. No attribution is made to fine artist, lithographic artist, or lithographer.[37]

The first folio edition of the lithographs was published in three volumes in 1842 and 1844. Osceola appears in volume 2, "Drawn, Printed, and Coloured at J. T. Bowen's Lithographic Establishment, No. 94, Walnut Strt" (see figure 19). The lithographic artist also initialed this plate "H. D."[38] The portfolio continued to be published through 1874 in various other folio, octavo, and royal octavo editions, both in England and America.

The original collection of King portraits was transferred to the National Institute in 1841, and its curator counted 130 Indian portraits in the collection in 1852.[39] In 1858 the collection was transferred to the Smithsonian Institution, and a report issued in the following year enumerated 147 paintings in the government collection. No portrait of Osceola was listed among them.[40] The Henry Inman copies of the King portraits also still exist, but there is no portrait of Osceola among them.

It now seems clear that Charles Bird King was not the source of the portrait of Osceola that appeared in the original folio edition of the McKenney-Hall portfolio. Two other questions remain, then, arising both from the McKenney-Hall plates and from the oft-quoted report on Osceola's portraits prepared in 1949 for the Jacksonville Historical Society by Joseph Edward McCarthy. McCarthy quotes the 1854 edition of McKenney-Hall as indicating that Osceola "was visited by many persons [while at Fort Moultrie], and among others by several artists, who took likenesses of him, one of the finest of which is that taken for the War Department."[41] He interprets this comment to refer to an unnamed artist who was sent to Charleston, on whose work a portrait was based by King, and upon which, in turn, the earliest McKenney-Hall plate was based.

There are several fallacies in this reasoning. By 1838, when the Charleston portraits were executed, Thomas McKenney had been out of office for eight years, and Charles Bird King had not painted any Seminole Indians for twelve years. Furthermore, the name of only one artist is recorded as having been sent to Charleston at the express request of the War Department—that of George Catlin. Thomas McKenney knew well Catlin's work and its public acclaim. James Hall had even tried, in 1836, to interest Catlin in a joint publication. It appears more reasonable to believe that the reference, which appears in the Osceola biographical text in the 1838, 1842–1844, 1854, and subsequent editions, was to Catlin's work.

The second question arising from McCarthy's article regards his assertion that Robert Matthew Sully painted the portrait of Osceola that appeared in the 1854 McKenney-Hall edition and that this portrait was different in both style and source from that published in earlier editions. This attribution seems highly unlikely, given a number of other known details. First, there is all the information discussed above that disproves King or Inman as artists. Second, there is the commentary provided by the editors of the 1934 annotated edition of McKenney-Hall, which also dismisses the King/Inman attribution but refers the reader only to the Catlin portrait.[42]

Third, there is the matter of Robert Matthew Sully's possible association with any of the images. As it happens, Sully is cited as a contributing artist in the 1842–1844 folio edition, but his contribution was the repainting, from an earlier and damaged work, of a portrait of Pocahontas, which he completed in 1830.[43] The principal source that McCarthy cites, out of context, is actually a monody on the death of Sully offered by a member of the Wisconsin Historical Society and published in 1856 as volume 2 of the society's *Collections*. It states: "He had devised liberal things for our Society. . . . He had also copied a fine sketch of Osceola, which he proposed enlarging into a portrait of that unfortunate Seminole chief, as an addition to our gallery. . . . But Sully is gone—these hopes and designs all frustrated."[44]

On the basis of this evidence, then, it seems more reasonable to conclude that Sully had sketched a copy of a work by some other artist, probably a known piece, and that he had not produced the painted version before he died. The article also indicates that Sully's reason for copying this and other works (he had already completed others) was to fill the Wisconsin Historical Society's gallery in the city where he intended to establish his residence. This source does not corroborate a connection between Sully and McKenney. It does yet again, however, illustrate the durability of Osceola's image in the national eye.

Beyond this evidence, there is also a fourth factor. The McKenney-Hall portraits of Osceola all share one common feature: a marked similarity to the Pierce/Currier lithograph, which in turn strongly reflects the Keenan engraving from Curtis's work. A background has been added to the McKenney-Hall plate, but it appears to be a generic Indian background consisting of a few tents—obviously not drawn by anyone familiar with Florida Indians—and several ambiguous rocks and tufts of grass.

Stylistically and ornamentally, the moccasins, leggings, and garters are similar. Although the long shirt has been deleted from beneath the hunting shirt, the garments depicted in the Curtis/Keenan, Pierce/Currier, and McKenney-Hall images are remarkably alike, especially in the unique Curtis treatment of the cape, which is portrayed as a linear slash across the shoulder. The geometrically patterned sash and belt are specifically those portrayed only in the Curtis portrait. The position of the arms has been changed, rather poorly, to bring the figure more into line with the Catlin full-length painting (no. 308, see figure 5). A generic gun has been placed in the left hand—smaller than Catlin's and now a mere device rather than an actual weapon. The classic earrings, turban, feathers, and hairstyle have been retained by the McKenney-Hall artist(s), but the face has been changed entirely.

All these details suggest one possibility. Thomas McKenney was fully aware of the national visibility of Osceola and the public interest in him, which was at its peak in 1838 after Osceola's ignominious capture and precipitous death. McKenney was also fully aware of the rewards that his competitor, George Catlin, was reaping from his association with Osceola. McKenney easily could have commissioned the lithographic press that was preparing the other plates to produce an image of Osceola by borrowing from the Keenan engraving (after Curtis) and/or the Ransom lithograph and the Catlin lithograph. Given the copyrights on the two individual prints, it would have been legally advantageous for the lithographic artist to change the face—which has indeed been changed, radically. This explanation would also account for the fact that the face bears no resemblance to those produced by anyone who actually saw Osceola. Then, the slight variances in the image that appear with the new, 1854, edition could easily be the result of a technical need to prepare a new stone for printing. By 1854, after all, the print had been reproduced for sixteen years from only one or two stones.

Finally, there is also the matter of the text that McKenney used to accompany the Osceola portrait. The Osceola text was obviously drawn from at least three, and possibly as many as five, separate sources, only one of which was prepared especially for McKenney, and that by a secondary source. The text names two of the sources, printed works by Woodburne Potter and Myer Cohen, and quotes from them directly. Mr. Hall further states, "Referring occasionally to these [Potter and Cohen] and some other authorities, we shall, in the remainder of this sketch, depend principally upon a manuscript statement in our possession, prepared with much care by an intelligent officer of the United States Army, serving in the Indian department throughout the whole of the Florida war."[45]

Judging by the types of information used and the specific events mentioned, it is possible that the "other authorities" were actually written reports submitted to the Indian Office by Major Phagan and Gen. Wiley Thompson, past Florida Indian agents. At any rate, the secondary and tertiary nature of the sources that were used for the text may be further evidence of McKenney's distance from this particular subject. Neither his text nor his image had been obtained through the regular channels that had been employed for the other subjects. This information, in turn, leaves us free, in the case of the image, to search for irregular sources, such as the Curtis/Keenan and Pierce/Currier prints, strong evidence for which is supplied visually in the prints themselves.

As for the identity of the officer who served in the Indian department throughout the Florida Wars period (1835–1842, at least), insufficient evidence is available upon which to identify this gentleman or his connection with the Osceola story. The fact that he was posted in Washington, however, rather than on the scene in Florida reinforces the secondary nature of

McKenney's information. This "intelligent officer" was still just a compiler, not an author.

Vinton, 1840

By 1840, with Osceola's national celebrity undiminished, John Rogers Vinton had produced his only painting of this familiar subject. In July he was contacted by a fellow officer with an offer regarding the production of yet another version. From the correspondence regarding the offer and one of the artworks under discussion (which is extant), we finally begin to understand Vinton's attitude toward the popularizing of history. In a letter dated "St. Augustine July 18th 1840," Vinton responded to a missive written in late April of that year by a close friend and fellow officer, Christopher Tompkins. Apparently, a "young Mr. Hubard," a burgeoning artist and acquaintance of Tompkins, was interested in obtaining sketches or other artwork that might aid him in the production of "an historic painting illustrative of Indians characters."[46] Vinton, flattered that some work of his might be useful to a professional artist, had tried in vain to find the time to produce some new drawings for consideration. He informed his friend that he had already completed an oil painting of Osceola but considered it too large to send by mail. He suggested, alternatively, that he and his friend might "concoct something, picturesque & striking" based upon their Florida adventures.[47]

Once again, Vinton stated that the only thing he had available at the moment, the large pasteboard painting of Osceola, would not be an accurate guide for Hubard's work, and he explained why. "You know how plain & vulgar the Seminoles dress in general & the artist must therefore borrow largely from his fancy if he wd. paint their vesture by any wiles of taste."[48] In other words, Vinton is offering us the rationale behind his graphic subversion of historical accuracy, and the tangible evidence of his attitude is available to us today. Through the gracious cooperation of a descendant of Lieutenant Tompkins, the St. Augustine Historical Society was able to reproduce the painting in full color, for the first time, in its 1982 issue of *El Escribano*.[49]

Beyond its inherent solid value as an original piece of Floridiana, the small painting, which measures ten by thirteen inches, has two further valuable facets. It depicts as background the wild, subtropical foliage of Florida. It also affords us another view of Osceola's face and physique, painted by a man who had personally observed him, even though these elements cannot be taken too seriously, given the highly stylized nature of the remaining details.

In what can only be interpreted as an attempt to endow the work with the classical beauty of the romantic savage in a wilderness domain, Vinton has produced an artistic parody. The Indian war leader has become a quasi-Roman general, outfitted as if for battle but frozen in a peaceful moment, surveying his forest battlefield. The rifle could be a staff, the hunting shirt a toga; the leggings have become soft boots. It is an interesting work in its exuberance, but hardly an accurate one in the depiction of its subject.

Hamerton/Day and Haghe, 1841

In 1841, perhaps to capitalize upon the popularity of Catlin's Indian Gallery, which was on exhibition at the Egyptian Hall in London, Andrew Welch brought out his publication on Oceola Nikkanochee, whom he had adopted as a ward and declared to be a young nephew of Osceola (see chapter 2).[50] Welch, a medical doctor, was also something of a sensationalist. In Charleston in 1837, he had published an offer to let visitors watch him dress the wounds of a woman who had been scalped by the Seminoles.[51]

His image of Osceola was drawn by R. J. Hamerton for the firm of Day and Haghe, Lithographers to the Queen, Piccadilly, London. This time, the lithographic artist drew from Catlin's bust-length portrait (no. 301, for the beaded sash, choker, and stance) and from the McKenney-Hall full-length print (for the face). The stance is reversed, a classical drape has been added covering the left arm, and an American Plains Indian fringe has been added to the leggings. Despite its hodgepodge of elements, the work was technically well executed.

Vinton, 1845

John Rogers Vinton produced one final image of Osceola before his death in 1847. He did so, it appears, for another fellow officer with whom he had served in Florida, Dr. Jacob Rhett Motte. Motte was revising his field notes in preparation for the publication of his own book about the war, and Vinton supplied five drawings, one of Osceola, to embellish the work. For unknown reasons, Motte did not publish his book, and the subsequent disposition of the five sketches was unknown until four of them passed into the possession of Mark F. Boyd of Tallahassee. Following Boyd's death, the sketches were transferred to the Boyd Collection, Otto G. Richter Library, University of Miami, Coral Gables.

This Osceola pencil sketch is another full-length depiction, unmistakably Vinton's, and interesting in its individual elements because it provides visual evidence partly of Vinton's memory of a subject whom he had been drawing for eight years and partly (once again) of the ambiguity of Vinton's attitude toward historical accuracy. As in all of his drawings, the topography and flora are handled with facility. The figure is still naive but pleasant, and the head and shoulders are almost exactly the same as those that Vinton first drew in the spring of 1837.

In this final drawing, Vinton has once again stylized the moccasins, and now he has even abbreviated the leggings so that they end, unconvincingly, below the knees. The buttons, however, do run up the front of the legs, leading to the conclusion that it was the lithographic artist who rearranged them in the 1838 print, and adding weight to the probability that this is, indeed, the way Osceola wore them.

Three further elements of the figure are inaccurate. First, Osceola holds his flintlock in his right hand, not his left. Second, the hunting pouch crosses from right to left instead of left to right, a detail that Catlin has explained for us. Finally and obviously inaccurately, the hunting shirt has short sleeves. This detail, however, appears to be a stylistic convention that Vinton has added, perhaps to complement Osceola's now bare knees.

Bowen, 1846

Among the many images of Osceola inspired directly by George Catlin's works was another that appeared in 1846 as an accompaniment to a book on the history of America's Indian wars.[52] The work was drawn by "Miss A. M. Bowen" for "A. Bowen, SC [South Carolina]." It is a very naive work and adds nothing except confirmation of the continuing interest in the subject.

N. Orr and Richardson, 1848

Unforgotten, Vinton's unmistakable little bust sketch of Osceola (cf. figure 2) appeared once again in 1848, the year after Vinton's death in the Mexican War, this time in John Sprague's history of the Second Seminole War.[53] For this publication, the illustrations were engraved, not lithographed, by the firm of N. Orr and Richardson of New York and South Carolina. It is obvious that the image is beginning to degenerate with this engraver's rendering, which may be attributable to the lack of an adequate image from which to work, a lack of skill on the part of the engraver, or both.

Catlin, 1849

The final members of this first-generation family of Osceola images came, once again, from the artist who had already produced the best known of its members. In 1849 George Catlin first adopted a method of editing and combining his original subjects in albums titled *Souvenir of the North*

Figure 6. *Seminolee. Wife and child of the Chief, Mik-e-no-pa, head chief* [seated, left]. *Os-ce-o-la, celebrated warrior* [standing]. *Two wives and child of Os-ce-o-la* (background]. Watercolor sketch by George Catlin, 1849. (Courtesy of the National Gallery of Art, Washington, D.C., Paul Mellon Collection.)

American Indians As They Were in the Middle of the Nineteenth Century.[54] Cartoon 68, plate 32, of one album depicts Osceola in the full-length stance depicted originally as no. 308, along with Micanopy and Micanopy's wife. In addition, however, this cartoon also gives us the only known representation of any of Osceola's nuclear family. It shows the two wives and a child who surrendered themselves after Osceola's capture and were transported to Fort Moultrie with him. The caption reads, "SEMINO LEE, Wife and child of the Chief. Mik-e-no-pa, head chief. Os-ce-o-Ia, celebrated warrior. Two wives and child of Os-ce-o-la" (see figure 6). Another copy of the plate, unbound, is titled only "Osceola and Four Seminole Indians."[55]

Waldo and Jewett, 1857

Osceola's image continued to be a popular one with writers of the nineteenth century, even those whose interest was not specifically in the Seminoles or Florida. Charles deWolf Brownell's *The Indian Races of North and*

South America, published in 1857, was accompanied by a colored lithograph of a full-length painting of Osceola created by a well-known team of American artists. The image was obviously taken from Catlin's full-length painting (no. 308), but the stance was reversed, and the artists used their imaginations to alter the physique and several of the ornamental elements—perhaps, again, to avoid Catlin's copyright. The vignette was produced by Samuel Lovett Waldo (1783–1861) and his partner, William Jewett (1792–1874).[56] The New York Historical Society also has in its collections a woodcut print by the firm of Babbit and Edmonds, South Carolina, after the Waldo and Jewett work. A semitropical background has been added, and the overweight figure is slightly more defined but still fanciful.

N. Orr Co., 1858

In 1858 John Rogers Vinton's popular bust sketch appeared again, apparently for the last time. Joshua Giddings, a famous abolitionist, used it for his antislavery book.[57] It was the same engraving (probably from the same plate) that had been produced for John Sprague's book ten years earlier, because the image was also produced by N. Orr Co., this time at their South Carolina shop.

Catlin, 1859

During the 1850s, Catlin also produced a number of "Albums Unique," containing "different numbers and combinations of outline drawings, but each . . . based on a master copy that Catlin must have maintained in his studio."[58] A page from one of these came on the market in 1985, inscribed by the artist on an accompanying sheet, "Seminolee. Os.ce.o.la (the Black Drink) a very celebrated Warrior, half caste, who signalized himself, and took the lead in the Seminolee War." The drawing is from an *Album Unique* executed for the Duke of Portland, containing 215 drawings and completed in 1859. The work was offered through David S. Ramus, Ltd., Fine Arts, of Atlanta, Georgia, for $32,000.[59] After 150 years, Osceola and George Catlin still were very popular, and profitable, associates, even though neither Catlin nor Osceola ever managed to benefit significantly from that profitability.

5 / A Lonely Grave

The third and final phase of the life of Osceola began and ended with ignominy. His seizure by American military forces in a setting where the Indians clearly had come hoping to parley and perhaps effect the release of Philip, lately captured, and to gain military détente, was the low point of the entire war. Such an end-justifies-the-means tactic was roundly condemned by the press. The *Niles National Register* editorialized, "We disclaim all participation in the 'glory' of this achievement of American generalship, which, if practised toward a civilized foe, would be characterized as a violation of all that is noble and generous in war."[1] Regardless of the broader range of civilian attitudes, the military generally concurred with General Jesup's method. Charlestonian Dr. Jacob Rhett Motte, who witnessed the capture, expressed it most clearly. "There was too much sympathy extended upon these treacherous, murderous savages. . . . General Jesup . . . was dealing with the very individuals who had repeatedly and treacherously trifled with the flag of truce; had forfeited their plighted faith, and flagrantly deceived him. . . . Public opinion ought not only to justify, but commend him for the transaction." Strategically, the capture was also considered a coup by the soldiers. With the capture of so many of the dominant spirits of the Indian resistance, they had "drawn the fangs of the reptile."[2]

Osceola, obviously, had viewed the parley as nothing more than that and still held out hope of a peaceful settlement. He had even sent a runner to

General Hernández to declare his intentions. An anonymous officer, who could only have been Motte himself, reported the message to the *New York Evening Star.* The quotation is, almost verbatim, the same as that which was recorded by Motte in his private (now published) journal. Furthermore, Motte informs us in his journal that he understood the "Seminole" (Hitchiti) language. Surely, his understanding of the message was excellent. He wrote:

> Two runners from Coa-hajo had an interview with Gen. Hernández. One who was the spokesman said that he came as a representative of Micanopy, Holatoochee and Jumper, that the road was white, and he had a short but straight talk from Powell and Coa-hajo, that a snake had two tongues, he had but one that his heart was white—that Powell sent him to say that he would be in to hold a talk in person; that a man, no matter how bad he was, would some day or the other be convinced of his errors—that he was sorry for what had past—that he had thrown away his rifle a long time since, and that he had not brought anything but his ball sticks. That he would hold a talk and then have one or two days ball play, when he hoped that they would be at peace once more. That they meant to trifle no longer with the white flag, would rub their faces with it, and play with it no longer. This was Powell's talk and as he received it so he gave it.[3]

"Powell's" talk came too late to change the mind of Hernández, much less Jesup. Thus it was that, on the Saturday morning of 21 October 1837, Osceola, Coe hadjo, some chiefs, and about eighty warriors were marched away from Fort Peyton between a double file of soldiers on the seven-mile trek to imprisonment at St. Augustine. Three of the captured, including Osceola, were provided with horses. The rest walked. Dr. Nathan Jarvis, who rode beside Osceola all the way to Fort Marion, spoke of him as "obviously unwell" but "in no manner downcast."[4] Throughout the weeks following this event, as word of the capture spread, other Indian warriors, women, children and blacks were captured or surrendered. A small party of Indians that surrendered at Fort Mellon on 30 November included Osceola's family—at least two wives (one of whom was accompanied by her sister), two children, his clan sister, and possibly his mother and other clan relatives.[5] (See figure 6.) All were funneled into the close confines of Fort Marion at St. Augustine, where Capt. Pitcairn Morrison, in charge of their emigration, had joined them on 13 November. Their total numbers were variously reported but ultimately reached approximately 237.[6]

No indication was given regarding the specific nature of the illness from which Osceola suffered as he entered captivity, although the possibility of malarial fever has been raised.[7] On 31 October Dr. Forry informed a friend that Osceola "now labored under an intermittent fever."[8] Shortly afterward, the *Tallahassee Floridian* ran an article stating, "A gentleman lately from St. Augustine states that Powell during the last year has suffered severely from chills and fever, which, with the injury he received by a shot through the hand at the Withlacoochee, has prevented him from taking much part in the war."[9] John Sprague also mentioned Osceola's having been wounded in the Battle of the Withlacoochee, which took place on 31 December 1835. He received the report from Alligator, who averred that Osceola had been hit "in the arm, which disabled him and was the cause of the Indians retreating."[10] During the summer of 1836, Osceola and his band occupied Fort Drane, a post that had recently been evacuated because of unhealthiness. The problem there may have been malaria. On 12 January 1837, General Jesup mentioned that Primus had seen Osceola again on the Withlacoochee and that he was sick.[11] In other words, during the entire twenty-two months in which Osceola had been leading and maneuvering his warriors in their arduous resistance and constant movements across Florida, he repeatedly had been fighting off some type of physical illness. In this respect, he was not very different from many of the white soldiers who were pursuing him, although it must be remembered how disparate were the resources that each might claim for aid in such debilitating circumstances.

There was one additional possible cause for the physical decline that Osceola experienced during November and December 1837 and January 1838. This possibility has become apparent only through a recent examination of the sole extant physical artifact from Osceola, a lock of his hair (see figure 18 in chapter 10). The hair sample was found to contain numerous egg cases of the head louse *Pediculus humanus capitis,* which is the source of relapsing fever among humans.[12] The disease is characterized by the sudden onset of violent fevers, which persist for about a week, and end with profuse sweating. The fevers remit, only to return again two to three times at approximately one-week intervals. Although the mortality rate is low, except in epidemic situations, the etiology of the disease is consistent with the poor and overcrowded conditions experienced by Osceola while he was confined in Fort Marion. The infection results from crushing the louse on the skin while scratching. Moreover, the symptoms of the recurrent fever are similar to those exhibited by malaria victims. The cause of this disease, however, was not isolated by medical researchers until 1867, so even though there is now ample proof of the possibility of its existence, its actual historical occurrences may never be known with certainty.

Many of the Indian prisoners were described as initially being in "desti-
tute condition." Captain Morrison tried to provide for their needs as best
he could under the strained conditions. To make matters even worse, a
measles epidemic swept the fort between 1 and 18 December 1837. From
the death reports, it appears to have reached its zenith on the eleventh. Fifteen of the Indians died, including men, women, and children.[13] Measles
had been spreading among the Indians for several months. In the preceding
June, Colonel Harney had written to General Jesup from Fort Mellon: "I
told Philip that I had received a good talk and a bad one from you [i.e.,
good news and bad news]—that all the people were all sick with measles."[14]
He was referring to the Indian people and to the fact that he was willing
to permit them to remain in Florida for an extra month to recuperate. In
mid-August, however, Capt. P. H. Galt wrote to Jesup from Fort King that
"the measles is committing great ravages in Philip's camp."[15] Philip's and
Osceola's people were camping together and had been for some months,
and it was Philip's and Osceola's people who were added to the already
cramped confines of Fort Marion in late October. Obviously, the measles
epidemic had not yet run its course.

Beyond, or perhaps exacerbated by, his physical debility, however, Osceola
seems to have reached a state of intellectual resignation. Dr. Motte had
taken notice of the radical change in his manner as soon as the warrior realized the fact of his capture. From "a good deal of uneasiness," he immediately became "perfectly quiet and calm" without "the slightest symptom
of emotion."[16] He was tired. He wanted to be reunited with his family—his
wives and children and his followers.[17] In an interview with a Cherokee
delegation sent in November to induce the Florida Indians to cease their
hostilities, Osceola was reported as saying that he was tired of fighting,
"that when he saw his Great Father [he] would tell him so, and then set out
for his new home toward the setting sun, but was too sick to say more."[18]
It is also reported that Osceola gave away two personal artifacts to Colonel
Sherbourne (Shelburne), the United States government agent who accompanied the Cherokee delegation. Giving the colonel one of his white feathers
and "a scarf," Osceola is reported to have said, "Present these to our white
father in token Osceola will do as you have said."[19]

Uchee Billy, whose "white man's name" was John Hicks, died at the
fort on 25 November 1837.[20] As we have learned, Coacoochee, together
with seventeen men and two women, escaped from the fort on the night of
29 November. Osceola himself reported the event to the commander and
sent word to General Jesup that he and his people could have left in the
same manner but had not chosen to do so.[21]

As a result of this escape, coupled with the growing number of confinees

in the fort at St. Augustine, General Jesup determined to transfer the prisoners to a position where they might be more securely held until transportation was available to Indian Territory in the West. Jesup allowed Captain
Morrison to choose between Savannah, Georgia, and Charleston, South
Carolina. Captain Morrison decided that "they would be much more comfortable at this season of the year in the quarters of either Castle Pinckney
or Fort Moultrie [Charleston harbor] than in the barracks at Savannah."[22]
The Indians were extremely reluctant to be moved from Florida. Perhaps
they hoped that some reprieve might yet be effected. They had fought—
some throughout their entire adult lives—specifically to be left in peace on
Florida soil. Dr. Weedon recorded in a personal diary the Indians' reaction
to the news of their transfer.

> On the day I met Capt Morrison on his way to the Fort he Informed
> me (what I new) that the Indians was unwilling to go to Charleston—
> soon after I went to the Fort Capt M & the chiefs was in Cohajos
> Room Capt M. told Micanopa that they must & should go, & there
> he would hold him responsible for the conduct of his young men—
> Cloud is equally unwilling to go but have sense enough to know that
> he has no choice, went through all the Motions, produced some Sea
> Sickness & said it would [ ] From Fort Mellon [ ] an Interpreter in-
> formed me that there was an Impression amongst them that they were
> to be carried to Charleston and there to be killd. I remonstrated with
> him respecting so absurd an Idea, pointing to the Soldiers on the Ram-
> parts ask if they could not Kill them as easy here as they could at
> Charleston, on my leaving the Fort Micanopa & Cloud sent for me. I
> went to their Room, they Expressed Great unwillingness at going to
> Charleston; ask if I would go with them, if compeld to go. I evaded an
> answer for the purpose of [ ] the object of the Enquiry.[23]

Another of the group also appealed to Dr. Weedon, who apparently had
come to know the Indians well and related to them without supercilious-
ness (albeit not with equanimity). A short time later he recorded:

> A few nights past Jno [John] Hicks a desperado who loves a Dram
> (& after having it) said to me what for Send Indian to Charleston In-
> dians no go, me no go, Governor [Micanopy] no go. I spoke Freely
> with him said Genl Jesop [Jesup] was unwilling to Keep them in so
> small a Space fearful they might Get more unhealthy, had concluded
> to Send them to an Island where they could have room & exercise
> until others came in, so as to send them to the west in a large Body [ ]

"no send us until those come in" was his reply with heat & anger [ ]
Hicks came close to me & putting a hand upon each of my Shoulders
said, "Talehassee [?], me see you, Father Eat Sofke you give him, me
Stoker [?] [ ] some, plenty & [ ] Flend [friend] each Jack [Indian?] you
Flend, Governor, you flend, Cloud you Flend, Cohago [Coe hadjo]
you Flend, Oceola, you Flend, No hurt [ ] no hurt you Squaw, no hurt
you Pickanenes [Negroes]; Philip no you Flend, [ ] cuche [Coacoochee]
no you Flend, Governor no let um, -hurt you [ ] white man think Indian Fool. Indian no Fool, bi & by Indian all together Take white man
lands Plenty, take um all"—I leave it to the Intelegent reader to draw
his own conclusions—Jno. Hicks & his Brother [ ] Joe (a chief) both
living with Oceola.[24]

Dr. Weedon then recounted an important exchange with Osceola.

[December?] 27 Found all the Indians better no new cases [of measles]
Oceola quite cheerful said he was Sorry that My Family had forgotten
him and laughingly said "Send me to Eat, plenty you no let me eat um,
now you say Oceola Eat, you no send um" [ ] while talking with him
his Brakefast arrives, requested me to parcel off what he should eat at
once, & when Eat again—asked the Steward to Boil the Eggs as I had
directed saying I had rather Eat 2 Eggs than have one Mustard plaster
both of his wives was in the room he set the plate aside until the Eggs
was boild, one of his wives uncoverd it and was looking at his Brakefast: he said with a quisical look, I know you want it no spare it eat
um myself get Strong give you some good, by & by they both laghd
& walkd out of the Room pushing & playing with each other.[25]

From this one report one may glean much useful information regarding
the character of Osceola and his interactions with whites generally and with
Dr. Weedon in particular. We see acceptable evidence of a sense of humor
and a playful nature that have been mentioned elsewhere in passing. We
also see inferential evidence that the Weedon family was acquainted with
Osceola, although this relationship should not be surprising given the size
of St. Augustine, the curiosity of whites concerning someone as well known
as Osceola, and the fact that Captain Morrison had given the Indians permission to move about freely within the confines of the fort. As a matter
of fact, Osceola seems to be saying that the Weedons had been visiting him
or remembering him with gifts of food. These diary fragments have no
months indicated and so must be calendared by the information they contain. If this entry was indeed written on 27 December, perhaps the family

members had curtailed their visits at the outbreak of the measles epidemic, about 8 December; a tacit local quarantine of the Indians could easily have made Osceola feel forgotten.

Interestingly enough, there is also evidence here of Osceola's listening to the medical advice of a white physician—a fact that will be corroborated by George Catlin later, even though, in extremis, this Indian leader would be forced, by pressure of cultural bias, to place ultimate confidence in his own medicine man. Here also is firsthand corroboration of his having had two wives with him in captivity, even if there is some confusion regarding their relationship to each other.[26] Dr. Lebby, who was also attached to the military contingent at Charleston, would also confirm this fact later, adding a white value judgment: "The Chief had two wives with him at Sullivan's Island, one of which appeared to be more in favour with him than the other—Neither were handsome."[27] Beauty is, indeed, in the eye of the beholder. Here also is evidence of another of the many qualities considered unusual among Creek and Seminole Indians that has been ascribed to Osceola by whites: his display of emotion and affection in full view of a white man.

Finally, and perhaps most important from the standpoint of historical inquiry, is the fact that Weedon is quoting Osceola, apparently verbatim, in broken English. From this exchange, one secures an understanding of Dr. Weedon's attitudes as well, for he continues the passage as follows:

I have made it my business to carefully scrutinise the Indians under my care and as Far as oportunity offered, others, and much opertunity fell to my lot having twice each 24 hours to visit every room in Fort M[arion] Ramparts & Casemates—am convinced that Education bestowed on a few Indians is lost, rumor have attributed to Oceola an English Education and the advantage of speaking the English language, neither of which is the Fact he is a savage in every sense, nor do I believe that I have ever seen one on whom Education would have been more uselessly bestowed from every thing that I have seen and my intercourse with him in sickness & health, & having many years of my life been a careful reader of men should without Hesitation say that I could not be made to believe that one Drop of Humane Blood ever passed through his Heart I have no unkind Feeling towards Oceola, on the contrary Sympathise for the wrongs his People & himself have sustained.[28]

Here we are allowed to view the interface of Indian and white in the midst of intense crisis and high human drama. They have lived as adversaries and yet interact on a nonthreatening basis. Their respective cultural affiliates have murdered each other, and still they have managed to recover shreds of the amenities of social intercourse. One must undoubtedly assign the larger credit to Osceola in this instance for being able to stabilize a relationship with an individual with whom he is at a decided disadvantage at the moment. Frederick Weedon represents the very power source that has destroyed the object for which Osceola has fought so intensely. At the same time, Weedon appears incapable of moving beyond his own cultural mindset, as he quotes the Indian in broken English and then immediately says that Osceola cannot speak English. One also sees that the doctor equates a white sympathy for humanity with intellectual ability—areas that are now understood as mutually exclusive facets of human development. As a consequence, one need not accept Weedon's belief that education would have been wasted on Osceola. Finally, also, this places in more accurate light the statement "I have no unkind Feeling towards Oceola, on the contrary Sympathise." Even in this nineteenth-century, paternalistic viewpoint, Dr. Weedon was beyond many of his peers.

The U.S. Army steam packet *Poinsett,* commanded by Capt. James Trathen, transferred the prisoners to Sullivan's Island, South Carolina, the site of Fort Moultrie.[29] The *St. Augustine Florida Herald* reported: "When they were told to prepare for their departure, they manifested much opposition to it, and some difficulty was anticipated. However, the presence of a strong guard, convinced them all that opposition would be unavailing, and they were marched on board with little trouble."[30] They disembarked on Monday, 1 January 1838. Although Osceola apparently had traveled in improved health and spirits, Captain Morrison had fallen ill. Lt. John Hatheway, second in command of the Indians' guard, took charge. The presence of Osceola at Charleston created a social stir. Charlestonians, who had been strong in their support of the citizens of East Florida and their fight against the Indian menace, were nevertheless inclined to sympathy for the highly publicized Indian leader. "No sooner was his arrival known, than he was visited by many persons, ladies and gentlemen, who manifested their good feelings by many acts of attention and kindness." Feeling the prisoner secure on the island, the military allowed him "liberty within the walls, and he roamed about at pleasure, or received visitors in his room."[31]

Thomas Storrow, although writing some six years after Osceola's death, obtained recollections from many eyewitnesses to the events that he recounted. Among his informants were Drs. Robert Lebby and Benjamin Strobel of Charleston. Some of his descriptions are slightly romanticized, in the style of nineteenth-century rhetoric, but through his firsthand observers, one learns numerous details that do not appear in larger accounts of the war. Storrow, for example, tells us that while at Fort Moultrie, Osceola was "more reserved than the rest [of the Indians], although he was not sullen. He had been ill some time previous to his confinement, which with his present misfortune had evidently an effect on his spirits. One circumstance was remarked, that while the others were constantly asking either for money, tobacco, or whiskey, he never made a request for either; and whatever may have been his previous habits, was not seen to use tobacco or whiskey during his stay at the Fort."[32]

Two other references bear on this last remark. First, one of the artifacts that has passed through the Weedon family is a brass pipe (see figure 14 in chapter 9). It would seem that, for his own reasons, Osceola chose not to smoke. Perhaps the smoke constituted a physical annoyance because of his debilitated condition (including the strep throat that we now know was coming on), or perhaps his pride precluded his asking for tobacco as the other Indians did. More likely, aware as he was of tobacco's principal value, that is, in medicine rituals, he simply had no use for it at the moment. Second, George Catlin, corroborated by the testimony of former Indian agent Gad Humphreys (who had known Osceola as a young man) stated that, contrary to unfounded rumors, Osceola was not a drunkard, as were many other Indians. Catlin never saw Osceola drink during the time that Catlin spent at Fort Moultrie, even when alcohol was offered to him "courteously, at table."[33]

On the evening of 6 January 1838, Osceola was still well enough to attend a theater performance at the New Charleston Theatre in Charleston, along with other Indians. The house was packed. The manager had gauged, shrewdly, that the presence of the Indians would draw a fine crowd. The play was a tried-and-true comedy by John Tobin titled *The Honey Moon*. James Birchett Ransom, a local poet and author, penned five verses in memory of the occasion. They were published in the local newspaper two days after the event and, later in the year, included in Ransom's highly fictionalized account of Osceola and the Seminole War.[34] In this poem, Ransom describes Osceola's attire with two lines:

With earrings, trinkets, necklaces, and bands,
Heads deck'd with feathers, rings upon their hands.

No other accounts have given any indication of rings as being among Osceola's personal adornments. Perhaps Ransom was simply speaking generally of the Indian group or exercising poetic license.

Storrow recounts another incident that occurred at Fort Moultrie during Osceola's stay there that he cites as evidence of the power and influence of

Osceola. It concerned an Indian who allegedly stole chickens from a resident of Sullivan's Island. The accused Indian hanged himself either out of guilt or out of chagrin at the prospect of suffering punishment in front of his peers for a crime that, as was later discovered, he had not committed. Storrow credits the former as reason for the Indian's action and cites Osceola's power among the Indians as having influenced the man to end his guilty existence.[35] Local news reports of the incident do not single out Osceola as having unilaterally adjudicated the crime.[36] Storrow's account, however, appears to have been taken, almost word for word, from the account furnished by Robert Lebby to Dr. Johnson only four months before Storrow's *Knickerbocker* magazine article appeared. Moreover, Lebby continues, "[Osceola's] influence appeared to be great over the Indians that were with him, and his word was the law, with them, not excepting Micanopy the Governor—He was sick most of the time, he lived at Fort Moultrie, but displayed much firmness and manly fortitude during his periods of pain."[37] Lebby's observations here hark to our new understanding of Osceola, a law enforcer of Bird Clan.

On the seventeenth of January, George Catlin wrote to inform the readers of the *New York Evening Star* from Fort Moultrie that

I arrived here this morning in three days, fine weather and well. I have just had an interview with Oseola, and other chiefs—had a talk with them, and begin in an hour from this [it was 9:00 a.m.] to paint.

I shall paint Oseola, Coahajo, Micanopy, Cloud, King Phillip, and several others, and hasten back with all speed to shew the citizens of New York how these brave fellows look.

You will think by this time that I am catering for the world at great expense to myself, and it is even so, "but things to be done, MUST be done."

Oseola is a fine and gentlemanly looking man, with a pleasant smile that would become the face of the most refined or delicate female—yet I can well imagine, that when roused or kindled into action, it would glow with a hero's fire and a lion's rage. His portrait has never yet been painted.

In haste, yours, GEO. CATLIN.

Osceola's health already had begun to wane once again. Crowds continued to press to see him, and whether from *noblesse oblige* or vanity, he permitted them. He sat long hours for the artists who came to capture him for posterity and spoke well into the night with Catlin, whom he apparently liked. During these conversations, Storrow reported, "He was usually pensive, and not over fond of conversing, except with those who had gained his confidence: with these he became sometimes animated, when he would laugh and talk freely. His thoughts were perpetually turned toward [Florida], of which he spoke with much feeling, and was ever eager to obtain news of the progress of military events."[38]

According to Lebby, Osceola also "manifested considerable reluctance to go to the West without his people, for he said, he knew that the family of Charley O'Mathla, (whom he shot) would kill him—This he told Dr. Wheedon several times—and I think communicated the same to Capt. Morrison."[39]

Storrow continued:

In one of his playful moods he ridiculed our mode of warfare, and gave an excellent pantomimic exhibition of the manner of the White man and the Indian in loading and firing. He evidently possessed a large portion of self esteem, mingled with no inconsiderable share of vain-glory. He said of "Wild Cat" that he was not fit to command a "big army," but was good to send out with a small party to murder and scalp women and children, and to rob. Such kind of work, he said, did not suit him. "It was always my pride," said he, "to fight with the big generals. I wore this plume when I whipped General Gaines; these spurs when I drove back General Clinch, and these moccasins when I Flogged General Call." His manners were quiet, and if he was not resigned to his lot, he gave no audible signs to the contrary. Yet sometimes he would complain in private, to the few friends he had made during his imprisonment, of the hardness of his fate, and at the same time dwell with fire on the great things he might have done could he have united all his people, and been obeyed.[40]

Osceola's fate quickly became harder still. During the evening of 26 January, his already poor health degenerated radically as he was attacked with the "violent Quinsy" (tonsillitis complicated by abscess), which would be the immediate cause of his death. He was not expected to live throughout the night. Through diary pages written in Dr. Weedon's own hand, preserved by various members of his family and first published here, we are able to reconstruct Osceola's last days (see figure 7).

[Friday, January] 26 if there is a change in Ociola it is for the Better Throat not so much swollen—& can lay down swallowed a little arrow Root with difficulty Capt. Morrison being So Ill, I concluded to call in a consulting Phisician (Dr. B. B. Strobel) of Charleston who

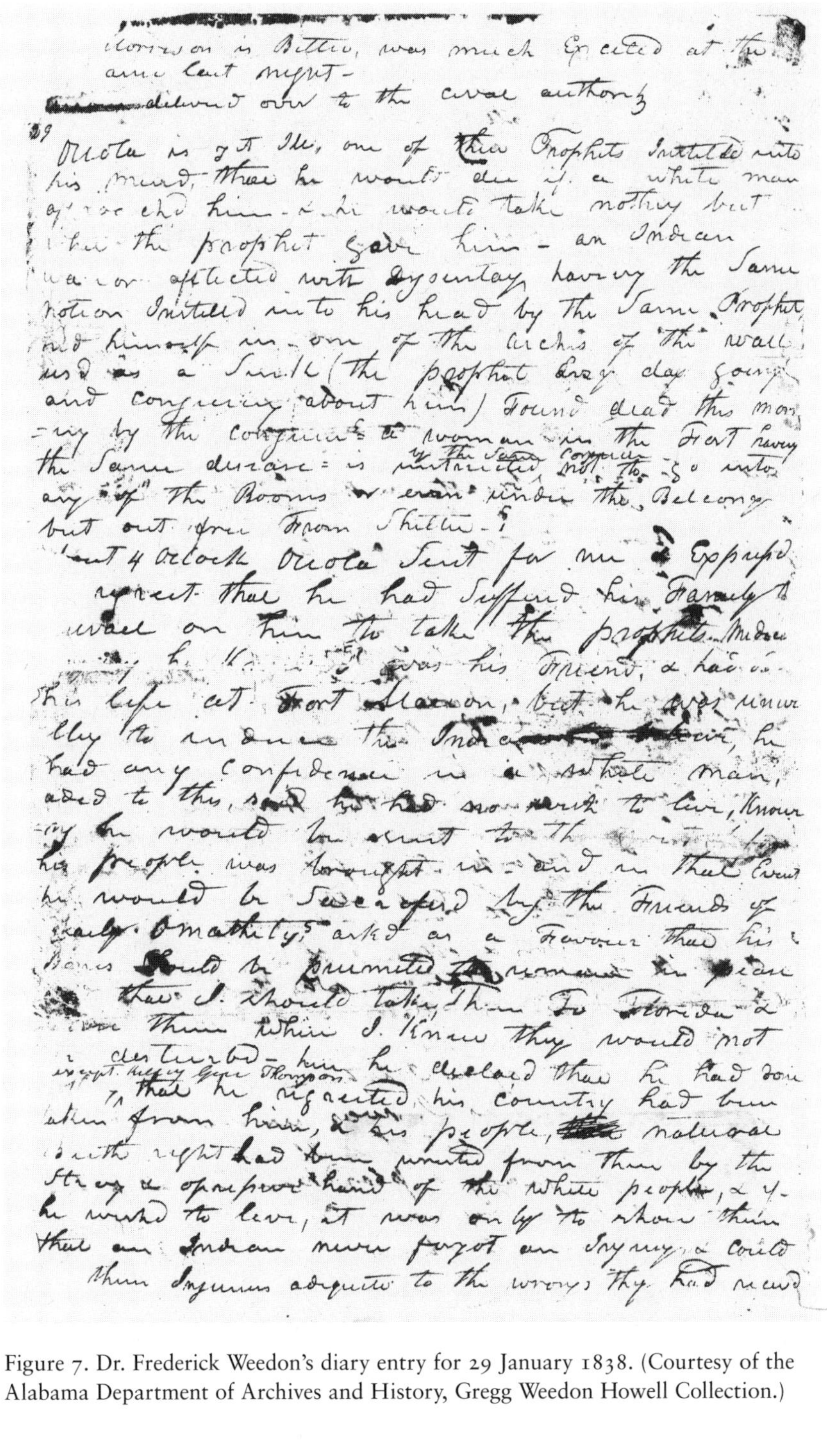

Figure 7. Dr. Frederick Weedon's diary entry for 29 January 1838. (Courtesy of the Alabama Department of Archives and History, Gregg Weedon Howell Collection.)

Kindly hasten to my assistance & staid all night Capt. M[orrison] is apparently Better, ague having gone off, his affliction is Dysentary, Intermitant & Hemroids.

27 this morning Capt. M. is very feeble—Oceola I think swallows with more Difficulty and cannot articulate so as to be understood—Extended his hand to me & made signs that he could Swallow his afflictions I am confident have been produced from his disposition to oblige everyone—he has for 6 or 7 Days been secured in a warm Room for Lemners [artists] Who wished to take his Likeness, & at the time he was not expected to live 2 hours. . . .

28 the press & confusion yet continues the hospital constantly besieged, to see Oceola, notwithstanding he is unable to Speak, & can only make Signs for people to Keep out of his room.[41]

[28, cont.] Morrison is Better, was much excited at the [al]arm last night—delivered over to the civil authority

29 Oceola is yet ill, one of their Prophets Instilld into his mind that he would die if a white man approached him—he would take nothing but what the prophet gave him—an Indian warrior afflicted with dysentary having the same notion Instilled into his head by the same Prophet, hid himself in one of the arches of the wall used as a sink (the prophet every day going and conjuring about him) Found dead this morning by the conjurer = a woman in the Fort having the same disease = is instructed by the same conjurer not to go into any of the Rooms or even under the Balcony but out free From shelter! about 4 oclock Oceola sent for me & expressd regret that he had suffered his Family to [pre]vail on him to take the prophets medicine [saying he knew that I] was his Friend, & had [saved] his life at Fort Marion, but he was unwilling to induce the Indians to believe he had any confidence in a white man, added to this, said he had no wish to live, knowing he would be sent to the west [before] his people was brought in—and in that event he would be [sacrificed] by the Friends of Charly Omathily! asked as a Favour that his Bones Should be permitted to remain in peace and that I should take them To Florida & place them where I Knew they would not be disturbed—here he declared that he had done nothing except killing Gen Thompson that he regretted his country had been taken from him, & his people natural Birth right had been wrested from them by the strong & oppressive hand of the

white people, & if he wished to live, it was only to show them that an Indian never forgot an Injury, & could [ ] them Injuries adequate to the wrongs they had receivd

30th this morning visit Oceola, find him remarkably Feeble—at Six Oclock visit him again, knew me & attempted to give me his hand but life was ebing Fast. all his trinkets, Belts Feathers Turbans & Knives was brought hastily (after I informed them he would live but a Few Hours) and attached to his belt a small whalebone cane he graspd in his Right & Knife in his left hand, & placing both hand by his sides adjusted himself & Died 20 minutes past 6—thus has a great savage sunk to the grave by the [un]bounded curiousity of the white people & conf. in their Prophets Superstition Day after Day has this poor Fellow been pent up in small warm Rooms for Painters to take his Likeness, Rooms Crowded until he could scarcely breath with the Handkerchiefs off his neck, then out in the cool wind, & into another Room to gratify another artist. the [Ca] Follows & such was the crowded State of the Rooms that a wite man ~~could Scarcely~~ was in danger of Being Suffocated—in vain [did I] solicit that more time should be taken his hea[lth] was delicate from a protracted illness in S. Augustine On ~~Thursday~~ 29th he sat some hours for W Gallan [George Catlin] to Finish as he was to leave the next morning—on his arrival at the Hospital informed me his throat was sore—appeared Exhausted but was cheerful, at 6 Oclock sent for me I found him labouring under a violent attack of quinsy.[42]

There is some confusion here regarding the date of the evening on which Osceola had his "violent attack." According to the timetable assembled by researcher Edwin Bearss, Catlin finished his portrait on 26 January, sat up through that night expecting Osceola to expire, and departed Fort Moultrie on the next day.[43] Weedon himself set the date of Osceola's death as the twenty-sixth in the account of the death that he sent to the newspapers.[44] According to Weedon's diary, however, "On 29th he [Osceola] sat some hours for W Gallan [George Catlin] to Finish as he was to leave the next morning." He crossed out the word Thursday and replaced it with the date, the "29th." However, 29 January 1838 fell on a Monday, and the previous Thursday would have been the twenty-fifth. His diary entries also indicate that Osceola had been seriously ill all week, however, and Captain Morrison had been sick enough to require a consultation with Dr. Strobel on the twenty-sixth as well. Here, in the confusion of the situation, Dr. Weedon seems to have erred in his notation.

Both Drs. Weedon and Strobel sent accounts of Osceola's death to the local newspapers, and Dr. Weedon also supplied George Catlin with details.[45] Catlin reported on Osceola's final days and moments in information sent to the editor of the *New York Evening Star,* and he confirms that the death occurred on the evening of the thirtieth. Catlin's report was published on 6 February, and his account—gleaned partly from his own observations and partly, as we are told, from Frederick Weedon—is clearly recognizable among the editor's own remarks. The editor reports: "Mr. Catlin informs us that a few days before he left, Osceola was suddenly attacked one night with a violent inflammation of the throat which proved Quinsey. The officers and surgeon thought him dying, and sat up with him. By copious bleeding in the arm, he recovered." This was certainly the instance in which Weedon first sent for his colleague, Benjamin Strobel. In this instance also Osceola forbore to be treated by a white physician. His family would not permit that again. And then we hear Catlin's voice:

In his extreme suffering he had torn off his Angola Turban, and his black clustering tresses now flowed in dishevelled wild [mass] down his nobly formed neck and shoulders, and over the lap of his favorite wife on whom his head reposed. The other was bathing his chest, and it was thus that the groups were arranged when the artist saw this graphic scene. Osceola, manfully as he breasted mortal nature, could not conceal the pain he endured. His features were distorted, or thrown into an expression of mingled despair and resolute firmness to meet his fate; the eye rolling in wild frenzy beneath the fretted brow; the chest heaving like the ocean billows; the throat laboring in the apparently last death struggle of the deep gurgling rattle, which gave to the fine mouth, that once could utter such winning eloquence, the expression of dark despair, that implored some pitying hand to put an end to his misery.[46]

Beyond the immediacy of the personal view that firsthand accounts of Catlin and the two doctors afford us, Weedon offers one unique and remarkable statement. Besides becoming the chronicler of part of Osceola's life and the guardian of much of his material legacy, Frederick Weedon also became the recorder of what amounts to Osceola's last will and testament. On 29 January Weedon recorded his final statement, his regrets, his desire to live, and his last request. He says that Osceola "asked as a Favour that his Bones Should be permitted to remain in peace and that I should take them To Florida & place them where I Knew they would not be disturbed."[47] There is no evidence that the doctor ever attempted to fulfill Osceola's dying request, although many others have tried since.

In 1844, when Thomas Storrow gathered information for his article, he apparently turned to Dr. Strobel for part of his material. On close examination, the accounts seem to complement each other, although they do differ in several details. Storrow may even have had a second informant for this scene, for after he completed the part of the account that was "derived entirely from [Dr. Strobel's] kind hand," he added that the doctor departed and "a visitor entered . . . and found him [Osceola] in a very feeble state."[48]

Unfortunately, we are not told who that visitor was. Nor does Weedon provide that information. It was Dr. Weedon, however, who noted that Osceola probably would have allowed himself to be treated by the white physicians if he had not been overruled by his family. There is every possibility, however, that the visitor of whom Storrow wrote was John Douglas Bemo, a clan nephew of Osceola who had been taken out of Florida as a child and was living his youth as a sailor with his adoptive father, a French seaman named Jean Bemeau (as we have discussed earlier in chapter 2 and will discuss further in chapter 11). In later years Bemo would become a Baptist preacher and return to work among his people in Indian Territory (Oklahoma). He is the one who would speak of having visited his famous uncle as Osceola lay on his deathbed, but he seems to have provided no details of the meeting other than the fact of its occurrence. Charleston was an important port, and it is certainly possible that the young Indian arrived there, accidentally or on purpose, at the propitious moment. Irrespective of his identity, however, the visitor's details add depth to the scene and, coupled with Weedon's published and unpublished information, delineate a number of personal items with which Osceola was surrounded or that he personally considered important in the last moments of his life. The articles mentioned were his blanket; full war dress, consisting of long shirt and great shirt, leggings, moccasins, war belt and bullet pouch (i.e., bandolier bag and belt), powder horn, knives, red paint, looking glass, knife sheath, turbans, and three ostrich plumes; a small whalebone cane; and the unique silver spurs.

At 6:20 on Tuesday evening, 30 January 1838, Osceola died, surrounded by wives with whom he had been close and familiar; children who were old enough to remember their father; Indian allies who respected his abilities even as they may have resented his ambitions; and whites who feared, admired, hated, and patronized him.

After the sensationalist nature of Osceola's life and death, the circumstances of his burial were apparently anticlimactic to all concerned, except the Indians. The two Charleston newspapers that had previously devoted so much space to his exploits now considered two paragraphs sufficient for his obituary.[49] Neither of the military commanders involved mentioned the service in official reports.[50]

Once again, however, Frederick Weedon's diary supplies heretofore undisclosed information concerning the details of the preparation of the body for burial and certain surrounding events. In a fragment of an entry for 31 January, the day of the funeral, he noted: "31st Sent to Charleston & obtained through the Politeness of Dr. Strobel on [Station], who took a cast of the Deceased in this matter I had much difficulty to encounter their Prejudices had to be alayd & Coehajo & Pompy the Interpreter I am indebted for the opportunity as I was unwilling to loos their confidence or get their ill will—at 4 Oclock the coffin was ready & plased him in it when another difficulty originated Capt. Morrison ordered that his ornaments should not be Buried, but brought to his quarters that they might be s[ent] to Washington—this order produsd considerable . . . "[51]

Thus the task of making the death cast fell to Strobel (and this will be discussed in detail in chapter 7), although we are not given to understand with whom the idea of making the cast originated. We also see that it was Coe hadjo, long-time ally of the whites, and Pompey, a black interpreter, who persuaded the Indians to allow the procedure. Unfortunately, we are still left to wonder about the rationale that Weedon used to induce these two to support his plan, which the Indians undoubtedly viewed not only as an effrontery to tradition but also as a potential source of bad medicine for all of them.

Then we are told that it was Pitcairn Morrison's decision—not the doctors'—to remove Osceola's personal effects. Tantalizingly, the diary entry ends there. What about the artifacts that the doctor reserved for himself? Had he already removed them, or was it Captain Morrison's order that first suggested the idea to him? Then, too, what about the head? Weedon says that the coffin had been readied and that the body had been placed in it, but with the head or without? It seems logical that Dr. Weedon would not have attempted to lift and handle the corpus by himself. Furthermore, we now know that the body was interred without a head. Therefore, some person(s) other than himself had to be aware that the body went into the coffin headless. Moreover, from the fact that the Indians had to be mollified regarding the making of the plaster cast, we may infer that the Indians were aware of details of the activities surrounding the preparation of the body. Weedon says that, as regarded his relationship with the Indians, he "was unwilling to loos their confidence or get their ill will." What, then, happened to the head, and how was its presence, separate from the body, kept hidden from the Indians? We will consider all of these events in chapter 7.

As for the details of the interment ceremony, only two acceptable sources have been located. The first is the sketch provided by Dr. Robert Lebby in June 1844 in which he indicated that he did attend the funeral but augmented his information with facts obtained from Dr. Weedon. This sketch was also part of the letter that was probably forwarded to Storrow by Lebby's correspondent, Dr. Johnson.

The second account was made public by Storrow in his November 1844 article. His details differ just enough from those of Lebby to indicate that he must have had another informant as well for this event. Storrow, however, gives no reason to believe that this informant was Strobel, contrary to the conclusion drawn by Bearss. Again, contrary to Bearss's conclusions, the romanticized, convoluted account published half a century later by an enthusiastic but subjective Charles Coe bears no discussion here either.[52]

According to Lebby, "He was buried in the Eastern Angle of the Fort with Military honors by the Garrison then composed of a part of the U.S. Infantry under Capt. Morrison—the Indians attending his remains as Mourners—and he was buried in the Indian custom, of committing to the coffin, with the body everything that belonged to him—I was not present but at the funeral, but most of my information I obtained from Dr. Wheedon."[53] Again, Dr. Weedon's diary entry for the day of the funeral may clear up one more detail. Weedon gave Lebby, a colleague, this account of the burial and specifically told him that Osceola's belongings had been interred with his body. Why did he think it necessary to conceal the truth? Perhaps Weedon was worried about allowing word to get out about the funerary irregularities until the Indians were sent on to the West. Word soon got out anyway, however, as we shall see.

Lebby and Storrow also reported that "a plain white marble headstone was erected to his memory, by Wm Patton Esqr of Charleston, with this simple inscription—Oceola—Such was the interest manifested in this Chief, that strangers frequently visited his grave, and took small fragments of the slab as a Memento of the Florida Chief. In consequence of which the slab has been very much mutilated." In addition, "one of the officers erected a paling round the grave."[54] (See Figure 8.)

Figure 8. Osceola's grave site, Fort Moultrie, Sullivan's Island (Charleston), South Carolina. Jimmie O'Toole Osceola (d. 2005) wears Seminole War period dress during tribal commemoration, 1998. (Courtesy of the Seminole Tribe of Florida.)

6 / The Forensic Report

In the deepening twilight of Wednesday evening, 31 January 1838, the body of the famous warrior patriot Osceola was conveyed to its grave. We know that the Indians, not traditionally used to accompanying a body to its final resting place, stood along the high gun deck of the tiny fort on Sullivan's Island and watched the sad and momentous procession. White soldiers had taken over Osceola's land and theirs—twice—in Alabama and again in Florida and had destroyed the peace of his life. White soldiers had sought him and fought him continuously for two years. White people had made him a tragic hero and raised a national outcry when he was finally captured while under the international sign of peace, a white flag. Now, even in death, the white people were making disposition of his body and all of his meager personal possessions in a manner totally inconsistent with his cultural beliefs, and, as the world would learn shortly, the white people had not even left him his own head.

A carpenter had constructed an old "toe pincher" style coffin, and four soldiers who had never known him had slung two ropes beneath the head and foot of the plain box and, grasping the ends, conveyed his body to a shallow grave beneath the earth of a land no longer his own. His family and most of his people would shortly be sent away forever. His last wishes, that his corpse be sent back to the land he had fought for in Florida, were ignored, and it would be left to other white people, over the coming years and centuries, to deal with the anxiety of his restless spirit. Ironically, the Maskókî tradition would have left the grave unmarked and undisturbed, but the desire of a white man to show respect for the fallen hero in white cultural terms by the placing of a headstone has provided all of us who are his legatees with a focal point for the controversy engendered by Osceola, whose story will not die either.

And so, the historical and archaeological investigations of non-Natives that have focused on the grave site and physical remains of Osceola have yielded information available from no other sources, as well as details critical to an accurate portrayal of this legendary figure and the continuing importance of his story. A researcher for the National Park Service (NPS) in 1968, for example, indicated that at least two, and possibly three, separate palings were placed around Osceola's grave after 1841.[1] The author was unable, however, to put forth a definitive argument concerning the gravestone that is extant at Fort Moultrie (currently held by the park among its historical exhibits inside the administration building).[2] He concluded that the spelling of the name, "Oceola," constituted proof that the stone is the same one originally placed on the grave by Charleston resident William Patton, Esq., sometime between 1838 and 1841. There are, however, various discrepancies among the references to this stone over the years. Some indicate only one word of text, some include drawings or photographs that conflict with the descriptions, some references indicate a high incidence of vandalism to the stone, and others refer to its fine state of preservation as a sign of continuing respect for the person it memorialized. The only verifiable fact is that the position of the stone was changed several times over the years, a conclusion confirmed now by archaeological evidence.

Beyond interest in the perpetuation of the markers at the grave, another aspect of the Osceola story has also occupied space in the press, mainly in the twentieth century. This is the subject of the removal of the remains and their return to Florida. It appears that, throughout the century following Osceola's death, the subject was not considered. In 1930, however, the United States War Department rejected a request made by the Florida Historical Society and endorsed by Florida's congressional delegation to return the bones to Florida for reinterment at a planned memorial near Silver Springs.[3]

In 1947, during a period after Fort Moultrie had been abandoned by the United States Army, state senator O. T. Wallace of Charleston urged his state's legislature to return the remains to the Seminole Tribe of Florida to "make amends" for the "disgrace" that Osceola had suffered.[4]

The controversy increased over the next five years as the Seminoles petitioned the South Carolina legislature, and Mike Osceola wrote to President

Harry Truman "to see that justice will be done."[5] A major issue of the controversy stemmed from the fact that South Carolina could not decide who actually had jurisdiction over the grave. The abandoned fort was classed as a war assets area and under federal control. The grave, however, was considered a special historical site and, under South Carolina public law, owned by state government. Furthermore, the federal government was then negotiating with Sullivan's Island Township to sell them the fort, including the Osceola grave site. To complicate the issue further, the South Carolina Forestry Commission was also making a bid for the fort and property for use as a park. The press reported that the entire question was "bogged down in red tape."[6]

Throughout 1950 and 1951 Florida and South Carolina engaged in a political tug-of-war over ownership of the remains. Florida governor Fuller Warren petitioned South Carolina governor J. Strom Thurmond to return Osceola. Charlestonians besieged their legislators, saying that Florida only wanted to make a tourist attraction out of the remains. Floridians responded that the grave was severely threatened by Charlestonians' neglect and that Floridians were not "ghoulish" enough to turn a respected Indian's grave into a mere money-making venture. Finally, the South Carolina House of Representatives killed the pending bill for the return of the bones, even though Floridians continued the fight.[7] United States senator George A. Smathers, a long-time friend of the Florida Indians, made an appeal to South Carolina governor James F. Byrnes in mid-1952, but the plea was once again rejected, and the dust began to settle—temporarily.[8]

The problem of the "ownership" of the grave and remains was finally resolved when Fort Moultrie became a part of the U.S. Department of the Interior, National Park Service, and became Fort Moultrie National Monument. Acts of vandalism diminished, the grave was properly maintained, and all seemed well until 8:30 a.m. on Saturday, 8 January 1966. NPS superintendent Paul Swartz of Fort Sumter National Monument (the authority site for Fort Moultrie) was notified by a park guard that he had discovered "diggings at the Osceola grave-site." Local police and Federal Bureau of Investigation agents were called in, and newsmen began to appear on the scene following an anonymous telephone call to the Associated Press office in Columbia, South Carolina. The following day, the Southeastern Regional Office of the NPS was also notified. Upon completion of an investigation, Superintendent Swartz reported that "nocturnal vandals tunneled beneath the enclosure fence of Osceola's grave with the intention of carrying his bones back to Florida and receiving publicity. They received only publicity and the damage was quickly repaired."[9]

But the story was still not over. In late March, stories began appearing in the Florida press containing assertions by a southern Florida businessman that he had stolen the bones and reburied them "somewhere in Florida."[10] Charleston County threatened to extradite the perpetrator to face charges of grave tampering, and NPS superintendent Swartz said the Floridian's boasts that he had obtained the bones were "a lot of bunk."[11]

The Floridian who had provided the impetus for this public turmoil was Otis W. Shiver of Miami, a former convenience-store owner and member of the Miami City Commission who was reputed to be seeking visibility for a possible statewide political run. Throughout 1967 Shiver maintained the mystery surrounding the disposition of the remains and kept public interest high. In December 1967 Shiver finally announced that the remains had been secreted in a Miami bank vault, awaiting their reinterment at a planned memorial at Rainbow Springs in central Florida.[12]

As early as three years prior to Shiver's publicity stunt, interestingly enough, announced plans for NPS restoration work at Fort Moultrie had impelled the Seminole Tribe of Florida's Tribal Council to pass a resolution asking that Osceola's remains be returned to them.[13] Considering the fame of Osceola, which had run so far beyond the Indian world, the tribe expressed its willingness to reinter the remains in a location that would have "a dignity and reverence about it that would appeal to everyone."[14] The wishes of the tribe were ignored, however, and the remains were not returned.

So it was that, when Otis Shiver returned to Florida from his surreptitious dig, Joe Dan Osceola, then chairman of the Tribal Council, was willing to meet with him, permit him to speak before the council, and allow himself to photographed by the Associated Press at the vault, draping the box of alleged remains with a tribal flag.[15]

In January 1968, Shiver was permitted to appear during a regular session of the Seminole Tribe of Florida's council and explain his plans for the remains. The council secretary reported that Shiver "has a romantic or sentimental feeling about the Seminoles." He knew that his digging at the grave in South Carolina was illegal but felt strongly that the bones should be brought back to Florida. The owners of Rainbow Springs had contacted him and offered their site, which, Shiver said, would be open to the public free of charge in order to honor Osceola and generate interest in the Seminoles. The plan was discussed by tribal citizens on each reservation. Only Big Cypress Reservation residents stated flatly that they wanted the tribe to fight to have the bones returned to the tribe rather than permit them to remain in the control of white men at Rainbow Springs.[16]

In the meantime, inquiries to Washington officials from Florida reporters continued, and in late 1967 the NPS determined that only a full archaeological investigation of the grave site could allay public concern and exonerate the NPS of any culpability. High water levels during the summer of 1968 precluded digging, but finally, in October of that year, John W. Griffin, chief of the NPS Archaeological Center, Macon, Georgia, began an examination of the site. The historical report, later published as the monograph *Osceola at Fort Moultrie,* by NPS historian Edwin C. Bearss, was the research document prepared as background for Griffin's investigations.

The archaeological work added a number of facts to the story of Osceola, laid to rest several rumors that had persisted over the years, and now adds tangible verification to the documentary evidence provided by the Weedon diary entries. Griffin reported, first, that the grave site lay between the walls of Fort Moultrie and a local street that passes the front of the fort. Indeed, the grave is literally a few feet to the right of the sally port as one enters the fort. The grave site was a rectangular area, approximately five feet wide and seven feet long that, by this time, included an ornate iron paling surround. Inside the fenced area was a headstone that had been broken sometime in the past and reassembled over the site with a poured concrete frame. It is this headstone that now (at the time of the writing) has been moved indoors and is exhibited inside the NPS Interpretive Center at the fort. In 1968, the headstone rested upon a brick platform that covered the entire area within the fence.[17]

The vandalism that had occasioned the investigation had occurred at the west end of the enclosure and had extended along the fence for almost five feet. The hole was about thirty inches wide, semicircular, and decreased to almost four feet in length as it descended to the water table. In order to enter the enclosed area, the vandals had demolished a portion of the three-course-high brick foundation of the fence. Finally, once inside the fence, they had scooped out soil from under the brick footer (the brick base, four courses high) that supported the horizontal headstone.

The soil matrix in which the vandals' hole had been dug was determined to be fill dirt, "apparently placed there sometime between the first Fort Moultrie of the 1776–1791 period and the 1838 burial of Osceola." The fill was heavy with ceramic shards, mortar and brick fragments, and faunal remains, all identified as dating from the first quarter of the nineteenth century. "It was obvious that the vandal hole had not disturbed the grave of Osceola, because its dimensions were not sufficient to have removed a full burial and there was no evidence of a grave in the undisturbed fill around it."[18] It was decided, however, to take the opportunity to complete the archaeological investigation of this unique site.

At the outset of the dig, researchers had hypothesized that soil conditions in the area were acid enough to have destroyed any physical evidence of the burial. The faunal remains discovered in the vandalized area suggested otherwise. Two tests were therefore conducted: one, on the site's soil, by scientists from the Citadel College, Charleston, and the other, on its groundwater, by staff of the United States Geological Survey. It was established that the deposit was nearly neutral or even somewhat alkaline and therefore that the possibility existed of finding physical evidence.

The local water table constituted a major problem at the dig site. The water level, always high in this low-lying area, had risen at least one foot since 1838. A bilge pump, lent by local coast guard officials, ameliorated conditions enough so that several boards were finally located near the northeast corner of the enclosure. "These were pulpy and rather thin, but definitely in place in the ground [that is, in their original place, obviously never having been disturbed]. By the end of the work day, [Griffin] had tumbled to the fact that [he] probably had the remains of a coffin."[19]

Further investigation yielded a left humerus (the upper part of the arm, from shoulder to elbow) in a remarkably good state of preservation. It now appeared that the site contained a human skeleton pressed between the collapsed top and bottom boards of a nineteenth-century "toe pincher" style wooden coffin. It became mandatory to deal with the water problem, however, before the entire skeleton could be removed.

The municipality of Sullivan's Island came to the rescue. It provided four well points, a heavy pump, and a crew. The coffin lay in moist, sterile soil, unlike the disturbed area adjacent. It was intact except for the corner that had been broken on discovery by the investigator. Sometime over the 150 years of its interment, the coffin's lid had collapsed onto the remains, and subsequently its sides had collapsed inward, some inches over the lid.

The lid was removed, and the sand was cleared away from the skeleton. Despite historical accounts of the burial by Lebby, Storrow, and later writers and conclusions drawn by Bearss from his research, Griffin reported that "not a single [material culture] object was found over, under, beside or inside the coffin. Not a button, not a bead. Not a speck of rust. Nothing."[20] Yet, this absence of personal and ornamental items, especially buttons and clasps of European manufacture, was taken by the investigator as corroborative evidence of an Indian burial. We now, of course, understand the reason for this lack of material culture evidence. Indeed, the traditional manner of "burial" for Osceola's people would have been to place the body in a hollow log, supine upon the ground, or, simply, to have placed the washed and dressed body *upon* (rather than *in*) the ground. Then, it would have been covered with the most personal possessions of the deceased, and the whole would have been covered with a low gable of logs, thatched with palmetto fronds in the manner of the *chikít* ("chickee") roof. Burying without possessions would not have been the Maskókî way. As Dr. Weedon's diary notes made clear, the decision to inter Osceola without so much as a button or a bead had been made by the military and medical authorities, not by the Indians.

Once the site was fully exposed, it could be seen quite clearly that the skeleton was headless. Moreover, the unbroken condition of the coffin lid and the disposition of the remains within the coffin indicated clearly that the corpus had been interred *sans* head, finally giving the lie to the public legend that the grave had been entered by vandals shortly after the burial and the head removed. As the skeleton lay, there was no room between the topmost remaining vertebra of the spinal column and the head-end wall of the coffin. It appeared that, when those four soldiers were lowering the coffin into the ground on that damp and chilly Wednesday evening in January of 1838, one of them had not been paying attention. The soldier who had been holding the rope at the head of the coffin, on Osceola's right side, had allowed the rope to slip and the coffin to tilt headward and toward his side so that the corpus slid in that direction. Such a relocation of the body would have been unnecessary, difficult, and messy had the head been taken even twenty-four hours after burial. Furthermore, the disturbance of the coffin lid and the redisturbance of the surrounding earth would have been very visible, forever.

"The skeleton was on its back. The left hand was folded across the body. The right—which had been folded across the left, clasping his knife, at the time of death—was now extended down the side of the body."[21] Griffin surmised that it may have been moved when the knife was taken. We now know, however, that the body was handled several times before burial: to remove the possessions, to remove the clothing, to make the plaster mold, and, finally, to remove the head, so the change in position is not significant. Finally, Griffin removed the skeletal remains and the coffin boards from the ground and transferred them to the interior of the fort for forensic examination.

In mid-December 1968, Erik Reed of the NPS and T. Dale Stewart of the National Museum of Natural History/Smithsonian Institution traveled to Charleston to examine the remains. Reed was responsible for the general comments made in the subsequent report, and Stewart added several points of considerable significance.[22] According to their report, the remains consisted of a postcranial skeleton (i.e., lacking the head), well preserved and almost complete. The first five cervical vertebrae and the hyoid bone had been removed with the head, and the topmost bones of the remaining vertebrae showed no signs of cutting. The decapitation had been accomplished in a "most workmanlike manner." In addition to these bones, the other anatomical portions missing from the skeleton as it was recovered included the coccyx (tailbone), three of the fourteen carpals and eleven of twenty-eight phalanges of the hand, and seventeen of the phalanges of the foot. In addition, several of the remaining bones were damaged. The loss of such small bones is not unusual, given the action of soil and rodents on skeletal remains.

No osteoarthritic growths had formed on the spine. The sacrum and innominates were mature and unquestionably male. The faces of the pubic synthesis corresponded most nearly to "Stage VII (age at death: between 33 and 38 years), but [appeared] to be more youthful than the typical standard form of that phase." Neither did the bones of the thorax and shoulder girdle exhibit "the faintest beginnings of . . . advancing age."[23]

The clavicles (shoulder bones), both fairly large and strongly curved, provided an exciting bit of corroboration that the remains were, indeed, those of Osceola. The left clavicle was noted as being markedly larger than the right. Stewart called to Reed's attention the fact that, on the death cast, these collarbones were clearly observable not only as being strongly curved but also as being of distinctly different sizes, the left being approximately a centimeter longer than the right (see figure 11 in chapter 7). Furthermore, Reed stated that "the bones of the left arm are just slightly larger than the corresponding bones on the right (while the reverse is a commoner situation)." It was Stewart's opinion that the enlarged size of the bones of the left arm did, indeed, constitute evidence that Osceola was left handed.[24] George Catlin had depicted Osceola as left handed and had described him as such to the world. Thus were the skeletal remains from the vandalized grave site at Fort Moultrie definitely identified as being those of Osceola.

In another observation, the bones of the arms and legs were noted as being "of moderate size . . . and normal muscular development . . . [with] no anomalies or pathological features."[25] This comment appears to contradict the contemporary reports that Osceola had been wounded in the arm during the Battle of the Withlacoochee in December 1835. It at least minimizes the seriousness of any such wound, because the bones of the arms showed no evidence of old traumas, such as fractures or breaks. Perhaps if Osceola were in fact hit, it was only a flesh wound, or the trauma involved only a hand—because some hand bones were missing from the skeleton and therefore not available for examination.

"An especially interesting aspect of the femora [long bones of the legs] was pointed out by Dr. Stewart while examining the bones on December 18. The femora are straight, unbowed, with little torsion, and hence suggest the Negroid rather than the Indian [Mongoloid] type."[26] In a telephone discussion with Stewart during the preparation of the first edition of this book, he expressed his belief that this feature was indicative of Negroid admixture, although the degree or generational source would be impossible to pinpoint.[27] Since that time, however, this interpretation has been challenged by physical and forensic anthropologists and can no longer be stated generally with any degree of certainty. Furthermore, no documentary indication of this admixture has been brought to light, although the absence of information concerning one of Osceola's ancestors, the maternal grandfather, Copinger, might provide the source for such osteologic evidence.

Ironically, although there is documentary evidence of Osceola's Caucasian ancestry, the single anatomical feature that would provide physical evidence on this point is also the one most conspicuously unavailable, namely, the cranium. As a consequence, by combining forensic and documentary evidence, only certain possible genetic parameters can be established for Osceola.

Even as many historical mysteries of the Osceola story were being solved by the archaeological investigation, however, one more was being created. Osceola's burial was not the only one contained in the grave site. Alongside the head of the larger, tapered coffin, about two inches from it and with its taper parallel to that of the larger box, was another, smaller coffin, just two feet in length. The skeletal remains contained in this coffin were determined to be those of a neonatal infant—either a very small newborn or possibly a premature stillborn. At such an early stage in its physical development, no determination could be made concerning the genetic assignment of this child. The archaeological evidence provided by the undisturbed soil indicated that the burials took place at the same time, however. For this reason, as well as the presumption that it would have been considered culturally unacceptable (to either group) to bury a white child next to an Indian, we may infer that the child belonged to one of the Indian prisoners. The two children reported to have accompanied Osceola and his wives to Fort Moultrie would have been too old to fit this description. One of the wives, however, was noticed to be "less in favor" with him than the other. Perhaps this perceived disfavor was a concomitant of a pregnancy, and perhaps she miscarried in the trauma of her husband's death. The child may also have been a victim of infanticide occasioned by the depression of severe cultural stress. Infanticide was a well-established practice among the Creek and Seminole Indians and occurred in times of natural famine, warfare, or the famine precipitated by warfare when a woman realized that she had no husband to provide nourishment and protection for the child. As an alternative possibility, we may consider a notation in Dr. Weedon's diary, made shortly before the death of Osceola, in which he mentions the death of an Indian boy.[28] Although he spoke of a "boy," as opposed to "infant" or "newborn," this is the only documented reference to the death of a subadult Indian at Fort Moultrie. It may never be possible to obtain an adequate answer for yet another mystery surrounding not only the life, but also the death, of Osceola.

7 / The Search for Osceola's Head

The life of Osceola was one of passion and determination in the face of terrible odds. His death was almost anticlimactic, given the sufferings of his people, but even in that final moment, he kept a personal dignity that the world denied him. His final wishes were totally disregarded: his body was not sent back to Florida as he had specified. His possessions were taken away, and he was buried without the benefit of any small part of his cultural traditions. And even the documentary record of his burial did not reveal what the archaeological record has finally confirmed: that he was buried without even his clothing—not so much as "a button . . . , a bead . . . , a speck of rust. Nothing."

But there was another indignity even beyond all of these. The body was taken to the tomb not only a lifeless but also a "headless corpse," as one white doctor would say later.[1] And what the white scientific practitioners saw as a superordinate goal of learning and the advancement of science had to be completely concealed from the Indians who were only a single closed door away from the act, for fear that they might, despite their extreme position, still rise up against their captors and begin yet another chapter in the war in which Osceola had fought so valiantly. As the act became public knowledge, the thought that Osceola's head had been taken from him shocked even the sensibilities of many white Americans, and more conjecture and controversy have arisen concerning this aspect of his story than any other.

There seems no doubt that the head was removed from the body *after* death and *before* interment. (Some gory rumors have circulated, nevertheless, that the head was removed while Osceola was still alive.) The Weedon family's oral traditions that the corpus was interred without the head are further corroborated by the private words of Weedon's son-in-law, Dr. Daniel Whitehurst when he commented in a letter that Osceola, "a child of the forest . . . [was] conveyed to the tomb, a headless corpse."[2] Certainly, Whitehurst was in an excellent position to know. In an even more tangible vein, the archaeological and forensic data discussed earlier also disprove the versions of this episode as promulgated by such later writers as Thomas Storrow and Charles Coe.[3]

Charles Coe, who did not gather the information for his publication *Red Patriots* until sixty years after the event, says that the coffin was opened "a few days after the burial" and that Charlestonians were aware of the action "at the time."[4] Coe cites no source for this information, but because only one earlier document that treats this subject has been located, it is probable that Coe repeated this detail from the 1844 *Knickerbocker Magazine* article of Thomas Storrow. Storrow was not a personal observer of any of the events upon which he reported, and the reliability of his information appears to vary somewhat with his sources. His account says that the grave was entered "some days" after the burial and the head separated from the body. He assumes a public knowledge of the action by commenting that this "violation" was "universally condemned" by the "inhabitants of Charleston."[5] Without further corroboration, it seems that both Storrow and Coe must have been taking significant poetic license with a long and unconnected series of events.

Furthermore, archaeological evidence from the grave site does not bear out the vandalism theory. The investigation (reported in chapter 6) indicated that the lid of the coffin did not exhibit damage consistent with vandalism and that the surrounding soil did not appear to have been sufficiently disturbed as to indicate secondary digging.

Even if his actions are now clear, the motives of Dr. Frederick Weedon, however, deserve reexamination. Did the removal of the head constitute an act of personal treachery and revenge on the part of the doctor who attended him? How could Weedon have sustained anything that could be characterized as a friendship with a man—and then cut off his head? Under what exact circumstances, and by what specific methods, was the head removed? And, very important for the search, how was it preserved? Is it reasonable to go on giving credence to the story first published by Edith Pope that Weedon used to *hang* Osceola's head on the bedpost of the young Weedon boys when they would not quiet down and go to sleep? Any discussion of this possibility must include the former discussion of preservation, which also sets the stage for the next set of questions.

This next set attaches to the story of this most personal of Osceola's possessions after it left the Weedon household in 1843 and passed into the possession of Dr. Valentine Mott, who was for many years one of the most famous surgeons in the nation. Where did Mott keep the head? Was it in his home or in his pathological teaching collection at one of the hospitals where he taught? Should we continue to believe that the head was eventually destroyed in the fire that consumed so much of that unique teaching collection? If not, then we must return to the question of preservation methods: how was the head preserved originally and in what condition might it still be in existence now, almost a century and three quarters later? Are there, for instance, other pathological specimen collections with samples as old as, or older than, Osceola's head is now? And, above all else, *if* it still exists— *where could it be*?

In order to answer even some of these questions, we must look to the individuals involved at the time and examine their own understandings of their art, their methods, and their motives, to the extent to which these can be discerned.

Frederick Weedon, M.D. (1784–1857)

I blame Tugby for all of this, you know. She's the one who started this whole thing. Of course, it was my fault, too, for talking so much! We were sitting around one day, talking about old Dr. Weedon, and I told her the story about the head. How did I know that she would go and write it in her book?
—Mary Weedon Keen, interview with the author, 6 November 1985.

"Tugby" was Edith E. Pope, wife of Florida's "Lion of the Senate," Verle Pope of St. Augustine, and an accomplished author in her own right. She included the story as a part of her historical novel *River in the Wind*, which was published by Charles Scribner's Sons in 1954. The story of Osceola's head was not introduced to the public by Edith Pope, however.

The demise of Osceola had not been a private event—partly because of his notoriety and the nature of the circumstances under which the death occurred, and partly because the cultural appurtenances of death among white societies in the early nineteenth century included vigilance by family, close friends, and "official" recorders such as clergy and medical practitioners. A clear and detailed firsthand account of the death was provided later, in writing, by Dr. Weedon (see chapter 5). But as for the interval between the death and the burial, the interval of so much importance to us today as we seek to reconstruct the movement of his possessions and, most of all, of his head, we are left to piece that together from various sources.

Admittedly, the fact that the death scene was documented by the very person to whom falsifying the scene would have been most advantageous, had his intentions been nefarious, might cloud our acceptance of the description. And, indeed, we know now that Dr. Frederick Weedon did issue some false information to the public (concerning Osceola's personal possessions), and his motive in that instance seems quite clear now. No evidence has been found, however, to indicate that Weedon ever personally acted toward his Indian charge with anything other than "the sense of duty which I owe to myself and to those entrusted with [my] safe-keeping," as he himself said.[6] Furthermore, he wrote, "I have no unkind Feeling towards Oceola, on the contrary Sympathise." Weedon was a man of science, not a vengeful predator.

In addition, one document specifically mentions a "friendship" between Weedon and Osceola. Thomas Storrow comments that, concerning Osceola's time of confinement at Fort Moultrie, "he was disposed to be melancholy; and when his *friend* Doctor Weedon, of the army, would speak kindly, and with words of encouragement to him, he would smile, as if grateful for the act, but was still uncheered" (emphasis added).[7] Unfortunately, Storrow gives no source for this detail, and he was writing after the fact, but Storrow's broad use of the term "friend" notwithstanding, there is no reason to deduce that Weedon ever violated his own sense of professional dignity in his dealings with Osceola. Perhaps Storrow's words would be more comprehensible in light of the relationship if friendship were to be interpreted as sympathy, paternalism, humanism, or even a "nobility of sentiment" for which individuals frequently were honored a century ago.

Another persistent line of argument against Weedon concerns the story of the alleged connection between Dr. Weedon's second wife, Mary Wells Thompson, and the removal of Osceola's head. This also may have begun well after the fact, with Dr. Weedon's son, Hamilton, also a physician. Sixty-seven years after the originating event, Hamilton Weedon wrote an article for the *Montgomery (Alabama) Advertiser*. It ran on Sunday, 17 December 1905. Weedon wrote that about mid-1835, Gen. Wiley Thompson "visited the home of a relative in St. Augustine (the mother of the writer), and on his departure, she warned him to be careful and beware of the treachery of the Indians." Later, imprisoned in Fort Moultrie, Osceola, Weedon says, expressed remorse for the killing of Thompson. The writer concluded, however, that "whether he really felt remorse or whether he said it because he knew that General Thompson was a relative of the doctor's wife, is a question."[8]

Certainly, it seems that Hamilton Weedon should be trustworthy on the subject of his own family tree, but so much of the rest of the article is a mixture of historical inaccuracy and cultural chauvinism that a pall of doubt is cast upon the whole. Perhaps the two people were distantly related; even Hamilton does not assert a close kinship. The extant family correspondence, however, does not even mention Wiley Thompson, much less a kinship. Furthermore, a letter written by Frederick Weedon's son-in-law, Daniel Winchester Whitehurst, just a few years after the taking of the head refers to the death of Thompson without any mention of an association of which a person so close to the family surely would have known (see below). Nevertheless, the personal correspondence of Frederick Weedon clearly shows him to be a true professional with a strong code of ethics that should have superseded any personal considerations. There appears to have been no sinister plotting here.

Contemporary accounts of Osceola's death and burial do not indicate any immediate public knowledge of the fact that Osceola's head had been separated from the corpus. Moreover, secondary historical accounts, up to and including those of the twentieth century, have assumed that Dr. Weedon was the lone actor in the process of decapitation, and guilt has been assigned to him both actively and passively. There were actually, however, not one but two white medical doctors who were present when Osceola's head was removed—two whose actions and motives should be examined and two who both knew the importance of keeping their actions secret, at least until they were well away from the Indians. The medical skills of Dr. Frederick Weedon and Dr. Benjamin Strobel may or may not have been equal, and their individual impacts on the story of Osceola were not equal. Over the century and three quarters since that moment in the tiny Charleston fort, however, one has come to be viewed as central to the story and the other as peripheral. Nevertheless, in order to understand the reality of the story, it is time to revisit and balance their actions and their subsequent roles in the drama.

Although Frederick Weedon was a generation older than Benjamin Strobel, they had come out of the same academic tradition. Weedon had been trained as a physician at one of the most prestigious medical universities in the nation, in Philadelphia, graduating in the first decade of the nineteenth century. He had practiced in Maryland, Alabama, and Florida. Dr. Benjamin Beard Strobel had an intellectual connection to Philadelphia and a personal connection to Charleston, to Florida, to the current Seminole

War, to medicine, to dissection, to the collection of anatomical specimens, and to a wide network of the background individuals who facilitated the events of 30 and 31 January 1838. Dr. Strobel's life was much more closely involved in the story of Osceola than we have previously realized.

Benjamin Beard Strobel, M.D. (1803-1849)

Benjamin Strobel was well known—and well connected—to a number of the men involved in the war in Florida. He was yet another native of the city of Charleston, he was another medical doctor, and he was trained in the same Philadelphia tradition as Frederick Weedon.

Benjamin Beard Strobel, "B. B.," was born in Charleston, South Carolina, on 5 December 1803. He was the fifth of twelve children born to Daniel Strobel and Mary Elizabeth Martin, both German nationals who had immigrated to the United States. Two brothers of Daniel, William Daniel and Philip Arthur, and a sister, Mrs. Nicodemus Aldrich, were also in the United States. The family was strongly Lutheran: B. B's mother was the daughter of a German minister; his father was for many years a vestryman of St. John's Lutheran Church in Charleston. Both uncles were Lutheran ministers, and the aunt was the wife of a Lutheran minister.[9] For many years, Benjamin Strobel was active in the Charleston Literary and Philosophical Society and in the German Friendly Society, which activities, together with his large and active extended family, would make him a well-known figure in Charleston society.

Young Benjamin digressed from the family tradition and took medical rather than theological training, graduating from the Medical College of South Carolina in 1826. This training was one more of the things that Strobel and Weedon undoubtedly found that they had in common. Weedon had pursued his medical studies at the University of Pennsylvania School of Medicine in Philadelphia. All the members of the entire first faculty of the young Charleston Medical College, where Strobel matriculated, had come directly from Philadelphia as well.[10] Even if the two men did not have professors in common, the Charleston faculty almost certainly were protégés of Weedon's former professors. Furthermore, Strobel's professor of anatomy, James Edwards Holbrook (1794-1871), had also taught at Philadelphia and had earlier studied in Edinburgh—the same medical tradition that had produced the mentors of Valentine Mott, M.D., and a tradition that was known for technical proficiency in the arts of dissection and preservation of specimens.[11]

Strobel was a lifelong member of the congregation of St. John's Lutheran Church in Charleston, where the pastor was another eminent German American, the Reverend Dr. John Bachman, a man who became a nexus in the social and cultural affairs of the city and, incidentally, in the life of Benjamin Strobel.[12] Bachman, a native of New York, served the Charleston congregation for sixty years. As had so many other northerners, Bachman had moved south for his health, and he had become an avocational naturalist as a recuperative hobby. His interests, abilities, and authority only increased over the years, both within Charleston and without, and he wrote numerous articles on natural history subjects and was invited to speak before learned societies.[13] He also collected bird and wildlife specimens. In this process he was aided by his friend and parishioner, Dr. Strobel. And, in this process, Bachman came to know the world-famous naturalist John James Audubon.

In 1831, Audubon and two companions, George Lehman (an artist/lithographer) and the prominent Henry Ward, traveled to Charleston to collect birds for Audubon's great *Birds of America*. They were received as guests by Bachman, and he and Audubon quickly formed a long-term and intimate relationship. As an Audubon biographer described it: "Audubon could have imagined nothing better than this chance meeting with a great-hearted man of science, one not seeking personal glory, but only eager to be of assistance. Blue-eyed, affable, his weathered cheeks deeply dimpled as if by inveterate smiling, Bachman possessed a sense of humor, penetrating mind, and good but plain manners that made their encounter seem luck itself." Bachman told Audubon of a childhood visit to the Oneida Indians and how Indians continued to fascinate him. By day, the two roamed the countryside in search of specimens. By night, the "two bosom companions wrote and studied in a library den amid stuffed owls and monkeys, atlases, books, bottled reptiles and freaks of nature, caged wild birds, and lively rodents." The close relationship formed by the two men soon extended to their families as well. Two of Bachman's daughters, Mary Eliza and Maria Rebecca, married two of Audubon's sons, Victor Gifford and John Woodhouse, respectively.[14]

Audubon made many friends and contacts in Charleston through Bachman. Dr. Edward Frederick Leitner (1811–1838), another Charleston physician and author of the *Charleston Botanical Chart,* also collected specimens for Audubon, from the Florida Keys. Audubon honored Leitner by including an image of a plant that Leitner collected in his illustration of the "Whistling Swan" (Havell Plate No. 411). While Audubon's book was being assembled for printing, however, Leitner was killed—in Florida—in a skirmish with the Seminoles.

Through Bachman, Audubon was also introduced to Dr. B. B. Strobel, but in Key West rather than in Charleston. Strobel married Mary J. Stewart on 30 June 1827.[15] Two years later, he and his wife and their first child moved to Key West. Strobel published the *Key West Gazette,* a weekly that lasted for eighteen months. He served as port physician and a contract surgeon to the U.S. Army.[16] He remained in Key West for four years, and his second child was born there. It was during this time that Audubon approached Strobel with a letter of introduction from Strobel's old friend, the Reverend Dr. Bachman.

His seventeen-day stay began yet another long-term association for Audubon; Strobel collected specimens for him for a number of years. It was in Bachman's home that Audubon first saw the Key West pigeon, or quail dove, collected by Strobel. It was Strobel who subsequently supplied Audubon with the story of the Florida wreckers, and in his third volume of his *Ornithological Biography,* Audubon gave Strobel full acknowledgment for his contribution of the "Wrecking Song."[17]

In September of 1832, Strobel returned to Charleston, for whatever reasons, where he apparently served as physician to the Charleston Marine Hospital before volunteering, with so many of his hometown friends, for army service in the Second Seminole War in Florida. Myer Cohen, a Charleston lawyer, obvious bon vivant, and lover of botany, mentioned Strobel several times in his book of experiences on the war. They crossed paths several times in 1836 during the relatively short terms of their service, at one point sharing "quarters" in the cockloft of a fowl house. Cohen was a staff officer of the Left Wing, under Gen. Abraham Eustis. Strobel was regimental surgeon in Brisbane's Regiment of South Carolina Volunteers, a contingent of the Left Wing.[18] W. W. Smith, the "Lieutenant of the Left Wing" and another Charlestonian, also knew Strobel and mentioned his collecting bird specimens in Smith's own book of Seminole War experiences.[19]

At one point, Cohen describes the scene at the encampment of the First Regiment of South Carolina Volunteers, in what was then the open field to the south of St. Francis Barracks in St. Augustine. He writes: "And in another [corner of the field], the ever diligent Dr. Strobel, is wiping alternately the lancet and the double barreled, wherewith he is so well qualified to draw blood."[20] Cohen credits Strobel with saving many lives, even to contributing his own personal stores to his care of the wounded when supplies were short. As they entered St. Augustine, nearing the end of their enlistment, on 1 May 1836, Cohen was particularly gracious to the doctor.

We entered the city the shabbiest, the most smoked, sun-burnt, torn down and worn out set. We had left it a trim, neat, fresh, and vigorous regiment. There have been five hundred and seven sick under the care of Dr. Strobel, our Regimental Surgeon, during the campaign, and of these, not one died under his treatment, a success attributable only to his medical skill and unceasing attentions to each and every patient. For Dr. S. was always at his post, and to his patients, not to his own ease or comfort, devoted himself, by day and by night. Messers Js. Simons and Jos. Bensadon (two students who volunteered for the purpose of obtaining experience in the practice of Medicine and Surgery,) have their hands full still.[21]

On the following day, General Eustis ordered the South Carolina regiments disbanded and transport arranged for their return to Charleston.

We have no specific documentary evidence that Dr. Benjamin Strobel met Dr. Frederick Weedon during his military visits to St. Augustine, but the likelihood is very high, especially because Weedon was also the mayor of the little city at that point—in addition to the fact that they were both medical men and both were closely associated with the military and with the Indians who were military prisoners. Daniel Winchester Whitehurst would have been there as well, and the three would have been natural acquaintances. In 1836 Whitehurst was a lawyer and in charge of a company of mounted volunteer militia from St. Augustine. In all probability he was already considering becoming a medical doctor as well, because in 1841 he would go to New York to study with none other than Dr. Valentine Mott (who will be discussed in more detail later).

Furthermore, late in 1838, after he had played his role in the events surrounding the death of Osceola, Strobel would be in Charleston during a yellow fever outbreak, during which time he became sufficiently interested in the etiology of the disease that he would return to St. Augustine in 1839 to observe an outbreak there. Both Weedon and Strobel would have been closely involved in the process of fighting the disease. In 1840 Strobel published *An Essay on the Subject of Yellow Fever Intended to Prove Its Transmissibility.* He was among the earliest physicians in the nation to use "spot maps" to track the spread of the disease. His theory was controversial among his peers, however. The Charleston quarantine officer, Dr. Robert Lebby, among others, remained of the opinion that yellow fever was local in origin. Strobel, a man secure in his own opinions and contemptuous of his critics, did not take disagreement well. He referred to one of his detractors as having been "endowed by nature with more whiskers than brains."[22]

Late in 1836, however, Strobel was living and practicing in Charleston, where he advertised in the *Charleston Courier* that he proposed to give a private course in anatomy "during the present season," to commence on 5 November, in his rooms at the west end of Queen Street. He stated that he would attend personally in his dissecting room three hours during the day and give lectures on the subject. He noted that "the subscriber possesses the same facilities of procuring subjects as the Demonstrators of Anatomy in the Colleges." The cost of the course was $10.[23] Thus it was that Dr. Benjamin Strobel was not only available but also a natural choice when Dr. Frederick Weedon invited him to confer on the minor indisposition of Capt. Pitcairn Morrison and when Weedon wanted a second opinion on Osceola's acute illness late in that cold, damp January of 1838. Thus it was that Weedon and Strobel made the perfect pair to make the death cast, to handle a corpse in full rigor, and to take Osceola's head in a most workmanlike manner.

According to Weedon family tradition, "After the death of the Seminole chief, Dr. Weedon was able to be alone with the body. During this time he cut off the head, but left it in the coffin with the scarf that Osceola habitually wore tied as usual around the neck. Not long before the funeral Dr. Weedon removed the head and closed the coffin."[24] From a practical standpoint, the Weedon family scenario makes sense, but only if it is viewed in context, that is, as a fragment of the story rather than the whole story. It does have one element that rings true immediately, and that is the obvious surreptitiousness of the process. Weedon and his colleague, Dr. Strobel, had to be very sure that the Indians did not realize what they were doing when they removed the head—but they had other tasks to perform first.

We understand now that a period of almost twenty-four hours elapsed between Osceola's death and the interment, during which period Weedon and Strobel had enough time with the body to perform this operation. Whether, and *when,* they had time *alone* with the body is another consideration, however. In fact, it is the very consideration that might lead us to ask, why was it necessary to permit such a period of time to elapse? In that interim between 6:20 p.m. on Tuesday, when Osceola expired, and sundown on Wednesday, when the body was buried, a number of actions occurred, no single one of which should have required so much time. Taken together, however, and taken together with heretofore unconsidered elements, the time interval makes sense.

The actions that certainly or probably occurred are these. First, a military carpenter had to have time to make a coffin. This action could have been set in motion on the evening of the death. In fact, it would have been expeditious to do so. If there was no military carpenter, or a soldier who might serve as such, available, then a local carpenter (from Sullivan's Island) had to be engaged to perform the task, or a carpenter from six miles across the bay in Charleston had to provide a coffin and transport it across the bay to the fort. This was certainly a matter of a few hours or half a day, but no more. A local carpenter on the island or in town probably would have had at least one coffin on hand, already made, because such items were in regular demand. Fort Moultrie, however, had not been manned by more than a minimal guard detail for some time, and most of the soldiers who were there at the moment were members of the detachment that had been sent up from Fort Marion in Florida with the Indian prisoners. Therefore, the probability is that Captain Morrison had to send out a military detail and that a coffin had to be procured from the island or the town. Because the death occurred when night was falling, a messenger might have been sent for a coffin, but there would have been no impetus to provide one that night, so it probably did not come until midday or later on the next day, Wednesday the thirty-first. Weedon noted in his diary that it had arrived before 4:00 p.m., but not how long before.

One other action might have taken place on the evening of Osceola's death. Weedon had earlier expressed the opinion that Osceola's life might have been saved had he not chosen to be controlled by the wishes of his family, who would not permit him to place any confidence in the treatments of a white medical doctor. In the acute case of a bacterial infection, and given the current white medical practice of leeching, the family may have been right—one type of treatment may have been no more efficacious than the other. We know, however, that Osceola had been willing to submit to at least one and perhaps several "bleedings," the old medical practice of releasing blood, which was thought to release the cause of an illness as well. But his family prevailed, and Osceola eschewed the white man's medicine in favor of his own tradition.

Osceola's ultimate adherence to his own cultural traditions leaves us with the probability that the medicine man also performed for Osceola the death rituals that were required of him. Part of these rituals, including laying a sacred fire, using powerful plants to waft smoke messages to the Giver of Breath, and singing to the *foos'hutki,* the white birds, to guide the spirit away from the living and over the bridge to the West, had to be arranged and performed immediately. The fire should have been kept burning continuously for four days. An unhappy and unguided spirit was a potentially malevolent spirit. Although there was, undoubtedly, a fireplace in the wooden house in the quadrangle where the infirmary and post surgeon's quarters were, the *hilis'haya,* the medicine man, would have laid a new fire, in the midst of the Indians and apart from their white captors, for the family. It is highly possible that Weedon notified Morrison to send for a coffin and then left the death chamber to those Indians—the clan men and the medicine men's assistants, who needed to be there all night.

Then, we know now, from the vantage point of history, that Dr. Weedon removed and kept certain of Osceola's possessions for himself—a brass pipe bowl and a silver concho. He might have taken these items the next morning, even as he waited for Dr. Strobel to arrive. He did not write this fact for the newspaper or even note it in his diary. These were small items and might easily have been secreted among the doctor's possessions; their removal was accomplished in the matter of a few minutes. (These items will be discussed separately in chapters 9 and 10).

Furthermore, we know that Capt. Pitcairn Morrison, the U.S. Army officer appointed to take charge of the emigration of this group of prisoners, also decided to take other of Osceola's personal possessions. In fact, the subsequent evidence indicates that it was Morrison, and not Weedon or Strobel, who determined that the death cast should be made. His declared intention was to send the artifacts to Washington. Although it is not made clear to which department, bureau, or individual he is referring, we now also have a clearer idea of this process. The logical inference seems to be to the War Department, and we know now that some of his artifacts did, indeed, wind up in Washington, D.C., but in private, rather than government, hands. Later on in this book (in chapter 12), we will discuss this set of items and their movements apart from the moment of Osceola's death.

We even know that Morrison did not decide until 4:00 p.m. on the day of the burial to keep the artifacts—just at the last minute, when Osceola's corpse was in the coffin, ready to be conveyed to the grave. Weedon specifically noted in his diary that "at 4 Oclock the coffin was ready & plased him in it when another difficulty originated Capt. Morrison ordered that his ornaments should not be Buried, but brought to his quarters that they might be s[ent] to Washington—this order produsd considerable . . . "

In fact, Morrison may have made the decision much earlier, but he had been unwell for several days—Weedon previously had called in his colleague, Dr. Strobel, to examine the captain, and Morrison may not have been completely "on top of things," as we might say today. Or he may have chosen to wait until the last minute to execute his order in the hope of avoiding any further difficulty with the Indians. But Morrison's order must have become known, and it must be his order that "produsd considerable . . . [difficulty?]," just as had the subject of making the cast. But the probability is equally great that it produced considerable difficulty for the doctors. Weedon's compliance with Morrison's order certainly would have been performed furtively, because Maskókî tradition required that the most intimate of a person's possessions (that is, those items the person used most) should be consigned to the burial site with the individual. It would have antagonized the Indians even more than they already had been antagonized if they had learned that Osceola was being buried in such an insulting manner. They would have been especially concerned lest an insulted and un-happy spirit—and one as powerful as Osceola's was—should fail to depart for the West, the land of the spirits, and instead remain close to the living, causing them sickness and unhappiness or worse.

The antagonism over the making of the plaster death cast had begun much earlier in the day, because by the time Morrison sent his order to sepa-rate Osceola's possessions from his body, that is, by 4:00 p.m., we know that Osceola's corpse had already been placed in the coffin, and the cast had to have been finished before then. Because we also know that the head and the body already had to have been separated before the moment when the body was ready for burial, this also was the most likely moment when the Weedon family's detail concerning the use of the handkerchiefs to mask the decapitation could have been accurate. Sundown was fast approach-ing on this short wintry day, and undoubtedly there was one more task to be performed. The Indian medicine man (the one the whites referred to as the "Prophet") would need to complete a medicine ritual for the dead warrior—and the Indians could not be permitted to learn that the warrior's body and his head had been separated.

Now, considering all the tasks we know had to be performed, we might ask not why there was a twenty-four-hour interval between the death and the burial but, rather, how Weedon might have managed to perform all of the requisite tasks so rapidly. The heretofore overlooked answer is in a no-tation Weedon made quite clearly in his diary: "31st Sent to Charleston & obtained through the Politeness of Dr. Strobel on [Station], who took a cast of the Deceased." This was the first entry in the diary for the thirty-first. Weedon's first action on the morning following Osceola's death was to send for Dr. Strobel, who was just across the bay, in Charleston, and, for all the actions that took place on that day, Dr. Strobel, as well as Dr. Weedon, was the key.

The casting process would have occupied several hours of the late morn-ing and midday. Osceola's clothing and possessions—at least those from above his waist—would have to have been removed to accommodate the casting process, which covered the head, shoulders, and upper torso (see figure 9). Weedon needed physical help to manipulate the corpse, which would have been fixed in rigor mortis about twelve hours after death, or by about 6:30 a.m. Removing the clothing after rigor was fixed would have been a somewhat difficult process, although a proficient dissectionist or em-balmer could have broken the rigor. Strobel was both of those.

In addition, Weedon probably did not have access to the necessary materials—the Paris plaster and the talc or oily substance—and so he called for help from Dr. Strobel, who had to be fetched by a soldier from his home,

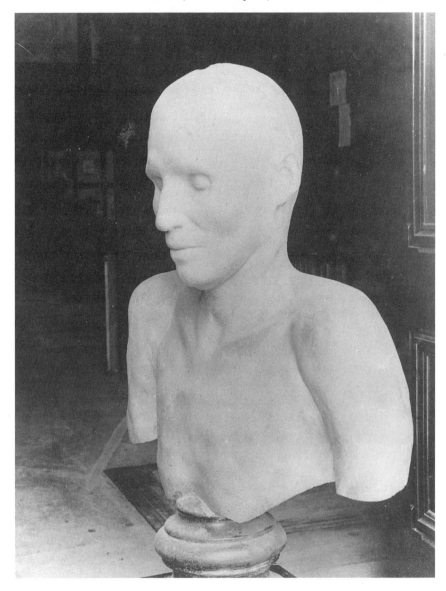

Figure 9. Mold taken from the death cast. (Courtesy of the National Anthropological Archives, Smithsonian Institution.)

had to gather the materials from his dissecting rooms, and had to return to the island from across the bay. The moment in which Dr. Strobel was notified of his colleague's request for assistance, and the message he was given, also would have been important. Although the trip across the bay by rowboat was not a long or particularly arduous one (along with a visit and a return trip, it could consume a leisurely day for a local visitor), it would have been time consuming if it had to be made more than once under time constraints. We have no way of knowing who delivered the message (probably another U.S. Army private), or its details, but there is every probability that Dr. Strobel was informed at the same time that he should bring along his dissecting instruments as well as the casting materials—if, that is, the idea to remove the head and keep it as a scientific specimen originated with Weedon. If the idea actually originated with Strobel, then that message need not have been conveyed. Given Strobel's background, there is every possibility that the idea originated with him and that his dissecting instruments were a permanent part of his medical bag accoutrements.

Furthermore, we know now—and, again, because Dr. Weedon himself has told us—that the casting process could not even begin until the discontent of the Indians had been allayed. It took all the persuasive powers of Coe hadjo and Pompey and, we infer, a good deal of discussion to calm their angers. All the while, lividity was progressing (i.e., the bodily fluids were settling to the lowest point in the body), and the features of the face and body would have been sinking into distortion, depending on the coldness of the ambient temperature and the mitigating warmth of the fire in the hospital room where the body was being kept. All these considerations lead us once again to the actual process of the removal—and preservation—of the head.

By noon on Wednesday, the coffin was in construction. We know that by 4:00 p.m. it had been delivered to the fort. By noon or soon thereafter, the cast would have been completed. For this process, the clothes covering Osceola's upper body had to have been removed, the body still had to be intact, and Strobel had to have arrived with Paris plaster to make the cast and either talc or a petroleum jelly–like substance to coat the body so that the plaster would not stick to the skin. This would have been the most likely, but not necessarily the only, moment for Dr. Weedon to have taken the long lock of hair that his daughter, Henrietta, would later plait. Osceola's traditional Maskókî warriors' hairstyle included long side locks and long hair at the base of the neck. George Catlin noticed this style and commented on it in his later report to the *New York Evening Star* (below). Either lock would have sufficed.

Then, once the plaster was in place on the body, it needed perhaps another hour or so to "set up" sufficiently that it could be removed in one piece. The casting covered only the front of the head and torso and as far around the shoulders as one might reach without lifting the body. The pressure of the weight of the plaster, together with the result of ongoing lividity, is clearly visible in the suppressed features of the resultant mold. This casting, made at Fort Moultrie, was the "mother," which no longer exists. It would have been destroyed in "pulling" the first mold, the one that was shortly displayed in a Charleston drugstore window and afterward escorted to Washington, D.C., by one of Captain Morrison's subordinates, Lt. John Fowler and, only much later, deposited among the anthropological collections of the National Museum of Natural History/Smithsonian Institution (see chapter 12). The first mold consequently was in Charleston. The maker and circumstances will be discussed in chapter 13.

Thus, it was only after all these actions had been completed that the two white doctors, the men of science, could have removed his head. But even then, there was one last element of the process to be considered. After Strobel arrived, after the Indians were mollified and the cast was taken, and before Osceola was placed in the coffin, the head had to be separated from the body. In that process, the body had to be drained of its blood and other fluids, or the neck had to be sealed with wax or tar to keep it from leaking through the wooden-board coffin on its short trip to the grave. The archaeological report discussed earlier has provided us with the knowledge that the head was removed "in a very workman-like manner," at the fifth cervical vertebra. If the body was lying supine on a flat surface, with the chin drooping toward the chest, as occurs when rigor relaxes, then the most efficient point below the chin at which to enter the throat and sever the neck was at the fifth cervical vertebra.[25] The draining process would have consumed at least an hour, assuming that the fluids were not forced out, which would have required less time but more apparatus. Permitting the body to drain naturally, between the moment when the mother mold was removed and the moment when the coffin was available, would have been by far the more practical solution. During that time, obviously, the Indians would have to have been excluded from the room.

When the coffin arrived, the reclothed body was placed in it, possibly with the head in place and the fact of the decapitation having been hidden by wrapping Osceola's own handkerchiefs around his neck, the detail supplied by Weedon family oral tradition. But it was at that moment when Morrison sent word that the personal possessions should be removed and sent to him, creating two difficulties: first, getting and keeping the Indians out of the room while the removal of the clothing and items was performed and, second, lifting and manipulating the body. This is also the point, however, when the head would finally have been removed from the body, probably just wrapped in cloths and stored temporarily in a wooden bucket or small keg. Then, the denuded body would have been hammered shut inside the old toe-pincher coffin and, as twilight melded their actions into obscurity, four soldiers would have slung two ropes beneath the head and foot ends of the coffin and begun the short walk from the surgery inside the quadrangle to the grave just outside of the sally port gate. The soldier at the head of the coffin and to Osceola's right was absorbed in his own thoughts, however. Perhaps he even dropped the coffin for a moment. That moment of abstraction, and the slack on his end of the rope, caused Osceola's headless body to slide up to the top wall of the coffin. That moment of a soldier's abstraction has provided the answer to a question that has occupied the thousands of people who remembered Osceola for the next century and a half.

⌐

And then what? One (more) conception that has obscured our understanding of events from this moment forward is our tacit belief that Weedon's action in taking an Indian's head was unique and, therefore, required a unique process and a unique rationalization. In fact, none of these beliefs is accurate.

Following the death and burial of Osceola, the Indian prisoners remained at Fort Moultrie for almost three weeks.[26] Although no documentation is available to corroborate this detail, Dr. Weedon probably fulfilled his contract with the United States government by remaining on Sullivan's Island until an army contract ship had been procured to take the Indians down and around the peninsula of Florida and northwestward across the Gulf of Mexico to the forts below New Orleans. From there they would begin their trek up the Mississippi River to Indian Territory (see chapter 11). What of Osceola's head during this period? Again, Weedon family tradition provides the detail that Dr. Weedon "embalmed the head according to a formula of his own devising."[27] But how, specifically, and when was this done, and was "a formula of his own devising" really necessary?

Weedon returned to St. Augustine at least by 25 March 1838 and carried the head with him. Samuel Forry, a regular army surgeon stationed in the city, wrote to a military compatriot on that date that "the Dr. has Osceola's head here in his possession."[28] This was a private correspondence, and we may not assume from its mere existence that the fact of Dr. Weedon's possession of the head was publicly known. Several other pieces of information indicate, however, that the reluctance that Dr. Weedon had displayed in Charleston to publicize his possession was rapidly diminishing.

First, there is the Weedon family tradition that, in addition to his medical practice, Weedon also maintained a drugstore in St. Augustine. The earliest public notice that Osceola had not been interred intact may, then, have been given by virtue of the fact that (also according to family tradition) Dr. Weedon displayed the head in his drugstore window.[29] Another Weedon family anecdote adds the detail that Dr. Weedon kept the head "in his home on Bridge Street, where he also had his office."[30] It was certainly a typical practice for medical doctors of this era to have their offices in one or two rooms of their homes and to maintain a drugstore (the erstwhile apothecary shop) in the front part of the building. Both family traditions, then, make sense.

One other observer who was in St. Augustine at the time and knew Dr. Weedon offers corroboration of this information. He is Andrew Welch, also trained as a physician, whose stories are sometimes sensational but frequently carry unique pieces of information that have a ring of truth. Welch mentions in his own later book about the young boy who may well have been Osceola's clan nephew that Weedon took Osceola's head with the knowledge and consent of the U.S. Army officers in charge. Given what we know now of Morrison's involvement in the story, and other parallel evidence that we will see shortly, this certainly seems accurate. But then, Welch says that Weedon took the head to New York, where he exhibited it in Peale's Museum on Broadway, among heads of New Zealand chiefs. Unfortunately, he reports, a crowd gathered there, angry at Osceola's capture and Weedon's treatment of the body, and Weedon was forced to withdraw.

Charles Coe, in his much later work titled *Red Patriots,* also asserted that the head had been exhibited in New York, but he seems to have confused two separate stories. He wrote: "Sometime afterward, according to the *New York Star,* of that period, the head was on exhibition at Stuyvesant Institute, New York City."[31] The Stuyvesant Institute was organized in 1834 and did operate in New York City, at 659 Broadway, opposite Bond Street, into the late nineteenth century. It was, in fact, a part of the University Medical College of New York, as well as the headquarters of the New York Historical Society during the mid-nineteenth century.[32] Several extant catalogs in the collections of the New York Historical Society indicate that it was a general fine-arts institute. In its issue of 10 January 1838, the *New York Evening Star* ran the following blurb: "CATLIN'S INDIAN GALLERY in the Stuyvesant Institute, though it has been closed, will re-open on Monday the 8th of January, and continue open during six days and evenings, and no longer, allowing the citizens of New York the *only opportunity* to see the *Portraits,* Villages, Religious and other ceremonies of the MANDANS, a nation recently extinguished."[33] This was before Catlin left for Fort Moultrie. Almost a month later, the *Evening Star* announced: "OS-CE-O-LA. MIC-E-NO-PAH, CO-A-HA-JO, CLOUD, KING PHILIP, &c.,—Stuyvesant Institute—Mr. Catlin has just returned from the South with the portraits of the above named Sem-i-no-le chiefs, and a half dozen others, which are placed upon the walls in his Indian Gallery, together with his whole collection. His rooms will, therefore, be re-opened on Monday, and remain open but a few days previous to their removal. Open day and evening."[34] Coe, it appears, used Catlin's recent association with Osceola to make an erroneous inference, and, thus far, no mention has been found of any New York City exhibit that included Osceola's head.[35]

Then, Welch tells us, Weedon took the head of Osceola back to St. Augustine, where he put it "in spirits on the counter of his 'drug store,' for the gratuitous gratification of poor Osceola's enemies."[36] Several points are interesting here. First, we are not given to understand whether Weedon went to New York directly from South Carolina and then returned to St. Augustine, or whether he returned to St. Augustine and then made the trip to New York and back. However, he certainly had sufficient time to go to New York from Charleston and then back to St. Augustine by 25 March, and that would have been the least complex route. Second, although Welch's penchant for hyperbole may have been unfortunate, his ability to observe and report details has been consistently underrated. It is Welch who, in passing, in a mere two words gives us the answer to the question of what method was used for the preservation of the head. The doctor preserved it "in spirits."[37] By this he undoubtedly meant that the head had been preserved, sealed inside a large jar of alcohol. This explains how the head had been preserved originally at Fort Moultrie and how it was transported. Not only is this the simplest and most practical answer, it also opens a door to our understanding that the doctor's action was neither unique nor unusual. A couple of examples will confirm this.

Myer Cohen and W. W. Smith, two Charlestonians who were devotees of the then-popular pseudoscience of phrenology (using the shape of the head to infer the propensities of the individual), both commented specifically on the general anatomical interest in the bodies of Indians, which stemmed partially from a popular interest in phrenology and partly from a (by this time) long-established national interest in natural history. In his book on his war experiences in Florida, Cohen offered a point-by-point comparison of the heads of two Indians, Yaha Hadjo and Euchee Billy. The former, the husband of one of Osceola's sisters, was erroneously reported killed in a skirmish on 29 March 1836. We have already seen, however, that he was still very much alive in November of 1837. The individual identified as Euchee Billy also was identified in error. Euchee Billy and his brother Euchee Jack would finally be imprisoned with Osceola and the others in St. Augustine in October 1837, and Euchee Billy would die there. Nevertheless, the fact remains that the officers collected and preserved two Indian heads and made "deliberate examinations" of them in phrenological terms.[38]

It would be Dr. Weedon, the assistant army surgeon on duty with the

Indian prisoners in Fort Marion late in 1837, who had already collected the head of Euchee Billy. Smith says of that action: "His head was preserved in the Dr's cabinet, and afforded a fine subject for the speculations of the phrenologists, of whom there were not a few in Camp, and if in other instances the followers of the science agreed as happily in their results as they did in this, Phrenology would not have to contend against so many opponents."[39]

Greater than the impetus of any interest in phrenology, however, was the long-standing national interest in the natural sciences, which easily had spilled over into an interest in human diversity and physiology that was present even before the United States was established. Welch's assertion that Weedon took Osceola's head to Peale's Museum in New York City opens the door to our understanding of this social phenomenon. Charles Willson Peale (1741–1827), prolific artist and lifelong proponent of a national museum, opened his own first museum in Philadelphia in 1784.[40]

Peale's dedication to the educational value of the world around us focused national attention on an already gathering trend. The city of Charleston, South Carolina, had laid the legal foundation for its own natural history museum in 1773, which plan was interrupted by the American Revolutionary War and revived in 1785. Dr. David Ramsay, another physician, was Charleston's connection to C. W. Peale. Dr. Ramsay was the brother of Col. Nathaniel Ramsay, Continental Line, who was married to Peale's sister, and although the colonel was not interested in the museum concept at all, Dr. Ramsay was, and he responded to Peale's requests for specimens. Peale informed prospective contributors that all but the largest specimens might "be put into spirits" and sent to him safely.[41]

Within the first five years, Peale had significant and growing Indian collections, including scalps and skeletons at least. Indians passing through Philadelphia visited the museum personally to view all of the collections. Presidents George Washington and Thomas Jefferson, also advocates of a national museum, hoped that Peale's collection would form its basis and gave him Indian rarities presented to them as presents or brought back by the great continental, government-sponsored expeditions, such as that of Lewis and Clark.

Peale was a prolific father in addition to prolific collector, and his children would travel far and wide, learning, increasing the Peale family's connections to the other great collectors, and obtaining specimens for him. Between June 1802 and September 1803, sons Rubens and Rembrandt traveled and studied in London. Rubens was permitted to attend the current lectures of Dr. John Heaviside, owner of an anatomical museum and brother-in-law of the great anatomist and surgeon Dr. John Hunter, FRS (1728–1793), whose own anatomical museum had just been transferred from government ownership to that of the Royal College of Surgeons in London.[42]

The great collections of the Royal College of Surgeons did, and do, include many fluid-preserved specimens, and many soft-tissue specimens, dating from periods earlier than that of Osceola's death. Unfortunately, both the collections and the accession records sustained significant damage during the Nazi bombings of World War II. Its Hunterian Institute was disbanded in 1954 when the Wellcome Institute of Pathology was founded, although the Hunterian collections continue to exist as a discrete element of the Royal College of Surgeons. Current records do not specifically contain any information on Osceola, or even correspondences between or among Drs. Weedon, Whitehurst, Mott, or Mott's mentor, Sir Astly Cooper, M.D.

During the winter and spring of 1818, Titian, another son of C. W. Peale, traveled to Florida and Georgia, together with friends George Ord, Thomas Say, and William Maclure. They spent their time "shooting alligators [and] opening an Indian mound."[43] Six years later, Titian would return to visit Florida and South Carolina, this time sponsored by the illegitimate nephew of the French emperor. A set of box-turtle-shell shakers, or stomp-dance rattles, collected on that trip eventually passed into the collections of Harvard's Peabody Museum, along with a number of other artifacts from Peale's collections—not, unfortunately, including Osceola's head.[44]

Not all of Peale's offspring inherited his dedication to the museum, and even among those who continued his collecting and public educational work, not all remained in Philadelphia with their father. By the time of the elder Peale's retirement in 1810, a new generation of "learned societies" was springing up to defend the advancement of knowledge against its popularization, or sensationalization, that is, to defend quality against the crass pursuit of profits. In 1814 Rembrandt Peale moved to Baltimore to open his own version of the Philadelphia museum. Control of the Baltimore museum was turned over to his brother Rubens in 1821, and ownership eventually passed to the city, where it is extant today as a municipal art and history museum.

After tiring of trying to make a success of the site in Baltimore, Rubens moved to New York City and, on 26 October 1825, opened Peale's New York Museum, also known as "The Parthenon," at 252 Broadway, an excellent location, facing the park and city hall. Rubens would preside there for more than a decade, including the moment of Osceola's death and decapitation. The museum would eventually be bought out by America's favorite sensationalist, P. T. Barnum. When the Barnum (erstwhile Peale) Museum burned early in 1868, the New York Times decried its commercialism and said the city needed a museum without "humbug."[45] Thus far, no record has been found of an exhibit of the heads of New Zealand chiefs in Rubens Peale's New York Museum, or of Frederick Weedon's having exhibited Osceola's head there, but the possibility exists nonetheless.

Thus we see that it was not only, or even primarily, an interest in phrenology that provided the impetus for the collection of Indian body parts during the Florida Wars of Indian Removal. Nor did this interest diminish over the years. During the Third Seminole War, the practice continued, and from the offhand manner in which it is mentioned, we discern the degree to which such investigations were a routine facet of the military/ medical experience. From the official files of the War Department, for example, comes information relative to an attack on a white Florida settler's home in 1856 in the escalation of antagonisms that became the Third Seminole War. The official report includes the notation that the body of one of the attacking Indian party was buried "in the stockade of Fort Meade, but was afterward disinterred by a U.S. government physician for ethnological purposes."[46]

What we are given in this official report is the understanding that "ethnological purposes" constituted a valid and, obviously, typical premise for the collection of Indian physical specimens. What we are not given here is any indication that the ethnological materials were sent to Washington, if we interpret "Washington" in an official, governmental, sense. In fact, that possibility could not have been realistic anyway because neither in 1838 nor in 1856 did the U.S. Army have any official governmental institution in Washington to receive them. The obvious institution to have received such specimens, the U.S. Army Medical Museum, was not established until twenty-four years later, in 1862. This institute is now the National Museum of Health and Medicine (NMHM), a part of the Armed Forces Institute of Pathology, at Walter Reed Army Medical Center. Even in 1862, that beginning was very modest, "consisting of three dried and varnished specimens placed on a little shelf above the inkstand on the desk of the recently appointed Curator."[47]

A month following his appointment and the creation of the museum, U.S. Surgeon General Hammond caused to be issued to his entire department an order requiring that specimens of "morbid anatomy, surgical or medical, which may be regarded as valuable" should be sent to the Office of the Surgeon General in order to create the collections of the new museum. Most important for our purposes, however, is the fact that in the order he specified the manner in which the specimens were to be preserved and shipped. He wrote that the specimens should be "immersed in diluted alcohol or whiskey [and] contained in a keg or small cask."[48] If other preservation methods were determined upon once the specimen reached the museum, they would be employed there, by the curatorial staff. Most often, they were not, however. Preservation in a sealed jar of alcohol was the simplest and most efficacious method of soft-tissue preservation in the nineteenth century, and it continues to be the simplest and most preferred method to this day, even though other methods of preservation certainly existed, both then and now.

The fluid-preserved soft-tissue pathological specimens in the NMHM collections (and today they are almost totally pathological, that is, anomalous, specimens) include examples dating to the American Civil War period, which specimens remain in an excellent state of preservation. Neither the accession records nor the actual anatomical collections of the NMHM, however, contain Indians' heads or even nonpathological specimens. There is some documentary evidence that anatomical specimens dating to the 1840s were once in the collections. In the late nineteenth century, however, a redefined collecting policy led curators to dispose of some specimens that were not pathological. In the same period, other specimens considered to be inconsistent with a further redefined collections policy were transferred to the Smithsonian Institution, and their original accession records were transferred with them. In the 1980s, the NMHM and the Smithsonian Institution cooperated in a survey of accession records that identified slightly more than three thousand items that had been included in the earlier transfer. Nothing even similar to Osceola's head was among them as either a fluid-preserved specimen or a dry-process soft-tissue specimen or even as a skeletonized skull.[49]

Neither was the great Smithsonian Institution available in 1838 to solicit or receive directly those anatomical specimens collected by military agents. James Smithson had made his bequest in 1826, but the negotiations with the U.S. government were lengthy. Among other concerns, the bequest was caught up in the same governmental controversy that had repeatedly stopped the attempts of Charles Willson Peale and his supporters (including several U.S. presidents) to have Peale's Museum bought by the U.S. government as the first national museum. There was no consensus that such an endeavor was within the purview of the federal government. In the final analysis, James Smithson's bequest brought the debate to a head, but the bequest was not confirmed, the monies were not transferred, and the Castle, the first building, did not open until 1855. The George Catlin collection, consisting of almost six hundred paintings of Indians made from life by the peripatetic artist, was not donated to the Smithsonian Institution until 1879.

According to Thomas Corwin Donaldson, who was instrumental in obtaining what remained of Catlin's Indian collections for the Smithsonian, and to the booklet created by the Smithsonian to celebrate its fiftieth anniversary (in 1886), while George Catlin and his collection were in Europe in 1840, the artist, chronically short of funding, mortgaged his painting collection to a Mr. Joseph Harrison for $40,000. Subsequently, Catlin returned to the United States and traveled to the West. Harrison, realizing that the debt would not be repaid, shipped the paintings and artifacts to Philadelphia and stored them in various of his warehouses. Soon afterward, a fire in one warehouse created the public impression that the paintings had been destroyed. Only much later was it discovered that such was not the case, and, following the death of her husband in 1879, Mrs. Harrison donated the collection to the Smithsonian Institution's Department of Ethnology, through the intercession of Mr. Donaldson. Some artifacts, badly damaged by moths and water over the years, were buried in the yard of the Harrison Boiler Works, where the paintings had been stored. The painting collection, together with the Smithsonian's Indian clothing collection, was exhibited on the first floor of the second building of the complex, known as the National Museum (now called the Arts and Industries Building). By this time, the infamous fire at the Smithsonian, which destroyed a significant collection of artifacts, had already occurred—in 1865—and it affected the upper floor of the Castle rather than the National Museum. Both of Catlin's famous images of Osceola (nos. 301 and 308) remain within the holdings of the Smithsonian today (see chapter 4).[50]

If no official, governmental institutions were available to receive anatomical specimens and cultural items in 1838, then where else may they have gone? The famous Gustave Heye, perhaps the best known of private collectors of Indiana, was not born until 1874. There were, however, as we now realize, numerous other private individuals whose interest in the expansion of knowledge, especially concerning the "vanishing" Indian tribes, led them to collect avidly in Indiana. In the case of Osceola, Captain Pitcairn Morrison directed that Osceola's death cast and his personal possessions should be "s[ent] to Washington," and he dispatched Lt. John Fowler directly from Fort Moultrie to escort them.

We know now that this collection, at least, was being sent to Maj. James Harvey Hook, the acting assistant commissary general of subsistence for the army and the personal possessor of a well-known collection of American Indiana. Captain Morrison's relationship with Major Hook and the major's relationship with the southern Indians will be explored further in chapter 12. Captain Morrison owed a debt of gratitude to Major Hook that led him to oblige the collector with artifacts that had a high popular visibility and, therefore, value. And so, suffice it to conclude here that some—

perhaps all—of the specimens being "s[ent] to Washington" in this period were being received by individuals as private collectors (even if they were also connected to the U.S. military establishment), rather than to government entities.

Meanwhile, as regards the whereabouts and disposition of the head during its time in St. Augustine, there are also the recounted stories of the two great-granddaughters, Mary Weedon Keen and May McNeer Ward. Besides exhibiting it in the family drugstore or storing it in the house (probably the same thing), Dr. Weedon also used the head to secure the submission of his overly energetic adolescent sons by affixing it to the bedstead and allowing it to remain there throughout the night if they misbehaved.[51] The youngest Weedon son, Hamilton, had just turned four years old when his father brought the head to their home. But there is no mention of what surely would have been a memorable event among the memories that Hamilton recorded for the *Montgomery Advertiser* years later. The other sons would have been seven, eight, ten, and thirteen when their father had Osceola's head in their house. Perhaps he did use such a threat to ensure their compliance—but the crassness seems improbable of such a serious individual. Nevertheless, he might have threatened to place it on a bureau, but he could hardly have hung it on a bedpost.

Documents preserved by the family do indicate, however, that Weedon intended to make the head available for public scrutiny, or even for sale. The first document is a page containing three holograph authentications that Weedon apparently solicited from army officers who had seen Osceola.

[St. Aug]ustine E. [Fl]or[ida] May [ ]
I have this day Examined an Indian head in the possession of Doctr. Weedon, and had no difficulty in ascertaining it to be the head of *As. ce. ola*; the distinguished Seminole Chief; who died at Fort Moultrie South Carolina, I was present at his capture, and have a distinct recollection of his Features
R. H. Peyton
1st Lieut. [ ]

I have examined the head of an Indian in possession of Dr. Weedon. I have no doubt but that it is that of Asin-Yahola (Oceola);—the chief was in my charge as Commander of this Post;—I am perfectly familiar with his features—
St. Augustine   Harvey Brown
May 3, 1838   Capt. 4th Rgt Artillery

St. Augustine 5th May 1838
I have examined the head above referred to and know it to be the head
of Oceola the Seminole Chief who died at Fort Moultrie So. Car. I was
present at his capture.
[I M] Hanson
Lt Col 2 Regt F[lorida] V[olunteers][52]

The process of obtaining "certificates of authenticity" to accompany artifacts of various types neither was nor is unusual. Weedon's specific intention in obtaining these attestations is unclear, however. Perhaps they represented nothing more than authentications collected to satisfy some personal
sense of order, or perhaps if Weedon's book on Osceola reached publication
and public favor, they might have increased the value of the specimen to
interested viewers. But there is also the possibility that the doctor contem-
plated selling the head, as is evidenced by the following letter.

New York
Sept. 9, 1839
Sir
    I learn through Dr. G. F. Towner of the U.S. Army that you have in
your possession the head of Osceola the Seminole chief; also the skull
of Uchee Billy.
    Learning the fact, I write for the purpose of ascertaining whether
you are willing to dispose of one or both of them, and on what terms.
I am engaged in collecting a Phrenological Cabinet, and the heads,
skulls, or casts of skulls of known persons are anxiously sought for.
If you will dispose of them, please state your lowest terms, payable
to your order in this city on the receipt of the heads, or sent to you
by mail.
    An answer to this, at your earliest convenience will much oblige.
                        Dr. Weedon   Yours Respectfully
                                      L. N. Fowler
                                      135 Nassau St. N. York[53]

First and foremost, it is valuable to realize that the writer differentiates between "head" and "skull" and refers to Osceola's as a head. He refers to
Euchee Billy's as a skull, whereas W. W. Smith uses the word "head."[54] Of
course, the writer is at some distance from the subject, and Euchee Billy was
less well known than was Osceola, but his words indicate that he was at
least aware of a differentiation. This seems to add corroboration to our
former assertion that Osceola's head was preserved as a head rather than as

a skull. The letter is docketed on the obverse, "answered the 24th & sent to Charleston by Capt _____ ."[55]

Valentine Mott, M.D. (1785–1865)

The next documentary information concerning the movements of Osceola's head also comes from the Weedon and Whitehurst family papers. Two letters, from and to the elder surviving daughter, Henrietta's husband, Dr. Daniel Winchester Whitehurst, indicate that the head was not sold to the New York collector in 1839 but was finally transferred out of the keeping of Weedon family members about four and a half years after its acquisition.

The erstwhile lawyer, now doctor, Whitehurst justified the original acquisition of the head on a strictly scientific basis. We may also read into his statement a slight defensiveness, possibly born of sentiments he heard expressed by members of the nonscientific community at the time. Dr. Weedon certainly had heard negative sentiments expressed, if we can believe Andrew Welch about the furor in New York that occurred when the head was exhibited in Peale's Museum. But Whitehurst was expressing his opinions to his former professor and mentor, Dr. Valentine Mott, a founder of the Medical College of the City of New York. With his letter of transmission to Dr. Mott and that doctor's positive response, the story of Osceola's head diverges from that of the Weedon family and, for now at least, passes into obscurity (although, perhaps, slightly less than heretofore). Daniel Winchester Whitehurst wrote:

St. Augustine, Fla. Oct. 2, 1843
Dr. Valentine Mott
New York
My Dear Sir;
    Accompanying this you will be handed the head of the celebrated Seminole Chief, Osceola, a man who in recent years filled a large space in the eye of the American public, if indeed not the civilized world. The strong sentiment which is manifested in the fate of the aborigines of this country and the policy of the government in consolidating them westward are as creditable to the feelings of humanity, as calculated to elicit apprehension at a result, which may ultimately prove a check to the adventurous enterprise of our countrymen. This territory, as you are aware, is but just relieved from scenes of a sanguinary character—too long protracted for its happiness, but growing out of a policy of the removal of the Red Man. Among those distin-

guished for [_____], in an eminent degree was Osceola: Brave and active in war,—he was equally docile in peace and from once having been a firm friend of the white man, he became his bitterest foe. He it was who killed General Thompson, the Indian Agent at Fort King, and by this act, buried the calumet of peace, and lit up the flame, which for six years, burned with such desolating waste over this unhappy land. In obtaining the head of such a man, I am aware that the sentiments of the ultra philanthropist would be shocked at what would be [_____] desecration of the grave, and much sympathy would be expended that a child of the forest with qualities commanding admiration and regard should be conveyed to the tomb, a headless corpse. But with the scientific and intelligent, such influences are of little worth, and in the preservation of the dead we do no violence to the feelings of humanity or even the strongest attachments of love. I am aware that the classic lands of Greece and Rome, the isles of the sea, many a well fought field of Europe, have alike given up their evidences of life, and in your cabinet of heads, we travel into the distant past, and hold communion with those of the times that were. In looking around me, where to place it, for preservation and [_____] I know of none more than yourself who would [_____] these intentions, and among the gifted and eminent of our own land, none to whom with more propriety I could make a tender of it. Be pleased to accept the [_____] of respect with which I am,

Your very obedient servant,
D. W Whitehurst, M.D.[56]

⌒

Valentine Mott was famous. He had studied in England with the leading surgeons of his day and had taught on two continents. He had performed more operations than any other surgeon up to that time (see figure 10). His personal medical library contained some four thousand books plus a collection of anatomical specimens numbering one thousand items. He did indeed seem a most likely repository for this unique specimen. Dr. Mott concurred:

My Dear Sir:
I am delayed returning you my thanks for the Head of Osceola, until Dr. Peck should do me this favor of [____ __] to you. I promised him a letter and had it [_____] but unfortunately [was] out when he [_____].
No one can realize such a [_____·__] than I do, and I esteem it as a particular favor that you have presented it to me. It will be deposited in the collection and preserved in my library at home, for I fear almost

Figure 10. Valentine Mott, M.D., 1857. Johnson, Fry & Co., Publishers, New York.

to place it in my museum at the University. [_____] temptation will be so strong for someone to take it. Your letter will be attached to the head, and I shall place as labels upon it—the name of the Donor.

I send you at this time our circular for the next academic year, which has just come from the press. You will be gratified to hear of the success of your Alma Mater.

Yours very truly,
Valentine Mott[57]

Several statements in these letters are of critical importance to our understanding of the next chapter in the story of the head. First, Daniel Whitehurst informs us that Osceola was a figure of international importance ("a man who in recent years filled a large space in the eye of the American public, if indeed not the civilized world"). This opinion is borne out by the ease with which he is still remembered, and the passions that attach to that remembrance, even to this day. Dr. Mott corroborates this evaluation when he surmises that "temptation will be so strong for someone to take it." Taken together, the statements imply that this artifact must have been highly visible—not one to be lost or forgotten easily.

Then, Whitehurst settles, quite clearly and simply, the controversy concerning the decapitation as an act of friendship versus the possibility that it was an act of revenge. He explains, "In obtaining the head of such a man, I am aware that the sentiments of the ultra philanthropist would be shocked at what would be [_____] desecration of the grave, and much sympathy would be expended that a child of the forest with qualities commanding admiration and regard should be conveyed to the tomb, a headless corpse. But with the scientific and intelligent, such influences are of little worth, and in the preservation of the dead we do no violence to the feelings of humanity or even the strongest attachments of love." In other words, science does not violate sentiment.

Next, Whitehurst wrote: "I am aware that the classic lands of Greece and Rome, the isles of the sea, many a well fought field of Europe, have alike given up their evidences of life." In this we find confirmed, once again, the long-standing practice of taking physical specimens of human beings for the purpose of scientific study.

Then, Dr. Mott informs Whitehurst that "it will be deposited in the collection and preserved in my library at home." Every researcher who has considered this point has failed to differentiate, although Dr. Mott obviously did, between the official act of cataloging or, in museum terms, *registering* the specimen into the collection—"depositing" it, as Dr. Mott termed it—and physically *placing* it among pieces of the collection. With this statement he quite clearly informs us that portions of his collection are located in at least two separate places: the utilitarian pieces—the teaching collections—are in the hospital; the unusual and/or valuable pieces are kept in his own home. Fifteen years later, on 1 April 1858, Dr. Mott issued a catalog of the specimens and paintings in his collection. At that time, two specimens numbered 1132 were listed, the first being "Head of Osceola, the great Seminole chief (undoubted). Presented by Dr. Whitehurst, of St. Augustine."[58]

When Mott first received Osceola's head, the study in which he placed it was within his relatively new and capacious home on New York's Upper West Side. One architectural historian places it within the growth of the city thusly: "During the post–Civil War era, the area bounded by Fifty-ninth and 110th Streets and Eighth Avenue and the Hudson River was transformed from a sparsely developed, almost rural landscape into a thriving urban district, known alternately as the West Side or the West End, with its own distinctive character. . . . In 1835 the celebrated surgeon Dr. Valentine Mott built his house at Ninety-fourth Street so far back from the river that in 1868 it had to be moved [by his widow and family, of course; Mott was dead by then] to make way for the construction of the Boulevard."[59] (See figure 11.)

Mott was not only a medical practitioner but also a widely hailed investor in the prosperity of the city of New York. A nominal Quaker and member of a wealthy and philanthropic Quaker family, Mott had studied medicine in Edinburgh and London and served on the faculty of the Columbia Medical College and the Medical College of New York University. He was a principal founder of the New York University Medical College and, for a long period, the president of the New York Academy of Medicine. In 1897, the *New York Sun* recapped "Wealth of Fifty Years Ago," naming the local citizens whose wealth in 1847 topped $100,000. Valentine Mott's was listed as $250,000, among the highest. Two of his sisters, who had inherited their father's estate, were worth $150,000, and his cousins William F. Mott and Samuel F. Mott, were worth $300,000 and $200,000, respectively.

Dr. Mott was not at all an elitist in his practice, despite his wealth. One historian described "the well-known gig of the world-renowned surgeon, whose neat Quaker garb, his highly-polished white top boots, and low-crowned, broad-brimmed beaver, was as familiar to all classes as the commonest necessity of daily life; for all, rich and poor, felt respect and love for Valentine Mott."[60]

To accommodate his work at the Fourteenth Street Medical College, as well as an active social life, Mott kept a home in town, on Bleecker Street, in what was then known as Depau Row, the block between Thompson and

Figure 11. Home of Valentine Mott, M.D., in the 1840s. (Collection of the New-York Historical Society, New York City.)

Sullivan streets. In 1840 Dr. Mott left his New York practice due to illness and traveled in England, France, and Egypt, making friends in the highest circles. On his return from his travels, the doctor wrote *Travels in Europe and the East*.[61] On the evening of 26 November 1841, Dr. and Mrs. Louisa Dunmore Munns Mott hosted a glittering event in honor of the Prince de Joinville, one of the acquaintances Dr. Mott had made in France. The ball was held in "the superb suite of rooms in Doctor Mott's mansion in Depau Place [*sic*], which is fitted up in a style of princely magnificence."[62] Almost three hundred guests attended, and the newspapers touted it as *the* event of the year.

In 1855, Mott commissioned the famous New York architect Richard Morris Hunt to build Stuyvesant House, also on Bleecker Street, a precursor of Hunt's future Stuyvesant Apartments, among the first apartment houses to be built in the city.[63] The building was built "on the Parisian model," on a large scale, with porte cochères, porters' lodges, courtyards, and a suspended veranda. . . . But was divided into separate houses, each of which must be occupied by a family."[64]

It was from the town house in 1858 that Mott finally completed and published the catalogue of his collections, including number 1132, "Head of Osceola, the great Seminole chief (undoubted)." Within the next few years, the town mansion in Depau Row was replaced by a more modest, albeit very comfortable, home that was also in town, at 1 Gramercy Park West, at the southwest corner of Twenty-first Street. This five-story building, on a lot facing Gramercy Park, is the only Mott residence still in existence.[65]

↝

Dr. Valentine Mott died on 26 April 1865. In his will he left an estate valued at $400,000 to be divided among his wife, seven surviving children, and two grandchildren. Among the contents of his residence, the will makes no specific mention of the head or any like objects. Regarding his specimen collection in its entirety, however, the will is most clear:

> Seventh—My museum is to remain under the guardianship of my son, Alexander B. Mott, at the Medical College in Fourteenth Street, on condition that said College shall take all the care and defray all the expenses needed for its perfect preservation; and on condition that my sons or grand sons practicing or studying medicine shall have free access to the same, under such restrictions as its safety and preservation shall require. In case this College shall be dissolved or discontinue to teach or object to comply with the conditions I have imposed, then my son Alexander, the appointed guardian of my museum, shall remove it to such place, medical school or public institution, as with the approbation of his mother, he shall decide upon. Expressly understanding that the Museum shall be preserved intact and the above conditions complied with. My sole object in making this arrangement in reference to my Museum of which a correct catalogue is kept is to make this labour of my life useful to my fellow creatures, as well as to my family. It is to be called the "Mott Museum" and never to be sold.[66]

Shortly after Valentine Mott's death, fire consumed the Medical College on Fourteenth Street, and many of the pathological specimens in the "Mott Museum" were lost.[67] His widow immediately gathered the surviving materials and reassembled them as the Mott Memorial Library at 64 Madison Avenue, New York. It was opened on 11 October 1866. The collection was later described only as being "choice . . . without being extensive."[68] It focused on his re-created study containing books, portraits, a bust of the owner, and a plaster cast of his right hand, taken after death. No further details are given, and no mention is made of Osceola's head.

One further available source of detailed information, however, might shed light on the whereabouts of the head at the time of the death of Dr. Mott. This is the detailed estate inventory of Valentine Mott's possessions, comprising several hundred pages, overseen by Mott's son and executor, Alexander Brown Mott, M.D. Dr. Alexander Mott, one of the founders of Bellevue Hospital Medical College, was devoted to his father's profession and to the Mott Museum. The estate inventory is on file in the Office of the Clerk of Surrogate's Court, New York. If the head were found to have remained in the residence library, as opposed to having been moved to the Medical College, then it would have escaped the fire. This certainly would seem to have been the case, given Mott's earlier statement to Whitehurst. Unfortunately, the estate inventory, which was in its proper file as recently as 1983, has since been misplaced and cannot be located now.

The Mott Memorial Library remained intact until 1929. The building was used as the headquarters and meeting site of the New York Academy of Medicine, to which organization it had been bequeathed in 1910. In that year, the collections were broken up and dispersed to various entities of like purpose. The New York Academy of Medicine, now headquartered on the Upper East Side at 103rd Street, still has among its collections Dr. Mott's medical case and instruments and the plaster cast of his right hand, as well as many of the books formerly in his library.[69] In addition, the New York Academy of Medicine holds manuscript items from Alexander Brown Mott, M.D., and his son, Valentine Mott, M.D. There is no known inventory of the Mott Memorial Library artifacts and, consequently, no evidence that Osceola's head may even have been among its collections.

The location of this unique artifact, then, is currently unknown. No definitive evidence has been found, however, to substantiate the conclusion that the head was destroyed in the Medical College fire, even though May McNeer Ward quotes her grandfather as saying that such was its fate.[70] On the contrary, the last word that we have on the subject from its last known possessor is that it specifically was not being held among the items that would be destroyed by fire.

The City of New York

For many of the participants in the events surrounding the removal and distribution of Osceola's clothing and personal possessions following his death at Fort Moultrie, all roads led to New York. So, too, in the story of his head and its movement outside of South Carolina and Florida does the road lead to New York. We already have discussed the Stuyvesant Institute, Peale's Museum, and Valentine Mott's collections. In many ways, the city of New York was itself as vibrant an actor in the story as were the humans who interacted with Osceola, with Weedon, with Whitehurst, and with each other. New York was a major U.S. port, a center of national culture and learning, and an international informational crossroads. There should be little surprise, then, that the lives, educations, professions, and activities of so many persons germane to Osceola's story should have had their vector there. There should be little wonder, then, that the city would have provided a number of tangential opportunities for seeking the whereabouts of Osceola's head over the last century and a half. Despite the fact that the head has not been located, it is appropriate to document some of the more obvious paths that have been explored.

One possibility focused on a contemporary and another medical colleague of Valentine Mott, Henry Abbott (1812–1859), who lived in New York City intermittently and who spent a great deal of time in Egypt acquiring a sizeable and significant collection of Egyptiana, even as Mott was collecting anatomical and pathological specimens. In 1854, Abbott's Egyptian collection was on exhibition at the Stuyvesant Institute.[71] For many years afterward, the collection was in the possession of the New York Historical Society, but on 17 November 1948, the New York Historical Society officially transferred the Abbott Collection to the Brooklyn Museum. In addition, "the following year the Brooklyn Museum secured full title to our collection of Pre-Columbian Spanish-American Indian artifacts and our small but choice collection of weapons and implements of the Indians of the Plains which [the museum] had had for several years on loan."[72] Information provided by museum staff and the curators of the Abbott Collection and the Native American Collection indicates that none of Mott's collections ever passed into the holdings of Henry Abbott. Neither did any of Mott's collections ever pass into the sizeable Native American collections of the Brooklyn Museum.[73]

Not only the number but also the obvious network of medical men involved in the story of Osceola's possessions is fascinating in itself. Yet another U.S. Army surgeon who served in Florida, a contemporary of Weedon, Whitehurst, Jacob Rhett Mott, Lebby, and others and a New Yorker was Nathan S. Jarvis, who was not only, not surprisingly, a collector of Indiana but also a former student of Dr. Valentine Mott as well. Jarvis, we recall, was with the unit that took Osceola prisoner at Fort Peyton in 1837, and Jarvis rode beside the captive warrior back to St. Augustine and Fort

Marion (see chapter 5). Jarvis collected artifacts during his tour of duty in Florida, and a number of his pieces passed into the collections of the Brooklyn Museum. Among them are several Seminole items, and a typescript list titled "Indian Materials available in 1950 as per 1848 deposit of Dr. Nathan S. Jarvis" enumerates them. They include a "Simonole bow," a "Chief's looking glass" (not a silver-banded mirror, however), "Ball clubs," and a "Seminole Indian hunting knife."[74] No attributions supplied by Jarvis link any of these artifacts to Osceola. Furthermore, no anatomical specimens are listed, and none are in the general collections of the Brooklyn Museum today.

A book in the collections of the New York Academy of Medicine offered another lead to New York avenues along which Mott's anatomical specimens might have passed. Actually, the lead was provided by two typewritten notes pasted on the first page. The book was titled *An Account of Bellevue Hospital with a Catalogue of the Medical and Surgical Staff from 1736 to 1894.* Valentine Mott was a staunch supporter of Bellevue and his son Alexander Brown Mott, M.D., was appointed a consulting surgeon there from 1847 to 1865 and again from 1884 to 1889. He was a visiting surgeon there from 1859 to 1882. Dr. James R. Wood, a director of the hospital, placed the Wood Pathological Museum on the new second floor of the hospital in 1857. The later-added notes indicate, first, that "the Curator of the Pathological Museum of the Bellevue Hospital reports that the Wood Museum is no longer in existence and that the specimens have been destroyed. March 22, 1956." The second note informs us that "the Museum of the N.Y.C. Medical Examiner's Office has a few items salvaged from the old Wood Museum of Bellevue Hospital. [n.d.]"[75]

A conversation with the chairman of the Pathology Department at Bellevue revealed that no anatomical or pathological collections are held there currently because there is insufficient space available.[76] A visit to New York's Office of the Chief Medical Examiner elicited the information that pathological collections formerly held by that office had been transferred over the years to the Armed Forces Institute of Pathology at Walter Reed Medical Center, Washington, D.C. A check by institute staff of the records associated with New York's Office of the Chief Medical Examiner's collections, however, includes no evidence that Osceola's head was ever among the items transferred to them.[77]

In 1994, a discussion with staff of the New York Academy of Medicine provided the information that a member of the Mott family had been researching there for information on his ancestors, and a blind letter forwarded by the staff to that individual obtained a cordial response. Unfortunately, the individual was a descendent of a collateral line and could provide no further information on Valentine Mott, Alexander Brown Mott, or their line of Mott descendents.[78]

Tentative Conclusions

Although the current location of the head remains unknown, many of our initial questions regarding its removal, preservation, and subsequent disposition have been answered now. For one thing, Osceola died a natural death; he was not murdered, as many people, including many Indians, have believed. Furthermore, although Dr. Weedon had the classic forensic triad—motive, means, and opportunity—we now see that Frederick Weedon was neither vengeful nor any kind of ghoul. Nevertheless, any discussion of friendship between the two individuals—at least friendship in twentieth-century terms—must be held separately from a discussion of the removal of the head. In fact, we now see that Osceola's head was probably removed by Dr. Strobel, even though Dr. Weedon did wind up as its possessor. We also know now that the head was not removed premortem, despite other persistent rumors, nor was the grave vandalized to remove it.

The head may have been exhibited for a short time in New York. But subsequently it was taken back to St. Augustine and remained there for five years before it was returned to New York, where it may still remain. It was preserved as a complete, rather than a skeletonized, specimen in a jar of alcohol, and at 168 years old (at the time of this writing), it is still a century younger than many other still-extant specimens of its type around the world. Its whereabouts are a persistent mystery among non-Indians and Indians alike, but in the strictest sense, its purview (along with that of the postcranial remains) lies with Osceola's descendents and cultural kin and not with us non-Indians—the passions of legislators, governors, tourist-attraction visitors, and mystery buffs notwithstanding. Osceola still belongs to his people. He spent his life proving that. He seems to be spending his death proving it as well.

8 / The Weedon Family

More than that of any other white man, the story of Frederick Weedon intersects the life of Osceola and remains involved with it over a longer period of time. Even more than simple length of interaction is the strength of that involvement, manifested even to this day in the continuing connection of the Weedon family descendants with the history, documents, and physical remainders of an Indian long since deceased. An examination of Frederick Weedon specifically, then, and his family will clarify much of the cultural setting of Osceola's life, as well as a great deal of the historical milieu through which many of those physical fragments of his material legacy have passed.

Frederick was born the first of six children of Col. William Weedon of Baltimore, Maryland, and his wife, Sarah Sands. William was a colonial descendent of a British family that traced its ancestors to the seventeenth century.[1] Family tradition, aided by sketchy research, has it that five brothers surnamed Weedon lived in England at that time. Two of these were early immigrants to Maryland in the American colonies, where one of the brothers, described merely as "young," died soon after arriving. He is reputed to have been interred at Kent Island on the Chesapeake Bay. The colonial branch of the Weedon family descended from the surviving brother.

William Weedon received his colonelcy during the American Revolution and married as the war drew to a close. Sarah Sands Weedon gave birth to her first child, a son whom they named Frederick, on 27 October 1784. Their next child was another son, John, whose destiny was also tied to that of Florida. John would die on 31 October 1840 at Picolata, west of St. Augustine on the St. Johns River, of chronic dysentery (an unfortunate but all-too-frequent effect of fighting in Florida's subtropical climate).[2] A third son, William, and three daughters, Henrietta, Ruth, and Sarah, completed the family.

Frederick followed a personal inclination to the practice of medicine. After study in Philadelphia, he returned to his home in Baltimore to practice. We are not given information concerning his father's civilian occupation, so we can only infer from historical evidence that it was Frederick's lifelong interest in medicine that gave rise to what would be the predominant family profession. As had his father, however, Frederick, we know, served in the military—during the War of 1812. He received his commission on 22 June 1808 as a captain of a company of cavalry attached to the Sixty-first Regiment of Virginia Militia. Captain Weedon did not enter the service until 1813, however, and between 9 March of that year and 1 March 1815, he saw active duty with his unit only intermittently.[3]

Sometime prior to 1816, Frederick married Mary Marable of Baltimore. She may have been older than her bridegroom and was very stable financially. She had a daughter, Frances, by a previous marriage, who was already old enough to marry. Frances soon married Frederick's youngest brother, William. Frederick and Mary had only one child, Julia, who died early. Their union ended with the death of Mary by 1816, and family tradition has it that disagreements about the inheritance of the senior Mrs. Weedon's estate caused a permanent estrangement between Frederick and William, as a result of which William changed the spelling of his surname to "Weeden." Shortly after the opening of Indian lands in Alabama at the end of the Creek War of 1813–1814, Frederick Weedon appears to have relocated to Huntsville, in northern Alabama, and shortly thereafter, William and Frances also moved there. By 1816, after Mary's death, the widower had begun to move into the public service arena. Also in that same year he remarried.[4]

Frederick Weedon's second wife, also named Mary, had been born Mary Wells Thompson in Elbert County, Georgia, on 25 January 1798 and thus was fourteen years her spouse's junior. (See figures 12 and 13.) "Polly," as her family called her, was the daughter of a wealthy Somerville, Alabama, planter who also may have moved into the area to take advantage of the newly available lands.[5] Despite assertions that still persist, no evidence has yet been found to link Mary Thompson to the Indian agent Wiley Thompson, who was killed in 1835 by Osceola. In a letter to his daughter and son-in-law written in 1830, William Thompson sent news of at least seven brothers and sisters, as well as seventeen nieces and nephews, but only one uncle was mentioned. This was Wilbur Thompson, who had a plantation in Baker County, Georgia, "on the Florida line a little East of the Chatahoche river."[6] In addition, no connection between the two individuals was noted in any of the contemporary accounts of Thompson's death and Osceola's exploits, even though Weedon's name was mentioned. Therefore, one is left with the conclusion, discussed earlier, that the revenge theme in the Weedon/Osceola relationship is a later embellishment of the story.

Although Mary Thompson Weedon also predeceased her husband, their relationship lasted for thirty-three years. The marriage also seems to have prospered in numerous ways. In 1818 their first child, whom they named Mary Euphrasia, was born. Within another year, Frederick had entered public service officially. William Garrett's *Reminiscences of Public Men in Alabama for Thirty Years* lists Frederick Weedon as the Madison County representative to the Alabama General Assembly in 1819, 1820, and 1821.[7]

In 1827 Frederick, Mary, and their family, which now included four children, moved to Florida, probably to Tallahassee. In addition to Mary Euphrasia, Mary had borne Caroline (died at birth, 1820), Henrietta Williams (25 January 1821), Julia Elizabeth (1823), and John Irving (1825). Another son, Frederick, Jr., joined the family in 1828, and on 25 November 1829 father Frederick took deed to a large piece of property in Leon County to serve as the homestead for his rapidly expanding group. The site included the crest of a hill at what is now the intersection of Jim Lee and Paul Russell roads in the southeastern quadrant of the county, as well as a twenty-acre corridor leading to it.[8] There is only one other bit of evidence regarding Frederick's life during this period. On 22 October 1832 he signed a letter of agreement governing a duel between James D. Wescott, Junior, and Thomas Baltzell, Esquire, as a second for one of the parties.[9]

During the five years that the Weedons lived in Tallahassee, three more children were born: George B. (1830), William Henry Harrison (1831), and Hamilton M. (15 March 1834). Hamilton's birth date is important because it effectually pinpoints the time at which the Weedons left Tallahassee for St. Augustine on the east coast. Within three months of the birth, Frederick and his wife had packed up their household and their eight offspring, half of whom were still under the age of ten years, and had moved almost two hundred miles across Florida Territory.

If Frederick was still actively practicing medicine (and he appears to have been), he was not, however, supporting his family solely from its proceeds. St. Johns County deed books yield information dated 12 June 1834 that a tract of "about six acres . . . near the redoubt of the first Ferry," planted with sweet oranges, was transferred from the estate of Mrs. Josepha F. Bravo to Gabriel Moore, trustee of Mary M. Weeden [*sic*], wife of Frederick Weedon.[10]

From the estate of his first wife, Dr. Weedon paid $2,821 for this property. Geographically, it was delineated on the west by the San Sebastian River, on the south by "a street leading to Veil's ferry," and on the east and north by lands of John Drysdale.[11] This acreage, approximately one mile north of Fort Marion, was known in the twentieth century as "Garnett's old orange grove" and seems to have been solely an income-producing property. The family dwelling was located in town.[12] A producing citrus grove certainly would have added to the family's economic base. Weedon kept this St. Augustine property throughout the rest of his life and passed it to his principal heirs, by whom it was sold out of the family in 1856.[13]

The Weedons' first year in St. Augustine was one of growing unrest and alarm—for their new friends in this small center of East Florida life, for proprietors of outlying sugar plantations, for territorial leaders anxious for statehood, and especially for that small percentage of Florida's population who were shepherding its precarious economic interests. State newspapers reported more and more frequently on the rumors, the reported sightings, and, finally, the depredations of the Florida Indians. Some specific Indians singled out by whites for their power or visibility among the dissident Seminoles were tracked by newspapers across the state. Osceola, or Powell, was one who rose particularly rapidly to white notoriety after 1834. White expansionists and Indian determinists were headed inexorably toward physical conflict. In response to the impending crisis, Weedon again joined the military, this time as a captain in Major Smith's company, Second Regiment of Florida Mounted Militia. His name appears on the company's muster rolls for seventy-one days, from 12 December 1835 to 20 February 1836.[14]

The year 1836 was one of anxiety and fear for the Weedons, as it was for other Floridians. For two months during the onset of the war, the doctor watched "night & day without dressing for to take repose."[15] Frederick Weedon was again occupying a position of authority and visibility. Besides his medical practice and agricultural responsibilities, he had been appointed justice of the peace in August 1835, and since December 1835 he had been mayor of the city. Outside of St. Augustine, however, East Florida suffered especially hard in the war. Almost all of East Florida's sugar plantations were ruined, and St. Augustine, a military garrison from its founding in the sixteenth century, continued to be a center for military activity. Captain Weedon enrolled in Company B, St. Augustine Veterans, Florida Militia. This time he served for three months, from 10 November 1836 to 10 February 1837, and then rejoined the company a week later at Fort Marion,

Figure 12. Frederick Weedon, M. D. (Courtesy of the Florida Photographic Collection, State Archives, Florida Department of State, Tallahassee, Florida. Gift of Mary Weedon Keen.)

Figure 13. Mary Wells Thompson Weedon (Mrs. Frederick). (Courtesy of the Florida Photographic Collection, State Archives, Florida Department of State, Tallahassee, Florida. Gift of Mary Weedon Keen.)

this time for six months—although the entire company was mustered out after only three months, on 29 May 1837.[16]

While Minorcan and Spanish inhabitants and American settlers banded together to form militia companies for physical protection, they also met compatriots in fraternal organizations. Frederick Weedon was a Freemason. Among the members of his lodge in little St. Augustine was a *criollo* (local-born Spaniard), Joseph M. Hernández, who was also the brigadier general commanding forces east of the St. Johns River. By at least mid-1837, Daniel Winchester Whitehurst, another Freemason, also was residing in St. Augustine. Whitehurst, originally of Norfolk, Virginia, was thirty years old that July when he became a lieutenant of a company of East Florida Mounted Volunteers in Col. John Warren's regiment. Whitehurst spent his six-month enlistment (13 July 1837 to 4 February 1838) at duty stations at Picolata and along the St. Johns River, close enough to St. Augustine to enhance his association with the Weedon family.

Dr. Weedon, although no longer officially affiliated with a unit, continued his association with the military establishment on a contract basis as a surgeon. He entered into an agreement dated 1 June 1837 for attendance on troops at Fort Lane (in present-day Seminole County).[17] Although this was undoubtedly an emergency situation where a shortage of medical assistance existed, the contract appears not to have been approved, and Dr. Weedon was discharged after only about twenty days' service.[18] The summer was the unhealthy season for campaigning in Florida, and soldiers were regularly dispersed to the most salubrious duty stations available. Moreover, the citizens of Florida, encouraged by the signing of a capitulation at Fort Dade on 6 March 1837, had begun to believe that the war was over.[19] The summer was a hot but welcome lull after more than a year of conflict and constant anxiety.

The records do not show when and where Whitehurst and Weedon met, but their overlapping spheres of interest in such a small town, and relative social stations must have thrown them together quickly. Mrs. Eliza C. Whitehurst, Daniel's mother, had been a resident of the city since November 1829. She and her daughter Elizabeth, along with a servant, had arrived aboard a schooner from Charleston. By the next year's census, the enterprising Mrs. Whitehurst was managing the boarding house on Hospital (now Aviles) Street, where they had taken up residence. Daniel had earlier attended New York University before embarking on a sea voyage to Africa for his health in mid-1832. After a shipwreck and an escape from hostile natives, he found refuge in Sierra Leone and recuperated there for more than three years. Sometime after 1835 and before 1837, however, he also had taken up residence at St. Augustine, where three tragedies in quick succession ended his family reunion. Daniel's brother-in-law, James M. Hanson, drowned in a shipwreck off Savannah in April 1837. Slightly more than one year later, in May 1838, Elizabeth Whitehurst Hanson would die, and in the next month Daniel's mother would pass away also.[20]

By the end of summer 1837, it became obvious that the Indians shared little of the whites' belief that the conflict would soon end. In October, at the order of General Jesup, Gen. Joseph Hernández seized an opportunity, took Osceola captive, and imprisoned him in Fort Marion at St. Augustine. Thus it was that, soon after the Indians were captured on 21 October and prior to their transport to Fort Moultrie on 31 December 1837, Frederick Weedon, a fifty-three-year-old physician, and Osceola, a warrior twenty years his junior, came to know each other for the first time. Dr. Weedon's military access to the post and the fort at St. Augustine assured him entreé to the Indians. His family visited Osceola as well and seems to have taken along gifts of food. Dr. Weedon would later be described as a "noble . . . gentleman."[21] Contemporary descriptions of Osceola's temperament refer repeatedly to his passion and intensity.[22] Perhaps each found something in the other with which he could identify. Perhaps their association was based only on proximity, or Frederick Weedon's professional curiosity, or on nothing more than fortuitous military expediency. A friend, T. Saunders, had written to Weedon at length the year before concerning the "state of your mind, which I cannot avoid perceiving . . . to be unhappy." Saunders commiserated with his friend on the many ills that had beset him as a result of the conflicts with the Indians but urged him strongly to "forgiveness" and reminded him that "the soul that fosters prejudice cannot be saved."[23] As we have learned from earlier discussions, the doctor took this reminder to heart.

When the steamer *Poinsett* left St. Augustine bar in late December 1837 bearing Osceola and his family and the other Seminole prisoners, Weedon traveled with them.[24] The Indians had persuaded him to go, and the army needed his services. In a contract dated 13 January 1838 and signed at Fort Moultrie, Charleston Harbor, Dr. Weedon agreed to perform the duties of "surgeon attending emmigrating Indians." The contract paid $150 per month and remained in force "during the pleasure of the parties." In a separate but companion document, Capt. Pitcairn Morrison certified that the persons then entitled to medical attention at Fort Moultrie included 40 soldiers, 3 company women, and 230 Indians and that "no competant physician could be obtained at a lower rate."[25]

Thus it was that Frederick Weedon attended on Osceola most intimately of all whites. The story of his involvement in Osceola's death is recorded elsewhere in this book, as is a discussion of his part in the survival of several of the personal possessions of his Indian charge, as well as Osceola's head. One other point, however, remains undocumented. Weedon's intellectual curiosity about Osceola's life, it seems, must have gone far beyond his medical interest. Two separate sources indicate that Weedon was assiduously collecting information for a written history of Osceola.

Dr. Robert Lebby, who had served as an assistant army surgeon during the Second Seminole War, reported later to an enquirer: "Dr. Wheedon of St. Augustine collected at different times a narrative of his life, and the reasons that produced the Florida troubles from the Chief himself . . . and I know [Osceola] communicated many facts of importance to this gentleman. . . . If Dr. Wheedon of St. Augustine is still alive, much information could be obtained from him, that would be interesting to the world."[26] Dr. Samuel Forry, another United States Army assistant surgeon stationed in St. Augustine in 1838, wrote to a friend, "Old Dr. Weedon is about publishing the life of Osceola. Powell has quized him (I don't know how to spell that word) most sublimely."[27]

Furthermore, on 12 July 1838 Weedon received a letter from John Inman, a New York newspaperman and publisher, advising him that he had "given Mr. Dearborn about 70 pages of copy, but I do not know whether he has yet commenced printing." Inman concluded, "I am very much pleased with the work, and have no doubt that we shall make a good thing of it—creditable both to you and me, and profitable besides. I will send you the proofsheets as I receive them."[28] To this date, no evidence of the manuscript or a finished product has been located.

Shortly after Osceola's death and burial, his family and the other Seminole prisoners were transported to Indian Territory in the West, and Dr. Weedon returned to St. Augustine, possibly via New York. The bustling little community of St. Augustine was still a military garrison, but Dr. Weedon tended to civilian ailments. Family tradition has it that he also operated a drugstore.[29]

Daniel Whitehurst became the owner and publisher of the *St. Augustine News* in November 1838. He also fell in love with sixteen-year-old Julia Weedon, and they planned to marry. Another sorrow intersected the Weedon family history, however, as Julia unexpectedly died in the winter of 1839–1840. The cause is not recorded, although there was yellow fever in St. Augustine in 1839.[30] Whitehurst, a man of many talents, submerged himself in work. In addition to his newspaper, which he maintained for two years more, he also practiced law.[31] Furthermore, as we have noted earlier, on 15 January 1841, journalist-cum-lawyer Whitehurst entered New York University to study medicine under Dr. Valentine Mott, one of the foremost surgeons in the country. He received his degree in 1843 and returned to St. Augustine to be married, on 13 April of that year, to Henrietta Weedon, the eldest surviving daughter of his friend Frederick.[32] Of Mr. and Mrs. Whitehurst's life during this period we have only one other piece of information, which indicates that he must have returned to St. Augustine. Several newspaper articles from 20 August 1842 announce the reinterment of the remains of the Dade's "Massacre" victims at the National Cemetery in St. Augustine. The services of several religious denominations were held, including a Masonic ritual in which "D. W. Whitehurst pronounced the monody on the dead" at the Presbyterian Church.[33]

Within the next two years, more of Florida's land became available, and Weedon was the first in the territory to take advantage of the opportunity. Under the Armed Occupation Act of 4 August 1842, he filed for the 160 acres that made up the abandoned military post of Fort Pierce.[34] According to family tradition, during the next year the Weedon sons were sent down to the fort to clean and clear the land, although only the two eldest sons, John and Frederick, Jr. (ages eighteen and fifteen) were old enough. Sometime in late 1843 Frederick must have moved down to the property also. Perhaps he took the younger sons, William (twelve) and Hamilton (nine), with him then.

It seems probable that Dr. Weedon had indeed moved to Fort Pierce because on 2 October 1843 it was Daniel, Frederick's son-in-law, rather than Weedon himself, who wrote to Daniel's mentor, Dr. Valentine Mott, in New York to offer him the unique specimen that Frederick had acquired at Fort Moultrie—Osceola's head.[35] Exactly why it had become within Dr. Whitehurst's purview to make disposition of the head is uncertain, but the Whitehursts would depart St. Augustine for Key West late in 1845 or early in 1846 so that Daniel might take up duties as post surgeon for Fort Jefferson in the Dry Tortugas. Perhaps because a major portion of the family appeared to be dispersing, other possessions were being disposed of as well.

Late in 1844 a tragedy struck Frederick Weedon's Fort Pierce settlement, and the news account also indicates that he must have been living at the fort for some time prior to the climactic event. According to the report, an alarm was cried out at midnight on 12 December 1844 as fire destroyed the buildings of the settlement. No lives were lost, due mainly to the heroic efforts of Dr. Weedon, although the settlers lost all of their supplies (reportedly enough for several years). Dr. Weedon was described as "the aged proprietor of the place . . . [who] occupied rooms north of the kitchen." His conduct in rushing to the aid of the other settlers deserved "the highest praise." He was a "noble old gentleman" who would be entitled to the "admiration of all others as long as memory remains." The narrative continued: "Fort Pierce ever since its abandonment by the U.S. Troops, has been a general stopping place for everyone who travelled through the region of country, and a favorite resort for all who located on St. Lucie and Indian River. Its hospitable proprietor Dr. Weedon, it is well known always extended the welcome hand for the way worn and the needy who ever found a welcome to his table and a shelter from the howling storm."[36] It may have been at this time that Weedon returned to St. Augustine.

On 2 November 1849 Mary Thompson Weedon died at St. Augustine at the age of fifty-one.[37] Henrietta returned to St. Augustine to visit her father at least once, in the winter of 1853–1854, and may have found him declining in health. She wrote to her family at Fort Jefferson on 17 January 1854 to inform them that she could not leave at that time because her father had fallen and broken his shoulder. Later that year Frederick transferred seven of his slaves to her.[38] The doctor seems to have been putting his affairs in order one last time, because he shortly moved to Key West, where he took up residence with his daughter and son-in-law. In September 1856 he wrote to his son Hamilton, who was then studying medicine in New York, that "the greatest difficulty I labour from apart from old age, is deafness." He was making a collection of seashells "and other curiosaties of the sea" to send to his son, and he reported, "I want for nothing, all my wants seem to be anticipated, I am kindly cared for."[39] Frederick remained with his family and died there in March 1857 at the age of seventy-three.

Henrietta and Daniel's first child, Clarence, was born while they were living in Key West, as well as Mason (1853–1881, also a physician). In 1858, the year after Frederick Weedon's death, Henrietta and Daniel's first daughter, Mary Katherine, was born. Two more children—Manning and Laura (1860–1925)—were born to the couple. Daniel maintained his varied intellectual interests throughout the remainder of his life. He was an avid reader, naturalist, and politician. He died in Key West in 1874. Henrietta moved her remaining family to Miami, where she resided until her death in 1885, when her body was returned to Key West for interment. Both Whitehurst daughters, Kate and Laura, are buried there also.

9 / The Weedon Artifacts

The second-largest known cache of artifacts that composed the personal property of Osceola left Fort Moultrie in February of 1838 with Dr. Frederick Weedon. (The largest group is discussed in chapter 12.) These pieces undoubtedly also constitute the single most important group of artifacts from the standpoint of the researcher because of their excellent provenance: most have remained in the possession of the descendants of Dr. Weedon ever since. It is intriguing to discover, however, that while he remained in Charleston, Weedon deliberately chose not to disclose his having acquired the pieces. Dr. Lebby reported to an interested party that Osceola "was buried in the Indian Custom, of committing to the coffin, with the body everything that belonged to him—I was not present but at the funeral, but most of my information I obtained from Dr. Wheedon."[1] On Weedon's return to Florida, however, and with the Indians safely on their way to the western reservations, his reticence diminished. Weedon family tradition indicates that the head (but only the head—the clothing and most of the personal effects are never mentioned) was displayed in the window of the doctor's drugstore. Altogether ten items belonging to or associated with Osceola may be considered the Weedon artifacts.

1. Carabine (carbine)
2. Powder horn

3. Lock of hair
4. Pencil sketch
5. Brass pipe
6. Silver concho
7–8. Two silver earrings
9. Garter
10. Sheath knife

Most of these items were taken back to St. Augustine by Dr. Weedon, although two were disposed of almost immediately: Osceola's gun, described as a "carabine," and his powder horn. Both artifacts were forwarded to Mr. J. W Jackson in Albany, New York, on 27 August 1838. The box was transported by the Hudson River Steam-Boat Association and arrived on 30 October 1838. The wording of a note that announced the transportation of the artifacts implies that the pieces were not sent as outright gifts to Mr. Jackson but rather were forwarded to him for further disposition. The note states, "Further instructions will follow by separate post."[2] Frederick Weedon gained possession of Osceola's gun and powder horn after Osceola's death. Evidence that the pieces were not given to the doctor before Osceola's demise is provided by two accounts of the death scene, supplied by Dr. Benjamin Strobel and later, through Strobel, by Thomas Storrow, which have been discussed elsewhere in this book.[3] Among the accoutrements of his full war dress, which Osceola donned as he prepared for death, was his powder horn. The disposition and current physical whereabouts of these two artifacts are unknown. As regards most of the artifacts, Dr. Weedon's daughter Henrietta seems to have been the pivotal family member. Henrietta exerted influence among her parents and siblings second only to that of her father. Documentation also remains to substantiate the fact that it was Henrietta's husband, Daniel Whitehurst, who took control (and apparently earlier, possession) of the head. Sometime in the years during which Henrietta had direct access to the head, she may have removed a lock of hair and plaited it in the fashion of nineteenth-century hair mementos and ornaments. To accompany the plait, she executed a pencil sketch of Osceola, which may have been copied directly from a pencil sketch drawn by John Rogers Vinton (figure 2 in chapter 4). This artifact will be discussed further in this chapter, because it presents several interesting points aside from its subject. She also kept a small brass pipe bowl and a coin silver concho, two more of the personal items that her father had acquired in Charleston. Her brother Hamilton, the youngest surviving male, took possession of two silver earrings and a finger-woven garter. In addition to the artifacts that are known among family members as having been the personal property of Osceola, there exists another that will also be considered in this chapter. It is a sheath knife that is currently in the possession of Josephine Weedon Stipe of Chapel Hill, North Carolina. She is a daughter of Frederick Renfroe Weedon, a grandson of Dr. Weedon. No traditional provenance connects this item with Osceola. In fact, no provenance at all is available for it. Because of its association with the Weedon family, however, it bears examination and discussion.

Provenance

Of the ten offspring of Frederick Weedon, only three children—Henrietta, William Henry Harrison, and Hamilton—had issue, and it is through their families that the artifacts passed and were preserved.

Henrietta Williams Weedon (1821–1885) and Daniel Winchester Whitehurst (1808–1874) had five children: Clarence (died at sea, no issue); Mason (1853–1881, also a physician); Mary Katherine, or "Kate" (1858–1924); Laura (1860–1925); and Manning. Laura never married. Kate was married to a Spanish military officer, but the two never lived together as man and wife. The two sisters spent the rest of their lives together. It was they who received the artifacts that had been their mother's.

William Henry Harrison Weedon (1831–1907), eighth child of Frederick and Mary, married Augusta Ann Renfroe. Six children were born to the couple: Hamilton, Oliver, William, Leslie Washington (1860–1937, also a physician), and twin daughters Mary Parmelia ("Aunt May") Yonge/Hagen (1865–1949), and Isabella Smythe ("Aunt Dumps") McNeer (1865–1937).

Among the children of Isabella Smythe McNeer was May McNeer Ward, whose romantic memories of Osceola are mentioned elsewhere in this book. Isabella's brother Leslie Washington married Blanche Henderson (1867–1957). Four children were born to this couple: Leslie William, Frederick Renfroe (1895–1980, also a physician), Harry Lee (1896–1977), and Mary Blanche/Keen (1905–1997). The four artifacts that had been held by Kate and Laura Weedon were passed by them to Frederick Renfroe, who gave them to his sister, Mary Blanche/Keen. In 1989 Mrs. Keen donated the artifacts to the Museum of Florida History, Division of Historical Resources, Tallahassee.

Hamilton M. Weedon (1834–1908) married Molly Dent. Their five offspring were Annie, Edward B., Mary (1883–1933), Hamilton, Jr. (also a physician), and Hubert (or Herbert). All except Hubert also had issue. Hamilton, Sr., passed his three artifacts (two earrings and one garter) to his son Hamilton, Jr.

Hamilton, Jr., married a Miss Henderson and moved to Troy, Alabama.

Hamilton Jr.'s. three artifacts passed to a daughter of his, Mrs. Robert Blount, who placed them with the Alabama Department of Archives and History, Montgomery, where they remain today.

Artifact Descriptions

Pencil Sketch

The pencil sketch is a right-profile bust, very similar to the one executed by John Rogers Vinton on 4 May 1837. Its similarity is so marked that the possibility should be considered that it was copied directly from the Vinton work. In addition, it has already been documented that the same Vinton sketch was made public, in the same year as its production, in John Lee Williams's *Territory of Florida,* and so it is also necessary to consider the Williams lithograph as the possible source.

Artistically, there seems little doubt, however, that the Vinton sketch and not the Williams lithograph provided the graphic source for the Weedon sketch. The lithographic artist's style is markedly different from that of Vinton; the sketch has been "cleaned up" by the lithographer. Henrietta Weedon was living in St. Augustine when Vinton drew the portrait. The Weedons, Whitehurst, and Vinton were in the same social circles. On the other hand, Henrietta certainly had an opportunity, later in 1837, to view the subject of the sketch firsthand and to execute the sketch from life. The formats of the two sketches, however, are too similar to be accidental.

The sketch is on a piece of writing paper 6″ high by 4⅞″ wide. The actual graphic area is only 2¾″ high and 2¼″ wide. Sometime after the sketch was drawn, the paper was used as a blotter or stored in conjunction with pieces of correspondence because reversed word "ghosts" are visible in several areas of the drawing. Later yet, the small sketch was affixed to a larger half-sheet of watermarked paper.

Directly beneath the image has been penciled the legend "Osceola— about 1833." The final "3" is a revision; the date had been shown as 1835. On the bottom of the larger mounting paper is the caption (in another hand) "A lock of Osceola's hair. The sketch is by Henrietta Weedon, daughter of Dr. Frederick Weedon." According to Mary Weedon Keen, neither legend was inscribed by the artist. She believes that later members of the family made the notations. Neither the 1833 nor the 1835 dates can be correct, of course. The more probable date is 1837, or even 1838, after Henrietta had obtained a more personal association with the subject. The mention of the lock of hair occurs because the plait of Osceola's hair that was also held by the Weedon family had been affixed to the sketch by a paper clip. The oxidation print created by the clip is still visible on the paper.

Brass Pipe

The brass pipe is a small item actually composed of two truncated cones (see figure 14). One forms the bowl of the pipe, and the other forms a perpendicular junction and serves as a permanent stem. The stem was extended by inserting a long hollow reed. The bowl measures 1 3/16″ high, 7/8″ diameter (mouth), and 7/16″ diameter across the truncated base. The stem is 1 1/8″ long and 3/8″ diameter (mouth).

The bowl of the pipe is decorated with four palmate repoussé motives arranged vertically and covering its entire surface. Its mouth exhibits an applied, plain brass lip. On the interior of the bowl may be seen, faintly, the brazed seam that closed the bowl after the repoussé work was completed. The apex of the stem protrudes into this cavity for one-eighth inch. Also visible in the bottom of the bowl is active oxidation, which has created a green scale, but no tobacco residue is readily visible.[4]

The secondary cone, which forms the abbreviated stem, is also of brass and undecorated. It has a lip that provides an aesthetic balance for the bowl but, unlike that of the bowl, has been worked rather than applied. The longitudinal brazed seam is readily visible, as is the brazing that joins the stem and bowl. According to the conclusion reached by John Goggin in 1955 in the only previous description of this artifact, the repoussé work was probably done by a white metalsmith and the finish work by an Indian craftsman.[5] The brazing work on the piece is not of high quality, but neither is it indicative of an untrained workman. The level of skill required to have completed the repoussé does not appear commensurate with the lesser quality of the finish workmanship. It is always possible, however, that the repoussé was created using a template or that the piece was poorly finished because it was intended specifically for the Indian trade.

Goggin also concludes that the pipe is an unusual piece, from an aesthetic standpoint, and cites only one contemporary reference to metal pipes as part of the Indians' ornamental lexicon. There are, however, two other references to smoking that place the habit inside Osceola's cultural frame of reference. Joshua Giddings, writing in 1858, mentioned that Osceola sent gifts to Philip by way of Wild Cat, consisting of a "neatly wrought bead pipe, together with a beautiful white plume."[6] Giddings cannot be considered a very reliable reporter, but aside from the obvious question of whether this was Seminole beadwork or a trade item, this mention does confirm once again that smoking implements had cultural significance among the

Figure 14. Osceola's brass pipe. (Courtesy of the Museum of Florida History, Florida Department of State, Tallahassee, Florida, gift of Mary Weedon Keen, and by permission of the Seminole Tribe of Florida.)

Indians. Indeed, pipe stems are a standard element of Florida Indian artifact assemblages recovered archaeologically. Furthermore, the use of tobacco as a basic element of Indian medicine among the Seminoles and their Maskókî kin in Florida and Oklahoma continues to the present day.

Thomas Storrow made specific mention of the Indian prisoners at Fort Moultrie constantly asking whites for "money, tobacco, or whiskey." From this reference one may infer that Osceola's cultural peers used tobacco regularly. Osceola, however, was not seen to smoke, regardless of "whatever may have been his previous habits," although, in the same paragraph, Storrow also comments on his subject's ill health.[7] Coupled with the physical evidence of the pipe itself, one may draw one of several possible conclusions from this information. First, the pipe, formerly in the possession of Mary Weedon Keen, was never the property of Osceola. This position seems unlikely, given the cumulative weight of the historical and aesthetic provenance of the Weedon family artifacts. Alternatively, one may deduce that the pipe, stylistically unusual for the Seminole Indians, was given to, or collected by, Osceola for personal reasons unconnected with the actual purpose of the pipe itself and, as such, was kept because of emotional rather than practical considerations. Or, finally, one may believe that the pipe was

Figure 15. Osceola's silver concho. (Courtesy of the Museum of Florida History, Florida Department of State, Tallahassee, Florida, gift of Mary Weedon Keen, and by permission of the Seminole Tribe of Florida.)

unusual and, as such, personally appealing to Osceola's vanity and that he had smoked it only on occasion or only prior to the onset of the illness from which he already seemed to be suffering at the time of his capture.

Silver Concho (Bangle)

The next artifact is an ornamental piece of hammered coin silver, 2⅛″ in diameter, with a very slight concavity (see figure 15). The concave side of the artifact appears to be the obverse and exhibits marked evidence of oxidation. A design has been sketched on the artifact reverse and punctated from the obverse with a flat-bladed instrument (such as a knife blade tip or chisel) approximately 1/16″ in width. The design is geometric and curvilinear and consists of six more-or-less equal arcs spaced around the circumference of the disc, facing outward. In the middle of the disc, a single dot marks the center of the circle, and four small triangles, with their apexes facing outward, are arranged at ninety-degree angles around it. At the outer edges of the disc are two small holes by which the concho may have been affixed to the clothing of the wearer.

According to the research of John Goggin, the use of silver for ornaments was introduced to the Florida Indians by the Spaniards and the British. By the late nineteenth century, a white observer wrote, "At different times they have had among them men who were quite noted as silversmiths and became celebrated throughout the tribe." The use of such silver ornaments appears to have been greater among the women than among the men, but a specimen, which has been sewn to the end of the fringe of a man's sash, is available in the collections of the Field Museum in Chicago.[8]

None of the graphic representations of Osceola depict silver conchos, although his use of other silver ornaments is obvious. It is also evident, from the variety of extant artifacts attributed to him, that the range of his personal possessions was not limited only to those documented graphically. As a consequence of these facts, together with the fact that this artifact has been held by the Weedon family, there is no reason to disbelieve its attribution.

Mention should be made of the fact that the concho and the pipe have been stored in a small twilled cotton flannelette bag, in which manner they were passed to their current owner, although there is no clear indication of the point of origin of this bag. The material is beige in color, with a curved seam handsewn with a single strand of cotton thread around three sides, in a running stitch. The nap faces inward, and the twill, outward. At the top, both lips have been turned in three-eighths inch (once) to accommodate opposing drawstrings. Although no strings are currently in place, the condition of the fabric indicates their regular past use.

Earrings

The earrings are the first two of the Osceola artifacts currently in the collections of the Alabama Department of Archives and History Museum, Montgomery, acc. nos. 85.17.2 and 85.17.3. The pieces have been hand hammered from a relatively low-grade silver that has oxidized over all surfaces but appears stable at this time. They are dangle-style earrings, made for pierced ears, and have an overall length of 3.7" (see figure 16).

The mechanical design of the post (a wire loop that passes through a 0.3" ball, through the ear, and back into the other side of the ball) indicates that the earrings were not meant to be removed easily or often. They were probably put in place soon after the ears were pierced and left there permanently. Below the post and ball is a conical dangle with two decorative bands and a double-domed base. These central elements are hollow and soldered to the post and to another ball finial that dangles separately from the bottom of the cone. The earrings are of relatively light weight; one specimen is complete (acc. no. 85.17.2), and the other lacks only one half of the ball from the post wire and the entire ball finial.

Figure 16. Osceola's silver earrings. (Courtesy of the Alabama Department of Archives and History, Montgomery.)

Garter

A garter is the third of the three artifacts that have been transferred by the Weedon family to the Alabama Department of Archives and History Museum, acc. no. 85.17.1 (see figure 17). Its relationship to the other documented garters that were in Osceola's possession and the other extant garters will be discussed further in chapter 13. This piece bears a strong resemblance to those depicted in the Catlin full-length portrait and the Catlin lithograph.

The garter is made of hand-spun, two-ply wool prepared by an experienced spinner. The colors are currently faded almost beyond recognition, but it is possible to determine that two, or possibly three, separate colors were incorporated into the piece originally. A darker color may have come from the indigo blue/green/brown range, whereas the lighter color appears to lie within the normal cream/gray/beige range of variation for undyed wool.

The piece was finger woven in a chevron pattern of alternating dark and light bands, beginning at the end that was meant to be worn on the outside of the leg. For approximately one-third of the length of the garter (also the portion that was meant to be worn on the outside), small white glass trade beads were worked into the border of each color band. For approximately the final two inches of the garter, the chevrons were allowed to degenerate into vertical bands, and both ends of the piece were finished with a horizontal, braided row to block the shape.

Braids of fibers (fifteen at the beginning and ten or twelve at the end) were arranged as tassels of mixed colors, which also served as ties for the garters. The current condition of the garter is poor. The fibers across the median of the piece are almost completely broken through, apparently as the result of prolonged stress, such as that occasioned by a fold. More than half of the tassels at the end of the garter are missing, which appears to be the result of use; repairs were made at some point during the original life of the piece by a person with little experience in the manufacture of such articles, possibly by the owner himself. The repair was made with an anomalous thread, possibly linen, of a light cocoa-brown color.

Two observations may be made relative to the dimensions of the artifact. First, the overall length is only 21¾″ long—barely long enough to wrap around the leg of a person of medium build or of a person of slight build whose calves were heavily muscled from constant walking and running. This fact correlates with the accounts of Osceola that describe him as a man of delicate-to-effeminate build. Second, the original length of the tassels is not sufficient to have allowed them to be tied into bows or other "fluffy"

Figure 17. Osceola's garter. (Courtesy of the Alabama Department of Archives and History, Montgomery.)

knots, such as are depicted in some of the graphics. In fact, they would have barely been sufficient for knotting. Because of their length and the blocking row behind them, however, they probably would have been more conveniently, or ornamentally, tied as two or three separate knots. This point may explain the disparities among depictions of the garter ties.

Sheath Knife

On 30 October 1956 William C. Sturtevant of the Bureau of American Ethnology/Smithsonian Institution responded to a letter from a member of the Weedon family in North Carolina. The letter asked for information concerning a sheath knife that had been passed down through the Weedon family and any possible association with Osceola. Several Osceola graphics depict a sheathed knife at his belt, but only two may be considered as potential sources of corroboration. The first is the Bufford/Currier lithograph of 1838, after Vinton, and the second is the Vinton full-length sketch of 1845. Both indicate a relatively short knife with an ornamented grip and knob finial of some light-colored material. The Weedon knife is 8¾" long with a carved ivory grip. The Weedon artifact also has an obscure maker's mark that Dr. Sturtevant was unable to identify. No graphic representation of this artifact is currently available.

10 / Osceola's Hair

By far the most important of all the extant Osceola artifacts is the only surviving remnant of the man himself—a small lock of hair (see figure 18). None of the earlier documenters have reported the existence of this physical remnant. Only one, Mark Boyd, appears to have been aware of it. Mrs. Keen reported that Boyd visited her during the preparation of his article for the *Florida Historical Quarterly* in 1955 and saw all the artifacts in her possession, including the hair.[1] Because no mention of it was made in the article and because no notes regarding it remain among Boyd's research papers, we may hypothesize that he either considered the lock irrelevant to his research or believed the disclosure of its existence indelicate. With the cooperation of Mrs. Keen, certain limited examinations of the lock of hair were begun on 2 December 1985. The following is a report of the results of those examinations.

Basic Microscopy

Initial contact was made with Jack Duncan, supervisor of the Crime Laboratory, Florida Department of Law Enforcement, Tallahassee. Linda Hensley, analyst at the laboratory, agreed to view the evidence in my presence and report on any verifiable conclusions. Constraints placed on the examination by the artifact's owner were as follows:

Figure 18. Plaited lock of Osceola's hair. (Courtesy of the Alabama Department of Archives and History, Montgomery.)

1. The hair was to be picked up personally by the researcher and re-turned within three hours (thus precluding any lengthy and more thorough analysis at this stage).
2. The plait was not to be materially disturbed (i.e., taken apart) for the sake of analysis.
3. No more than one strand of the hair might be removed for individual examination.
4. All testing must be of a nondestructive nature.

With these conditions in mind, then, the first stage of the examination consisted only of measuring the plait, establishing its physical description, and observing the entire plait under a stereoscopic (8 ×–40 ×) microscope.

The plait measures approximately 5¾″ long and consists of nine bunches of hair. The original lock of hair, however, appears to have been doubled back on itself to shorten the finished plait, provide sufficient bunches for the wide, flat braid, or both. Consequently, the original lock must have been approximately 12″ to 14″ long in order to allow for doubling and plaiting. If one accepts the male Seminole hairstyle as reported and sketched later by United States government agent Clay MacCauley, then for a lock of this length to be obtained, it would have to have been taken from the crown of the head or the nape of the neck, but most probably from the nape of the neck.[2] However, in the contemporary drawings of Osceola, he also appears to have earlocks of sufficient length to have accommodated such a lock. Because the MacCauley information was obtained slightly more than two generations after Osceola's death and neither possibility precludes the other, either source of the hair may be correct.

Plaited locks of hair were extremely popular personal mementoes of both the living and the deceased throughout most of the nineteenth century, and their collection constituted a fad that finally culminated in the high Victorian rage for hair mourning jewelry. The *St. Augustine Florida Herald* in 1834 defined the cultural mood clearly: "*A Lock of Hair.* Few things in the world are so delightful as keepsakes. Nor do they ever, to my heart at best, nor to my eye, lose their tender, their powerful charm! How light how small, how tiny a memorial, saves a beloved one from oblivion."[3]

There are any number of moments in which it would have been simple to separate such a lock from Osceola's head. The first was when the cast of the head and torso was taken, which, as we have discussed earlier, was done at Fort Moultrie, before the head was removed. The second was a few hours later, after the head was removed and before it was preserved in alcohol. We now know as well that Dr. Weedon probably transported the head to New York and back to St. Augustine, and after he returned to St. Augustine the head was in his possession for almost six years. It seems most likely, however, that it was Henrietta, through whom all the other family-held artifacts had passed, who plaited the lock—perhaps as a final keepsake when her husband, Dr. Whitehurst, determined to present the head to Dr. Valentine Mott of New York and the Whitehursts were readying for their move to Key West. Why would the family have been interested in the plait earlier, when they still had the entire head? The alcohol in which the head had been preserved would have maintained the hair in excellent condition. The flat, small plait would certainly have made a more transportable keepsake than would the head.

Once the lock was doubled to halve its length, the doubled end was woven (approximately one-eighth inch from the bend), using two single-ply strands of commercial sewing thread. As the plait was completed, tapering slightly, the combined distal and root ends were closed inside a small cloth square that was neatly folded to the inside and sewn together to form a "bag" to secure the loose ends. The thread used to sew the bag was comparable to one of the two types of threads used to weave the hair strands at the opposite end.

At the woven end, numerous individual hairs were observed to have broken under the stress of the radical bend. As a result, several strands of comparable length were protruding from the plait, one of which was chosen for closer examination. It was carefully removed from the plait and set aside. Primary investigation revealed three facts. First, the shape of the individual strands was extremely rounded, as opposed to flat or elliptical, a condition generally indicative of the Mongoloid (including Amerindian) groups. Second, the color of the hair strands was a deep mahogany red/brown, which color is not inconsistent with Amerindian genetic types.[4]

Third, in addition to these two items, an interesting anomaly was noted. Scattered throughout the strands of hair were numerous lice egg cases. These appeared to be of two varieties: a smaller, translucent variety and a larger, more opaque type. The presence of this information is certainly not unexpected in view of the debased lifestyle that Osceola had been living during the last three months of his life. After a few months in captivity, even George Catlin remarked to Commissioner of Indian Affairs Carey A. Harris regarding the "modes of life & filthiness" of the Indian prisoners at Fort Moultrie.[5] Although one must accept a certain amount of uncleanliness as a concomitant of the Indians' earlier, outdoor lifestyle, one is nevertheless constrained to remember that the conditions under which the prisoners were forced to exist in captivity were undoubtedly far more degraded ones from their point of view as well.

Following the examination of the plait, the single strand was prepared for closer inspection. This strand, one end of which had been projecting from the plait at the woven end, was carefully removed with a pair of tweezers in order not to disturb the main body of the plait. It was finally cut away from the covered end with a small scissors. The total length of the single removed strand was 5⅜". It was then set on a laboratory slide mount in Permount®, a xylene-soluble mounting medium.

Closer investigation (under 10 ×, 25 ×, and 40 ×) revealed that all of the cuticle layer of the sample strand was missing, which was probably due to bacterial and insect damage that had occurred after the hair had been separated from the head. Without this outer layer or natural hair surface, it became impossible to discern the direction of growth of the hair lock, discuss original treatment of the hair (for example, brushing vs. combing), or discover information regarding oils, pomades, or powders that might have been used on the hair regularly (the use of bear grease, for example, was common among the Creeks). This lack of evidence available on the single strand did not, however, preclude the possibility that an extant cuticle layer might be found on other strands and might be available for analysis during future testing. Still well formed and highly visible, moreover, were the reddish-brown, striated body of the hair and the dark, obvious medulla, both of which formations are also indicative of Mongoloid genetic stock.

Finally, single-fiber samples were removed from each of the three discrete types of materials that had been used to secure the plait. Sample A, a bluish fiber, was taken from the woven end of the plait. Sample B, an elongated brownish fiber, was also recovered from the woven end, where it had been entwined with the first in what appeared to be a hair-weavers knot. Sample C was removed from the covered end of the plait. Results of a separate examination of these textile fibers by Crime Laboratory analyst James G. Luten indicated the following findings.

Sample A, the bluish white fiber from the woven end of the plait, obtained its blue color from dyeing. The fiber, although damaged and deteriorated, appeared to be flax. Sample B, the brownish fiber that had been woven together with Sample A, was apparently undyed, but no determination could be made regarding the fiber's type because of its deteriorated condition. Sample C, a sample of the material that was used to cover the end of the plait, was also a natural fiber and had a brown substance adhering to its entire length. This may have been indicative of dye over the chemical compound used to "weight" the fabric for commercial production, as the fiber was determined to be silk.[6]

This information also tends to support the hypothesis that the plait was prepared in the nineteenth century because of the prevalence of weighted silk fabrics during that era. It also tends to support the hypothesis that Henrietta Weedon prepared the plait, because weighted silk was a well-known ladies' dress fabric.

Louse Egg Case Examination

On 14 August 1986 the plaited hair sample was examined by John Mulrennan, director of the Department of Entomology, Department of Health and Rehabilitative Services, Jacksonville. The examination took place in the conservation laboratory, Bureau of Archaeological Research, Division of Historical Resources, R. A. Gray Building, Tallahassee. Mulrennan had been recommended by the Centers for Disease Control in Atlanta, Georgia, as the Florida expert on lice and lice-borne diseases. He concurred that the translucent cases present in the hair sample were indeed egg sacs of the *Pediculus humanus capitis,* or head louse, as they were firmly attached to the individual shafts of hair. The disparity in sizes among the cases was due simply to their variant stages of desiccation.

Mulrennan also indicated that lice eggs were most commonly found among the hairs around the ears and along the nape of the neck. This information tends to support the earlier hypothesis that the lock was originally a part of the area of longest hair growth on the male Seminole head, the nape of the neck. In addition, the doctor also reported that lice infestations were seldom the result of living in the wild but, rather, were concomitants of uncleanliness in crowded living conditions. In other words, lice need living human hosts and are passed on by living humans. Therefore, it is much more likely that Osceola's lice infestation was the result of his captivity than of his earlier, forest lifestyle. It is also obvious, by virtue of this information, that this infestation had to have taken place while Osceola was still alive to suffer its unpleasant consequences. It is but one more irony in the story of Native Americans that one of the facets of the Indian life considered most reprehensible by whites may well have been a facet created, or at least exacerbated, by those same whites.

11 / Descendents East and West

On 28 February 1838, the *New York Evening Star* reported to the nation: "Indian Captives.—Micanopy and the other Indians who have been confined on Sullivan's Island, were to leave Charleston on the 22d, on the brig Homer, for their destination in the West, via New Orleans."[1] The order had been given to remove the prisoners a month before, on the same day on which Osceola died. Commissioner of Indian Affairs Carey A. Harris sent the instructions to Capt. Pitcairn Morrison, who was still in charge of the prisoners at Fort Moultrie.

> Sir:
> It has been determined by this department that the party of Indians now at Fort Moultrie, with such exceptions as will be provided for below, shall be removed forthwith, to the country assigned them west of the Mississippi River; and you will, therefore, proceed to make every necessary arrangement for that purpose with all possible despatch—the conveyance will be by water as far as practicable, via New Orleans to Fort Gibson where the party will be turned over to Capt. J. R. Stephenson, USA, Disbursing Agent for Creeks and Seminoles West. Should there be other Indians of this tribe who can at the time of the departure of the party be added to it, or join it on the route without too great expense of time and funds, you will send them off also. It is understood that there is a small party at Fort Pike [below

New Orleans], of this description; and that others may be collected at other places—upon these points you will obtain such information as your means will permit.

In carrying the above mentioned determination into effect you will please to observe that it is the intention of the department to retain as prisoners all the Chiefs whose return, if it should take place, to the Seminole Nation east would be attended with danger to the peace and tranquillity of the country—The designation of these individuals is submitted to your judgement, and such as you design ought to be retained in custody you will keep as prisoners with all necessary precaution against escape—The families of these prisoners will be permitted to remain with them—It is believed that Micanopy may with safety go to the West, as he is not considered as within the exception above stated. Oceola, Cloud &c &c certainly are within it—Lieut. J. G. Reynolds, U S Marine Corps will join you with all possible expedition, and will act in this service under your direction—From his business talents and long experience in Emigration I anticipate that you will find in him a valuable assistant—Enclosed is a copy of instructions this day given to Lieut Reynolds—It is presumed that you will give to him the conducting of the party to its destination, and that he will also officiate as Disbursing Officer—He will be furnished by you with all necessary assistance—It is expected that your duties will require your presence in Florida so soon as your health shall be so far established as to enable [you] to resume them—In case of your departure you will make such arrangements as your judgment shall dictate for the safe keeping of the prisoners remaining at Fort Moultrie.

> Very respectfully
> Yr. Most Obt Servt
> (Signed)   C. A. Harris
> Comg.

I certify that this is a true copy.

> (Signed)   Jno. G. Reynolds
> 1st Lieut, U S. M C.
> & Disbg. Agt. Ind. Deptr.

In obedience to this Order I was directed by
Captain Morrison to repair to Fort Pike and
remove such Indians as may be at that post.

> [words blotted out]
> (Signed)   Jno. G. Reynolds

Fort Pike
14th March 1838[2]

The route they took was already an old one. Hundreds, more than a thousand, of their clan and cultural kin had been forced to emigrate since the Creek War had begun in Alabama in 1813. It was the Seminole Trail of Tears, and it would continue for an entire generation longer than that of any of the other Indians of the Southeast, until the end of the Third Seminole War in 1858. In that year would occur the final withdrawal of U.S. troops from Florida, after almost half a century of desultory and open warfare that had nearly bankrupted the territory and materially delayed statehood as most Florida Natives were pushed out of their homelands. In that year would occur the departure of Billy Bowlegs and many of his people from Fort Brooke, on Tampa Bay—the last of Florida's Native people to depart.

Osceola's family and the others held at Fort Moultrie in Charleston Harbor in 1838 were taken by boat down the peninsula of Florida. There is nothing to indicate that any of the war leaders were held back to prevent their becoming a rallying point for further resistance, although this same system of dividing and conquering would be used by the United States in its Indian wars for the rest of the century. The Charleston prisoners were taken around the Florida Keys and across the Gulf of Mexico to one of the two forts below New Orleans: New Orleans Barracks or Fort Pike. New Orleans Barracks, now Jackson Barracks and the headquarters of the Louisiana Army National Guard, received many of the prisoners. Old Jumper and at least two of his sons, James and John, and part of the Jumper family had passed through there already. Old Jumper, Osceola's compatriot, had died there. He was certainly not the only Florida Indian to die there, but their graves were never marked. Part of Jumper's family would remain in Florida, however, and some others would return shortly, sent by the U.S. government to convince more to depart. The plan backfired, however. Instead of convincing others to leave, some of the Jumper family stayed in Florida with their other Panther Clan kin, and in Florida the Jumpers remain to this day. Fort Pike, on the island of Les Petit Coquilles, also received many of the Florida Indians. The tiny fortification, a masonry structure in the style of the Second System forts being constructed all along the coastline of the eastern and southern United States, remains today as a part of the Louisiana state park system.

From Louisiana and the delta of the Mississippi River, the Indians were transshipped to smaller vessels, if such could be obtained, for travel up the river as far as it was navigable. In many instances, however, the prisoners were obliged to walk, with foodstuffs and supplies in wagons behind them. It was a terrible march to Forts Gibson and Smith in the Arkansas Territory, the disbursing point for the Creek and Seminoles into lands promised them as theirs in perpetuity, lands that would, irrespective of that national promise, later become Oklahoma.

Lt. J. Van Horne of the Third Infantry, who was appointed a disbursing agent to General Gibson, the commissary general of subsistence, had been in charge of a party of Seminole prisoners who had been taken over the same route two years earlier. His report stated, all too clearly, the realities of the travel.

> Choctaw Agency, May 23, 1836
> Since my last we have made only about 71 miles. . . . We have had every difficulty to contend with. A constant scene of vexation and toil. About half the party have been and still are sick. Many continue very low and must die. Three dead yesterday. Three this morning. It has rained powerfully every day flooding the streams and making the roads deep and miery. Some places almost impassable. We have been obliged to fasten 10 or 12 yoke of oxen to each wagon in succession and drag them through deep mire for long distances.

The lieutenant's "vexation" with the weather was great, but his vexation with the humans in his charge seems to have been greater. Despite the pain and suffering that had been visited upon them already, he continued,

> these people seem to have been pampered and indulged to such a degree that nothing can satisfy them or equal their extravagant expectations. Their inertness and stubborn immobility exceed all conception. Myself and Mr. Chase my assistant have strained every nerve have shrunk from no toil or difficulties. The Indians have contested every inch of the way and we have been obliged in effect to force them each day from their camp. The great number of those desperately sick is their pleas for delaying. . . .
>
> The wife and daughter of Black Dirt 2nd Chief and Tusteenugge Hago principal warrior have just died. They begged urgently as usual to be allowed to lay by for the day. Col. A. seemed to think the circumstances required it, and much against my will I yielded, when at the conclusion of the interval, I found them obstinately bent on remaining. In the after part of the day it rained powerfully.[3]

As a result of the fact that the U.S. military neither knew nor wanted to understand Maskókî kinship systems, coupled with the fact that so many of the "emigrants" were individuals captured away from their families and camps (as opposed to those entire families that turned themselves in to the U.S. military), the toll of forced removal was even far greater than non-Indians could have known. Clan camps were fragmented. Nuclear families were broken apart. Collateral kinship lines that would have grown old together in the same clan camp or multiclan community were broken apart and forced to live and die without knowing each other again. To this day, relatives in two widely separated states seek the old connections that bound them for thousands of years.

In Indian Territory, much of which would become the U.S. state of Oklahoma within the first decade of the twentieth century, many clans were never able to reassemble. The dislocated "emigrants" clung to their "bands" — that is, to the groups of loose affiliation with which they had been captured or had turned themselves in, and they reassembled along these band lines. This process of fragmentation and reassembly was further enforced by the fact that U.S. government agents paid relocation allotments only to band representatives and required them to account for the individuals for whom the allotments were being paid. As a result, the people for whom the bands were themselves nontraditional were forced to accept and perpetuate a nontraditional system. The bands became fictive clans, and many of the emigrants forsook even the memories of their fragmented birth clans in favor of the critical affiliation with a band that all too frequently was also their only source of hard-money income.

In Florida, the valuable element of physical isolation protected the relative handful of survivors for the rest of the nineteenth century, at least. The peace and isolation, even in such a hostile environment, gave the survivors time to reconfirm the "old ways" and the social systems that buttressed them. Most basic of all, the clan system remained intact and continued to function as a survival mechanism (as it continues to this day). Furthermore, and of critical importance, the traditional systems of polygamy and sororate polygyny reinforced the clan system. Older men who had not been directly involved in the fighting, and younger warriors who had managed to escape capture and removal, took multiple wives, sometimes including sisters and younger women (women well under the traditional marriage age of their late twenties) as partners. As a result, despite a significant infant mortality rate, the birth rate managed to meet or exceed the death rate, and the Florida "Seminoles" did not slowly disappear into oblivion, as state and national predictions had assured white settlers. The most obvious evidence of this process and its success is the fact that "Seminoles," "Creeks," and "Miccosukees" continue to survive to this day in Florida as sovereign tribes and are recognized as such by the U.S. government.

The non-Indian world learned very little about the families that had, with fierce determination, remained in their homelands. The few government agents and proselytizing missionaries who were able to contact the Florida Indians in peace in the last quarter of the nineteenth century obtained limited information, and oftentimes that information was deliberately misleading.[4] Indian distrust of white authority ran deep and continues to run deep to the present day. The twentieth-century demographic boom in south Florida that began in the 1920s would once again threaten the very survival of the Florida Indians, however, and they struggle today against the myriad insidious elements of non-Indian cultural encroachment and political assaults in what I have characterized as the Fourth Seminole War.

But, despite what they have or have not told non-Indians in the past, their own memories of ancestors and of families ripped apart remains stronger than non-Indians could realize. In the case of Osceola and his descendents, significant pieces of information remain.

The Southeastern Descendents

In Florida today, three separate family lines lay claim to an Osceola connection. In Seminole terms, each carries its own internal potential for validity, and each family has carried and transmitted this information for all the generations since the wars. In addition to these lines, which continue to flourish inside the Seminole Tribe of Florida today, two other lines of Osceola's relatives have their genesis in Florida but leave it too soon. They should be included here nevertheless. One ends almost as abruptly as it begins. The other is at least as strange as the many other stories surrounding the life of the charismatic Osceola.

Line 1

The first line is that represented in the late nineteenth century by Charlie Osceola (ca. 1823–1898) and his wife, Nancy (ca. 1815–ca. 1898), known also as Old Nancy. This was the principal line investigated by Sturtevant in his article "Notes on Modern Seminole Traditions of Osceola," although he "tended to believe" that the surname was only an honorific and implied no genetic affiliation.[5] The evidence, I believe, supports the opposite conclusion.

Charlie and Nancy had at least five sons and two daughters (that is, they had seven children who survived to adulthood). Each child took a surname, and they took the same surname, "Osceola." Taking a surname was atypical for Florida Indians of the later nineteenth century, and finding a biological family in which all the siblings used the *same* surname was atypical as well. Nevertheless, naming traditions supported attachment to names of power, that is, to names earlier attached to individuals publicly considered to have been powerful. The larger Maskókî tradition also contained a well-established mechanism for transmitting such names across descending generations.[6] In the second of the three Florida lines, we will see this process in action.

Minnie Moore Willson, who spoke with some Florida Indians on a fairly regular basis over a period of years, particularly with members of the "Tallahassee band" (a group that included Old Tallahassee and the Florida Chupco family), reported that Charlie Osceola was the half brother of Osceola.[7] What appear to be contradictory assertions by other reporters that a son of Charlie was a nephew of Osceola are, nonetheless, reconcilable if one takes into account the Maskókî kinship system.[8] That is, if Charlie Osceola and Osceola the warrior were related because they had the same mother, then they were brothers in the Maskókî system, because they were the same clan, because clan membership is transmitted through the mother, and kinship is conferred and gauged by clan affiliation. Consequently, a son of Charlie would indeed be a nephew of Osceola. Furthermore, men who had the same mother would be clan brothers to each other as well, irrespective of whether they also had the same fathers.

On the basis of the information presented in chapter 2, there is little doubt that Osceola's mother, Polly Copinger, came into Florida and was still young enough, and was in Florida long enough, to have taken one or several more partners and to have given birth to other children. We know enough about Charley Osceola to establish a plausible scenario. Polly Copinger was born about 1770 and probably lived until sometime after 1838. She reached Florida with her son, Billy Powell—later Osceola—about 1814, when she was only in her forties. Given the childbearing span of other women of her culture, it would not have been unusual for her to have borne children at any time during the next twenty years. Other documented children have been discussed in chapter 2.

An Indian "friend" told Smithsonian ethnographer Bill Sturtevant that Charlie's mother was Bird Clan and that his father was Snake. Indeed, Charlie's Indian "name" was *Fos'yaholî*, which appears to corroborate this. *Fos'* is the contraction of *foóswa* or bird in Maskókî, and *yaholî* is a ceremonial position, a wolf singer, the same position given to Asse Yahola, or Osceola, at his first Green Corn Ceremony (see chapter 2). The position of *yaholî* was one occupied by many men over time, however, and implies no other connection. The difference in the final vowel sound—î versus a—can be accounted for in two ways: by the slight differences in pronunciation that occur among clans and by the orthographic differences among hearers and writers in English.

The Seminole Tribe has recorded that the children of Charlie and Old Nancy were (at least):

Lucy Osceola (1872–1928), who married (1) Tom Tiger and (2) Willie Tiger
Robert Osceola/*Katsamatalki* (ca. 1870–1914), father of Cory Osceola
Charlie Osceola/*E-faw-le-hadjo* (1843–1914), who married Nancy of Deer Clan
Tommy Osceola (?–1919), who married but had no children of his own
Jim or Old Jimmy Osceola (1852–1947), who married twice, to an Otter and a Bird
Little Nancy Osceola (1870–1929), who married Billy Conapatchie/Cornpatch
John Osceola (1868–1939), who married an Otter Clan woman.[9]

Robert (ca. 1870–1914) was the father of the well-known Cory Osceola, who died before Sturtevant did his fieldwork in Florida. Little Nancy was the mother of Josie Billie, who was the "friend" and paid confidante of Sturtevant. Josie and Ingraham/Ingram, one of his brothers, were "strong medicine" (both "good" and "bad") and, as such, holders of much esoteric information. Nevertheless, the story persists among the Florida Seminoles that Josie deliberately misled Sturtevant, on the premise of safeguarding much of their esoteric information. This is a complex subject, as Josie was a particularly complex person, and does not appear to bear further on the current research.

Line 2

The second line that may be a collateral line of descent in the same clan as Osceola is that of a daughter of Old Tommie Tiger, Bird Clan (personal name unknown), whose husband was Billy Martin (?–1914). The possibility of association exists here partly because of the ceremonial title Asse Yahola, which has been reserved by, and passed down within, this family to the present day. Coupled with the fact that this is a Bird Clan line, there well may be a clan connection between it and Osceola, who was Bird Clan, but the specific point of connection is unclear. The mother of Mrs. Billy Martin was Martha, of Bird Clan, whose own mother was a sister of Old Tallahassee (ca. 1815–ca. 1910). Martha's mother and Old Tallahassee, consequently, were also of Bird Clan, as was their own mother. It is through this woman, the mother of Martha and Old Tallahassee, personal name unknown, that the connection to Osceola probably occurred. Perhaps this woman was a biological sister or a clan sister of Polly Copinger.

The father of Old Tallahassee and Martha's mother was Icho hadjo chupco, Deer Clan, who died in 1817 in a battle with whites at the Suwannee River. One of Icho hadjo chupco's sisters was Mary (Chupco), Deer Clan, who was the second or young wife of Billy Bowlegs (II). (See figure 19.) Mary went to Indian Territory with the Bowlegs party in 1858. Another of her brothers, Fixico hadjo chupco, aka Long Jack (see figure 20), also emigrated to Indian Territory in the Bowlegs party, along with his wife, who was Eliza Bowlegs, the daughter of Mary Chupco and Billy Bowlegs (II), and one child. Their descendents remain in Oklahoma today, although the surname "Bowlegs" no longer attaches.

One of the sisters of Bowlegs (I), Panther Clan, and maternal uncle to Billy Bowlegs (II), had as husband "Solachoppo"/Chupco, aka Long Tom. This woman and Bowlegs (I) were also brother and sister to "King" Payne. Their father was Cowkeeper (*mikkî(t) anópî(t),* in Hitchiti, a "keeper" of domesticated animals, including "cows") (ca. 1712–1785), and their mother, a woman of Panther Clan, was a daughter of "Emperor Brim."

This sister of Bowlegs (I) and Solachoppo had a daughter, possibly known as Mena, who took as husband Old Jumper, the father of Jim and John Jumper who emigrated to Indian Territory, as well as father to those Jumpers who returned to Florida. Old Jumper died en route, as mentioned earlier, and the Jumper line continues today as Jumpers in Florida and in the Brown/Davis family in Oklahoma. One of Mena's brothers is known to history as Micanopy, also Panther Clan, and another sister took as husband Philip, called Emathla (a title of respect). Philip is recalled among the Indians as a Spaniard and as the father of Coacoochee or Wild Cat. (Osceola himself is also recalled by the Indians as "a Spanish man." See chapter 2.) One of Coacoochee's sisters, not his fraternal twin but another sister known to later generations as Grandmother Smith, was born about 1825 and died in Florida in 1917. She was Wildcat Clan (which was later subsumed by Panther), as was Coacoochee. The modern descendents of this line in Florida include Morgan Smith, Frank Shore, Sam Jones, Laura Mae Osceola, and Betty May Tiger Jumper. This family tree has produced many excellent blossoms.

Line 3

The third line that may have genetic associations with Osceola is proposed here solely on the basis of information provided by one of the most respected Florida medicine men of the twentieth century.[10] Asked some years ago by another Seminole citizen which Florida family he considered the most likely to have been related to Osceola, this man gave the question much thought and finally responded, "The Jimmie family." He provided no

YOUNG WIFE OF BILLY BOWLEGS.

Figure 19. Young wife of Billy Bowlegs. *Harper's Weekly,* 12 June 1858. (Courtesy of the Florida Photographic Collection, State Archives, Florida Department of State, Tallahassee, Florida.)

LONG JACK, BILLY BOWLEGS'S LIEUTENANT.

Figure 20. Fixico hadjo chupco or "Long Jack." (Courtesy of the Florida Photographic Collection, State Archives, Florida Department of State, Tallahassee, Florida.)

further explanation. The oldest tribal record of this line begins with Lucy Miami (?–1914), who was Wind Clan, and this may have been the impetus for the medicine man's response. She was married to Old Lazy Jim, aka Doctor Jim (ca. 1850–1914), clan unknown. Osceola's clan grandfather (maternal great-uncle), Peter McQueen, who spent some years in Florida and died in the state, was married to Betsy Durant of Wind Clan. The Jimmie family has carried, and continues to carry, a tradition of a relationship to Osceola, but nothing more specific than that. If Wind Clan is indeed that connection, then the family's descent may be from a daughter of Betsy Durant and Peter McQueen who remained in Florida when Betsy returned to Alabama after Peter's death and married one of Peter's nephews. Alternatively, the family connection may be through Jim Boy, an English name for the one-time "war chief" of Peter McQueen.[11] That English name has passed down through this family in various convolutions at least since the middle of the nineteenth century.

Line 4

The denouement of the story of one of Osceola's nephews, Nikkanochee, is far too short (see figure 21). He was a son of one of Osceola's sisters, possibly named Maunee, and the old Micco of Econchatti. We know from his own information (albeit transmitted through Andrew Welch, the sensationalist) that his mother died prior to or during 1835. From chapter 2, we recall that Welch, the English physician, adopted him. He returned to England with the Welch family in 1840; Welch was ready to go home, and he was concerned for the safety of the boy in Florida, where feelings ran so highly against the Indians. In London, Nikkanochee frequently visited the Egyptian Gallery where George Catlin's collection of Indian portraits, drawings, and artifacts was on exhibit. There, the famous artist painted his portrait and recorded Welch's story, which Catlin accepted.[12] A life cast of his head was taken by Mr. Donovan, principal of the London Phrenological Institution, King William Street, in the Strand. In addition, "a splendid painting of the Young Prince, similar to the frontispiece, has been made by Mr. Wilkin—which is now on exhibition at the Royal Academy, Trafalgar Square."[13] Welch wrote his *Narrative* in 1841, when his ward was still only eleven years old, and we have no further information concerning his later life. Consequently, we have no way of knowing whether he ever chose to, or was able to, return to his people. Once again, however, there is nothing implausible in his story.

Line 5

Among the many other fascinating stories connected to Osceola's life, there is yet another that begins in Florida, and although it has no satisfactory

Figure 21. Oceola Nikkanochee. Lithograph by Day and Haghe, London. Published in Andrew Welch, *A Narrative of the Early Days and Remembrances of Oceola Nikkanochee, Prince of Econchatti . . .* (1841), frontispiece.

ending, it deserves to be included here for its unique, and certainly dramatic, value, if nothing else. It is the newspaper story of a man who died "of very intemperate habits," in New York in 1877 and may have been a clan nephew of Osceola and possibly even a brother of Fos'yaholî, aka Charlie Osceola. In late-nineteenth-century rhetorical fashion, the *New York Times* article begins, "A ROMANCE OF THE SEMINOLES. Death of a Nephew of the Great Seminole Chief—A Curious History of Savage and Civilized Life. Osceola Cooper, a man who claimed to be a nephew of Osceola, the renowned Chief of the Seminole Indians, died suddenly yesterday of acute disease of the kidneys, accelerated by other aliments, at No. 35 Bond-street, a lodging house."

The reporter acknowledged that history did not record Osceola's having had a brother, but we have already seen that Osceola's fame eclipsed that of all the other members of his family, both nuclear and extended, and we now have some better idea of how many relatives there were and may have been. Friends of the dead man averred that "he [Osceola] had one [brother], several years his junior, who was adopted by Solomon Cooper, of New York, at the close of the Seminole war."

According to the story, "A small band of Seminoles, a remnant of Osceola's scattered tribe, encountered, a few days succeeding the capture of their chief, a hostile party of Indians, from whom they rescued Mr. Cooper [a white man]." No reason is given for the presence of Cooper in the area, unless he was a soldier, settler, or sutler, and the report says that, at first, Osceola's people were also inclined to treat Cooper as a prisoner. They were, the article asserts, also fleeing from hostiles at this point. But because Osceola's people were "hostile" to the United States, the only Indians who were "hostile" to them were those Indian friendlies who were allied with the U.S. troops. If Indian friendlies had Cooper with them, then the white man should not have needed rescuing. This portion of the story (among others) may be confused.

There is, however, one very short window in which this incident might have occurred: between 21 October and 30 November 1837, the date when Osceola was taken prisoner and the date when his family surrendered themselves at Fort Mellon at his instructions. Furthermore, the notation that Osceola's brother was still a boy indicates that he must have been less than fourteen years old (or he would have gone through his rite of passage into manhood and would have been traveling as a warrior with the men). Consequently, he was probably born about 1824 or later. At any rate, Osceola's brother interceded on Cooper's behalf, and "the half-breed Indian boy" became greatly attached to Cooper and was subsequently adopted by him and taken with him to New York. The reporter gives no reason for describing the boy as a "half-breed" either.

Young Solomon Cooper, Jr. (named after his adoptive father), eventually inherited considerable property, went to Barcelona, Spain, and there married "a woman of good family." Their first child, Osceola (the subject of the obituary), and a daughter were born in Spain. The family soon returned to the United States and "settled on a farm near the homestead of the Greeley family at Chappaqua. Cooper, Jr., our Osceola's putative half brother, became famous there as an 'Indian doctor,' and through his professional exertions, gained considerable wealth."[14]

Sometime after 1861 Dr. Cooper, Jr., joined the Confederate army and reportedly was killed in battle. His son, Osceola Cooper, unaware of his father's actions, ran away from college and served in the Union army as a courier for Gen. W. T. Sherman. Following the war, Osceola Cooper found that his mother had relocated within New York City and learned from her of his father's death.

The sister of Osceola Cooper married a Colonel Marshall, CSA, who died at Pavonia, New Jersey, about 1872. Mrs. Marshall died two years later. The Marshalls left two children, Jennie and Willie Osceola Marshall, to the guardianship of their uncle Osceola Cooper, who placed them in the home of a Mrs. Post in Pavonia. "About six months ago Alfreta Powell, an Indian woman, who claimed Osceola Cooper as her brother, but who was only recognized by him as an adopted sister, surreptitiously removed little Willie Osceola Marshall from Mrs. Post's house and disappeared with the boy." Up to the time of his death on Thursday, 2 August, Osceola Cooper had been unable to locate the child. It was believed that Mr. Cooper left "property, including real estate, amounting in value to $50,000."[15]

What the reporter composed here is a patchwork quilt containing numerous errors of fact. Amazingly enough, however, the basic facts of this story as they relate to the Florida War are plausible, and there is a significant amount of peripheral and later information that appears to substantiate parts of it. If Osceola's mother formed another union, or more than one, during the period 1815 to, say, 1830, and there is no reason not to accept this, then the boy whom Solomon Cooper took back to New York could have been between seven and thirteen years old. Other events in the life of the boy and his own later son, however, tighten the time frame even more. If Polly Copinger had a son in 1824, who was therefore thirteen years old when he was taken to New York, then he, as the man Solomon Cooper, Jr., could have married in his nineteenth year, in 1846, and produced a son, Osceola Cooper, in 1847, who could have been sufficiently old enough to serve in the American Civil War, but young enough, at only fourteen years of age, to serve only as a drummer, a powder monkey, or a courier.

To comply with the story as presented, however, Solomon Cooper would have to have traveled all the way to Spain and back—and found a wife in the midst of the trip (as a seaman, a la John Bemo?)—and would have been in his forties when he was killed in action. Osceola Cooper died in 1877 after a short life of "intemperate habits," at only about thirty years of age. Osceola Cooper's sister, Mrs. Marshall, would also have to have died at a very young age, in her late twenties, although her husband, who was old enough to have attained the rank of colonel in the Confederate army, would have been significantly older than she.

The basic relationships in this story are partly supported by the U.S. census of 1860, which shows Family No. 39 living at New Castle, Westchester, New York: Cooper, Solomon, fifty years old, an "Indian Doctor," with real estate valued at $15,000 and personal resources of $860.00 (not the $50,000 reported in the newspaper article, but a respectable worth nonetheless). He states that he was born in New York, but this is not definitive. Solomon's wife, Eliza, is thirty-eight years old and states that she was born in New York as well. In addition, there are seven women and one man in the household with relationships to each other and to the Coopers unspecified, among them Margaret Powell, eighty years old, and Mary Powell, twenty-three. Benona Cooper, a twenty-year-old female and probably either a sister or a daughter to Solomon, is included. A Chevors(?) Cooper, a thirty-year-old male, is also present with his two children, P. Cooper, a fifteen-year-old female, and Osceola Cooper, listed as a ten-year-old *female*. He could be a brother or a son, but, if a son, then Solomon must have had an earlier wife.[16]

A decade later, on 20 June 1870, the U.S. census of 1870 lists the remnants of the previous group as Family No. 11, living at Fordham, Township of West Farms, Westchester, New York (Chappaquah was in Westchester). Eliza Cooper is now fifty years old and listed by the enumerator as a "Mulatto." Solomon, reportedly killed in the Civil War in the intervening decade, is not listed. Eliza is listed as the head of the household, which also includes her daughter, identified only as "F. C.," and F. C's husband, the erstwhile Col. William Marshall. F. C. is twenty years old, and Marshall is forty. Their children, Virginia and Willie, are three and one years, respectively. The Marshall family is listed as "white." Eliza's child, Osceola Cooper, now accurately identified as a male and as almost twenty years old, has a young wife, Sarah, eighteen years old, with him. Osceola and Sarah are shown as "Mulatto." Again, the entire family is listed as having been born in New York, but census data are frequently undependable.[17]

This certainly seems to be the family outlined in the obituary article that will appear a short seven years later. Osceola Cooper is younger than we might expect, but given the vagaries of census enumerations, he still would have been close to thirty years old at his death.

In the process of attempting to clarify this fascinating story further, however, an entirely new element came to light, and it adds yet another dimension of pathos to the story. The *New York Herald* of 2 August 1870 provided the following.

The Williamsburg Suicide
Another Sensation Exploded

Notwithstanding the extravagant intimations of "foul play," as set forth in a sensational morning paper, in connection with the suicide of Sarah Cooper, at Williamsbridge, Westchester County, on the 24th ult., the belief that she died by her own hands exists in the minds of all those most familiar with the circumstances attendant upon the finding and examination of the body. It was ascertained yesterday from Sergeant Steers, of the Tremont police, that Osceola Cooper, the husband of the deceased, after discovering the body of his wife suspended from the rafters of the house, hastened to the police station and announced the fact. Having accompanied Cooper to his abode, a short distance from Williamsbridge, the Sergeant was conducted to an upper room, where he made a thorough survey of the premises. The body was still hanging, suspended by a small shawl, and with the feet some distance from the floor. Close by was a soap box, which deceased had evidently stood upon while adjusting the fatal noose, and which apparently served as a platform from which she stepped into mid-air. After cutting her down the Sergeant examined the neck, and the marks here visible, together with other unmistakable evidences, convinced him that it was a clear case of self-murder, and in his opinion he was fully sustained by the verdict of the Coroner's jury.

The remains were subsequently interred at Woodlawn Cemetery, and had not been disturbed up to noon yesterday. It appears that the deceased woman's relatives disliked Cooper and his family on account of their aboriginal extraction, and on Friday they obtained a permit from Coroner Bathgate to exhume the body that it might be examined by a physician of their acquaintance. It was agreed upon by the relatives of the deceased that they should exhume the remains on Saturday, the attendance of the Coroner being requested on the occasion. In accordance with his promise that official proceeded to the cemetery at the appointed time, and having waited several hours without seeing the parties to whom he granted the permit, returned home, determined not to be "fooled" a second time.

Instead of Cooper having disappeared from the neighborhood, he called at the Tremont station house yesterday afternoon, and having indignantly exhibited the sensational newspaper alluded to, ruefully inquired as to what steps he might take in order to obtain redress for the malicious imputation it contained.[18]

This is a sad and fascinating story. Sarah Cooper hanged herself. A scant month after the census taker had enumerated the family, she had found her life so unbearable that she chose to end it. The cause of her profound disquiet seems to have been the pressures placed upon her by the bigotry of her own family. This certainly could explain the next seven years of her young husband's "intemperate habits." Two years after the death of his wife, Osceola had to deal with the death of his brother-in-law, William Marshall, and in another two years "F. C.," Osceola's sister, was also gone.

His mother, Eliza, outlived them. She is still living in 1900 and possibly in 1910. One Eliza Cooper is living with her son, William F., a locomotive engineer, in Kansas in 1900. She is shown as eighty-one years old (born June 1818) and reports having had four children, of whom all four are still living. This is the right birth date, but includes two children about whom we have not been informed. In 1910, an Eliza Cooper is living in Iowa, boarding with a seemingly unrelated family. She is eighty-three, a widow, and has her "own income." She reports having had five children, of whom three still are living. This may not be the same woman.[19]

Of an "Alfreta Powell" there is no trace. She does not appear in U.S. census records of the period anywhere. She does not appear on the Dawes Rolls of the Creeks in Oklahoma. Nevertheless, both a Margaret and a Mary Powell were living with Solomon and his extended family in 1860. The newspaper account says that the Powell woman who took Willie Osceola Marshall called herself a sister, but was recognized by him only as an adopted sister. This accords with the census information. Margaret Powell was eighty years old in 1870. She certainly could have passed away by 1877. "Alfreta" (Mary?) took the child from the care of a woman in Pavonia, New Jersey. Although there are several cities of the same name, the most likely Pavonia is now a part of greater Jersey City, but a search of the records indicates that there are no relevant deaths or wills recorded.[20]

One (more) intriguing detail in the original *New York Times* 1877 article reports that two years prior to his death, Osceola Cooper visited "the tribe of his father in Oregon"! Such an error would be sufficient to discredit the entire story were it not for the other names and details and for an entire recap of the story of Osceola, correctly placing him in Florida and included in the original article but not included here. Was "Oregon" a simple reporter's error? Did Osceola Cooper really visit "his father's tribe"—in Oklahoma? Which relatives might he have found or what arrangements might he have made to reconnect his family to that of the war leader Osceola? Why does the article identify Alfreta Powell as a sister or even an adopted sister? And, finally, what connection might this story have to the story of a "white" boy adopted by Lucy Powell, one of Osceola's sisters, in Indian Territory? More of this is below.

The (Removed) Oklahoma Descendents

The McQueen Line

Among the Muscogee (Creek) and Seminole Nations of Okalahoma, the McQueen family is represented by several lines. Milly, Nancy, and Tallassee McQueen, the three daughters of Peter McQueen and Betsy Durant, emigrated to Indian Territory with their communal husband, Yagee, who was a son of Menawa or Big Warrior the Micco of Tuckabatchee (Alabama). He was also known in Indian Territory as Captain Checotah Yargee. Tallassee's children with Yagee, if she had any, are undocumented. The children of Nancy and Yagee (spelled with the anomalous English "r" in Oklahoma) were Lucinda Yargee/Yarger, Mitchell Yarger, and a daughter who married into the Asbal family. Milly or Malee and Yagee had (at least) Louise Yargee, John Yargee, Muscogee Yargee, and a son who died en route to Indian Territory. Louise had a son and a daughter, with whom her line seems to have ended. John had children, and they had children. Muscogee married Joshua Ross, a Cherokee and nephew of Lewis and John Ross, Cherokee leaders. Many of the descendents of these lines are living in Oklahoma today and are enrolled in the Muscogee (Creek) Nation.

When Betsy Durant returned to Alabama following Peter's death, she married Willy McQueen, a son of a brother of Peter McQueen, possibly either his brother Bob (although he was cited by Tom Woodward as having been "a very old man" when Woodward first met him) or Fulunny (ca'lánî or yellow hair). Betsy and Willy had (at least) Sophia McQueen, Muscogee McQueen, and two or three sons. Sophia married a white man, Robert W. Stewart, and her children have carried on the McQueen surname in Oklahoma, as well as intermarrying with the Creek families of Buck, McCosar, and Faulkner.

The Powell Line

Several things are known about the life of William Powell after the split that sent Polly Copinger and her son, Billy Powell, into Florida in 1814 along with members of her clan family. First, we know that William turned eastward and stopped at the Chattahoochee River in Georgia, in the middle of Creek Country, near West Point and then Coweta. Second, we have a

248 / Chapter 11

census document indicating that he was living with three females there in 1832. Third, we know that he finally left the Southeast and migrated to Indian Territory in 1838. This information has been discussed earlier in chapter 2. We have no reason to believe that Osceola was his only child; in fact, there is much reason to believe that he did have other children.

The evidence indicates that William Powell or Powel had at least three wives, and possibly four, at least three of them Creek women and, possibly, all clan sisters. In his case, however, he seems to have taken his wives consecutively rather than collectively. His first wife was the "pretty little woman" with whom Benjamin Hawkins found him in 1796 (see chapter 2). William, born about 1777, was not quite twenty years old when he established himself in this part of the Creek country, and with this first wife he had two daughters. One was Lucy Powel or Lucy *hutkî* (white Lucy, probably because she was half white). This would have been the child whom Hawkins mentioned. The other was Martha Powell, aka Lucy *laní* or Larney (probably blond Lucy). Both children would have been born between 1794 and 1797.

With Polly Copinger, William Powell had at least three children. Probably the first was a son, Billy Powell, born about 1804, who would be known to the world as Osceola. Another was a daughter, possibly known as Maunee, who became the wife of old Econchatti Micco, the pacifist, and the mother of Osceola Nikkanochee. She died prior to 1835 in Florida and almost certainly could have left other children behind. A second daughter became the wife of Yaha hadjo, who fought alongside Osceola in the Second Seminole War. She was quite possibly the mother of the child who would later be known as John Douglas Bemo (of whom more below). Yaha hadjo was imprisoned with Osceola and transported to Indian Territory. She certainly could have had other children and probably was the sister who was imprisoned with her husband and brother in Fort Marion and Fort Moultrie and subsequently transported to Indian Territory as well.

Following the family split that impelled Polly Copinger and her son southward into Florida with the family group headed by Peter McQueen, William Powell and his two eldest daughters, as mentioned earlier, traveled eastward to West Point and Coweta. With a Creek woman of Coweta, William had at least two more daughters, Hepsy Powell, born about 1824, and Priscilla or Silla Powell, born about 1826. In the 1832 Creek census, we find William and three females living together and his two older daughters living individually beside him (see chapter 2). After almost a quarter century of relative peace in that area, William and his four daughters once again became caught up in a war with whites, the (Second) Creek War of 1836. This time, however, they did not follow other resisters into Florida but rather moved westward to join relatives already established in Indian Territory. Hepsy's memories of their emigration do not mention a mother who traveled with them, and it is likely that she had passed away prior to their move.

Once in Indian Territory, William Powell seems to disappear from historical view. It is certainly possible that he found another Creek wife, or even a white wife, and had other children. When he emigrated in 1838, he would have been around sixty years old. Thus far, however, no information has been found to document his later life.

Hepsy, his daughter by the Coweta woman, married, first, a "Homarty," undoubtedly a variant of Emarthee, itself an English corruption of *Emathla*, a Maskókî term of respect, and, second, a Leader/Leeder. It appears that she died prior to the creation of the Dawes Rolls. It may also be that her second family (if there was one) is on the rolls of the Chickasaw Nation, because the Leader/Leeder surname is well known among the Chickasaws.

Her sister, Silla, became the wife of Sam Checote (1821–1899) (var. Checotah, Chocote), who was chosen as principal chief of the (removed) Muscogee (Creeks) several times before the American Civil War. Sam and Silla (his first wife) had five children: Rachel (1867/70–1900), Hettie (1873–?), Martha (1855–1901), Melissa (d. young), and Martin (1859–1899).[21] In 1867 a tribal roll indicated that Sam and Silla were still living together, and Martha and Martin were with them. Sometime between that year and 1874, Silla died, and Sam took another partner, Lizzie, with whom he had at least two children, both daughters, who also had children. In the 1882 Creek tribal roll, Samuel Checote is sixty-one years old and living alone. Several of his children, along with their own children, are living together in another town. Each of these children had offspring in Indian Territory whose own descendents remain in Oklahoma to this day.

Martha Powell, daughter of William Powell and his first wife, the "pretty little Indian woman," married Noble Perryman in Indian Territory. Although both partners died before the Dawes Rolls were created, a daughter, Mollie, was enrolled as a full-blood Creek, Roll No. 2698. Her husband, Ceasar Rogers, also a full-blood, was Dawes Creek Roll No. 2697.

Lucy Powell, sister of Martha by the same mother, does not appear on the Creek or Seminole Dawes Rolls. We know nothing of her husband or any biological family.[22] Information does exist, however, concerning one other individual who was an adopted part of her family, and once again the ephemeral details are tantalizing. They are provided, this time, by Bishop Orrie Tuggle who earlier provided useful information concerning Osceola's sister Hepsy. Tuggle is making notes to himself concerning a sermon delivered to the Creek Baptists on 12 September 1879 by "Bro[ther] John McIntosh." McIntosh is the grandson of William McIntosh, the Indian who had been executed by Creek resistance fighters in Georgia for signing a treaty with the whites. Tuggle is unable to understand anything McIntosh is saying, but knows that the sermon is based on the Biblical text, "Ye have not chosen me, but I have chosen you" and calls the sermon "magnetic and eloqiuent." He continues:

> Osceola the Seminole chief killed the whites—& here sat John Powell—a white man raised by Lucy Powell, Osceola's sister. His parents were a Spaniard & English woman & they died when he was a baby—He lives among the Seminoles, is a Baptist, an interpreter & an [e]x[h]orter.
>
> Osceola's sister raising an orphan white baby to preach & sing to the Indians the white man's religion. He loves to sing & sang one of Levi Mitchells songs—(a Creek poet, who died in Mch 1879 & who made many beautiful songs, words & tunes) at close of Bro John's sermon—
>
> (Get the song)
>
> Powell is about 35—has blue eyes—roman nose, light curly hair, medium height, stout built, & wore today a loose striped blouse—like a sack coat, wide colar & ruffles all around the edge of entire coat. He has married a Creek woman & after her death married his present wife—a Seminole, & lives in Canadian [on the Canadian River] near John Jumper.[23]

A page or so further on Tuggle left space to include the words to one of Levi Mitchell's songs but apparently never obtained them. Nevertheless, he provides pertinent material for the present investigations.

One scenario is that John Powell is the son and last child of William Powell with a fourth wife, Creek or white, in Indian Territory. Powell immigrated to Indian Territory in 1838, and Tuggle judges that John is about thirty-five years old, in which case he was born about 1844. He further believes that the young man, John Powell, is white, but this is not a universal view. On the Seminole Dawes Rolls created in Indian Territory in 1898, John Powell is "non" (non-Indian) in one family and a full blood in another.[24] Such discrepancies are not unusual on the Dawes Rolls, however, and may have been the result of racial stereotyping on the part of the Dawes commissioners or the result of the way John Powell, certainly a mixed blood, was imaged by his relatives.

Another and more fascinating scenario is that the John Powell who was adopted by Lucy Powell was somehow connected to the family of Solomon

Cooper, Jr., and Osceola Cooper. The single clue to this possibility lies in Tuggle's report that John's parents were "a Spaniard & English woman & they died when he was a baby—." Tuggle had not been in Indian Territory very long. Surely he got this tidbit from Hepsy, Lucy, or John himself. The story of Solomon Cooper, Jr., as reported in the *New York Times* article in 1877 says that Cooper, Jr., the brother of the war leader Osceola, went to Spain and married there and that his first two children were born there. Tuggle's estimation makes John Powell older than Willie Osceola Powell would have been, but we have no idea on what Tuggle based his estimation, other than his own perception.

John Powell married, first, a Creek woman with whom he does not appear to have had children. With his second wife, Melissa, John had three children: Sophrona (1873–1899); Willie Powell (1874–1898); and James (1873–ca. 1901). Sophrona married into the Cosar family and had offspring. She and her husband and at least one child were enrolled on the Dawes Roll of the Seminoles.

Willie Powell, son of John Powell and Melissa, was twenty-four years old in July of 1898 and living alone near Sasakwa, soon to be Seminole County, Oklahoma. Within three years, however, Willie had had offspring with two partners in the course of one short and one continuing relationship. With Cinda (half blood, born 1865) he had a daughter, Hannah (1896–1904). With "Hoktoche Cotcha" (*hóktochî*, little girl, and *gatcha*, Panther, in Maskókî), he had a son, George Powell, born 31 July 1901. These two children were born early enough to be enumerated on the Dawes Rolls. Subsequently, Willie and Hoktoche had a total of six boys and four or five girls, among whom were Dave, John, Shorty, Ramsey, William, and Bobby Lee Powell (1932–ca. 1994). According to family history, Willie was abusive to his sons and especially to the one who was a young teenager in 1933. One day the boy followed his father to the outhouse, waited for him to go in, and leveled a shotgun at him and fired.

James married Lizzie (1870–1899) and had two children, "Cheparney" (*chebán*, son/little boy, born ca. 1895) Powell and Jennie Powell (born ca. 1896), both of whom were enrolled as Seminoles by the Dawes commissioners. It may be a complete coincidence, but it is interesting to see the names "Willie" and "Jennie" occur in this particular family.

The Powell family in Oklahoma today has preserved the information that Melissa, second wife of John Powell, was in Tusekia Hadjo Band. The family has not been able to preserve the names of either John Powell's clan or his band. They do recall, however, that the current adult Powells are the seventh generation removed from Osceola. That tells us that there are three generations of ancestors above John Powell for whom we have not yet accounted. Without further hard information, it is possible to speculate end-lessly on the connections.

One final piece of information is offered here only for its interest. In 1998, during the devastating forest fires that burned so much of south and central Florida, one of Osceola's Powell family descendents was among the Oklahoma firefighters who volunteered to come to Florida and help save its forests and white men's houses. He was proud, he said, to be able to per-form this service for what he still thinks of as his ancestral home.

The Bemo Line

In chapter 2 we began the story of John Douglas Bemo (ca. 1824–1890), a nephew of Osceola (see figure 22). We return to the story here because the Bemo family is a large one that continues in Oklahoma to the present day and maintains the tradition of its association to Osceola.

As we saw earlier, John Douglas Bemo was a Seminole Indian and the nephew of Osceola. In 1834, when he was about ten years old, he was car-ried away from his home in Florida. One of his abductors was a man named Jean Bemeau, from whom the boy received his name. He was taken to sea for eight years. In 1842 his ship made the port of Philadelphia, and while there he visited the [Presbyterian] Mariner's Church and met the pastor, Rev. Orson Douglas. The reverend reported that Bemo was greatly con-cerned about the persecution of the Seminole Tribe at the hands of the gov-ernment and expressed a strong desire to return to and serve his unhappy people.

Bemo was received into the church and plans were made to fit him to teach and preach to the Seminole people in their western home. Mr. Douglas in September 1842 "put him into the best schools our city affords, so that all the instruction needful to prepare him to be a blessing to his people had been furnished. He is so desirous to do them good that his mind is bent on returning" to them in the fall of 1843, "to live or die with them & for them." It seems to us a singu-lar providence, that, while they are so prejudiced against the whites, one of their number should be raised up of God for their welfare. When Osceola died at the fort near Charleston, John was present and sent word by the warriors that so soon as they ceased fighting he would 'return & be their chief.' It is the Rev. Orson Douglas who is writing . . . for assistance in sending John Bemo to the Seminole Na-tion in the West; he offers to take the Indian to Washington for the commissioner to interview him.[25]

Figure 22. John Douglas Bemo, clan nephew of Osceola. (Courtesy of the Florida Photographic Collection, State Archives, Florida Department of State, Tallahassee, Florida.)

That the boy who would be known henceforth as John Douglas Bemo was, indeed, a nephew of Osceola seems credible. As a man, he told the story himself. We do not have to rely on second- or third-hand reports. If he was also a nephew because he was the son of one of Osceola's biological or clan sisters and the warrior Yaha hadjo, then the story is even more credible. Bemo does not seem to have supplied the names of his mother and father publicly. Osceola's sister and Yaha hadjo were removed to Indian Territory in 1838. Both appear to have died prior to the Dawes Rolls enumerations but may well have had at least two other sons, who were enrolled as Seminoles.

Bemeau and the Indian boy must have remained close to the southern Atlantic coastline for several years. Otherwise, it would have been impossible for Bemo to have been in port at Charleston, South Carolina, while Osceola and the others were imprisoned there. Bemo tells us that he was literally in the room with Osceola when the famous warrior died, and as strange as that may seem, we have no reason to discredit it. Between that moment at the end of January 1838 and late 1841 or early 1842, however, he sailed the seas. One often-reported evidence of this is the fact that Bemo named his only daughter Iona, called "Onie," after the Ionian Isles, which he visited.[26]

It was when Bemo began speaking at the church in Philadelphia in 1842 that he met Mrs. Mary A. Lilley and her husband, John, whom he would guide to Oklahoma in 1847–1848 to join him in working among his Seminole people.[27] He began to preach his newfound beliefs immediately upon reaching Maskókî lands in Indian Territory. The *Van Buren (Arkansas) Intelligencer* of 14 October 1843 reported that "a Seminole Indian, Husticolu-chee, half brother to Osceola, has recently been successfully preaching the doctrines of Christianity to the members of the tribe. He preached at Little Rock, Ark., on the 15th ult."[28] When he preached in Indian Territory, John Douglas Bemo's Indian "name" is usually given as *talamasmico*, but this is merely an epithet, not a name. It is the contraction of *tala machúsî mikkó*, "a new leader."

Bemo was only about twenty years old when he reached the Seminole lands in Indian Territory in late 1843. He had been out of Florida for almost a decade. When he was taken away from his family in 1835, at about eleven years old, the antagonisms between whites and the Florida Indians were building rapidly. One Oklahoma researcher had written that the young man's father was a "chief" who carried furs to St. Augustine to trade and died there after a drunken brawl with another "chief" of the same tribe.[29] An Oklahoma Indian who knew Bemo, however, recalled in 1937 that Bemo had told him of being captured in Florida by federal troops.[30] This seems the less fanciful and more likely version. The implication of either version, however, is that it was, consequently, from St. Augustine that the boy was taken away by the French seaman Jean Bemeau. Certainly, if Bemeau and the lad left Florida by water, St. Augustine was the logical place from which to depart at that time.

It was in Philadelphia in 1842 that Bemo's dream of returning to his people became capable of realization. The wife of the Reverend Mr. Loughridge, missionary to the western Seminoles, passed away, and Loughridge wrote to the mission board in New York asking for help in his work. This is the same Loughridge who a few years later compiled an excellent Muscogee-English dictionary.[31] Mary A. Lilley, John Lilley, and John Douglas Bemo were sent to augment the missionary team in Indian Territory. Mrs. Lilley recorded the trip and the story of her life for her family.[32]

Five years later, Mr. and Mrs. Lilley shared a house that Bemo helped to build for them and his own family in Seminole country, and all worked together preaching and ministering for several years. Mrs. Lilley recorded several situations in which Mr. Bemo's kindness and caring were invaluable to her.

Under the influence of the Reverend Joseph Murrow, the first Baptist missionary to proselytize among the removed Seminoles, Bemo became a Baptist preacher. His switch from the Presbyterian to the Baptist belief system did not occur easily. Reportedly "he prayed and meditated on it" for almost three years. The Baptists did not proselytize him; he offered himself for conversion at a meeting. In 1860, as a Baptist preacher, Bemo baptized another well-known Seminole, John Jumper, whose father, Old Jumper, had been a war leader in Florida.[33]

John Douglas Bemo married a Creek woman, Harriet Lewis, a daughter of Kendle Lewis, a Creek slave owner who had entered Indian Territory with the Roley McIntosh party in 1832.[34] They had four children: Alex, Alson Douglas, John, and a daughter, Iona.[35] Bemo reportedly died in 1890, but his children were still living when the Dawes Rolls were created. Iona, or Onie, died at eighteen years of age without offspring. Alexander (1854–1901) was listed as a citizen of the Creek Nation by the Dawes Commission. Douglas, who may have been the same as Alson Douglas, died prior to 1901. John Douglas "Benmore" (as listed on the Creek Nation Dawes Roll) died in 1900.

Alexander married Molly, a Seminole woman, and had eight children. One daughter married a Larney. The youngest son, George (born 1896), was the father of Richard Bemo and Madeline Lutus Bemo; Madeline later married William Burgess, a Seminole. Richard was one of the founders of the American Indian Movement (AIM) in Oklahoma and passed away only within the last few years. He had a large family enrolled in the Seminole Nation of Oklahoma.

Douglas married Katie, a non-Indian, and had at least one child, Leon. John Douglas married twice, both times to non-Indians. His second wife was Mary Alice Erikson, a Swede. Both marriages may have produced off-spring. One daughter married a white man, and their children continue to reside in Oklahoma to this day.

⌐

The information provided in this chapter, though significant, was never meant to be exhaustive. Undoubtedly, many other direct and collateral descendents of Osceola continue the family lines to the present day as well. Conspicuous by its absence here is any mention of Osceola's two wives and their children, who also were removed to Indian Territory following his death. The wives would not, of course, have been of his clan, and, consequently, neither would the children. His line, in his own cultural terms, was continued by those sisters who were also children of his mother.

The objective of including this information here has not been to identify them specifically, however. Indeed, in order to protect their privacy and the larger part of the information they have shared with me, I have sought only to sketch them here. The real objective of including this information has been to take Osceola out of the historical past—the "disconnected" past—and make him live on in the minds of my readers, in the persons of the family he loved and the descendents who keep his memory alive. In the minds of the Florida Indians, as well as their removed kin in Oklahoma, the pain of the wars lives on, and the passion of the fight remains strong.

12 / Pitcairn Morrison's Mementos

The largest single cache of personal items removed from Osceola left Fort Moultrie via Charleston. Fifteen "mementos" were obtained by Pitcairn Morrison, the officer who had been placed in charge of the Indian prisoners while they were in custody at Fort Marion, St. Augustine. As we have learned, Dr. Weedon noted in his diary entry for the day of the funeral that, at the last minute, Morrison had "ordered that [Osceola's] ornaments should not be Buried, but brought to his quarters that they might be s[ent] to Washington."[1] The newspaper article from the *Army and Navy Chronicle,* quoted below, also makes it clear that the items were not collected for any official reasons but rather were intended to be bestowed as gifts, on the personal initiative of Captain Morrison.

> OCEOLA—The ornaments which belonged to this noted warrior, and on which every Indian prides himself, have been presented to Major J. H. Hook, of the U.S. Army. Major H. has at his hospitable mansion a larger collection of Indian curiosities, perhaps, than any individual in the city, and these, in addition to his estimable social qualities, render a visit to his quarters very agreeable. The Major's known liberality of conduct and feeling, in aiding poor soldiers to recover their rights, and in furthering the interests of the army generally, no doubt pointed him out to the officer into whose hands Oceola's ornaments fell after

his death, as the most proper person to whom they should be confided. The annexed letter accompanied the ornaments, and we are glad to learn that the gallant and worthy young officer who was the bearer of them has arrived in this city, much improved in health.

St. Augustine,
March 25, 1838.
My Dear Major:
My gallant young friend, Lieut. Fowler, 1st regiment Artillery, has taken charge of a box, containing a bust of the celebrated Oceola, and the ornaments which he wore at the time of his death, which he will deliver to you, and which I beg you to accept as a mark of my esteem and friendship.
Yours sincerely,

P. MORRISON
Captain 4th Infantry
Commanding Indian Guard

To Major J. H. Hook, Washington, D.C.
List of the Ornaments.
Four black and two white ostrich feathers.
Large silk shawl, for head-dress.
Splendid belt, composed of ornamented beads.
Indian belt, ornamented with beads.
Blue guard, composed of beads.
Three silver gorgets.
Hair brush, with glass mirror on the back.[2]

After eighteen years in the army and ten years in grade, Morrison, a native of New York, had obtained his captaincy only a short year before his Florida assignment.[3] His career had begun in the artillery in 1820, but he had transferred to the infantry two years later. Promotion was slow in coming, as it was for so many in a nineteenth-century American military of career soldiers, limited officerships, and insufficient warfare. In September 1836, when First Lieutenant Morrison was finally promoted to captain, at least six companies of his regiment, the Fourth Infantry, were already engaged in the Indian war in Florida. The regiment lost 113 men—84 percent of its total losses—to disease in that year, although none of the losses occurred at St. Augustine, where the clean sea air was generally thought to provide a healthful climate.[4]

On 2 September 1837 Secretary of War Joel R. Poinsett named Captain

Morrison superintendent of emigration for the Seminoles. He proceeded immediately to Fort Brooke (Tampa) to report to General Jesup, whereupon he was ordered to St. Augustine to take charge of the Indians being held in Fort Marion. On 13 November 1837 the captain arrived in St. Augustine, where Osceola and other Seminoles who had been captured by General Hernández had been imprisoned.[5]

By late December the number of Indian prisoners had increased by almost 30 percent, and health conditions inside the fort could not be ameliorated even by St. Augustine's excellent climate. A measles epidemic killed fifteen of the Indians, a number that Morrison considered quite high and attributed to their "improvident habits and want of care [of] themselves." Moreover, a party of nineteen Indians led by Coacoochee (Wild Cat) had escaped from the fort in late November. General Jesup determined to transport the prisoners west before the victory of their capture should become defeat through attrition. He offered Captain Morrison the choice of moving them either to Savannah, Georgia, or Charleston, South Carolina, upon which the captain chose Charleston on the humane grounds that their comfort would be greater "at this season of the year" in quarters available there than in those provided at Savannah.[6]

Accordingly, the Seminole Indian prisoners were transferred from Florida to Charleston, and Captain Morrison traveled in command of the guard. The other officers of the guard were 2nd Lt. John Samuel Hatheway, First Artillery, another New Yorker as well as an 1836 graduate of West Point, and 2nd Lt. Henry W. Wharton, Sixth Infantry, a native of Washington, D.C., who had entered the army in Alabama only two months before this assignment.[7] Dr. Weedon also went along as surgeon.

Morrison was certainly in an excellent position to obtain access to the belongings of a member of the Indian prisoners group, even though his own health was apparently tenuous during his sojourn at Fort Moultrie. He arrived in Charleston still ill, and on 2 January Weedon ordered him to bed. When Osceola died on 30 January, Morrison, in command of the garrison, must have given at least tacit approval to the arrangements for his funeral service.[8] Neither he nor his second in command, Lieutenant Hatheway, made any official report of the event, however.[9]

Dr. Robert Lebby says that Dr. Weedon told him that all of Osceola's possessions were interred with the body, in the Indian fashion.[10] At the time of the event, however, it was obviously public knowledge that the removal of a sizable group of artifacts had been arranged by Pitcairn Morrison. One wonders whether Dr. Weedon felt some personal reluctance to disclose the nature or extent of his involvement in the expropriation of other of Osceola's possessions.

The next individual to whom these mementos passed, Maj. James Harvey Hook, was a fascinating man in his own right, and his ownership would circumscribe a second generation in the genealogy of extant Osceola artifacts. I uncovered the details of his life, however, only fortuitously and only after two weeks of telephone calls and questioning, which described a trail across half of the United States and right back to Florida.

Standard military and genealogical printed sources had failed to yield more than the barest references to a J. H. Hook. He was from Maryland, had a lifelong military career, and was not a West Point graduate.[11] Inquiries to the Maryland State Archives and the Maryland Historical Society also yielded no further specific information. A telephone call to a fellow military history researcher at the United States Navel Academy Museum in Annapolis, however, finally uncovered the trail that led Major Hook out of his 150-year quietude.[12]

I was advised to contact the Historical Research Division of the National Park Service at Harper's Ferry, Virginia, where historian William Brown suggested that I try the Old Military Records Branch of the National Archives.[13] Michael Musick of the National Archives fortunately recalled that an article on Hook had been published a few years earlier and offered the telephone number of the author. James S. Hutchins, historian of the Dwight D. Eisenhower Institute for Historical Research at the Smithsonian Institution, Washington, was graciously willing to share his research. He immediately forwarded copies of his article on Hook, as well as photo-duplicates of obituaries and other pertinent materials.[14] His research provided no clues to any association that led Morrison to choose Hook as the recipient of the artifacts. It did, however, provide the critical information that Hook's Indian collection eventually passed to another United States Army officer, John C. Casey, whom I recognized as having served in Florida during the Third Seminole War. I already knew that many of Casey's papers were in the collections of the Thomas Gilcrease Institute of History and Art, Tulsa, but ironically, copies of a number of those documents had recently come to rest in my own file cabinet.

James Harvey Hook was born in Baltimore, Maryland, on 17 February 1792. He began his military career as an ensign of infantry just prior to the War of 1812, and as a captain he saw duty in command of Fort (Benjamin) Hawkins, on the Georgia frontier with the Fourth Infantry under the command of Lt. (later Gen.) Duncan L. Clinch. There, in 1816, a dispute with a fellow officer over a horseshoe ended in a duel that crippled Hook for life. (The ball of his opponent's pistol passed through his lungs and injured his spine, resulting in paraplegia.[15]) Thereafter he could walk only with the aid of a crutch and, in 1818, was assigned to a desk job in the Office of the Commissary General of Subsistence, a newly established bureau of the War Department.[16] Hutchins's appraisal encapsulates this officer and explains the cryptic newspaper statement concerning "the Major's known liberality of conduct and feeling."[17]

> Ever genial and possessing great tact, Hook was a popular figure in the little War Department of the 1820s and 1830s. Officers high and low, anxious for inside word about promotion, reassignment, or a rumored troop movement, civilians desirous of a contract to furnish army rations or favorable settlement of some old transaction, and would-be pensioners alike sought out the affable, influential Hook. Friendships grew up between him and a number of the officers with whom he came in contact. To these Hook threw open his bachelor's lodgings when they visited Washington; with some of them he corresponded for years. With the help of such acquaintances who served in the west, he assembled what must have been a substantial collection of Indian artifacts and drawings of Indian life.[18]

Hook was spoken of as "one of the most genial gentlemen that the Army has ever produced."[19]

In July of 1836, it was Major Hook who penned a public appeal to the readers of the *New York Times* for funds in aid of "Ransom" Clarke. This is the same Ransome Clarke who had been the lone survivor of Maj. Francis Dade's fateful battle with the Seminoles in Florida on 28 December 1835. Clarke, still desperately ill from wounds sustained in that battle, had expended all of his funds in traveling to Washington to obtain the pension that had been allotted to him by an act of Congress. Hook, ever the champion of justice, made the appeal "with the view of procuring donations for his immediate relief."[20]

Major Hook's collection of Indian artifacts was also well known. It was described consistently as "a Museum, containing Indian and other curiosities too numerous to enumerate"; "a museum, consisting of Indian Costumes, War Implements, &c., together with a series of rare and beautiful Indian and other Paintings, by a Swiss artist"; and an "interesting collection of curiosities and paintings, illustrative of the Indian character and habits."[21] The memorabilia of so popular an Indian as Osceola were undoubtedly a welcome addition to such a collection.

James Hook, erstwhile bachelor, finally married on New Year's Eve 1840, and the bride, Mary Bronaugh, joined her husband in his residence at F and Twenty-first streets. Their life together was short lived, however. Hook died late in the following year, on 30 November 1841, at age forty-nine. His much-applauded liberality of nature apparently left a heavy burden upon his widow; within two weeks, his estate was being sold at auction to satisfy debts.[22] The administrators of the estate, who superintended the sale, were Richard Gott and Marcus C. Buck. An inventory of the estate's contents, dated 14 December 1841, placed a value of only $300 on the Indian collection.[23] As Hutchins pointed out, at $325, Hook's "Carriage and Harness" were valued higher than the entire contents of the "museum."[24]

In another, undated list in the Hook file are the notations concerning monies received for the individual items in the estate. Capt. John C. Casey, Second Artillery, who was then on duty in Washington, D.C., as assistant commissary of subsistence and therefore in a position to take advantage of the offering, paid $460 "(—$5 discount on New York notes) $455.00" for the museum, with the contents not itemized. In a separate notation contained in the same document and immediately following the former is the citation, "For 'Bas Relief' 25.00."

Of the artifacts in the museum, we are able to trace the subsequent movements of only two elements. The first is a substantial group of paintings of Indian life by the celebrated Swiss artist Peter Rindisbacher. Hook had been collecting the artist's work for more than a decade through the agency of another military friend, Reuben Holmes, whom Hook had assisted in gaining military promotions.[25] This group of artworks, at least eighteen pieces, apparently passed to Casey with the rest. The location of this portion of the Hook collections is known today. Eighteen Rindisbacher paintings are currently among the collections of the United States Military Academy, West Point. Hutchins opines that "it may well be that Casey, their subsequent owner, had something to do with the drawings' arrival at West Point. Regrettably, West Point's earliest record of the presence there of these drawings is an 1898 catalogue of the contents of West Point museum and the catalogue is silent regarding the donor."[26]

As for the second element, the 1838 *Army and Navy Chronicle* article said that one of the items transferred from Morrison to Hook was "a box, containing a bust of the celebrated Oceola." The Hook estate inventory mentioned a "Bas Relief." In each instance, this item was separated from the personal effects, possibly because of its secondary nature. Might not the bust and the bas relief have been one and the same? Sometime by or before 1885 the collections of the Smithsonian Institution acquired a cast of the head and shoulders of Osceola made from the original casting that was taken immediately following his demise. The casting is marked on the inside, "C. Recli Fecit" (see figure 9).[27] Charles Coe also mentioned this acquisition, saying that "a death-cast of the head and shoulders of the dead chief was taken before burial, this is now in the Smithsonian Museum, Washington, D.C."[28] John M. Goggin, in an article for the *Florida Historical Quarterly,* indicated that in 1954 Smithsonian officials found no evidence of such a mask or of their ever having possessed it.[29] The files of the St. Augustine Historical Society, however, currently contain a black-and-white photograph of such a cast (not to be confused with its descendant, the so-called Colin Bust) with a Smithsonian Institution negative number appended.[30] Through this negative number it was possible to trace the artifact to the place where it remains today, the National Museum of Natural History at the Smithsonian Institution, cat. no. 381 237.[31]

On 21 March 1838, one month after the Indians departed Charleston for the West, an article appeared in the *Charleston Mercury* stating, "The cast, taken from Oseola, after death [is] to be seen at Dr. Cohen's."[32] Morrison, who had remained ill throughout most of February, had left the mother cast and Osceola's ornaments behind in Charleston in charge of a friend, Lieutenant Fowler, who would deliver them to Washington. In the meantime, from the mother cast, Carlo Recli, a local medallion and statue maker made a first casting. We are not given to understand who commissioned the work; perhaps Dr. Strobel paid for it, or Morrison may have left the money, or Recli may have made it as advertising for his craft. This first casting was placed in public view in the window of Dr. P. Melvin Cohen's drugstore at 61 Broad Street in Charleston.

Upon his return to St. Augustine, Morrison wrote to Major Hook to inform him that the gifts were on the way. This was the note, dated 25 March 1838, that was published in the *Army and Navy Chronicle* along with the article and list quoted earlier. Why did Weedon give the cast to Morrison rather than keep it for himself? It seems to have been Weedon's decision to make the cast, not Morrison's. Might the two men have struck some bargain regarding the division of the artifacts? Subsequently, the Recli cast passed from Morrison to Fowler to Hook to Casey to the Smithsonian, where it has remained to the present time. Several molds taken from this first casting also survive today, and their provenance is discussed in chapter 13.

It is also interesting to speculate on another of the items given to Major Hook—the blue "guard," composed of beads. This was almost certainly a colloquialism for a garter, an accoutrement familiar to soldiers of the eighteenth and early nineteenth centuries. Soldiers used it to secure their gaiters, or leggings, and Osceola used it for the same purpose. If so, the fact that it was blue and beaded and occurs only as a single item rather than as a pair in the published list fits well with the fact that a single, blue, beaded garter passed through the Weedon family and into the Alabama Archives and

History Museum. Perhaps Captain Morrison claimed one of the pair, and Weedon took the other. This also corroborates the conclusion that Weedon and Morrison came to some arrangement regarding a split of Osceola's possessions.

We have no concrete information regarding the rest of the fourteen artifacts. Several important clues, however, do exist. Capt. John C. Casey came to Florida as an invalid in 1848, suffering from tuberculosis. In October 1850 he was appointed a special commissioner for the Seminoles and, for the most part, continued in that capacity until his death at Fort Brooke on 25 December 1856. Casey was eulogized as a true and faithful friend of the Indians who won their respect and confidence through strict veracity. In an interesting irony, the steamer that bore his body away for burial in Philadelphia also carried the Seminole leader Billy Bowlegs and his party to the United States government's western reservation in Indian Territory. No copy of Casey's will has yet been located. Therefore, the location of the artifacts that he obtained from the Hook estate, with the exception of the Rindisbacher paintings, is undocumented. Coe, however, in his preface to the original edition of *Red Patriots,* offered incidental information regarding the disposition of certain of Casey's possessions. The author acknowledged his obligation "to Maj. Wm. S. Beebe, late of the Ordnance Department, U.S. Army, who kindly placed at my disposal old letters, diaries, and other valuable material, left by his late uncle, Capt. John C. Casey, prominent in the Seminole War and later as agent among the remnant." It is also known that at least one Seminole artifact collected in Florida by Casey—a white-feather "flag of truce"—was preserved by Beebe, who had been living in Brooklyn, New York.[33] Beebe, himself a decorated career soldier, died on 12 October 1898, even as Coe's acknowledgment was being published for the first time.[34]

Efforts to locate further information concerning Casey or Beebe family descendants have thus far been unsuccessful. It is exciting to consider, however, that another entire group of Osceola artifacts may still exist today.[35]

13 / A Far-Flung Legacy

The total range of artifacts that can be attributed to Osceola through literary and graphic sources falls into three categories. The first, and the largest, is composed of those items for which no further information is available beyond their citation in documents or their appearance in the graphic sources. The second category is made up of artifacts that are cited and for which a provenance has been established but which have thus far not been located. The third category consists solely of extant pieces, of both proven and unproven attribution, for which a provenance or a current location has been established.

Artifact Types

Appendix A displays the complete range of these artifacts. The abbreviated chart presented here totals the three categories by type, as they will be discussed in this chapter. The margin for error in the table lies in the calculation of the total number of artifacts. Some of the citations undoubtedly refer to the same artifacts, whereas most citations specify unique details. The margin for error we may estimate as approximately forty-six artifacts, or 37 percent.

Artifact Types

Type	Cited or in Graphics	Provenance Established	Extant
Clothing			
Hunting shirt	7	1	5
Shirt	1	—	—
Moccasins	6	—	—
Leggings	4	—	—
Headgear			
Turban	5	1	—
Accoutrements			
Gun	4	1	—
Knife	8	1	1
Sheath	1	—	—
Powder horn	3	1	—
Spurs	2	—	—
Tomahawk	1	—	—
Personal adornments			
Bullet pouch	1	—	—
Feathers	24+	7	—
Handkerchief	2	—	—
Scarf	1	1	—
Concho	1	1	—
Gorget	8	4	1
Wrist bands	4	—	—
Beads	8	—	—
Earrings	4	2	2
Pouch/strap	2	1	1
Belt	5	4	2
Sash	3	1	—
Garter	6	4	3
Personal possessions			
Pencil	1	1	1
Pipe	1	1	1
Hairbrush	2	1	—
Paint	1	—	—
Cane	1	—	—
Other			
Hair	1	1	1
Cast/casting	7	7	7
Total	125	41	25
% of total		32%	19%

Less up to 37% duplication	79		
% of total		51%	30%

The Artifacts

Clothing

A primary component of nineteenth-century male apparel of the southeastern Indians was an outer cloth or buckskin coat, which appears to have had its antecedents in colonial frontier garments that date at least to the American Revolutionary War period and probably to the Middle Ages in Europe. During the American Revolutionary War period it was known as a hunting shirt (or rifle shirt, or rifle frock, when worn by riflemen).[1] "The hunting or rifle shirt . . . was the familiar frontier garment. In its most common form it was made of deerskin for winter and linen for summer, reaching often to the knees and having one or more capes. Being open down the front and without buttons, it had to be held together by a broad leather belt by which was carried a knife or hatchet."[2] It is uncertain whether the garment originated in Europe or in the colonies.[3] Some sources attribute it to the American Indians, others to the trappers, and, therefore, the garment may represent a colonial syncretism. Available information, however, clearly indicates that the style can be documented at least as early as the third quarter of the eighteenth century.[4] It is the garment that East Florida governor Patrick Tonyn was indicating in 1777 when he described the East Florida Rangers, British military irregulars, as "Split Shirt Banditti."[5] It was an eminently practical, inexpensive piece of clothing that was extremely common in the frontier areas of the colonies. Little wonder, then, that it has remained in general use among the Creek and Seminole Indians almost until the present time, although cultural isolation has allowed it to evolve in a manner that is uniquely Seminole.

Five hunting shirts attributed to Osceola are extant today, and a sixth can be partially accounted for. Of these, two have sufficient provenance to link them clearly to Osceola. The first is a buckskin coat, acc. no. 22/9750, in the collections of the Museum of the American Indian, Heye Foundation, New York City (appendix A, no. 1; subsequent reference numbers are all to the list in appendix A). The catalog card indicates that the garment was worn at the treaty meeting in 1837 (that is, the capitulation or armistice of 6 March 1837 at Fort Dade). It was collected by "Dr. Motte in St. Augustine," undoubtedly Jacob Rhett Motte, who was garrisoned at Fort Mellon during the armistice. Two more of Osceola's possessions also collected by Motte at this time will be discussed later in this chapter. Motte gave the hunting shirt to Dr. George Jackson Fisher (1825–1893) in 1848. Fisher received his medical degree from the University of New York in 1849, but otherwise there is no specific information concerning the relationship between Motte and Fisher. Two years later, Dr. Fisher moved to Sing Sing (now Ossining), New York, where he continued to practice until his death. Fisher was an eminent physician with an extensive library of four to five thousand volumes and a collection of medals and portraits. On his death the collection was dispersed. His library was sold intact, as per a stipulation of his will, to the Vassar Brothers Hospital in Poughkeepsie, New York. On the expiration of the stipulation that the library be kept intact, which occurred about 1908, some two thousand of the six thousand titles (those not already duplicated in its collections) were purchased by the Medical Society of the County of Kings.[6] Many of the portraits went to the Johns Hopkins Hospital Library. The Osceola artifacts, however, were a part of the "Dr. George Jackson Fisher Collection, Formed at Ossining, 1840–1890" and presented to the Heye Foundation by Union Free School District One of Ossining, New York.[7]

The hunting shirt is forty-three inches long. Because such garments commonly reached from the shoulders of the wearer to just about the knees, the length of this item indicates that its wearer was approximately five feet ten inches in height, which is consistent with other information we have about Osceola. It is totally devoid of ornamentation, with the exception of a short buckskin fringe applied to the neck, the edges of the pointed cape, the front vertical edges, the hem, and a band about six inches above the hem all the way around the garment. The sleeves are finished by means of a rawhide thong about three inches from the wrist, which draws them into gathered cuffs. This hunting shirt may also account for the deerskin hunting shirt cited as no. 6 in appendix A. It is highly possible that this garment did indeed belong to Osceola.

The second hunting shirt of buckskin is currently held by the Denver Museum of Natural History, Denver, Colorado (no. 2). It is similar in style to the one in which Osceola is depicted in the McKenney-Hall portrait. The provenance associated with this artifact, however, is insufficient to link it to Osceola in any way, even though it does appear to date from the period. Nor does its similarity to the McKenney-Hall portrait lend it any credence, because the provenance of that image has been disproved.

The third hunting shirt (no. 3, catalogued as a "jacket") also has no acceptable documentation; furthermore, the style of the garment places its manufacture in the Great Lakes area. This artifact is held by the Moravian Historical Society, Nazareth, Pennsylvania, and is discussed in articles by John Goggin and William Sturtevant.[8] Its only documentation, as quoted by Sturtevant, was an "old label, partly obliterated, reading 'ap[praised?] $____ [illegible] Worn by Oceola ____ [illegible] War.'"[9] A conversation with the curator of that agency indicates, however, that the attribution must have been removed because no artifact in the collection is currently attributed to any southeastern Indian.[10]

A hunting shirt for which a provenance has been established but which is no longer in existence (no. 10) was acquired by Osceola's close friend John Graham. In the correspondence between Graham's grandnephew John Tharpe Lawrence and Florida's secretary of state R. A. Gray in 1939, Mr. Lawrence recalled that "Osceola presented [Graham] with a full dress suit of buckskin, beautifully worked with beads and a silver headband and breast plate. Unfortunately, the suit was destroyed but I still have the headband [no. 60] and breast plate [no. 59]. I also have a beaded sash [no. 78] which I believe was part of the suit, but of this I am not positive."[11]

In a short and tantalizing series of only three more letters, Mr. Lawrence offered the artifacts to the state of Florida for permanent safekeeping. Secretary Gray responded positively and referred the matter to then state librarian, W. T. Cash. Mr. Cash assured Lawrence that the state would be pleased to receive the artifacts, and the final letter in the series from Lawrence, dated 21 February 1939, begins, "I am mailing you the relics of Osceola, and hope they will reach you in good condition."[12] After this point, the artifacts completely disappear.

Two further hunting shirts (nos. 4–5) attributed to Osceola are extant, and even though they appear to be excellent examples of Seminole clothing from the appropriate period, they have insufficient provenance—both documentarily and stylistically—to link them to our subject. Both are textile garments, and both are held among the collections of the Berlin Museum fur Volkerkunde (acc. nos. IV B 247 and IV B 248). Of the two, only the former is large enough to have been worn by a man of Osceola's size. It is forty-four inches long and would reach just to the knee or below, the length at which colonial soldiers wore their hunting shirts and the length at which Osceola is most frequently depicted wearing his. The other is only thirty-two inches long, barely hip length for a grown man. Both appear to be excellent examples of the syncretistic nature of Seminole clothing, combining European design (especially the cape, gussets, and fringes) and Seminole style (the ruffles and intensified ornamentation, the complex decorative patterns, and the use of more and brighter colors). Sturtevant describes them as "the oldest dated Seminole clothing." They were purchased by the Prussian state in 1845.[13] Now, however, this discussion should be broadened to include the Heye Foundation hunting shirt described earlier. Although it did not enter the collections of the museum until the early twentieth century, its provenance and style are compelling enough to place it in the same category as these early specimens.

As regards the textile hunting shirt shown by George Catlin in his Fort Moultrie portrait of Osceola (figure 4), no firm information is currently available. In her 1942 thesis Helen Wellington, however, cites the presence of an unidentified textile hunting shirt in the collections of the Museum of the American Indian, Heye Foundation, New York City (no. 7), which bears a striking resemblance to the one pictured in the Catlin portrait.[14] At this time, no further information is available concerning this piece.

Item nos. 8 and 9, both great shirts, an over-the-head garment worn by both Indians and whites under the hunting shirt and made on the same pattern, cannot be located. From the archaeological report, it is clear that no evidence of clothing was found with the skeletal remains. Such pieces, however, made generally of low-grade cotton trade cloth during this period and worn constantly in direct contact with the skin, would have been particularly consumable items. It is highly unlikely that such items would have survived, if indeed they were dispersed to white ownership at the time of the burial rather than simply discarded.

The citation regarding Osceola's "trappings" (no. 11) was recorded in the family history papers of Capt. Paul Quattlebaum, a member of Colonel Brisbane's Regiment of South Carolina Volunteers. The unit was raised in Charleston in February 1836 and mustered out at St. Augustine on 4 May of the same year.[15] Senator Paul Quattlebaum, grandson of Capt. Paul Quattlebaum, wrote of his ancestor, "While serving in Florida, Captain Quattlebaum and his men came so near surrounding Osceola in a farm house that the wiley chief was able to escape only by leaving behind all his trappings, including a handsome head-gear of beautiful ostrich plumes [no. 39], a prized trophy that was later given to a superior officer."[16]

No more specific information is available within the family concerning this incident. Paul Quattlebaum, Jr., son of Senator Quattlebaum, recalls, however, that a strong oral tradition has survived among family members concerning this story and well remembers his grandfather (Captain Paul's son) telling it. He believes that the site of this escapade was Volusia, where Captain Quattlebaum was stationed, and that the artifacts, although passed down through the family for many years, were ultimately lost or destroyed some time ago.[17]

Two such encounters are recorded as having taken place at Volusia and in which Brisbane's Regiment of South Carolina Volunteers participated: a skirmish at the river crossing on 22 March 1836 and an attack on the blockhouse on 14 April 1836.[18] During this period, however, Osceola appears to have been engaged nearer the Cove of the Withlacoochee and is not reported to have participated in the Volusia attacks. One is therefore left with two alternative conclusions. Either the entire episode is accurate as it is preserved inside the Quattlebaum family, despite the lack of documentation, or else the Indian notable involved in this incident was mistakenly identified as Osceola. Neither possibility is implausible, although we have already seen that Osceola's passion and resolve made him a highly visible figure to whom numerous disparate exploits were attributed erroneously.

Another group of artifacts that remains unaccounted for is that composed of Osceola's moccasins (nos. 12–15) and his leggings (nos. 16–17). Although two accounts mention only "moccasins," the Catlin portrait, the documents that accompanied one of the Catlin lithographs, and Ransom's fictionalized account indicate that Osceola wore ornamented moccasins. The Catlin lithograph document says specifically that they were decorated with porcupine quills, a style common among western plains Indians but not among the southeastern Indians. It is possible that this detail is correct, however, and that the ornamented moccasins were obtained through trade among the Indians. Osceola's personal penchant for exotic accoutrements has been evidenced a number of times.

The same document also gives the detail that Osceola's leggings were red and made of broadcloth. Broadcloth seems an unlikely choice of fabric (as opposed to osnaburg or stroud, for example, which would have provided much more body and durability), but the term may have been used as a generic designator, and the color rings true. Micanopy was very proud of his pair of red leggings and chose them specifically when he sat for Catlin. It is also interesting to note that the Catlin lithograph drawing, taken from his first full-length image of Osceola (no. 308, figure 5), shows his leggings buttoned up the front of the leg. The only contemporary sketch that places the leggings' closures on the side of the legs is one of John Rogers Vinton's drawings, but Vinton cannot be accepted as completely reliable for details of dress.

Headgear

The next item of apparel for which citations are available is the textile piece that was commonly folded and wrapped as a turban by the southeastern Indians. A "large silk shawl for head-dress" (no. 18) was sent to Major Hook by Capt. Pitcairn Morrison. If this item was the same as the "India shawl of bright colors, tied in the form of a turban" (no. 19), which was mentioned in the Catlin lithograph document, then Morrison's reference to silk may be a mistake or indicative more of quality or appearance than of manufacture. In this period, several fabrics were available (some more easily obtained than others) that would have provided the requisite weight and body for a turban: silk, silk/wool, wool challis, cotton/wool, or cotton. The "India" spectrum of fabrics indicates a cotton-based cloth, which could be block printed in bright colors. Weedon also mentioned a turban (no. 21), but without details, and Ransom again chose to specify a red cloth turban (no. 20), which may tell us more about Ransom's mind-set than Osceola's clothing. None of these pieces appears to have survived into the twentieth century.

Accoutrements

The evidence provided by documents (a letter and a freight bill) indicates that Osceola's gun (nos. 22–25) and his powder horn (nos. 33–35) were obtained by Dr. Frederick Weedon and given away or sold to a friend. Weedon gave no indication that the powder horn was of the exotic manufacture cited in the Catlin lithograph document ("a silver mounted buffalo horn"), nor does the lithograph itself show such a piece.

The gun, however, does appear in the lithograph as a long-barrel flintlock, rifled, with metal butt plate and ornate metal patch box and trigger guard. W. W. Smith specified that Osceola had a silver-mounted rifle, possibly the gift from Indian agent Wiley Thompson. This reference does not conflict with the weapon depicted by Catlin. It does conflict, however, with the specification "carbine" in Weedon's note transferring the gun and powder horn. Because not even one gun with a reasonable provenance attributed to Osceola has been located, this point must remain enigmatic for the time being. Osceola's other weapon, however—his knife (nos. 26–31)—may be extant within the Weedon family, although the sheath for the knife (no. 32) remains unaccounted for, as does a tomahawk (no. 37), if indeed Osceola owned one.

Two other items remain tantalizingly vague. Storrow mentions twice that Osceola wore spurs (no. 36). Two lithographs that appeared in 1838 actually show spurs on Osceola's feet. The source of one of the graphics, and probably of the other as well, was Robert John Curtis, one of the artists who painted Osceola from life. There is no indication, however, that Osceola ever rode a horse. On the contrary, there is the direct quotation of an Indian woman, from the Prince diary, to the effect that Osceola never even owned a horse.[19] It is possible, however, that this was another of Osceola's personal affectations. If so, there is no information at this time concerning the current existence of such artifacts.

Personal Adornments

Neither can the feathers that Osceola wore in his turban be accounted for today (nos. 39–40, 43–44, 46–48). There seems little doubt, given the agreement of the numerous references and the graphic sources, that Osceola was distinguished by the number, color, and placement of these items. His habit was to wear at least one, and no more than three, solid black and solid white ostrich plumes, affixed jauntily in the back of his turban (not in the front, as the others wore them). He also appears to have carried extra feathers, as Pitcairn Morrison sent a total of six ostrich plumes to Major Hook (nos. 41–42). The social traditions among southeastern Maskókî warriors did not permit purely decorative items, however. Consequently, we may accept that Osceola was permitted to wear them and that they had military significance.

The feathers that Osceola is reputed to have given away as a gift to his friend John Graham, however, were crane feathers (no. 49), not ostrich plumes. We are not given to understand whether any special significance was attached to this choice (or even whether the report was accurate), but crane feathers were available to the Florida Indians for free (obtainable from an indigenous bird), whereas ostrich plumes were exotic and had to be obtained from the traders. On the other hand, the crane feathers had an intrinsic value of relative rarity, because they are the "marriage" plumage of the cranes, appearing at their fullest only once a year, during the mating season, and therefore had a uniqueness and, perhaps, a higher personal value in themselves as a gift. Indeed, because we now know that Osceola was Bird Clan, the gift may have had an additional layer of significance.

Of the scarf (no. 53) and the scarlet handkerchief and the blue handkerchief that Osceola wore around his neck (nos. 50–51), a usage typical among the Indians of Florida, there is no trace. Neither do we know the whereabouts of a single white ostrich plume (no. 45) that Osceola reputedly gave as a gift to the United States government agent accompanying the Cherokee delegation to Florida in late 1837. It was intended as a token of good faith for the Indians' "white father," the president, but we have no evidence that it ever arrived in Washington.

Two more scarves (no. 54), one pendant from each wrist and used to secure silver wristbands (nos. 61–62), have vanished along with the bands. Five silver items have survived, however, and the current location of each is known, although a reliable provenance is available for only four. A silver concho, or decorative bangle, of coin silver (no. 55) and two silver dangle earrings (no. 67) remained in the Weedon family. There seems no reason to doubt the authenticity of these pieces. From the graphic evidence, the two extant earrings also appear to be the same as those depicted by Vinton, Catlin, Curtis, and others and mentioned in the Catlin lithograph document (no. 68).

The fourth artifact is a silver gorget. The Vinton sketches of Osceola show him wearing four gorgets, whereas the Curtis and Catlin portraits, executed about eight months later, show only three (figures 3, 4), and the Catlin lithograph document lists only three (no. 58). It is now known from the Lawrence information discussed earlier in this chapter that Osceola gave one gorget to his friend John Graham. It is also known that three gorgets, presumably the three depicted by Curtis and Catlin (no. 57) passed from Morrison to Major Hook to John Casey to his nephew Beebe.

The one gorget that is extant, then, appears not to fit with the known information but has several interesting points in its favor. This one (no. 56) is currently in the collections of the National Museums of Scotland, Edinburgh, acc. no. 1921.1700. According to the accession records, "The gorget is the familiar crescentric silver form, 5 ins. in length and engraved with the figure of a boar running to the left. Below is the name 'Osceola.' The item was purchased in 1921 from a Mr. George Day and has no further provenance."[20]

The style of manufacture of the gorget itself is thoroughly consistent with others of the period circa 1760–1820, the high point and stylistic model for this genre of artifact. The crescent shape has an applied, fluted, surround and two silver bosses, or buttons, presumably with the standard looped shank, one in the apex of each point. The artifact itself could have been in existence during Osceola's lifetime. Both the engraving and the attribution require documentation to be totally acceptable, however. The engraved motif contains an excellent likeness of a southern razorback boar hog, charging (viewer's) left on a low, grassy, and possibly marshy tuft of land. Directly beneath this element, in clean, uppercase lettering, is engraved the single word, "OSCEOLA." The entire motif is centered and occupies approximately 30 percent of the available space. The work appears to have been professionally executed, but the style is not ornate. Although it is difficult to reach any definitive conclusions from only a photograph, both elements of the motif appear to have been executed at the same time. Stylistically, the motif is not anomalous for the first half of the nineteenth century. Because the National Museums of Scotland can supply no information concerning the previous owner, Mr. George Day, we may never know whether this fascinating item was a presentation piece, perhaps also commissioned especially for Osceola (by Wiley Thompson?), or simply a commemorative of some type, made by an unassociated admirer after his death.

The fifth silver artifact is another anomalous piece, but with strong provenance. It is a silver mechanical pencil (no. 84) that is currently among the collections of the National Park Service, El Castillo de San Marcos National Monument, St. Augustine, acc. no. 22, cat. no 551. The piece is three inches long, with point retracted. It has a simple, fluted barrel with an ornate, beaded tip (almost one-fourth of the overall length) and flat head. The point opens and retracts by a direct slide mechanism that is operated manually. The barrel is marked "W M. & C. [I.]." The artifact was donated to the Castillo in 1946 by Dr. Edward F. Corson of Philadelphia.

At the same time that Dr. Corson gave the artifact to the Castillo, he also donated several fragmented documents to the Florida Historical Society, and these currently are held in the collections of that organization at its library. These indicate that Dr. Corson's grandfather, William A. Carter, fought and worked in Florida during and following the Second Seminole War. Carter, of Prince William County, Virginia, enlisted in the United States Army at Warrenton, Virginia, on 1 July 1836. He was then eighteen years and three months old, and he listed his previous occupation as farmer.[21]

From his service record and the fragmented letters, one learns that Carter was assigned to Company A, Second Dragoons, and fought with them at the Battle of Camp Monroe (Fort Mellon), which took place on 8 February 1837.[22] Later that same year, on 12 August, Carter was discharged at St. Augustine as a sergeant. He was therefore, ostensibly, in St. Augustine when Osceola was brought to Fort Marion (the Castillo) as a prisoner two months later, although earlier in 1836 the two might have had the opportunity to meet elsewhere. Sometime following his discharge on disability, Carter went into business as a sutler, with his headquarters at Palatka, west of St. Augustine on the St. Johns River. There is no further information concerning the duration of his life and business in Florida or his subsequent movements.

At any rate, the pencil donated to the National Park Service, St. Augustine, was supposedly given to William Carter by Osceola and held until 1949 by the Carter/Corson family. The alleged provenance for this artifact is not disproved by the documents. Moreover, mechanical pencils had been available commercially since the eighteenth century, so the artifact type is not anachronistic either. Even though we are missing the specific documentation that would link Osceola, a mechanical pencil, and William Carter together, we have already seen that much less plausible incidents did occur in the life of Osceola.

None of the necklaces depicted in the Catlin portraits and drawings have survived, and nothing is known of their provenance. Interestingly enough, Catlin is the only artist known to have drawn Osceola from life who depicted him wearing necklaces (nos. 63 and 65). Neither Vinton nor Curtis shows beads. The Catlin lithograph document also describes these as a gold joint chain around his neck (that is, a gold choker) and two strings of wampum beads (that is, two long strands of trade beads [nos. 64 and 66]).

The subject of the belts, sashes, pouches, and garters that may have belonged to Osceola is a very confusing one. There is substantial disparity among the documented types, the graphic images, and the extant pieces, and the issue is further obfuscated by semantics. It is highly possible that Osceola had several of each item at any one time and a number of each over the period 1834–1838. The two techniques generally used by the Creek and Seminole Indians for the fabrication of such items were finger weaving and sewing, both of which methods were highly portable. Production required only manual dexterity and a small number of lightweight materials, but the skill of the maker and the beauty of the finished product combined to make them highly prized trade items. Because a number of these have survived to this day in white men's collections, it is possible that the Florida Indians thought of these items as appropriate for gift giving or perceived the white men's interest in the beautiful items and, thus, made them with some frequency.

The Catlin lithograph document indicates that Osceola is wearing an otter-skin bullet pouch (no. 38), and Frederick Weedon mentions a bullet pouch (no. 70) but does not specify its construction. The pouch shown in Catlin's full-length painting and lithograph and in subsequent drawings does indeed appear to be made of skin. Its shape is analogous to classic Seminole and Creek pouches, with a square or nearly square bag and elongated triangular flag. Its strap, however, is anomalous, appearing as a very narrow (hide?) thong, unlike those generally used by the Creeks and Seminoles.[23] No known artifact of this design is attributed to Osceola.

In the formal portrait that Catlin substantially completed at Fort Moultrie (figure 4), Osceola appears to be wearing a sash rather than a pouch and strap. The sash was a decorated item, an over-the-shoulder, tied belt that was not used to support a pouch. Although the width of the one in the portrait is comparable to typical Creek and Seminole pieces, its decorative design is not. Neither, however, are the one extant pouch and sash attributed to Osceola comparable to this depicted one, although they do appear to be the typical Creek-Seminole type. The extant set (no. 69) was formerly on loan to the Florida State Museum of Natural History, Gainesville, acc. no. E-693/79-3. The limited provenance available indicates that the artifacts were collected by Thomas P. Roberts in 1869 (but from whom we are not told) and stored in a family bank vault. They were subsequently lent to the museum in 1979 by a descendant, Gen. J. Milnor Roberts.

The pouch is of red wool and is muslin lined, with spot-stitched seed beads worked in a dense, curvilinear design on the elongated flap, and the bag is edged with a border of blue beads. The flap is finished with double-tab strap ends and has navy blue tassels on the tabs and across the bottom of the bag. The bag measures 6½″ wide and is 8¼″ long, including the flap ends and tassels. The strap is also of red wool and lined with red printed cotton. The strap is decorated with beadwork in curvilinear designs that differ on each of the strap halves, edged with beads, and finished with short tassels. The strap is 28″ long, including the tassels, and 3⅜″ wide.

General Roberts's loan also included a belt, acc. no. E-694/79-4 (no. 73), which is attributed to Osceola and bears a strong resemblance to the belt and sash depicted in the portrait by Robert John Curtis (figure 3). This could be the same belt mentioned by Weedon (no. 74) and Ransom (no. 75). It is finger woven, of black and dark blue wool yarns. The belt is woven on a diagonal, three-over-two, diamond pattern, with white beads strung on blue yarn creating the diamond centers. The edges are trimmed with white beads, and the ends have long, loom-woven fringes, eight at each end (although two are missing from one end), alternating blue and black, and finished with white bead edges. The belt itself is 3⅝″ wide and 20″ long, and the fringes are each 36″ long. In 1997 both items (nos. 69 and 73) were recalled from loan by the Roberts family and offered for sale at public auction. The beaded pouch and sash set subsequently sold for $195,000, and the blue beaded sash, in poorer condition, brought $28,750.[24]

The Catlin lithograph document also indicates that Osceola wore a red sash (or belt) ornamented with beads (no. 77) and a blue sash (belt) ornamented with beads (no. 78). Only the beaded fringes are discernible in the lithograph, and in the portrait the belt is indistinguishable, so we have no way of knowing whether they were meant to depict the same items. The lithograph document says that the blue belt was given to Catlin by Osceola as a parting gift and was placed in the extensive Catlin collection of Indian artifacts.

The splendid belt of ornamented beads (no. 71) and the Indian belt ornamented with beads (no. 72) were collected by Pitcairn Morrison and passed through the nineteenth century as described in chapter 12. One of these two items may well have been a sash, not a belt. Osceola gave away yet another of his beaded belts as a gift, this time before he left St. Augustine (no. 74). The recipient was Capt. Lucien B. Webster, First Artillery, acting assistant quartermaster for the post and commanding officer at Fort Marion, where Osceola and the other prisoners were held from late October until the end of December 1837. Consequently, it was Webster who was in command when Coacoochee and the others made their escape from the

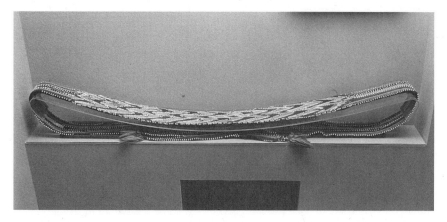

Figure 23. Osceola's beaded belt; a gift to Capt. Lucien B. Webster. (Collection of the Rochester Museum and Science Center. May not be reprinted without permission of the RMSC.)

fort, and it was Captain Webster who was exonerated of any misconduct in the event by the panel of inquiry. The belt remained within the Webster family for three succeeding generations until a granddaughter of the captain sold it to the Rochester Museum (now the Rochester Museum and Science Center), Rochester, New York (see figure 23). The belt is "wool woven in a tan and dark brown herringbone pattern with white glass beads along the border. The overall length is 8 feet with a 26 inch central band."[25]

So far, then, we have seen that Osceola may have possessed at least two separate bullet pouches with straps, four belts, and two sashes. In addition, he appears, from the graphic sources, to have had and worn four garters—two on each leg. The Catlin lithograph illustrates this usage most clearly, and the accompanying document mentions "gaiters" (that is, leggings, garters) of bead-worked netting (no. 83), although the number is not specified. Four garters, however, can be accounted for today; three are extant.

A single beaded garter (no. 80) was collected by Frederick Weedon and survives today in the Alabama Department of Archives and History Museum in Montgomery (figure 17). A blue "guard," or garter, which may have been the mate to Weedon's, was sent to Major Hook with the rest of Pitcairn Morrison's artifacts. Its current location is unknown. The third and fourth garters, a pair, were collected by Jacob Rhett Motte and passed to the collections of the Museum of the American Indian, Heye Foundation, New York City, acc. no. 22/9751, by the route described for the other Motte artifacts earlier in this chapter (no. 81).

Personal Possessions

Among his other personal possessions, Osceola also had a brass pipe (no. 85), which is currently held by the Museum of Florida History, Tallahassee (figure 14). A beaded pipe (no. 86) is cited by Joshua Giddings, but Giddings may or may not be a reliable source. Another personal item, a hairbrush with a glass mirror on the back (no. 87), was also among the items Morrison sent to Hook and was probably the same item that Weedon called Osceola's "looking glass" (no. 88). Finally, it is reported in the death scene accounts that Osceola had with him a parcel of red paint (no. 89) and a "small whalebone cane" (no. 90).[26] The paint was probably a red ocher that could be transported and stored in powder form. This was a consumable item and could have been used up at that time. The mention of the cane is interesting, because it lends credence to other anomalous attributions, such as the mechanical pencil, but no indication exists as to the disposition of these artifacts.

Physical Remains and Associated Artifacts

One final class of items must be considered that is by far the most personal of all. Although only three of the items can be considered as primary, taken together they constitute the only physical evidence concerning Osceola the man. The primary extant item is, of course, the lock of hair (no. 91), which was a part of the Weedon family's holdings and is discussed at length in chapter 9. The second, the head (nos. 97–98), has not yet been located, although there is no longer any reason to believe that it could not be extant. The skeletal remains, the third primary item (no. 99), although extant, cannot now be examined further because of their reinterment. As we have previously seen, however, much critical information has already been gathered from them by forensic anthropologists.

A group of secondary artifacts directly associated with the physical remains consists of several extant plaster molds and castings. The earliest was the death cast (the so-called mother, or postmortem, mold; no. 93) of the head and upper torso made at Fort Moultrie at the time of Osceola's death. This mold was destroyed in pulling the first casting, the one that was exhibited in Dr. Cohen's drugstore in Charleston and afterward transferred to Major Hook. The subsequent transferal of this cast to the National Museum of Natural History/Smithsonian Institution, Washington, D.C., and its current location were discussed in chapter 12. Among the collections of the National Museum of Natural History/Smithsonian Institution there still exists today this first-generation, unpainted, three-dimensional casting pulled from the original mold made at Fort Moultrie by Carlo Recli (no. 94). This casting is cat. no. 381 237, neg. no. 44262H.

According to Smithsonian records, the next use made of this casting was in the production of a three-dimensional casting of the complete head and torso (cat. no. 76,181), made about 1885 by staff member Achille Colin for an exhibition at the Smithsonian. This is the so-called Colin Bust, which was referred to in John Goggin's article on Osceola for the *Florida Historical Quarterly*.[27] Colin also used the Catlin portrait (no. 301, figure 14), which was held by the Division of Ethnology at the Smithsonian as a further model for the detailing of his casting.

In addition, a torso and legs were sculpted for the bust, in order to make it a free-standing figure, by Theodore A. Mills of the Smithsonian staff, and the bust and torso were then painted by A. Zeno Shindler, who was a staff artist for the Smithsonian from 1876 until his death in 1898. "About 1950, when Hall[s] 9 and 11 of the U.S.N.M. were being prepared for modernization of the exhibits, this figure was separated as it had been made, the bust was retained, and the lower part was condemned and destroyed as not being of any further use to the museum under present conditions."[28]

Sometime in the early twentieth century, Chief Preparator William H. Egberts of the National Museum of Natural History/Smithsonian Institution made a secondary, two-piece mold of the face only, undoubtedly to preserve the original from the degeneration of time and use (no. 94). From this secondary, two-piece mold, four castings were subsequently made, and their initial disposition was recorded. The first casting was made on 10 December 1928 and was presented as a gift to the St. Augustine Historical Society by Robert Ransom. The face is set in high relief on a plaster base and inscribed "R. R. 12/10/28." This cast is still held by the St. Augustine Historical Society. The second casting was made on 3 April 1958 for "Mrs. M. Park, Sculptor." No notation was made concerning her location, and nothing is currently known about this cast. The next was made in February 1959 for the "Southeast Museum of the North American Indian, Marathon, Florida." This institution no longer exists, and although a number of its artifacts are known to have passed into the holdings of a large private collector, no information is currently available regarding the disposition of this artifact. The fourth and last casting was made on 28 October 1965 for the Division of Cultural Anthropology, National Museum of Natural History/Smithsonian Institution.

Finally, today there exists in the National Museum of Natural History/Smithsonian Institution a series of casts made from the skeletal remains (no. 96). These consist of casts of the pelvic girdle, one of the long bones of the legs, and one of the bones of the forearm.[29] These castings were taken from the skeletal remains uncovered by John Griffin and examined by Stewart and Reed. This, then, constitutes all the information that is currently available concerning the material legacy of Osceola.

Epilogue

Two Very Expensive Alleged Osceola Artifacts

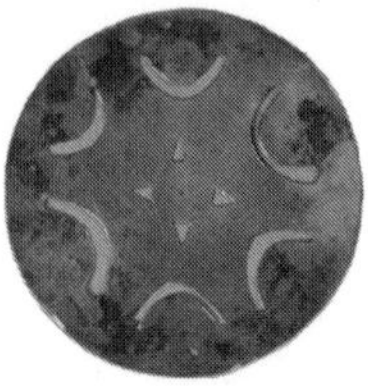

I am not a believer in coincidence. The story of the two artifacts presented here was the impetus for all of the researches presented elsewhere in this book, and the fact that enough information has presented itself since the original publication to warrant a revised edition is sufficient evidence of the persistent nature of Osceola's story. I have said this repeatedly. He has a powerful hold on our collective imagination. Over the intervening years since the story of these artifacts was first published, I have heard a few more rumors of their movements, but none recently. Nevertheless, their story is worth retelling in this revised edition, if only as a cautionary tale. In Osceola's case, however, there is little doubt that they will turn up yet again.

It was only a line or two written in passing—even less, actually, because the information was not corroborated by all the contemporary sources. One slightly romanticized modern account referred to Osceola's firearm as "an expensive gun."[1] Other sources merely indicated a generic "gun" or "rifle," but the only real attention paid to Osceola's weapon by those who saw him (or purported to have seen him) was by W. W. Smith, a young "Lieutenant of the Left Wing," and later by George Catlin. Smith observed, "His rifle is the only costly thing about him, and is a silver mounted one, which his friend Thompson made him a present of, and which he bought in New York for one hundred dollars."[2] George Catlin, who was a close and excellent observer, specifically mentioned that Osceola's weapon was "a long barrel Spanish rifle, with plain flint-lock."[3] Indeed, such a weapon is depicted in Catlin's full-length sketch.

None of the sources indicated a powder horn presentation piece as well, although a powder horn is also delineated in Catlin's full-length lithograph (figure 15 in chapter 4), and the accompanying flyer describes it as a "silver mounted buffalo horn."[4] Dr. Frederick Weedon mentioned a powder horn as one of the accoutrements that Osceola had with him at the time of his death.[5] These scattered, conflicting references, however, were enough to kindle a spark of excitement, and coupled with two small, aged pieces of paper, they were almost enough to occasion the expenditure of a sizable amount of money in the 1980s on two Osceola artifacts that almost certainly are spurious. Moreover, the existence of the artifacts and their interesting story were enough, ironically, to provide the impetus for an entire research project: this epilogue was, in reality, the prologue to *Osceola's Legacy*.

It is every museum's dream to find artifacts so tantalizing that they are almost too good to be true; it is also too often every museum's nightmare, after making the purchases, to discover that they *are* too good to be true. In one recent instance, it was possible to make the critical discovery beforehand and thereby avoid everything—except a week or so of feverish activity and, of course, the disappointment.

The entire story began innocently enough. I had made the two-and-one-half-hour trip from Tallahassee to Gainesville to spend the day at the Florida State Museum (FSM, now the Florida State Museum of Natural History) conducting graphic research for a forthcoming traveling exhibit on Florida's Seminole Indians. Our Museum of Florida History registrar, Dennis Pullen, had also come along in order to deliver artifacts to our "sister" museum. Upon our arrival, FSM's registrar, Deborah Harding, immediately invited us to examine and comment upon two artifacts that had just been received: a carbine and a powder horn purported to have been the property of Osceola. We were soon joined by Jerald Milanich, then chairman of FSM's Department of Anthropology, who explained the provenance of the pieces and the circumstances by which they had been offered for sale to the museum.

The circuitous route by which the artifacts and their alleged documentation had returned to Florida was not of itself unusual, even though it had begun almost eighty years earlier. A private individual had purchased a house in Albany, New York, about 1912 and had ostensibly discovered the pieces in the attic. Along with the gun and the horn were two small, yellowed pieces of paper. One, a note penned at St. Augustine, "Florida Territory," in August 1838, indicated shipment of a carabine (carbine) and a powder horn. The other was a freight bill form filled in to certify delivery of, and payment for, one box, contents unspecified, to the gentleman to whom the note had been addressed. The text of the note read:

St. Augustine
Florida Territory August 27, 1838

Mr. J. W. Jackson
Dear Sir:
I am instructed by Doctor Weedon to notify you that the enclosed carabine and powder horn were once the possessions of the savage Osceola.
Further instructions will follow by separate post.

Yours very respectfully,
Samuel Pond

Over the years since 1912, the artifacts had subsequently been sold at a New York gun show in 1982 to a dealer in Native American artifacts whose headquarters were in Salt Lake City, Utah. This dealer now offered the pieces, along with their documentation, to FSM—for the not inconsequential sum of $100,000.

The descriptions of the pieces were unpretentious enough, as well may have been the pieces themselves in an earlier day. In 1983, however, the gun and horn that accompanied the notes were rare enough to generate much intense interest across at least four hundred miles of modern Florida territory. The gun indeed appeared to be a carbine, but its stock and forearm had been ornamented with trade beads of various colors, and the ventral spine of the stock bore the beaded legend, "ASIYAHOLO OSCEOLA." The powder horn was carved throughout with longitudinal friezes of repetitious geometric motives interspersed with bands containing naive but recognizable representations of Florida wildlife. In addition, two of the friezes bore legends—one had "SEMNOOLOSCEOLA," and the other had "JULIT 1835."

On the basis of just a visual examination, we did not find either artifact to have any anomalies that would immediately disqualify it from consideration as a legitimate piece. That is to say, the carbine did not exhibit any style of manufacture that was obviously post-1830s, although some of its individual parts did appear incongruous in context with each other. The beads also appeared to be of a shape, color, size, and material consistent with the period, although the presence of the beadwork as ornamentation on a weapon was unusual among Creek and Seminole Indian material-culture traditions. Many museum curators, however, have built their entire reputations on locating the rare exceptions to material-culture "rules." The coloration of the powder horn marked it as being at least nineteenth century, and the style of its ornamentation was consistent with Osceola's period.

Beyond the physical characteristics of the pieces, the spelling of the legends presented something of a mystery. They were either authentic misspellings by an unschooled individual or a non-English speaker or were perhaps poor phoneticisms chosen by a modern forger as crude approximations of 1830s illiteracy. Closer examination of the engraving technique with the aid of a microscope and ultraviolet light would possibly solve this mystery.

The carbine had two immediate strikes against its authenticity: it was neither a rifle nor silver mounted. Neither point was enough to preclude further investigation of the weapon, however, for several reasons.

1. Smith's description, although containing more detail than any other, was also not substantiated by any other contemporary sources.
2. Smith admitted in his dedication that the early portion of his book covered events that took place before his arrival in Florida and that he had relied upon the accounts of others, upon whose names and characters he did not elucidate.[6]
3. There was no reason to assume that Osceola had only one gun or that a highly ornamented "presentation" gun would have been used every day.
4. One of the few remaining lacunae of Second Seminole War documentation regards the types, numbers, and sources of longarms used by the Indians in the prosecution of the war.[7] As a consequence, the carbine in question could not be ruled out, if indeed it had been manufactured early enough.
5. Although numerous graphic representations of Osceola show him holding a longarm, none contains enough detail to permit definite identification or comparison. Painters of American Indians during the middle two quarters of the nineteenth century were fascinated with the color and drama of the Indians' unique dress style. A few, such as George Catlin, were also intrigued by the cultural context of Indian scenes. White artists, nevertheless, were primarily purveyors of a white mindset and as such were little interested in examining specific facets of the unique whole.[8]

Obviously, no identification of this import could be made on the basis of one cursory visual examination. I asked for and received permission to have the artifacts transferred to Tallahassee for further investigation at the

Conservation Laboratory of the Bureau of Archaeological Research. In the meantime, some research in the records of the Florida State Archives might shed light on the information contained in the paper documents that accompanied the pieces.

Unfortunately, the available intermittent tax rolls from St. Johns County covering the period 1838 to 1848 showed no taxpaying citizen named Samuel Pond. Nor did the files of the St. Augustine Historical Society identify Mr. Pond. A search of printed genealogical materials covering Albany, New York, in the late 1830s also failed to yield information concerning J. W. Jackson. In the limited time available, then, only one corroborative point was established concerning the pieces of paper. Examination of both sheets by technicians at the Florida State Archives Paper Conservation Laboratory indicated paper, ink, and writing styles consistent with the dates shown. The mention of Dr. Weedon was, of course, a slightly esoteric and important point in favor of the accuracy of one of the documents. The critical point regarding the sheets of paper, however, was that even if their provenance could be established beyond a shadow of a doubt, their primary value was still only documentary, not artifactual. That is to say, the fact that these two "good" pieces of paper and two artifacts were available together in 1983 did not automatically make the artifacts "good" by association or prove that these were the same two artifacts referred to in the documents.

Within the week, the artifacts were transported to the headquarters of the Division of Historical Resources in Tallahassee by Deborah Harding. There, an extensive microscopic examination was conducted by members of the technical staff of the Museum of Florida History and the Bureau of Archaeological Research.[9]

Close inspection quickly discounted the powder horn. It had an overall length of 11½" and a base diameter of 2½". The horn itself exhibited coloration, striations, and wear patterns that indicted it was at least old enough to have been in use in the early nineteenth century. The engraving, however, was discovered to have been executed with a modern drilling tool. Although this information certainly tainted the rest of the group, it did not constitute prima facie evidence for rejection of the other artifact. The weapon would not be disproved so easily.

The gun was a late-style flintlock, transitional to the percussion-cap design. It bore no maker's marks, contract numbers, proof marks, or other civilian or military designations. The weapon's dimensions were consistent with those of other nineteenth-century carbines: it had an overall length of 40⁹⁄₁₆", a barrel length (muzzle face to tang) of 24¾", and a .68 caliber bore. The muzzle face, however, had anomalous tool marks on its interior rim that suggested the barrel may have been shortened at some time. Although an unmarked weapon was not particularly unusual for the period, it was perplexing to find a weapon that appeared to have been assembled from so many disparate parts. This fact might simply mark the piece as "homemade" (a rather inexpensive choice if it were a gift) or as a trade gun (one of a variety of poor-grade weapons that the English frequently reserved for colonial Natives). On the other hand, such a weapon would be useful from the viewpoint of anyone interested in disposing of a spurious artifact, because each of the gun's parts would now have to be treated separately for dating purposes.

There was one important fact in our favor in this regard, however. It quickly became obvious that the forward barrel band could not be removed because it was obstructed by the beading on the forearm. The majority of the carbine's parts therefore had to have been assembled before the beading was done, and because it was the beaded legend that created the cultural link with Osceola, any one of several of the parts might provide the terminus post quem for the entire weapon. The barrel bands were brass and had been altered to fit the weapon. The ramrod was metal and of the appropriate length and diameter to fit the barrel. The frizzen was fairly clean; that is, it did not exhibit wear consistent with the sustained firings that might be expected if it had indeed been used in warfare over almost three years.

The side lock plate was small, oval, and plain and held in place by only one screw. This detail was suggestive of sporting arms rather than grosser military weapons. The trigger was of brass, which was also out of context with other parts. The trigger guard closely resembled the M1841 military contract guards produced by the Ames Company of Springfield, Massachusetts, for its government-contract navy revolver. This trigger guard plate had been straightened out to accommodate the configuration of the less-curved "fish belly" stock. A wooden plug on the ventral side of the stock might have been used to fill a previous sling-swivel mount, which lent credence to the theory that the barrel had been shortened.

The lock was crisp and appeared to have original oxidation inside and out, although the sear and bridle were replacement parts. This repair had been made during the twentieth century, however, because inside the lock cavity a modern drill bit tip was found, along with electric drill marks corresponding to the replaced parts.

While the weapon was partially disassembled for inspection, color photographs were taken to document the points thus far noted. In addition, F. E. ("Jack") Williams III, a well-known gun collector from St. Augustine, was invited to inspect the carbine at this time. He also noted that the tang screw was a modern 10-32 (machine made) replacement part and that the corresponding screw hole had been retapped all the way through the trigger guard bow. Williams suggested that several of the parts, especially the barrel bands, were reminiscent of those produced by Ames, under contract, for the Jenks breech-loading percussion carbine.[10] If this source could be substantiated, then the artifact's authenticity would have to be discounted because Jenks patented his new breech-loading invention at Columbia, South Carolina, on 25 May 1838—almost four months after Osceola's death at Charleston. Obviously, more research was in order.

One of the better-known firearms experts in the country is Harry Hunter at the National Museum of American History/Smithsonian Institution, Washington, D.C., and it was to him that I turned next, hoping for some definitive answer. After a telephone conversation describing the situation, I forwarded 35-mm color slides of the carbine for his inspection. His opinion, although not entirely unexpected at this point, was still disappointing.[11] The likelihood of our having found two heretofore unknown Osceola artifacts was remote. Mr. Hunter advised that the weapon appeared to be an English-style carbine, not a Jenks, and probably from the period 1820–1840. Many merchants and middlemen arms dealers (for example, the Wilkes family that operated in England from about 1827 through the early 1850s) bought up cheap and obsolete arms and sold them throughout the world. The carbine in question was most reminiscent of those sold in the Balkans. Hunter's advice was essentially the same as that of Norman Flayderman (now deceased), international gun dealer, with whom I had consulted regarding the artifacts.[12] It is, beyond all technical expertise, the sine qua non for curators, collectors, and dealers alike. According to Flayderman, "If the artifact doesn't jump right up and 'talk' to you, and if the dealer can't offer overwhelming proof of its validity, then don't buy with your heart."

The story of these purported Osceola artifacts has two ironic postscripts. Several months after the artifacts had been returned to the Utah dealer, the topic of their attempted sale came up in a conversation with another Florida dealer.[13] By this coincidence it was revealed that the Utah dealer had brought the artifacts into Florida for gun shows at least twice before they were offered to the Florida State Museum—and the price had been less than half of that asked of the state of Florida. Then, in April 1986, the artifacts and their owner surfaced again. During a research visit with Mary Weedon Keen in Tallahassee, I was apprised of a letter she had received, dated 3 March 1986. The letter was from Glenn C. Anderson of Sun Dance Gallery, Salt Lake City, Utah. It was the follow-up to a telephone call in which the dealer had discussed the artifacts belonging to Mrs. Keen (the lock of hair, pipe, and so on). It also included a photoduplicate of a letter that Anderson had sent on the same day to Josephine Weedon Stipe in

North Carolina. One letter outlined Anderson's historical justification for his belief in the authenticity of the artifacts. It was filled with misconceptions and inaccuracies. Mr. Anderson never mentioned his interest in selling the artifacts, however, nor were values or money discussed. I advised both Mrs. Stipe and Mrs. Keen to offer no further information.[14] But even then the story did not end. As late as 1988 the two pieces were still on the market; no buyer had yet been found who was willing to accept a very expensive offer of two alleged Osceola artifacts.

Appendix A

Summary of Osceola Artifacts

Artifact[a]	Provenance[b]	Text Reference/ Citation[b]
CLOTHING		
1. *Hunting shirt, buckskin*	Motte/Fisher/N.Y./Heye	Chap. 13
2. *Hunting shirt, buckskin*	Denver	—
3. Jacket	Moravian Historical Society	Boyd, "Asi-Yaholo"
4. *Hunting shirt, textile*	Germany	—
5. *Hunting shirt, textile*	Germany	—
6. Deerskin hunting shirt	—	Ransom, *Osceola*
7. Hunting shirt of chintz or calico	—	Catlin litho. doc.[c]
8. Tunic [shirt] of chintz or calico, brighter than the hunting shirt	—	Catlin litho. doc.
9. Shirt	—	Weedon (in Ward, "Disappearance")
10. Full-dress suit [hunting shirt, leggings] of buckskin, beautifully worked with beads	Graham/Lawrence/Fla.	SLF
11. All his trappings	Quattlebaum	Quattlebaum, "Family"
12. 2 low and ornamented moccasins	—	Ransom, *Osceola*
13. 2 moccasins	—	Storrow, "Osceola"

14. 2 moccasins	—	Weedon (in Ward, "Disappearance")
15. 2 moccasins of buckskin, garnished with porcupine quills	—	Catlin litho. doc.
16. 2 leggings	—	Weedon (in Ward, "Disappearance")
17. 2 leggings of red broadcloth	—	Catlin litho. doc.

HEADGEAR

18. Large silk shawl, for head-dress	Morrison/Hook/ Casey/Beebe	A-NC; Foreman, *Indian Removal;*
19. India shawl of bright colors, tied in the form of a turban	—	Catlin litho. doc.
20. Red cloth turban	—	Ransom, *Osceola*
21. Turban	—	Weedon (in Ward, "Disappearance")

ACCOUTREMENTS

22. Rifle	—	Potter, *War*
23. Silver mounted rifle	—	Smith, *Sketch*
24. Carabine	Weedon/Pond/Jackson	—
25. Long barrel Spanish rifle, with plain flintlock	—	Catlin litho. doc.
26. *Belt knife*	Weedon/Stipe	Chap. 9
27. Long sharp knife	—	Ransom, *Osceola*
28. Knife	—	A-NC; Bemrose, *Reminiscences;* Welch, *Narrative;* Cohen, *Notices*
29. War knife	—	Storrow, "Osceola"
30. Knives	—	Weedon (in Ward, "Disappearance")
31. Knife	—	Catlin litho. doc.
32. Sheath (for knife)	—	Weedon (in Ward, "Disappearance")
33. Powder horn	Weedon/Pond/Jackson	—
34. Powder horn	—	Weedon (in Ward, "Disappearance")
35. Silver mounted buffalo horn [powder horn]	—	Catlin litho. doc.
36. 2 spurs	—	Storrow, "Osceola"
37. Keen-edged tomahawk	—	Ransom, *Osceola*

PERSONAL ADORNMENTS

38. Otter-skin bullet pouch	—	Catlin litho. doc.
39. Handsome headgear of beautiful ostrich plumes	Quattlebaum	Quattlebaum, "Family"

40. Black ostrich feather	—	Smith, *Sketch*
41. 4 black ostrich feathers	Morrison/Hook/ Casey/Beebe	A-NC; Foreman, *Indian Removal*
42. 2 white ostrich feathers	Morrison/Hook/ Casey/Beebe	A-NC; Foreman, *Indian Removal*
43. 3 ostrich plumes	—	Weedon (in Ward, "Disappearance")
44. 3 ostrich plumes surmounting the turban	—	Catlin litho. doc.
45. White plume	—	Giddings, *Exiles*; Boyd, "Asi-Yaholo"
46. Tall, nodding plume	—	Ransom, *Osceola*
47. Plume	—	Storrow, "Osceola"
48. Many odd feathers	—	Ransom, *Osceola*
49. White crane feathers	Graham	*St. Augustine Florida Herald*
50. Scarlet handkerchief	—	Smith, *Sketch*
51. Blue handkerchief	—	Smith, *Sketch*
52. Handkerchiefs	—	Weedon diary
53. Scarf	—	Boyd, "Asi-Yaholo"
54. 2 scarves, pendant from each wrist	—	Catlin litho. doc.
55. *Silver concho*	Weedon/Keen/MFH	Chap. 9, fig. 15
56. *Silver gorget*	Royal Scottish Museum	Chap. 13
57. 3 silver gorgets	Morrison/Hook/Casey/ Beebe	A-NC; Foreman, *Indian Removal*
58. 3 silver half moons [gorgets]	—	Catlin litho. doc.
59. Breastplate [gorget]	Graham/Lawrence/Fla	SLF
60. Silver head band [turban band]	Graham/Lawrence/Fla.	SLF
61. 2 silver wristbands	—	Catlin portrait (app. B, no. 7)
62. 2 silver wristbands	—	Catlin litho. doc.
63. Beads, choker, single strand	—	Catlin portrait (chap. 4, fig. 4)
64. Gold joint chain around the neck	—	Catlin litho. doc.
65. 3–4 beads, long strands	—	Catlin portrait (chap. 4, fig. 4)
66. 2 strings of wampum beads	—	Catlin litho. doc.
67. *2 silver earrings*	Weedon/Blount/ADAH	Chap. 9, fig. 16
68. 2 ear drops [earrings]	—	Catlin litho. doc.
69. *Red wool pouch with strap*	Roberts/FSM	Chap. 9, fig. 16
70. Bullet pouch	—	Weedon (in Ward, "Disappearance")
71. Splendid belt of ornamented beads	Morrison/Hook/ Casey/Beebe	A-NC; Foreman, *Indian Removal*

72. Indian belt ornamented with beads	Morrison/Hook/ Casey/Beebe	*A-NC*; Foreman, *Indian Removal*
73. *Beaded belt*	Roberts/FSM	Chap. 13
74. *Beaded belt*	Webster/Rochester Museum	—
75. War belt	—	Weedon (in Ward, "Disappearance")
76. Narrow belt	—	Ransom, *Osceola*
77. Red sash [belt] ornamented with beads	—	Catlin litho. doc.
78. Blue sash [belt] ornamented with beads	Catlin collection	Catlin litho. doc.
79. Beaded sash	Graham/Lawrence/Fla.	SLF
80. *Beaded garter*	Weedon/Blount/ADAH	Chap. 13
81. *2 beaded garters*	Motte/Fisher/N.Y./Heye	Chap. 13
82. Blue guard [garter] composed of beads	Morrison/Hook/ Casey/Beebe	*A-NC*; Foreman, *Indian Removal*
83. 2 gaiters [garters] of bead-worked netting	—	Catlin litho. doc.

PERSONAL POSSESSIONS

84. *Silver mechanical pencil*	Carter/Corson/NPS	Chap. 13
85. *Brass pipe*	Weedon/Keen/MFH	Chap. 9, fig. 14
86. Beaded pipe	—	Giddings, *Exiles*
87. Hairbrush, with glass mirror on the back	Morrison/Hook/ Casey/Beebe	*A-NC*; Foreman, *Indian Removal*
88. Looking glass	—	Weedon (in Ward, "Disappearance")
89. Red paint	—	Weedon (in Ward, "Disappearance")
90. Small whalebone cane	—	Weedon diary/HFP

PHYSICAL AND ASSOCIATED ARTIFACTS

91. *Lock of hair, plaited*	Weedon/Keen/MFH	Chap. 10, fig. 18
92. *Bust* (mold from death cast)	Recli/Morrison/Hook/ Casey/Beebe/NMNH,SI	Chap. 7, fig. 9
93. Death cast (original mold)	—	*Charleston Mercury*, 21 Mar. 1838
94. *Death cast* (first casting from original mold)	NMNH,SI	Chap. 7, fig. 9
95. *Death casts* (second casting from original mold)	NMNH,SI/Ransom/ SAHS/PE	—
96. *Bone casts* (original molds)	Stewart/NMNH,SI	Chap. 6
97. Head	—	"Letters of Forry"
98. Head	Weedon/Whitehurst/ Mott	—
99. Skeleton	NPS	Chap. 6

[a]Artifacts in italics are extant, and locations are as indicated in the text.
[b]In these columns, items are abbreviated as follows:

ADAH	Alabama Department of Archives and History Museum, Montgomery
A-NC	*Army and Navy Chronicle*
Fla.	State of Florida (items now missing)
FSM	Florida State Museum of Natural History, Gainesville
Germany	Museum fur Völkerkunde, Berlin
Heye	Museum of the American Indian, Heye Foundation, New York City
HFP	Howell Family Papers, ADAH
MFH	Museum of Florida History, Tallahassee
NMNH,SI	National Museum of Natural History, Smithsonian Institution
NPS	National Park Service, St. Augustine
SAHS	St. Augustine Historical Society
SLF	State Library of Florida, Tallallassee
WWFP	Weedon and Whitehurst Family Papers, Chapel Hill, N.C.

[c]Catlin Lithograph Document, from about 1838, in the Osceola file, St. Augustine Historical Society.

Appendix B

Graphic Representations of Osceola

This list gives fuller information for the various graphic representations of Osceola referred to in chapter 4. All dimensions appear in inches, with height preceding width. The location indicates the current or last-known place where the work may be found. (See the bibliography for full information on sources cited here.)

1. Figure 1
Title: [Osceola]
Artist: "Drawn, Engraved, and Printed by W[illiam] Keenan"
Executed: Charleston, S.C., 1836
Medium: Black and white
Size: Page: 6⅝ × 3⅞; image: full-page bleed
Location: Cohen, *Notices of Florida*, facing p. 45

2. Figure 2
Title: Oseola
Artist: Capt. John Rogers Vinton, USA
Executed: St. Augustine, Fla., 4 May 1837
Medium: Pencil sketch, right-profile bust
Size: Paper: 3⅛ × 3¼
Location: Museum of the American Indian, Heye Foundation, New York, neg. no. 26048

3. (Not reproduced here)

Title:	OSEOLA
Artist:	[Greene and McGowran's Lithography], lithographic artist unknown; after Vinton (no. 2 above)
Executed:	[New York], 1837
Medium:	Black and white stone lithograph
Size:	Page: 6⅜ × 3⅛; image: 3 × 3¾
Location:	Williams, *Territory of Florida*, frontispiece

4. (Not reproduced here)

Title:	Osceola, Chief of the Seminoles
Artist:	William L. Laning
Executed:	Charleston, S.C., 1837(–38)
Medium:	Oil on canvas
Size:	Image: 36⅛ × 28
Location:	Chrysler Museum, Norfolk, Va.

5. Figure 3

Title:	Osceola
Artist:	Robert John Curtis
Executed:	Charleston, S.C., January 1838
Medium:	Oil on canvas
Size:	Image: 30 × 24
Location:	Charleston Museum, Charleston, S.C., acc. no. AZ-76

6. Figure 4

Title:	Osceola, the Black Drink, a warrior of great distinction
Artist:	George Catlin
Executed:	Charleston, S.C. [and New York?], January 1838
Medium:	Oil on canvas, no. 301
Size:	Image 30⅞ × 25⅞
Location:	National Museum of American Art, Smithsonian Institution, acc. no. 1985.66.301

7. Figure 5

Title:	Osceola, The Black Drink
Artist:	George Catlin
Executed:	Charleston, S.C. [and New York?], January 1838
Medium:	Oil on canvas, no. 308
Size:	Image: 28 × 23⅛
Location:	American Museum of Natural History, New York City

8. (Not reproduced here)

Title:	O.CE.O.LA OBT. JANY. 30. 1838
Artist:	William Keenan, after Curtis
Executed:	Charleston, S.C., 1838
Medium:	Steel engraving
Size:	Image: 14¾ × 11½
Location:	Largest Print File, "Osceola," South Caroliniana Library, University of South Carolina, Columbia

9. (Not reproduced here)

Title:	O.CE.O.LA OBT. JANY. 30. 1838
Artist:	William Keenan, after Curtis
Executed:	Charleston, S.C., 1838
Medium:	Steel engraving, colored by hand
Size:	Image: 14¾ × 11½
Location:	Largest Print File, "Osceola," South Caroliniana Library, University of South Carolina, Columbia

10. (Not reproduced here)

Title:	Osceola, of Florida
Artist:	George Catlin
Executed:	New York, 1838
Medium:	Stone lithograph by the artist, colored by hand
Size:	Image: 26¼ × 19½
Location:	Various, including Library of Congress, acc. no. PGA-D-Catlin; National Archives, acc. no. 111-SC-93123; National Portrait Gallery, Smithsonian Institution, acc. no. S/81.5; New-York Historical Society, New York, neg. no. 33950; Thomas Gilcrease Institute of American History and Art, Tulsa, Okla.; St. Augustine Historical Society, St. Augustine; Museum of Florida History, Tallahassee; State Library of Florida, Tallahassee

111. (Not reproduced here)

Title:	[Osceola]
Artist:	Robert John Curtis, att.
Executed:	[Charleston, S.C., 1838]
Medium:	Oil on canvas
Size:	Bust, in the small
Location:	Flagler College, St. Augustine

12. (Not reproduced here)

Title:	[Osceola]
Artist:	Robert John Curtis, att.
Executed:	[Charleston, S.C., 1838]
Medium:	Oil on canvas
Size:	Image: 35 × 28
Location:	Elmerside, Inc., Art Dealers, New York

13. (Not reproduced here)

Title:	Osceola, the Great Seminole Chief
Artist:	John Neagle
Executed:	[Philadelphia], between 1838 and 1865
Medium:	Oil on canvas
Size:	Image: 30 × 25
Location:	Unknown

14. (Not reproduced here)

Title:	OSEOLA
Artist:	John H. Bufford, lithographic artist for Nathaniel Currier's Lithography, after Vinton (no. 2 above)
Executed:	New York, 1838
Medium:	Stone lithograph
Size:	Image: 10⅛ × 8¼
Location:	Various, including New-York Historical Society, New York, neg. no. 26041; P. K. Yonge Library of Florida History, University of Florida Library, Gainesville

15. (Not reproduced here)

Title:	Os.ce.o.la
Artist:	F. Pierce, lithographic artist for Nathaniel Currier's Lithography, after Keenan's engraving from Curtis (no. 8 above)
Executed:	New York, 1838
Medium:	Stone lithograph
Size:	Image: 6½ × 3
Location:	Ransom, *Osceola*, frontispiece

16. (Not reproduced here)

Title:	ASSEOLA, a Seminole Leader
Artist:	[J. T. Bowen's Lithographic Establishment], lithographic artist unknown

Executed: Philadelphia, 1838
Medium: Stone lithograph, colored by hand
Size: Page: folio
Location: McKenney and Hall, *History of the Indian Tribes*
                 (1838), vol. 2, facing p. 40

17. (Not reproduced here)
Title: ASSEOLA, a Seminole Leader
Artist: J. T. Bowen's Lithographic Establishment, lithographic
                 artist "H. D."
Executed: Philadelphia, 1838
Medium: Stone lithograph, colored by hand
Size: Page: folio; image: 15½ × 12¾
Location: McKenney and Hall, *History of the Indian Tribes* (1842–
                 44), vol. 2, facing p. 203

18. (Not reproduced here)
Title: [Osceola]
Artist: John Rogers Vinton
Executed: Florida, 1840
Medium: Oil on pasteboard
Size: Image: 13 × 10
Location: Private collection of Christopher Tompkins, New Orleans

19. (Not reproduced here)
Title: [Osceola]
Artist: Day and Haghe, Lithographers to the Queen, London,
                 lithographic artist R. J. Hamerton, after Catlin
Executed: London, 1841
Medium: Stone lithograph
Size: Image: 7 × 4¼
Location: Welch, *Narrative of the Early Days,* facing p. 20

20. (Not reproduced here)
Title: Oseola at Lake Monroe during the Armistice, May 1837
Artist: John Rogers Vinton
Executed: [Mexico], 1845
Medium: Pencil sketch
Size: Image: 8¾ × 5⅜
Location: Mark F. Boyd Collection, Otto G. Richter Library, Spe-
                 cial Collections, University of Miami, Coral Gables

21. (Not reproduced here)

Title: OSCEOLA
Artist: A. Bowen [Lithographic Establishment], lithographic art-
            ist, Miss A. M. Bowen
Executed: Charleston, S.C., 1846
Medium: Stone lithograph, colored
Size: Image: 6 × 4⅝
Location: Trumbull, *History of the Indian Wars*, facing p. 305

22. (Not reproduced here)

Title: As-se-se-he-ho-lar, Black Drink (known as Oceola or
            Powell)
Artist: N. Orr and Richardson, after Vinton (no. 2 above)
Executed: South Carolina and New York, 1848
Medium: Steel engraving
Size: Page: 7³⁄₁₆ × 3⅜; image: 3⁷⁄₁₆ × 3
Location: Sprague, *Florida War*, facing p. 101

23. Figure 6

Title: Seminolee. [Osceola and Four Seminole Indians]
Artist: George Catlin
Executed: [New York], 1849
Medium: Pencil drawing, watercolored by hand
Size: Page: 8 × 10¼
Location: Catlin, *Souvenir of the North American Indians as They
            Were in the Middle of the Nineteenth Century*, cartoon 68,
            pl. 32; Phillipps Collection, Thomas Gilcrease Institute of
            American History and Art, Tulsa, Okla.; New York Pub-
            lic Library; National Gallery of Art, acc. no. 1965.16.119

24. (Not reproduced here)

Title: Osceola
Artist: Samuel Lovett Waldo and William Jewett, after Catlin
Executed: [Boston], 1857
Medium: Lithograph, colored by hand
Size: Page: 8¾ × 4¾; image: 6¾ × 3¾
Location: Brownell, *Indian Races*, facing p. 129

25. (Not reproduced here)

Title: Osceola
Artist: Babbitt and Edmonds, after Waldo and Jewett (no. 24
            above)

Executed: South Carolina, ca. 1857
Medium: Woodcut
Size: Page: 8⅝ × 6⅝; image: 8⅛ × 5⅛
Location: New-York Historical Society, New York, neg. no. 26043

26. (Not reproduced here)
Title: As-se-he-ho-lar (known as Osceola, or Powell)
Artist: N. Orr Co., after Vinton (no. 2 above), probably the
                same plate as no. 22 above
Executed: South Carolina, 1858
Medium: Engraving
Size: Page: 6 × 3⅛; image: 3⅜ × 2⅞
Location: Giddings, *Exiles of Florida*, facing p. 112

27. (Not reproduced here)
Title: Seminolee. Os.ce.o.la (the Black Drink) a very celebrated
                Warrior, half caste, who signalized himself, and took the
                lead in the Seminolee War
Artist: George Catlin, "Album Unique" for the Duke of Portland
Executed: London, 1859
Medium: Pencil drawing
Size: Page: 14 × 10½
Location: Hirschl and Adler Galleries, Inc., New York

Notes

The following abbreviations are used in the notes:

ADAH   Alabama Department of Archives and History, Montgomery
CGS   Commissary General of Subsistence
FHQ   *Florida Historical Quarterly*
NARA   National Archives and Record Administration, Washington, D.C.
OAG   Office of the Adjutant General
RG   Record Group
SAHS   St. Augustine Historical Society, St. Augustine

Preface

1. John Whiteclay Chambers II, ed., *Oxford Companion to American Military History* (Oxford: Oxford University Press, 1999), 519.

Introduction

1. See John M. Goggin, "Osceola: Portraits, Features, and Dress," *FHQ* 33 (January–April 1955): 161–92; and William C. Sturtevant, "Osceola's Coats?" *FHQ* 34 (April 1956): 315–28.

2. Thomas J. Schlereth, *Artifacts and the American Past* (Nashville: American Association for State and Local History, 1980), 2–3.

Chapter 1

1. Throughout this book, I refer to its subject primarily as Osceola because this is the name by which he is most commonly remembered and recognized today, even in Indian Country, and because such usage will preclude making a complex story any more confusing. I deviate from this spelling only within direct quotations.

2. The terms "Maskókî" and "Creek" are sometimes synonymous but not always useful because they may obscure more than they clarify. For a fuller explanation of the terms in their historical and geographical settings, I refer readers to my book *The Tree That Bends: Discourse, Power, and the Survival of the Maskókî People* (Tuscaloosa: University of Alabama Press, 1999). For the purposes of furthering the story of Osceola within the larger history of the southeastern Maskókî peoples, I will retain the term "Creek" wherever it helps or at least does not confuse the story.

3. An excellent example of the tradition that children remained with their mothers' clans comes from the life of the U.S. Indian agent Benjamin Hawkins. Shortly after his arrival in Creek territory, the Indian mother of his assistant, Timothy Bernard, offered one of her daughters to Hawkins. He considered the union (its duration left undetermined), but the offer was withdrawn as the result of their disagreement over the custody of potential offspring. Hawkins expected that the children would be his. The mother would not agree that her daughter's "children should be under the direction of the father, and the negotiation ended there." See "Letters of Benjamin Hawkins, 1796–1806," *Collections of the Georgia Historical Society*, vol. 9 (Savannah, 1916), 85, cited in Merritt B. Pound, *Benjamin Hawkins—Indian Agent* (Athens: University of Georgia Press, 1951), 148–49.

4. Robert V. Remini, *Andrew Jackson and His Indian Wars* (New York: Viking Penguin Books, 2001), 1–4, 78, 89, 90; for more detailed discussion, see Robert V. Remini, *Andrew Jackson and the Course of American Empire, 1767–1821*, vol. 1 (New York: Harper and Row, 1977).

5. Remini, *Andrew Jackson and the Course of American Empire*. For further discussion of the Creek War of 1813–1814, see also H. S. Halbert and T. H. Ball, *The Creek War of 1813 and 1814* (1895; repr., Tuscaloosa: University of Alabama Press, 1995).

6. On this topic, see John R. Swanton, "The Indians of the Southeastern United States," *Bureau of American Ethnology*, Bulletin 137 (1946; repr., Washington, D.C.: Smithsonian Institution Press, 1976), 81; Lawrence A. Clayton, Vernon James Knight, Jr., and Edward C. Moore, eds., *The DeSoto Chronicles: The Expedition of Hernando de Soto to North America in 1539–1543*, 2 vols. (Tuscaloosa: University of Alabama Press, 1993).

7. James W. Covington, "The British Meet the Seminoles: Negotiations between British Authorities in East Florida and the Indians, 1763–1768," *Contributions of the Florida State Museum*, Social Sciences, No. 7 (Gainesville: Florida State Museum, 1961).

8. John Lee Williams, *The Territory of Florida; or, Sketches of the Topography,*

Civil, and Natural History, of the Country, the Climate, and the Indian Tribes, from the First Discovery to the Present Time (1837; repr., Gainesville: University Presses of Florida, 1962), 275.

9. Susie Jim Billie (ca. 1890–2000), the eldest medicine practitioner in the Seminole Tribe of Florida, was fluent in an old form of Mikísuúkî (Hitchiti) the medicine language of core Maskókî. When I asked her whether she recalled the man Abiákî, she responded immediately "Abeca?" Susie Jim Billie, personal communication, 1994.

10. John T. Sprague, *The Origin, Progress, and Conclusion of the Florida War; to which is appended a record of Officers, Non-Commissioned Officers, Musicians, and Privates of the U.S. Army, Navy, and Marine Corps, who were killed in battle or died of disease. As also the names of Officers Who Were Distinguished by Brevets, and the Names of Others Recommended. Together with the order for collecting the remains of the dead in Florida, and the ceremony of interest at St. Augustine, East Florida, on the fourteenth day of August, 1842* (1848; repr., Gainesville: University Presses of Florida, 1964).

11. Susie Jim Billie, among other Florida and Oklahoma Seminoles and Maskókî (Creeks), confirmed this as well. Susie recalled that Cowácuchî(t) (Coacoochee) was much more powerful than Osceola in leadership terms, which was to say in terms of heredity as well. Susie Jim Billie, personal communication, 1994.

12. Wickman, *Tree That Bends*, 95–104.

13. Sprague, *Origin, Progress, and Conclusion*, 80.

14. General T. S. Jesup to Colonel Z. Taylor, "Headquarters Army of the South, St. Augustine, Oct. 27th 1837," NARA, RG 94, OAG, Generals' Papers and Books, Letters Sent by Staff, July–October 1837, box 28.

15. NARA, RG 192, CGS, "1835 Seminoles, Emigration," Item no. 35, "Hon. Wiley Thompson (Reports murder of Charley Emathla)"; and holograph copy, Wiley Thompson to S. V. Walker, Seminole Agency, 23 June 1835, ibid.

16. NARA, RG 192, CGS, "1835 Seminoles, Emigration," File [3], "Hon. Wiley Thompson, Spec. Agent (Punishment & Repentance of Powell? Chief Osceola"; and Wiley Thompson to Gen. George Gibson, Seminole Agency [Fort King], 3 June 1835, ibid.

17. Sprague, *Origin, Progress and Conclusion*, 88.

18. NARA, RG 192, CGS, "1835 Seminoles, Emigration"; and Wiley Thompson to Gen. George Gibson, Seminole Agency [Fort King], 30 November 1835, ibid.

19. Richard Keith Call to Andrew Jackson, 22 December 1835, in *Territorial Papers of the United States*, vol. 25, *Florida*, ed. and comp. by Clarence E. Carter and John P. Bloom (Washington, D.C.: U.S. Government Printing Office, 1944-), 216–17; Mark Boyd, "Florida Aflame: Background and Onset of the Seminole War, 1835," *FHQ* 30 (July 1951): 56–57; Mark Boyd, "Jacksonville and the Seminole War, 1835, 1836" *FHQ* 3 (January–April 1925): 17–19; [Woodburne Potter], *The War in Florida, Being an Exposition of Its Causes and an Accurate History of the Campaigns of Generals Clinch, Gaines, and Scott. By a late staff officer* (1836; repr., n.p.: Readex Microprint, 1966), 100–101.

20. John K. Mahon, *History of the Second Seminole War, 1835–1842* (Gaines-

ville: University Presses of Florida, 1967), 104–6. For an in-depth account of this event, see Frank Laumer, *Dade's Last Command* (Gainesville: University Presses of Florida, 1995).

21. Wickman, *Tree That Bends*, 221.

22. Sprague reports that he had it from another war leader, Alligator, that Osceola "was hit in the arm, which disabled him, and was the cause of the Indians' retreating." See Sprague, *Origin, Progress, and Conclusion*, 92–93. W. W. Smith, in his *Sketch of the Seminole War and Sketches during a Campaign. By a Lieutenant of the Left Wing* (Charleston, S.C.: Dan J. Dowling, 1836), 47, says that Osceola was only wounded in the left hand, although "for some time after the battle, he was not heard of, and it was supposed that he had been severely wounded or killed." Henry Prince, in his diary entry for 17 February 1836, noted that an express rider from Tallahassee said that "Powel received two shots and is recovering." See Henry Prince, *Amidst a Storm of Bullets: 1836–1842, the Diary of Lt. Henry Prince of Florida*, ed. Frank Laumer, Seminole Wars Historic Foundation, Inc., Contribution Number One (Tampa: University of Tampa Press, 1998).

23. Smith, *Sketch of the Seminole War*, 67.

24. Ibid., 67–68.

25. M[yer] M. Cohen, *Notices of Florida and the Campaigns* (1836; repr., Gainesville: University of Florida Press, 1964), 125–26.

26. John Bemrose, *Reminiscences of the Second Seminole War*, ed. John K. Mahon (Gainesville: University of Florida Presses, 1966), 77.

27. Williams, *Territory of Florida*, 227–28; Cohen, *Notices of Florida*, 100–101. See also [Potter], *War in Florida*, 156–59; Prince, *Amidst a Storm of Bullets*, entry for 6 March 1836; Bemrose, *Reminiscences*, 77; and Mahon, *Second Seminole War*, 147–49.

28. Sprague, *Origin, Progress, and Conclusion*, 158–59; Williams, *Territory of Florida*, 245, 252; Mahon, *Second Seminole War*, 173–74.

29. Mahon, *Second Seminole War*, 173.

30. Thomas Sydney Jesup, *Seminole Saga: The Jesup Report* (Fort Myers Beach, Fla.: Island Press, 1973), 36–37.

31. Sprague, *Origin, Progress, and Conclusion*, 167.

32. Prince, *Amidst a Storm of Bullets*, entry for 21 March 1837, 90.

33. Col. William S. Harney to Gen. T. S. Jesup, Fort Mellon, East Florida, 26 May 1837, NARA, RG 94, OAG, Generals' Papers and Books, Genl. T. S. Jesup Papers, box 5, "Col. Wm. S. Harney" folder no. 2.

34. Sprague, *Origin, Progress, and Conclusion*, 187–88.

35. Williams, *Territory of Florida*, 270; Capt. J. R. Vinton to Lt. James A. Chambers, Fort Mellon, East Florida, 3 May 1837, NARA, RG 94, OAG, Generals' Papers and Books, Genl. T. S. Jesup Papers, box 9, "Capt. J. R. Vinton" folder.

36. Col. William S. Harney to Gen. T. S. Jesup, Fort Mellon, East Florida, 21 May 1837, NARA, RG 94, OAG, Generals' Papers and Books, Genl. T. S. Jesup Papers, box 5, "Col. Wm. S. Harney" folder no. 2.

37. Ibid.

38. Williams, *Territory of Florida,* 270; Sprague, *Origin, Progress, and Conclusion,* 180; Mahon, *Second Seminole War,* 103–4.

39. Col. William S. Harney to Gen. T. S. Jesup, Fort Mellon, East Florida, 6 June 1837, NARA, RG 94, OAG, Generals' Papers and Books, Genl. T. S. Jesup Papers, box 5, "Col. Wm. S. Harney" folder no. 2.

40. Ibid.

41. Gen. T. S. Jesup to Brig. Gen. W. K. Armistead, 6 June 1837, NARA, RG 94, OAG, Letters Received, Jesup 117.

42. Mahon, *Second Seminole War,* 201.

43. Lt. R. H. Peyton to Col. W. S. Harney, Fort Mellon, East Florida, 24 May 1837, NARA, RG 94, OAG, Generals' Papers and Books, Genl. T. S. Jesup Papers, box 5, "Col. Wm. S. Harney" folder no. 2.

44. The memory that Philip was a Spaniard is held by various Oklahoma Seminoles. I had it first from a personal conversation with Richmond Tiger (now deceased) in 1997.

45. Jacob Rhett Motte, *Journey into Wilderness: An Army Surgeon's Account of Life in Camp and Field during the Creek and Seminole Wars, 1836–1838* (Gainesville: University of Florida Presses, 1953), 138–39.

46. General T. S. Jesup to Colonel Z. Taylor, "Headquarters Army of the South, St. Augustine, Oct. 27th 1837," NARA, RG 94, OAG, Generals' Papers and Books, Letters Sent by Staff, July–October 1837, box 28.

47. Capt. J. R. Vinton to Gen. T. S. Jesup, New York, 22 November 1837, NARA, RG 94, OAG, Generals' Papers and Books, Genl. T. S. Jesup Papers, box 9, "Capt. J. R. Vinton" folder.

48. John Ross, "Report of the Cherokee Deputation into Florida, Washington City, D. C., Feby. 17th, 1838," *Chronicles of Oklahoma* 9, no. 4 (December 1931): 426, 428, 438.

49. *New York Evening Star,* 5 January 1838.

50. Thomas W. Storrow, "Osceola, the Seminole War-Chief," *Knickerbocker Magazine* 24 (November 1844), 447–48.

Chapter 2

1. See Goggin, "Osceola: Portraits, Features, and Dress," 161–92; and Sturtevant, "Osceola's Coats?" 315–28.

2. For a discussion of this topic, see Wickman, *Tree That Bends,* 25–34.

3. Ibid.

4. The people themselves, however, have never forgotten that the term "Maskókî" is a Native term for their ancestors, even though they did not coin it, and they prefer it to the English term "Creek." So, for example, the removed tribe in Oklahoma call themselves the "Muscogee (Creek) Nation of Oklahoma." In the nineteenth century, George Stiggins, a half blood, wrote his valuable *Creek Indian*

History: A Historical Narrative of the Genealogy, Traditions, and Downfall of the Ispocoga or Creek Indian Tribe of Indians by One of the Tribe (Tuscaloosa: University of Alabama Press, 1989).

5. Swanton, "Indians of the Southeastern United States," 218.

6. Ibid.

7. Interestingly, the Maskókî descendents in both Florida and Oklahoma continue to use the word *tchlokî(t)* now and to make their old enemies, today's Cherokee people, the butt of many of their jokes.

8. I have found no definitive translation of the compound word *Tallassee*. Its root is the Maskókî word *tal-*, which is a generic for anyplace where people live as a coherent group bound by Maskókî traditions. The root recurs in numerous forms throughout the language: *talwa; italwa* (which may combine the old word, *ikon*, for earth or land); *talófa* (a place taken in battle); *tallahassee* (old fields; they grew food there, but they are gone). These understandings have been gleaned from many discussions with native Maskókî speakers in Florida and Oklahoma and from R. M. Loughridge, *English and Muskokee Dictionary: Collected from Various Sources and Revised* (ca. 1884); repr., Okmulgee, Okla.: B. Frank Belvin, Baptist Home Mission Board, 1964), esp. 44, 83, 201.

9. See Thomas Woodward, *Woodward's Reminiscences of the Creek, or Muscogee Indians, Contained in Letters to Friends in Georgia and Alabama* (1859; repr., Tuscaloosa, Ala.: Weatherford Printing, 1939), 21.

10. See "Letters of Col. Benjamin Hawkins," 168, cited in John R. Swanton, "Early History of the Creek Indians and Their Neighbors," *Bureau of American Ethnology*, Bulletin 73 (Washington, D.C.: U.S. Government Printing Office, 1922), 244.

11. "Letters of Col. Benjamin Hawkins, 1796–1806," in *Collections of the Georgia Historical Society*, vol. 9 (Savannah, 1916), cited in Mark Boyd, "Asi-Yaholo or Osceola," *FHQ* 33 (January–April 1955): 253.

12. Merton E. Coulter, "A List of the First Shipload of Georgia Settlers," *Georgia Historical Quarterly* 31, no. 4 (December 1947): 282.

13. Don Martini, "Who Was Who among the Southern Indians: A Genealogical Notebook, 1698–1907," typescript in the Collections of the Oklahoma Historical Society, Oklahoma City, 466.

14. Larry Ivers, "The Battle of Fort Mose," *Georgia Historical Quarterly* 51, no. 2 (June 1967): 149.

15. Woodward, *Woodward's Reminiscences*, 9.

16. Joyce Elizabeth Harmon, *Trade and Privateering in Spanish Florida, 1732–1763* (St. Augustine: St. Augustine Historical Society, 1969), ch. 2 passim.

17. This information concerning Scotsmen in the English navy and Scottish commercial presence in Spanish colonies was received in personal correspondence from David Dobson, St. Andrews, Scotland, 11 June 1993. For further discussion of these issues, see his published works: *Directory of Scots Banished to the American Plantations* (Baltimore: Genealogical Publishing, 1983); and *The Original Scots Colonists of Early America* (Baltimore: Genealogical Publishing, 1989).

18. Woodward, *Woodward's Reminiscences*.

19. Ibid., 110, 77, 42.

20. Ibid., 77, 84, 110.

21. James McQueen, christening record of 18 October 1695, County of Edinburgh, Parish of Edinburgh, Old Parochial Register, General Register Office, Edinburgh, Scotland.

22. Wickman, *Tree That Bends*, ch. 4.

23. Woodward, *Woodward's Reminiscences*, 9. A curious but fascinating story concerning the birth of Polly Copinger's son has been passed down through the Frank family in Florida. Even though it does not fit with other information, it does not conflict either. As the story goes, "When Osceola was born, they wanted to leave him out to die [because his father was not an Indian]. They put him away from his mother and left him. At night, he cried and cried and cried all night. The old women told them they must go and get him and bring him back because he was special—he was going to be someone special. When they got him, the ants had eaten off his lips. They had eaten all around his mouth. But he was still handsome when he grew up. He was a Spanish man" (personal communication with the author; source unnamed at the citizen's request). The practice of leaving half-blood infants out on the banks of a river to die or be eaten was still occurring in Florida in the 1930s.

24. *Narrative of a Voyage to the Spanish Main in the Ship "Two Friends," the occupation of Amelia Island, by M'Gregor etc.,—Sketches of the Province of East Florida, and anecdotes illustrative of the Habits and Manners of the Indians; with an Appendix, containing a Detail of the Seminole war, and the execution of Arbuthnot and Ambrister* (1819; repr., Gainesville: University Presses of Florida, 1978), 167.

25. Benjamin Hawkins, "A Sketch of the Creek Country in 1798 and 1799," *Collections of the Georgia Historical Society*, vol. 3, pt. 1 (1848; repr., New York: Kraus Reprint, 1971), 26. See also Swanton, "Early History," 244.

26. Thomas L. McKenney and James Hall, *History of the Indian Tribes of North America, with Biographical Sketches and Anecdotes of the Principal Chiefs. Embellished with One Hundred and Twenty Portraits, from the Indian Gallery in the Department of War, at Washington*, 3 vols. (Philadelphia: Daniel Rice and James G. Clark, 1842–44), 2:225.

27. Woodward, *Woodward's Reminiscences*, 21–22.

28. Ibid., 110, 77, 42.

29. Ibid., 59, 9, 111.

30. Benjamin Hawkins, *The Collected Works of Benjamin Hawkins, 1796–1810*, ed. H. Thomas Foster II (Tuscaloosa: University of Alabama Press, 2003), 50.

31. The widely circulated rumors in southeastern Georgia, all of which link a woman named Missouri Powell Canaday, a Coppinger family, and the Osceola who is the subject of the present researches, do not appear to have validity here. Other than the Irish/Spanish governor of East Florida, José Coppinger of Cuba, the earliest record located thus far for a Coppinger in the lower southeast is for a Joseph Coppinger, who entered the colonies through the port of Charleston, South Carolina, in 1819–20 aboard the schooner *Margaret*. Joseph Coppinger was a merchant who listed the country to which he belonged as Spain and who intended to remain in

Charleston. This date is too late to place him in Tallassee as early as necessary. Nevertheless, there is the possibility that this Joseph Coppinger is the José Mária Coppinger y Saravia who was a son of the East Florida governor José Coppinger. Governor Coppinger married in 1797, and although we have no birth date for his son, José, we do know that he married a *criolla*—a Spanish woman born in St. Augustine, Florida—and that the marriage took place on 6 April 1825. Even if the José who was the son of Governor Coppinger and the Joseph who entered the port of Charleston in 1819-20 were, indeed, the same person, then the scenario is still too late. See: United States of America, *Passenger Arrivals, 1819–1820* (Washington, D.C.: Gales and Seaton, 1821), 27. The surname Coppinger also occurs among Revolutionary War service records of soldiers from Massachusetts and New Jersey, but these individuals do not appear to be connected to the Irish Coppingers who went to Cuba and Florida (Ancestry, Inc., 1999, Orem, Utah, direct data capture from Rolls 35 and 59).

32. El Conde de San Juan de Jaruco, *Historia de Familias Cubanas,* 7 vols. (Miami: Ediciones Universal, 1985), 7:109. This set is considered to be the bible for researchers of Cuban genealogy.

33. Mrs. Morgan John O'Connell, *The Coppingers of Ballyvolane and Barryscourt,* pt. 2 (Manchester, England: Guardian Letterpress, 1883), 188.

34. Patricia R. Wickman to Nestor A. Moreno, St. Augustine, 2 September 1970, SAHS, Coppinger file. See also *National Intelligencer,* 24 July 1819, 3.

35. In the Spanish Florida documents, her name is given as "Senavia." Patricia R. Wickman to Nestor A. Moreno, St. Augustine, 2 September 1970, SAHS, Coppinger file.

36. Benjamin Hawkins knew Ecun hutki, or White Ground, well. He described it as a small village just below Coo-loo-me, on the same side of the Tallapoosa River. See Hawkins, *Collected Works,* 34s. John Swanton cites it as Kan-Hatki, having accepted the Maskókî word for land or ground, *ékon,* without its first syllable. Its nearest neighbor was Fus-hatchee (*foóswa hatchî* or bird tail). It was well established by 1733, at least, but lost much of its population to Florida over the period of the Creek wars. See Swanton, "Indians of the Southeastern United States," 142.

37. Hawkins, *Collected Works,* 195.

38. United States of America, *Passenger Arrivals,* 27.

39. "Last Spanish Governor: Irish and Born in Cuba," article contributed by Coppinger family member Mrs. L. Vianello (Adriana Alacán y Lastres), *Miami Herald,* 5 May 1965; research report on Governor José Coppinger (1816-1821) prepared by Patricia R. Wickman, from the files of the SAHS, "Coppinger," St. Augustine; and El Conde de San Juan de Jaruco, *Historia de Familias Cubanas,* 7:109.

40. Lorene Gopher, a Florida Seminole, recalls the memory of her maternal grandmother, Lucy Pierce (Snake Clan; 1882-1965; daughter of Charley Peacock and Old Nancy) that Osceola was *tathálgî*—a person who spoke a different language. She also recalled that his father (i.e., William Powell) had made a personal choice not to come to Florida with Billy Powell and his mother (Lorene Gopher, personal conversation, 1994).

41. Hawkins, *Collected Works*, 50.

42. Boyd, "Asi-Yaholo or Osceola," passim.

43. Hawkins to Mrs. Eliza Trist, Coweta, 25 November 1797, in Hawkins, *Collected Works*, 254. A Powell family of Columbus County, North Carolina, holds another anecdotal connection to Osceola as well, and I have received information from several of this family's lines but cannot make any connection to known information.

44. Leon Saxon Powell, "Powell Records of Virginia, North Carolina, South Carolina, Georgia," typescript provided by Leon Saxon Powell, in the personal files of Patricia R. Wickman.

45. Ibid.

46. Eugene Current-Garcia, ed., *Shem, Ham, and Japeth: The Papers of W. O. Tuggle, Comprising His Indian Diary, Sketches, and Observations, Myths, and Washington Journal in the Territory and at the Capital, 1879–1882* (Athens: University of Georgia Press, 1973), 131.

47. Ibid., 49.

48. There is no female "Leader" on the Dawes final rolls of the Chickasaws whose age corresponds with that of Hepsy, however. The only female of seventy or older is Jane Leader, No. 107, on the Chickasaw freedman list. There is a list, among the holdings of NARA, Southwest Region, Fort Worth, titled "List of Persons Enrolled on Creek Cards Whose Names May Be on the Rolls of the Cherokee, Choctaw, and Chickasaw Nation." In the section headed "Part Chickasaw," we find Lucy Leader and Nancy Leader, but neither of these individuals is listed on the final Dawes Rolls of the Chickasaws.

49. Parsons-Abbott Census, *1832 Creek Census,* trans. James L. Douthat (Signal Mountain, Tenn.: Institute of Historic Research, 1995), 66. This is a transcription from the original in NARA, micro. T275.

50. Woodward, *Woodward's Reminiscences,* 88; also Dr. Marion Elisha Tarvin [Turvin], "The Mascogees or Creek Indians," typescript, Oklahoma Historical Society, Oklahoma City. Dr. Tarvin was the great-great-grandson of Sehoy Marchand (II) and her first husband, Malcolm McPherson, through their daughter, Sehoy (who was also the mother of the famous William Weatherford, or Red Eagle). Sehoy Marchand (II) later became the wife of Lachlan McGillivray, with whom she had four more children: Sophia, the ambitious Alexander, Jeanne, and Elizabeth. This Sophia and Benjamin Durant were the parents of Betsy, who married first Peter McQueen and, after his death, his nephew Willy McQueen. Halbert and Ball, in their *Creek War of 1813 and 1814,* do not include an alliance between Sehoy Marchand (II) and Malcolm McPherson. They assert that her first partner was a "Tabacha chief" by whom she had Sehoy (III), the great-grandmother of Dr. Marion Elisha Tarvin. Halbert and Ball collected information from numerous sources second- and third-hand, however, and Woodward discusses, courteously, the errors into which they fell. Halbert and Ball also discuss Woodward with respect, and I have found Woodward to be more reliable. In the case of Dr. Tarvin, he was discussing his own family, albeit from a chronological and geographical distance and, admit-

tedly, with help from old friends. I conclude that Sehoy (II) certainly may well have had three men as partners at various times, but a "Tabacha chief" (Tuckabatchee?) is an anomaly, and Dr. Tarvin is, on the whole, the more credible of the two sources.

51. For further discussion of the politics of this period, one excellent source is Michael D. Green, *The Politics of Indian Removal: Creek Government and Society in Crisis* (Lincoln: University of Nebraska Press, 1982), 14–42.

52. Ibid.

53. See Remini, *Andrew Jackson and His Indian Wars,* 87–93. See also Halbert and Ball, *Creek War;* Mahon, *Second Seminole War,* 6–7.

54. Remini, *Andrew Jackson and His Indian Wars,* 87–93.

55. Woodward, *Woodward's Reminiscences,* 43–44.

56. Lorene Bowers Gopher, from her grandmother, Lucy Pearce, personal communication, 1994.

57. Sprague, *Origin, Progress, and Conclusion,* 100.

58. Hawkins, "Sketch of Creek Country," 74.

59. Sprague, *Origin, Progress, and Conclusion,* 100–101.

60. Col. Benjamin Hawkins to Governor Early, 14 June 1814 and 20 February 1815, in the Telemon Cuyler Collection, University of Georgia, Athens, cited in Boyd, "Asi-Yaholo or Osceola," 256.

61. The British were serious about rewarding the Creeks, who had fought with them against the Americans in parts of the War of 1812. Article 9 of the Treaty of Ghent, which closed that war, required the United States to return "all possessions" of the Creeks, that is, their lands, to the extent they had encompassed in 1811, before the war. In yet another instance of disregard, however, the United States chose to ignore article 9.

62. Woodward, *Woodward's Reminiscences,* 153.

63. *American State Papers: Indian Affairs,* 2:156, cited in Charles H. Fairbanks, *Ethnohistorical Report of the Florida Indians,* Indian Land Claims Commission, Dockets no. 73, 151 (1957; repr., New York: Garland Press, 1974), 224.

64. Col. John Banks to the Editor, *Columbus (Ga.) Sun,* 27 May 1858, in Woodward, *Woodward's Reminiscences,* 50–51.

65. Woodward, *Woodward's Reminiscences,* 45.

66. Andrew Jackson to Calhoun, 20 April 1818, in *American State Papers: Military Affairs,* 700; Jackson, *Papers,* 4:193n1; and Andrew Jackson to Calhoun, 26 April 1818, in Jackson, *Correspondence,* 2:363; all cited in Remini, *Andrew Jackson and His Indian Wars,* 151.

67. Hawkins, "Sketch of Creek Country," 69.

68. The clearest explanation of this word comes from Henry John Billie, Seminole Tribe of Florida, personal communications, 1992–99.

69. See the example cited in my publication *Tree That Bends,* chapter 4, concerning the Escampaba leader Calos and his successor, Don Felipe. For translations and discussion of the Spanish documents, see Felix Zubillaga, ed., *Monumenta Antiquae Floridae* (Rome: Monumenta Missionum Societas Iesu, 1946), as docs. 41 and 85, in *Missions to the Calusa,* trans. and ed. John H. Hann (Gainesville: University

Presses of Florida, 1991), 230–85. For the reproductions of sixteenth-century images and text of Florida natives, see Stefan Lorant, ed., *The New World: The First Pictures of America* (New York: Duell, Sloan and Pearce, 1946).

70. *American State Papers: Indian Affairs,* 1:847, 849, 851, 852, 857; *American State Papers: Military Affairs,* 1:682, 683, 700, 749; Woodward, *Woodward's Reminiscences,* 9, 21, 25, 42, 44, 48, 97, 110, 153; Halbert and Ball, *Creek War,* 125–49.

71. Fairbanks, *Ethnohistorical Report,* 245. This same list and variants appear in several other sources that are most lucidly compared and examined by Fairbanks.

72. See my exposition of the process of linguistic transference that brought this term into the Florida Indian lexicon, in Wickman, *Tree That Bends,* 192–98.

73. Woodward, *Woodward's Reminiscences,* 25.

74. Fairbanks, *Ethnohistorical Report,* 245. Again, Fairbanks presents the most cogent synthesis of a number of cited figures.

75. Sprague, *Origin, Progress, and Conclusion,* 100–101.

76. Ibid.

77. *American Anti-Slavery Almanac* (New York: Webster and Southard, 1839), 25.

78. Joshua Giddings, *The Exiles of Florida; or, the Crimes Committed by Our Government against the Maroons, Who Fled from South Carolina and Other Slave States, Seeking Protection under Spanish Law* (1858; repr., Gainesville: University Presses of Florida, 1964), 98; and Cohen, *Notices of Florida.* Cohen should not be accepted at face value but evaluated only in conjunction with other primary sources. Taken together with these others, however, he provides many fascinating details.

79. See also Kenneth W. Porter, "The Episode of Osceola's Wife: Fact or Fiction," *FHQ* 26 (July 1947): 92–98.

80. List of prisoners held at Fort Marion, East Florida, in November 1837 from the personal papers of Capt. Lucien B. Webster, who was the commanding officer at Fort Marion, in Lucien B. Webster Papers, SAHS.

81. Rev. Orson Douglas to Commissioner of Indian Affairs Crawford, 15 August 1843, NARA, RG 75, Office of Indian Affairs, Seminole File D816, cited in Grant Foreman, *The Five Civilized Tribes: Cherokee, Chickasaw, Choctaw, Creek, Seminole,* 5th ed. (Norman: University of Oklahoma Press, 1974), 239.

82. Lt. Col. A. G. W. Fanning to Lt. James Chambers, St. Augustine, 16 December 1837, NARA, RG 94, OAG, Generals' Papers and Books, Genl. T. S. Jesup, box 4, "Col. A. G. W. Fanning" folder no. 2.

83. Smith, *Sketch of the Seminole War,* 247; Cohen, *Notices of Florida,* 169; and Mahon, *Second Seminole War,* 157, 341n40.

84. [Andrew Welch], *A Narrative of the Early Days and Remembrances of Oceola Nikkanichee, Prince of Econchatti, a Young Seminole Indian; Son of Econchatti-Mico, King of the Red Hills, in Florida; with a Brief History of His Nation, and His Renowned Uncle, Oceola, and His Parents, Written by His Guardian* (1841; repr., Gainesville: University Presses of Florida, 1977).

85. James M. Gould, "Dr. Andrew Welch," *St. Augustine Florida Herald and Southern Democrat,* 24 July 1843.

86. [Welch], *Narrative of the Early Days,* 49.

87. Boyd, "Asi-Yaholo or Osceola," 260.

88. Swanton, "Indians of the Southeastern United States," 81, follows Hawkins concerning the town and the people. Halbert and Ball, *Creek War*, 21, regard the people of Econchatti as Alibamos.

89. Archibald Smith to General George Gibson, Gadsden County, Florida, 12 and 25 July 1836, NARA, RG 192, CGS, Seminole Emigration File (Apalachicolas), nos. 222 and 224.

90. [Welch], *Narrative of the Early Days,* 124–25.

91. Ibid., 67–70.

92. Ibid., 82–83.

93. Arthur E. Francke, Jr., *Fort Mellon, 1837–42: A Microcosm of the Second Seminole War* (Miami: Banyan Books, 1977), 122.

94. [Welch], *Narrative of the Early Days.*

95. Prince, *Amidst a Storm of Bullets,* entry for 25 April 1837.

96. Lt. John C. Casey to Gen. T. S. Jesup, Seminole Agency, Tampa Bay, Fla., 24 July 1837, NARA, RG 94, OAG, Generals' Papers and Books, Genl. T. S. Jesup, box 2, "Lt. John C. Casey" folder.

Chapter 3

1. Woodward, *Woodward's Reminiscences,* 45.

2. Ibid.

3. Capt. J. R. Vinton to Gen. Thos. S. Jesup, Fort Mellon Lake Monroe, 7 May 1837, NARA, RG 94, OAG, Generals' Papers and Books, Genl. T. S. Jesup Papers, box 9, "Capt. J. R. Vinton" folder.

4. For a further discussion of equilibrium and reciprocity as the twin elements of the Maskókî world, see Wickman, *Tree That Bends,* ch. 3.

5. Col. Wm. S. Harney to Gen. Thos. S. Jesup, Fort Mellon, East Florida, [n.d.] April 1837, NARA, RG 94, OAG, Generals' Papers and Books, Genl. T. S. Jesup Papers, box 5, "Col. Wm. S. Harney" folder no. 1.

6. Mark F. Boyd, "The Seminole War: Its Background and Onset," *FHQ* 30 (July 1951): 44.

7. Woodward, *Woodward's Reminiscences,* 110.

8. [Potter], *War in Florida,* 75–76.

9. *St. Augustine Florida Herald,* 13 January 1836.

10. [Potter], *War in Florida,* 10–11.

11. Motte, *Journey into Wilderness,* 140.

12. William C. Sturtevant, "Notes on Modern Seminole Traditions of Osceola," *FHQ* 33 (January–April 1955), 206–7.

13. Woodward, in *Woodward's Reminiscences,* differentiates between the Osceola of Second Seminole War fame and the Creek Indian in Georgia whose name is similar.

14. Sturtevant, "Notes on Modern Seminole Traditions," 208.

15. [Potter], *War in Florida*, 10, vi–vii.

16. Ibid., 68.

17. Ibid., 158.

18. Dr. Robert Lebby to Dr. Johnson, 21 June 1844, in E. Detreville Ellis, *Nathaniel Lebby, Patriot, and Some of His Descendents* (n.p.: privately printed, 1967), 317.

19. Ibid.

20. *Charleston Courier*, 7 February 1838.

21. George Catlin, *Letters and Notes on the Manners, Customs, and Conditions of the North American Indians* (London: published by the author, 1841), 2:219–20.

22. Cohen, *Notices of Florida*, 237.

23. Giddings, *Exiles of Florida*, 166.

24. [Potter], *War in Florida*, 111.

25. Among others are the comments of several Brighton Reservation (Florida) elders and those of Jimmy O'Toole Osceola, David Jumper, Betty May Jumper, Louise and Lewis Carpitche, and Maude Frank, personal communications, 1992–2003.

26. Lt. John C. Casey to Gen. Thos. S. Jesup, Tampa Bay, 4 June 1837, NARA, RG 94, OAG, Generals' Papers and Books, Genl. T. S. Jesup Papers, box 2, "Lt. John C. Casey" folder. It is highly possible that this Spanish-Indian relationship during the war years constituted the genesis for the "Big Town" Clan that continues to this day. Indian women who eschewed their traditional matrilocal marriage pattern and went to live with their non-Indian husbands formed a fictitious clan in order to replicate traditional relationships. There are several likely places where this might have occurred, because of the historic Spanish presence: around Tampa Bay, around Fort Dade (Miami), and around St. Augustine (in the St. Augustine-Piccolata-Volusia triangle). It may have occurred in any or all of these, or it may have predated the close association during this period. Today, the general Seminole attitude toward the Spaniards, among both the Florida and the removed Seminoles, is very positive.

27. "A Bit of Indian History," *St. Augustine Tatler*, 4 April 1896, 4.

28. Bemrose, *Reminiscences*, 21.

29. Cohen, *Notices of Florida*, 237.

30. *St. Augustine Florida Herald*, July 1837.

31. [Welch], *Narrative of the Early Days*, 49–62.

32. Storrow, "Osceola, the Seminole War Chief," 440.

33. Bemrose, *Reminiscences*, 52.

34. [Potter], *War in Florida*, 157–58.

35. Sturtevant, "Notes on Modern Seminole Traditions," 213.

36. Nathan S. Jarvis, "An Army Surgeon's Notes on Frontier Service, 1833–1848," *Journal of Military Service Institution of the United States* 39 (September–October 1906): 277.

37. John Tharpe Lawrence, Delavan, Minnesota, to Secretary of State, Jacksonville [*sic*], Florida, 10 February 1939, photoreproduction in Osceola, Biography File,

Dorothy Dodd Florida History Collection, State Library of Florida, Tallahassee. Location of original documents unknown.

38. Bemrose, *Reminiscences*, 25.

39. Ibid., 21.

40. *National Intelligencer*, 23 February 1838.

41. Bemrose, *Reminiscences*, 25

42. William H. Powell, *A History of the Organization and Movements of the Fourth Regiment of Infantry, United States Army, from May 30, 1796, to December 31, 1870; Together with a record of the Military Services of All Officers Who Have at Any Time Belonged to the Regiment* (Washington, D.C.: n.p., 1871), 160; *Army and Navy Chronicle* 7 (19 July 1838): 41.

43. Bemrose, *Reminiscences*, 55.

44. *Army and Navy Chronicle* 7 (19 July 1838): 41.

45. Ibid., 7 (28 July 1836): 57–58.

46. Bemrose, *Reminiscences*, 31.

47. Sprague, *Origin, Progress, and Conclusion*, 88.

48. Lt. R. H. Peyton to Lt. J. A. Chambers, Fort Mellon, 26 May 1837, NARA, RG 94, OAG, Generals' Papers and Books, Genl. T. S. Jesup Papers, box 5, "Col. Wm. S. Harney" folder no. 2.

49. Ellis, *Nathaniel Lebby*, 317.

50. Frederick Weedon, diary entry, 29 January 1838, in the collections of the Alabama Department of Archives and History, Montgomery (hereinafter cited as Howell Family Papers, ADAH).

51. "List of Creek Indians who came in from the Seminoles, & joined the Friendly Indians in the Spring of 1837," NARA, RG 94, OAG, Generals' Papers and Books, Genl. T. S. Jesup Papers, box 4, "Major W. G. Freeman" folder.

52. Howell Family Papers, Weedon diary, ADAH, 29 January 1838.

53. Bemrose, *Reminiscences*, 39; and [Potter], *War in Florida*, 111.

54. Lt. Joseph W. Harris, disbursing agent to the Florida Indians, Fort King, to Gen. George Gibson, commissary general of subsistence, Washington, D.C., 30 December 1835, *American State Papers, Military Affairs*, 6:561, cited in Boyd, "Seminole War," 72.

55. Sprague, *Origin, Progress, and Conclusion*, 92–93.

56. [Smith], *Sketch of the Seminole War*, 47.

57. Prince, *Amidst a Storm of Bullets*, entry for 17 February 1836.

58. [Smith], *Sketch of the Seminole War*, 47; Boyd, "Seminole War," 79.

59. Boyd, "Asi-Yaholo or Osceola," 273–74.

60. Bemrose, *Reminiscences*, 25.

61. Viator, "From the New Bern, N.C., Spectator, Feb. 26, FLORIDA," in *Army and Navy Chronicle* 2, no. 13 (31 March 1836): 199.

62. [Welch], *Narrative of the Early Days*, 47.

63. Storrow, "Osceola," 430.

64. Sprague, *Origin, Progress, and Conclusion*, 80.

65. Williams, *Territory of Florida*, 227–28; Cohen, *Notices of Florida*, 100–101;

[Potter], *War in Florida*, 156–59; Prince, *Amidst a Storm of Bullets*, entry for 6 March 1836; Mahon, *History of Second Seminole War*, 149.

66. Dr. Robert Lebby to Dr. Johnson, 21 June 1844, in Ellis, *Nathaniel Lebby*, 316.

67. Sprague, *Origin, Progress, and Conclusion*, 167.

68. Prince, *Amidst a Storm of Bullets,* entry for 21 January 1837.

69. Williams, *Territory of Florida*, 27.

70. Jesup's report to Congress is contained in "A Message From the President of the United States Transmitting A report from Major General Jesup of his operations whilst commanding the army in Florida, in compliance with a resolution of the Senate of the 6th instant," U.S. Congress, 25th Congress, 2nd Sess., S Doc, 7 July 1838. The report was published in the twentieth century as *Seminole Saga*.

71. Ibid.

72. Thomas S. Jesup, "The Case of Osceola," *Magazine of American History* 5 (1880): 447–50. Potter was reprising Jesup's 1858 defense because recently he had seen "Osceola the Seminole mentioned in a newspaper." No further details of the newspaper article are given, but this certainly could have been the *New York Times* article concerning Solomon and Osceola Cooper discussed in chapter 11.

73. "Reminiscences: General Jesup on the Capture of the Chief Osceola," *New York Times*, 25 October 1858.

74. Jesup, "Case of Osceola," 449.

75. "Reminiscences: General Jesup on the Capture of the Chief Osceola."

76. Ibid.

77. Gen. Joseph M. Hernández to Gen. Thos. S. Jesup, St. Augustine, 29 September 1837, NARA, RG 94, OAG, Generals' Letters and Papers, Genl. T. S. Jesup, box 21, folder 3 (A&G 1).

78. Gen. Joseph M. Hernández to Gen. Thos. S. Jesup, St. Augustine, 17 October 1837, NARA, RG 94, OAG, Generals' Letters and Papers, Genl. T. S. Jesup, box 21, folder 3 (A&G 1).

79. Memorandum of a letter addressed to Gen. Joseph M. Hernández, 21 October [1837], NARA, RG 94, OAG, Generals' Letters and Papers, Genl. T. S. Jesup, box 21, folder 3 (A&G 1).

80. Ibid.

81. Lt. John C. Casey to Gen. Thos. S. Jesup, Tampa Bay, 20 September 1837, NARA, RG 94, OAG, Generals' Letters and Papers, Genl. T. S. Jesup, box 2, "Lt. John C. Casey" folder.

82. Dr. Robert Lebby to Dr. Johnson, 21 June 1844, in Ellis, *Nathaniel Lebby*, 317.

83. Francke, *Fort Mellon*, 122.

84. Asst. Surgeon George F. Turner to Capt. Pitcairn Morrison, Fort Marion, 12 December 1837, NARA, RG 94, OAG, Generals' Letters and Papers, Genl. T. S. Jesup, box 4, "Col. A. G. W. Fanning" folder 2.

85. Sources for this event are reviewed in Kenneth W. Porter, "Seminole Flight from Fort Marion," *FHQ* 22, no. 3 (January 1944): 119. They include the *Charleston Courier,* the *Army and Navy Chronicle,* Jacob Rhett Motte, John T. Sprague, and the *Savannah Georgian.*

86. "Philip's People: List of the prisoners who made their escape from Fort St. Marks [San Marcos] on the night of the 29th of November 1837," Capt. Lucien B. Webster Papers, SAHS.

87. Harvey Brown to Captain Webster, Fort Marion, 4 December 1837, in Webster Papers, SAHS.

88. "Report of the Board of Officers on the escape of the Indian Prisoners from Fort St. Mark [sic] Novr. 30th 1837," in Webster Papers, SAHS.

89. This tradition was passed down through the family of Oklahoma Seminole Woodrow Haney and told to me by his son, Enoch Kelly Haney, artist and state legislator in Oklahoma.

90. See Wickman, *Tree That Bends,* for a discussion of the cultural significance of the number four.

91. Gary E. Moulton, ed., *The Papers of Chief John Ross, Volume 1: 1807–1839* (Norman: University of Oklahoma Press, 1985), 566.

Chapter 4

1. See Joseph Edward McCarthy's assertion in his article "Portraits of Osceola and the Artists Who Painted Them," *Papers of the Jacksonville Historical Society* 2:24, 26.

2. Cohen, *Notices of Florida,* facing p. 45.

3. [Potter], *War in Florida.*

4. Cohen, *Notices of Florida,* facing p. 45.

5. *Charleston Courier,* 18 December 1828, cited in Anna Wells Rutledge, *Artists in the Life of Charleston: Through Colony and State from Restoration to Reconstruction* (1949; repr., Columbia: University of South Carolina Press, 1980), 156.

6. *National Cyclopaedia of American Biography* (New York: James T. White, 1907), 9:370–71; Francke, *Fort Mellon,* 7.

7. *National Cyclopaedia of American Biography,* 9:370–71.

8. Green, *Politics of Indian Removal,* 133.

9. Originally copied "For Mrs. Chester Smith from Charles Mayer Va[n], New York, 1933," photoduplicate in Osceola file, WPA Files, Florida Historical Society Collection, University of South Florida Library, Tampa.

10. See, for example, Jean Parker Waterbury, "' . . . Really an Amiable Looking Indian . . . ,' John Rogers Vinton's Portrait of Osceola," *El Escribano* 19(1982): 30.

11. *St. Augustine Florida Herald,* 7 July 1837. Francke confuses this citation badly by concluding that the sketch was given to Osceola by Vinton and by citing the 8 July 1837 newspaper. See Francke, *Fort Mellon,* 7.

12. Williams, *Territory of Florida,* frontispiece and illustrations facing pp. 56 and 268.

13. Winthrop Williams to Mrs. Susan M. S. Crouch, 6 January 1838, in "A Description of Osceola," *South Carolina Historical Magazine* 65(April 1964): 85–86.

14. William H. Truettner, *The Natural Man Observed: A Study of Catlin's Indian Gallery* (Washington, D.C.: Smithsonian Institution Press, 1979), 36.

15. Edwin C. Bearss, *Osceola at Fort Moultrie, Sullivan's Island, South Carolina, Fort Sumter National Monument* (Washington, D.C.: Division of History, Office of Archaeology and Historic Preservation, 1968), 16.

16. Ibid.

17. Storrow, "Osceola," 444–45.

18. Frederick Weedon, diary entry (n.d. January 1838), Frederick Weedon Papers, SPR 251, folder 2, Manuscript Collection, ADAH.

19. *Charleston Courier,* 6, 13, 16, 18 December 1837; *Charleston Mercury,* 12 December 1837; cited in Rutledge, *Artists in the Life of Charleston,* 244.

20. George C. Groce and David H. Wallace, *New York Historical Society's Dictionary of Artists in America* (New Haven, Conn.: Yale University Press, 1957), 384, in Emma Lila Fundaburke, ed., *Southeastern Indians Life Portraits: A Catalogue of Pictures, 1564–1860* (Luverne, Ala.: Emma Lila Fundaburke, 1958), 128n287.

21. Rutledge, *Artists in the Life of Charleston,* 156.

22. *Charleston Mercury,* 23 January 1838, cited in Rutledge, *Artists in the Life of Charleston,* 156.

23. Dr. Robert Lebby to Dr. Johnson, 21 June 1844, cited in Ellis, *Nathaniel Lebby,* 317.

24. Rutledge, *Artists in the Life of Charleston,* 192.

25. Storrow, "Osceola," 443, 446.

26. Truettner, *Natural Man Observed,* 36. Truettner cites the *New York Evening Star,* 1 February 1838, regarding the location of this exhibit. Charles H. Coe, *Red Patriots* (1898; repr., Gainesville: University Presses of Florida, 1974), 112, uses this also. See chapter 7 for a fuller discussion of this topic.

27. Hammer Galleries, *Art Objects and Furnishings from the William Randolph Hearst Collection* (New York: Hammer Galleries, 1941), 35.

28. William H. Truettner, curator of eighteenth- and nineteenth-century painting and sculpture, National Collection of Fine Arts, Smithsonian Institution, Washington, D.C., telephone conversation with the author, 19 September 1986.

29. *Marquis's Who Was Who in America, Historical Volume, 1607–1896* (Chicago: A. N. Marquis, 1963), 83.

30. Ransom signed the preface to his book on 4 July 1838 from Camp Street, New Orleans.

31. James D. Horan, *The McKenney-Hall Portrait Gallery of American Indians* (New York: Crown Publishers, 1972), 22.

32. Ibid.; John C. Ewers, "Charles Bird King, Painter of Indian Visitors to the Nation's Capital," *Annual Report of the Smithsonian Institution for 1953* (Washington, D.C.: U.S. Government Printing Office, 1954), 472.

33. Horan, *McKenney-Hall Portrait Gallery,* 23; Thomas L. McKenney and James Hall, *The Indian Tribes of North America, with Biographical Sketches and Anecdotes of the Principal Chiefs,* ed. Frederick Webb Hodge and David I. Bushnell, Jr. (Edinburgh: John Grant, 1934), 2:xxxiv–xxxvi.

34. William DuVal to Secretary of War John C. Calhoun, Washington City, 11 February 1825, photoduplicate in MS Collections, box 9, P. K. Yonge Library of

Florida History, George A. Smathers Libraries, University of Florida, Gainesville; and Thomas L. McKenney, Washington, D.C., to Governor DuVal, "now in Washington," 21 February 1825, NARA, War Dept., Office of Indian Affairs, Letters Sent, book 1, cited in Clarence Edward Carter, comp. and ed., *The Territorial Papers of the United States* (Washington, D.C.: U.S. Government Printing Office, 1958), 23:185.

35. Horan, *McKenney-Hall Portrait Gallery,* 106.

36. Thomas L. McKenney, *Catalogue of the One Hundred and Fifteen Indian Portraits, Representing Eighteen Different Tribes, Accompanied by a Few Brief Remarks on the Character etc. of Most of Them* (Philadelphia: [Edward C. Biddle], 1836).

37. Thomas L. McKenney and James Hall, *History of the Indian Tribes of North America with Biographical Sketches and Anecdotes of the Principal Chiefs. Embellished with One Hundred and Twenty Portraits, from the Indian Gallery in the Department of War, at Washington* (Philadelphia: Greenough, 1838), 2:facing p. 40.

38. Ibid., facing p. 203. The lithographic artist, "H. D.," begins to appear on the latter plates of volume 2, which was printed in 1842, and continues through some of the plates in volume 3, printed in 1844. Thus far, however, the artist's name has not been established.

39. Ewers, "Charles Bird King," 466.

40. William H. Rhees, *An Account of the Smithsonian Institution, Its Founder, Its Buildings, Operations, etc., Prepared from the Reports of Prof. Henry to the Regents, and other Authentic Sources* (Washington, D.C.: Smithsonian Institution, 1859), 55–58.

41. McCarthy, "Portraits of Osceola," 30.

42. McKenney and Hall, *Indian Tribes* (1934), 391.

43. McKenney and Hall, *History of the Indian Tribes* (1842–44), 2:197–98.

44. Wisconsin Historical Society, *Second Annual Report and Collections of the State Historical Society of Wisconsin, for the Year 1855* (Madison: Wisconsin Historical Society, 1856), 70.

45. McKenney and Hall, *History of the Indian Tribes* (1842–44), 2:203.

46. J. R. Vinton, St. Augustine, to Lt. C. Tompkins, Frederickstown, Maryland, 18 July 1840, original in the possession of Christopher Tompkins, New Orleans, Louisiana, cited in John Goggin, "Osceola," 166–67. There is some doubt as to the identity of the artist referred to by Tompkins. Waterbury ("Really an Amiable Looking Indian," 34) posits that it was Richard William Hubbard, a landscape artist then studying with Samuel F. B. Morse in New York. Checks of various standard art references have failed to corroborate this identification but suggest, rather, William James Hubbard (1807–1862), an English-born silhouettist who was studying oil painting with Gilbert Stuart at this time and living in Boston and Virginia. He would thus have had good access to the Neagle-Inman-Curtis-King circle of painters of American Indians. See, for example, *Marquis's Who Was Who in America,* 264.

47. J. R. Vinton to Lt. C. Tompkins, 18 July 1840, cited in Goggin, "Osceola," 166–67.

48. Ibid.

49. Accompanying this print is a short article that misrepresents much information. See Waterbury, "Really an Amiable Looking Indian," 29–36.

50. [Welch], *Narrative of the Early Days*.

51. Rutledge, *Artists in the Life of Charleston*, 156. The woman was Mrs. Jane Johns, about whose misadventures Welch also produced a book.

52. Henry Trumbull, *History of the Indian Wars* (Boston: N. C. Barton, 1846), facing p. 305.

53. Sprague, *Origin, Progress, and Conclusion*, facing p. 101.

54. Truettner, *Natural Man Observed*, 133. This souvenir album is now among the collections of the Gilcrease Institute of History and Art, Tulsa, Oklahoma.

55. Fundaburke, *Southeast Indians Life Portraits*, pl. 275, gives the detailed legend that accompanies a copy held by the New York Public Library. The single sheet is held by the National Gallery of Art, Washington, D.C.

56. McCarthy discusses this piece in his article "Portraits of Osceola," but mentions the Catlin attribution only indirectly and even finds the work acceptable (pp. 39–41).

57. Giddings, *Exiles of Florida*, facing p. 112.

58. Truettner, *Natural Man Observed*, 134.

59. C. Duncan Connelly, President, Corporate/Contract Division, David S. Ramus, Ltd., Atlanta, Ga., to Erik Robinson, Museum of Florida History, Tallahassee, 25 October 1985. The work is the property of Hirschl and Adler Galleries, New York City.

Chapter 5

1. *Niles National Register*, 4 November 1837, cited in Motte, *Journey into Wilderness*, 286.

2. Motte, *Journey into Wilderness*, 139, 140–41.

3. "Further from Florida—The Capture of Osceola," *New York Evening Star*, 1 November 1837, p. 2, col. 1; cf. Motte, *Journey into Wilderness*, 137, 139.

4. Jarvis, "Army Surgeon's Notes," 278, cited in Boyd, "Asi-Yaholo or Osceola," 297.

5. "List of Indian Prisoners at Fort Marion, October–December 1837," Webster Papers, SAHS; Jarvis, "Army Surgeon's Notes," 285; *Savannah Republican*, n.d.; *Savannah Georgian*, 8 December 1837; *Army and Navy Chronicle* 5(21 December 1837): 394, all cited in Boyd, "Asi-Yaholo or Osceola," 301; Storrow, "Osceola," 443; Lt. John Pickell, "Journal," 30 November 1837, in Francke, *Fort Mellon*, 122. Although the designator "family" is used promiscuously throughout the military and civil documents of the period, for the most part its users did not know or understand the southeastern Indian clan system and used "family" to indicate a nuclear family of mother, father, and children. The designator "band," wholly a superimposed term, was used by military and civil officials to refer to any group of any size that came under their control through capture or capitulation. Consid-

ering the traditional living patterns of the Creek and Seminole people and the pressures on those patterns occasioned by the war, it is highly probable that Osceola's "people" comprised members of his own clan, along with members of his wives' clan(s), warriors who followed him because of clan connections, and ex-slaves who had placed themselves under his protection or control voluntarily or who had been captured by him. Certainly, however, not all of the individuals related to Osceola by blood would have been traveling with him.

6. This number is taken from the assessment made by Edwin Bearss, *Osceola at Fort Moultrie,* 3–5, who drew them from Pitcairn Morrison's reports.

7. See the hypothesis propounded by Mark Boyd, malariologist and historical researcher, in his "Asi-Yaholo or Osceola," 298–99.

8. Samuel Forry to J. W. Phelps, 31 October 1837, in "Letters of Samuel Forry, Surgeon U.S. Army, 1837–1838," pt. 3, *FHQ* 7(July 1928): 95.

9. *Tallahassee Floridian,* 16 December 1837.

10. Sprague, *Origin, Progress, and Conclusion,* 92–93. The date reported was 12 January 1837.

11. See chapter 2 for a discussion of these sources.

12. Report on the examination of the hair sample by Dr. John Mulrunnan, director, Department of Entomology, Florida Department of Health and Rehabilitative Services, Jacksonville, 14 August 1986, conversation with the author.

13. Bearss, *Osceola at Fort Moultrie,* 3–5.

14. Col. William S. Harney to Gen. T. S. Jesup, Fort Mellon, East Florida, 6 June 1837, NARA, RG 94, OAG, Generals' Papers and Books, Gen. T. S. Jesup Papers, box 5, "Col. Wm. S. Harney" folder no. 2.

15. Capt. P. H. Galt to Gen. T. S. Jesup, Fort King, 14 August 1837, NARA, RG 94, OAG, Generals' Papers and Books, Gen. T. S. Jesup Papers, box 5, "Capt. P. H. Galt" folder no. 1.

16. Motte, *Journey into Wilderness,* 139.

17. Samuel Forry to J. W. Phelps, 31 October 1837, in "Letters of Samuel Forry," 95.

18. *Augusta Constitutionalist,* n.d., 384, cited in Boyd, "Asi-Yaholo or Osceola," 298.

19. Gen. Jesup to Secretary of War Joel Poinsett, *American State Papers: Military Affairs,* 7:891, cited in Boyd, "Asi-Yaholo or Osceola," 303.

20. Motte, *Journey into Wilderness,* 280. Yuchi (Euchi, Uchi) Billy was a prominent warrior whose death had been reported, erroneously, a year earlier. See Cohen, *Notices of Florida,* 169, and Smith *Sketch of the Seminole War,* 247.

21. Jarvis, "Army Surgeon's Notes," cited in Boyd, "Asi-Yaholo or Osceola," 298–99.

22. Pitcairn Morrison to Carey A. Harris, 20 December 1837, and Gen. Jesup to Pitcairn Morrison, 16 December 1837, NARA, RG 75, Office of Indian Affairs, Florida Emigration, cited in Bearss, *Osceola at Fort Moultrie,* 5–6.

23. Frederick Weedon, [December 1837], Frederick Weedon Papers, ADAH.

24. Ibid.

25. Frederick Weedon, "27" [27 December 1837?], Frederick Weedon Papers, ADAH.

26. Storrow, "Osceola," 443, says that the two wives were sisters. He offers no source for this statement but apparently thinks that their relationship is corroborated by their obviousness closeness. The explicit nature of the list of prisoners made at Fort Marion (and discussed in chapter 2) and its clear notation that the two wives were not sisters but, rather, that one of the wives had *a* sister with her, supersedes this misunderstanding, however. In this instance, we have no way of accounting for all of the rumors that circulated even among firsthand witnesses.

27. Dr. Robert Lebby to Dr. Johnson, 21 June 1844, in Ellis, *Nathaniel Lebby,* 317.

28. Frederick Weedon, [January 1838], Frederick Weedon Papers, ADAH.

29. NARA, RG 92, Office of the QM General, Water Transportation, 1834–1900, box 81, Planter-Point City, Vessel File of the USS *Poinsett* 1837, 7 October–27 November: List of types and amounts of foodstuffs and supplies (e.g., coffee, white sugar, tea, mustard, turkeys, gallons of molasses, dozens of eggs, sperm oil, hinges, hooks, eyes, and pounds of cocoa). These were among the supplies that were taken on board to subsist the crew and passengers during the period immediately preceding 1 January 1838, when the *Poinsett* disembarked Osceola and the others at Charleston. There is no captain's log for this period, however.

30. *St. Augustine Florida Herald,* n.s., 3:32, 1 January 1838, p. 2.

31. Storrow, "Osceola," 442.

32. Ibid.

33. Documents appended to the Catlin lithograph of Osceola, 1838, now in the collections of the SAHS.

34. *Charleston Courier,* 8 January 1838; [James Birchett Ransom], *Osceola; or, Fact and Fiction: A Tale of the Seminole War, by a Southerner* (New York: Harper and Brothers, 1838), 145–46.

35. Storrow, "Osceola," 444.

36. *Southern Patriot,* 9 January 1838; George Catlin to Cary A. Harris, 31 January 1838, NARA, RG 75, Office of Indian Affairs, Florida Emigration, cited in Bearss, *Osceola at Fort Moultrie,* 12–13; the *New York Evening Star* edition of 17 January 1838 reported the event simply but evocatively: "*Indian Feeling.*—One of the Indian Braves confined in Charleston harbor has hung himself. The warrior could not brook the indignity of a prison. He was found suspended by a piece of cow-hide his dress almost touching the ground."

37. Dr. Robert Lebby to Dr. Johnson, 21 June 1844, in Ellis, *Nathaniel Lebby,* 316.

38. Storrow, "Osceola," 443.

39. Dr. Robert Lebby to Dr. Johnson, 21 June 1844, in Ellis, *Nathaniel Lebby,* 317.

40. Storrow, "Osceola," 443.

41. Frederick Weedon, [January 1838], Frederick Weedon Papers, ADAH.

42. Frederick Weedon, "28," "29," "30" [28–30 January 1838], Frederick Weedon Papers, ADAH.

43. Bearss, *Osceola at Fort Moultrie*, 22–23.

44. See, for example, the *Apalachicola Gazette*, 26 February 1838, although the *St. Augustine Florida Herald*, 15 February 1838, complicated the issue further by misprinting the date as "16" January 1838.

45. *Charleston Courier*, 7 February 1838, and *Apalachicola Gazette*, 26 February 1838, cited in May McNeer Ward, "The Disappearance of the Head of Osceola," *FHQ* 33(January–April 1955): 195–97; George Catlin, *North American Indians, Being Letters, Notes on Their Manners, Customs, and Conditions during Eight Years' Travel Among the Wildest Tribes of Indians in North America, 1832–1839*, 2 vols. (1866; repr., Edinburgh: J. Grant, 1926), 251.

46. "DEATH OF OSCEOLA," *New York Evening Star*, 6 February 1838, p. 2, col. 1.

47. Frederick Weedon, "29" [29 January 1838], Frederick Weedon Papers, ADAH.

48. Storrow, "Osceola," 445–46.

49. *Southern Patriot*, 31 January 1838; *Charleston Courier*, 1 February 1838.

50. Bearss, *Osceola at Fort Moultrie*, 34.

51. Frederick Weedon, "31st" [31 January 1838], Frederick Weedon Papers, ADAH.

52. Coe, *Red Patriots*, 112.

53. Dr. Robert Lebby to Dr. Johnson, 21 June 1844, in Ellis, *Nathaniel Lebby,* 316.

54. Ibid.

Chapter 6

1. Bearss, *Osceola at Fort Moultrie*, 51.

2. Jack Duggan, NPS Interpretive Specialist, Fort Sumter National Monument (Fort Moultrie), Charleston, South Carolina, telephone conversation with the author, 24 January 1985.

3. "Bones of Osceola will not be moved to Florida grave," *Ocala Star*, n.d., in WPA files, "Osceola" file, SAHS.

4. "Osceola Reburial Urged," *New York Times*, 1 September 1947.

5. "Seminoles Want Return of Chief Osceola's Body," *Miami Herald*, 18 August 1948; "Return of Osceola's Bones Asked of Truman," *Tampa Tribune*, 26 March 1951.

6. "What to Do with Osceola Still Problem after Death," *Jacksonville Florida Times-Union*, 10 March 1950.

7. Among myriad articles on this topic, see "Governor Warren Joins Effort to Bring Osceola to County," *Collier County News*, 24 March 1950; "Saga of Osceola Is Revived by Latest Campaign to Return Bones to Florida," *Jacksonville Florida Times-Union*, 18 February 1951; "Florida Apparently Losing Fight for Return of Infamous Osceola's Bones from S. Carolina," *Tampa Tribune*, 18 February 1951; "Chief Osceola's Grave Still There," *Charleston News and Courier*, 8 April 1951; "U.S. Rebuffs Osceola Kin over Chief's Bones," *Miami Herald*, 15 April 1951.

8. "Osceola Plea Refused," *New York Times*, 27 June 1952. Comparable articles

also appeared in the *Miami Herald* and the *Jacksonville Florida Times-Union* at about the same time.

9. Bearss, *Osceola at Fort Moultrie,* 54.

10. Among other accounts, see "Osceola's Bones Stolen by Floridian," *St. Petersburg Times,* 31 March 1966; "Floridian Says He Stole Remains of Indian Chief," *New York Times,* 31 March 1966; "Old Chief Osceola On the Move Again," *Tallahassee Democrat,* 3 July 1966; "They're Still Rattling Osceola's Bones," *Tampa Tribune,* 1 April 1966.

11. "Charges Pend in 'Theft' of Osceola's Bones," *Tampa Tribune,* 1 April 1966.

12. "Osceola's 'Remains' Returned to State; Put in Miami Bank," *Tallahassee Democrat,* 22 December 1967.

13. Seminole Tribe of Florida Council Resolution C-25-64.

14. Ibid.

15. Associated Press, *Tallahassee Democrat,* 22 December 1967.

16. Seminole Tribe of Florida, Minutes of the Tribal Council Meeting, 12 January 1968, and Special Council Meeting, 9 February 1968, Betty Mae Jumper, Council Chairman, and Fred Smith, Tribal Secretary-Treasurer.

17. John W. Griffin, "The Search for Osceola," n.d., typescript of slide/talk, personal files of (John W. Griffin, now deceased) Patricia Griffin, St. Augustine, and personal conversations with the author, 1986.

18. Griffin, "Search for Osceola," 9.

19. Ibid., 11.

20. Ibid., 13.

21. Ibid., 14.

22. John W. Griffin to Erik K. Reed, 3 January 1969, and Erik K. Reed to T. Dale Stewart, 31 December 1968, with attached "Report," photocopies in the personal files of (John W. Griffin, now deceased) Patricia Griffin, St. Augustine.

23. Ibid., 1–2.

24. T. Dale Stewart, telephone conversation with the author, 11 August 1986.

25. Reed to Stewart, "Report," 2.

26. Ibid., 3.

27. T. Dale Stewart, telephone conversation with the author, 11 August 1986.

28. Frederick Weedon, diary (n.d.), Frederick Weedon Papers, ADAH.

Chapter 7

1. D. W. Whitehurst, M.D., to Valentine Mott, M.D., 2 October 1843, Weedon and Whitehurst Family Papers, Southern Historical Collection, University of North Carolina, Chapel Hill.

2. Ibid.

3. Storrow, "Osceola," 447; Coe, *Red Patriots,* 112.

4. Coe, *Red Patriots,* 112.

5. Storrow, "Osceola," 447.

6. Frederick Weedon, in his letter to the *Charleston Courier,* February 1838, reprinted in the *Apalachicola Gazette,* 26 February 1838.

7. Storrow, "Osceola," 443.

8. Hamilton M. Weedon, "Osceola: Stories of the Seminole War Heard as a Youth," *Montgomery (Alabama) Advertiser,* 17 December 1905.

9. Genealogical materials prepared by a descendent in Salt Lake City, Utah, and provided by Dr. Ashby Hammond to the author, 1998.

10. Jane Brown, Curator, Waring Historical Library, Medical University of South Carolina, personal communication to the author, 17 June 2004.

11. Joseph I. Waring, *A History of Medicine in South Carolina, 1825–1900* (Columbia: South Carolina Medical Association, 1967), 243–45.

12. George J. Gongaware, *The History of the German Friendly Society of Charleston, South Carolina, 1766–1916* (Richmond: Garrett and Massie Publishers, 1935), makes thirty-six references to Bachman.

13. See, for example, two Bachman items offered for sale by the prestigious auction house of Christie, Manson, and Woods International, Inc., on 26 May 1977, and advertised in their sale catalogue of *Highly Important Natural History Books and autographs including Audubon's Birds of America and an extensive collection of his manuscripts.* The items were as follows: No. 48 "Bachman (Rev. John): On the Different Species of Hares [Genus Lepus] Inhabiting the U.S. of America: The original and corrected copy of remarks read before the Charleston Library and Philosophical Society, Nov. 8 1832 and later published in the Journal of the Academy of Natural Science, Philadelphia, 1837," and No. 49 "Bachman (Rev. John): On the mammalia of the United States . . . , Delivered before the Apprentices Society, South Carolina Hall, Charleston, July 6 1836." This latter presentation dealt specifically with the disparate physiognomies of ethnic U.S. populations.

14. Alice Ford, *John James Audubon* (Norman: University of Oklahoma Press, 1964), 284–85, cited in G. E. Gifford, Jr., "John James Audubon and His Charleston Physician-Friends," *Journal of the South Carolina Medical Association* 75, no. 6 (June 1979): 257–63.

15. *Charleston Observer,* 30 June 1827.

16. Waring, *History of Medicine,* 304.

17. Ashby Hammond, M.D., personal communication to the author, August 1999; see also Strobel's article on Audubon in the *Charleston Courier,* 28 June 1833.

18. Cohen, *Notices of Florida,* 142, 159.

19. [Smith], *Sketch of the Seminole War,* 70, 302.

20. Cohen, *Notices of Florida,* 137–38. St. Francis Barracks is extant today as the core of the headquarters building of the Florida National Guard on Marine Street.

21. Ibid., 220.

22. Waring, *History of Medicine,* 305.

23. *Southern Christian Herald,* 10 February 1836, cited in Waring, *History of Medicine,* 304–5.

24. Ward, "Disappearance of the Head," 198. Mrs. Ward, also a great-

granddaughter of Dr. Frederick Weedon, is the only source of information regarding this detail. Mary Weedon Keen did not remember this story. She did, however, remember to insist that Osceola was, in fact, never a chief.

25. This is the method preferred by anatomists and by criminals to this day. The author deeply appreciates the information and guidance of Dr. William Maples (deceased) and his worthy successor, Dr. Anthony Falsetti, founder and director of the C. A. Pound Human Identification Laboratory at the University of Florida, Gainesville, who have shared their expertise in various esoteric discussions on this and allied topics.

26. Bearss, *Osceola at Fort Moultrie*, 52–53; Coe, *Red Patriots*, 119.

27. Mary Weedon Keen, conversation with the author, 15 October 1985.

28. "Letters of Samuel Forry," 101.

29. Mary Weedon Keen, conversation with the author, 15 October 1985. Records of the SAHS have thus far failed to yield the exact location of such a business, although other properties owned by Dr. Weedon in St. Augustine have been documented.

30. Ward, "Disappearance of the Head," 198. Although Bridge Street is near Weedon Street in the southwest quadrant of peninsular St. Augustine, no evidence has yet been located to indicate that the street was named for its occupant or that the Weedon family residence was nearby on Bridge Street.

31. Coe, *Red Patriots*, 112.

32. Henry Le Roy Fairchild, *A History of the New York Academy of Sciences, Formerly the Lyceum of Natural History by Henry Le Roy Fairchild, Recording Secretary* (New York: published by the author, 1887). The book contains an illustration of the building. See also Phelps Stokes, *The Iconography of Manhattan Island, 1498–1909* (New York: Robert H. Dodd, 1928), 51.

33. *New York Evening Star*, 10 January 1838, p. 3, col. 3.

34. Ibid., 3 February 1838, p. 3, col. 3.

35. Mary Carey, librarian, New York Historical Society, conversation with the author, 18 July 1986.

36. [Welch], *Narrative*, 201–2.

37. In addition to Welch, another source reports that on the day Osceola died, his head "was severed from his body, and placed in a vase of spirits, and now adorns the shelf of an apothecary in St. Augustine, Florida." This appears to be the report of Colonel Shelburne, the man appointed by the War Department to accompany the Cherokee delegation that visited Osceola and the others in Fort Marion. Shelburne, it seems, took to England an interesting but fanciful portrait purported to be of a wife of Osceola and one of his children, with the intention of presenting it to the queen; possibly from the *London Times*, n.d., from the files of the SAHS, "Osceola" file. The report of a vase of spirits and of the head being in an apothecary shop in St. Augustine certainly supports Welch's assertion and accords with the other facts. The rest of the Sherburne article is so inaccurate, however, that it is worth no further discussion.

38. Cohen, *Notices of Florida*, 169–71.

39. [Smith], *Sketch of the Seminole War,* 249–50.

40. Charles Coleman Sellers, *Mr. Peale's Museum: Charles Willson Peale and the First Popular Museum of Natural Science and Art* (New York: W. W. Norton, 1980), 9.

41. Ibid., 201.

42. Dr. Caroline Grigson, assistant conservator, Odontological Museum, Royal College of Surgeons, to the author, 28 July 1993; and Ms. E. Allen, Qvist curator, Hunterian Museum, Royal College of Surgeons, to the author, 20 August 1993.

43. Sellers, *Mr. Peale's Museum,* 235.

44. Gloria Greis, manager of the archaeology and osteology collections, Peabody Museum of Archaeology and Ethnology, Harvard University, in letter to the author, 15 September 1998.

45. *New York Times,* 18 March 1868, in Sellers, *Mr. Peale's Museum,* 333.

46. "Original Narratives of Indian Attacks in Florida: An Indian Attack of 1856 on the Home of Willoughby Tillis. Narrative of James Dallas Tillis," *FHQ* 8, no. 4 (April 1930): 179–87.

47. J. K. Barnes, acting surgeon general, circular letter of 24 June 1862, in D. S. Lamb, "A History of the United States Army Medical Museum, 1862 to 1917, Compiled from the Official Records," 28–29, unpublished manuscript on file at the Otis Historical Archives, National Museum of Health and Medicine, Armed Forces Institute of Pathology (Walter Reed Medical Center), Washington, D.C.

48. Ibid.

49. Lenore Barbian, manager of the anatomical collections, National Museum of Health and Medicine, personal interview with the author, July 2004. It was through the good offices of Dr. Barbian that I was permitted to review the records of the Smithsonian Institution transfer and discuss the holdings in the NMHM collections. The list of the specimens transferred to the Smithsonian includes a significant number of *craniums* (skulls, complete except for the lower jaws), *calveria* (vault of the skull only), and other skeletal remains from Florida Indians. For the most part, however, these were collected in the late nineteenth century by Clarence B. Moore, an independent avocational archaeologist, or by Smithsonian expeditionist J. W. Powell, who collected principally in the 1870s.

50. Thomas [Corwin] Donaldson, *George Catlin's Indian Gallery in the U.S. National Museum (Smithsonian Institution), with Memoir and Statistics,* author's edition (Washington, D.C.: U.S. Government Printing Office, 1887), 4–6.

51. Ward, "Disappearance of the Head," 198; Mary Weedon Keen, conversation with the author, 15 October 1985.

52. Holograph page, May 1838, Weedon Family Papers.

53. L. N. Fowler to Dr. Weedon, 9 September 1839, Howell Family Papers.

54. Mr. Fowler also spells the name "Uchee" rather than "Euchee." These are but two of the variations in spelling that occur among written Seminole names. The same word also is spelled "Yuchi" in this period.

55. L. N. Fowler to Dr. Weedon, 9 September 1839, Howell Family Papers.

56. D. W. Whitehurst to Valentine Mott, 2 October 1843, Weedon and Whitehurst Family Papers.

57. Weedon and Whitehurst Family Papers.

58. *Catalogue of the Surgical and Pathological Museum of Valentine Mott, M.D., LL.D.* (New York, 1858); Bound Pamphlets No. 68, New York Academy of Medicine Rare Books Collection, New York.

59. Robert A. M. Stern, Thomas Mellins, and David Fishman, *New York, 1880: Architecture and Urbanism in the Gilded Age* (New York: Monacelli Press, 1999), 736, 737; and Peter Salwen, *Upper West Side Story: A History and Guide* (New York: Abbeville Press, 1989), 34, 43–44.

60. Abram C. Dayton, *Last Days of Knickerbocker Life* (New York: G. P. Putnam's Sons, 1897), 316.

61. Valentine Mott, *Travels in Europe and the East* (n.p.: published by the author, 1841).

62. *New York Weekly Herald,* 27 November 1841.

63. Stern, Mellins, and Fishman, *New York, 1880,* 533.

64. Lewis W. Leeds, "Parisian Flats," cited in Stern, Mellins, and Fishman, *New York, 1880,* 533.

65. "Old Mott House Figures in Sale," *New York Times,* 24 September 1941.

66. Certified copy of the petition of the last will and testament of Valentine Mott, County of New York, Clerk of Surrogate's Court, Liber 156, p. 228, proved date 24 May 1865.

67. *International Art Treasures Exhibition Catalogue, Presented by the British Antique Dealers Association* (Bath, England: n.p., 1973), 1.

68. S. D. Gross, *Memoir of Valentine Mott, M.D., LL.D., professor of surgery in the City of New York; member of the Institute of France* (Philadelphia: Lindsay and Blakiston, 1868), 74; Moses King, *King's Handbook of New York City* (Boston: Moses King, 1893), 333.

69. New York Academy of Medicine, Adriane Fabio, personal communication with the author and personal interview with the author, April and June 1992.

70. Ward, "Disappearance of the Head," 201.

71. Henry Abbott, *Catalogue of a Collection of Egyptian Antiquities . . . now exhibiting at the Stuyvesant Institute. . . .* (New York: J. W. Watson, 1854).

72. R. W. G. Vail, *Knickerbocker Birthday: A Sesqui-Centennial History of the New York Historical Society* (New York: New York Historical Society, 1954), 190–91.

73. Diana Fane, curator, Native American Collections, Brooklyn Museum, personal conversation with the author, July 1993; Mary McKurtcher and Richard Fazzini, curators, Abbott Egyptiana Collection, Brooklyn Museum, personal conversation with the author, July 1993.

74. "Indian materials available in 1950 as per 1848 deposit of Dr. Nathan S. Jarvis," typescript provided by Diana Fane, curator, Native American Collections, Brooklyn Museum.

75. Robert J. Carlisle, M.D., *An Account of Bellevue Hospital with a Catalogue of the Medical and Surgical Staff from 1736 to 1894* (New York: Society of the Alumni of Bellevue Hospital, 1893).

76. Dr. John Pierson, chairman, Bellevue Medical Services, Pathology Department, personal conversation with the author, 25 June 1993.

77. Paul S. Sledzik, Armed Forces Institute of Pathology, personal correspondence with the author, 23 November 1999.

78. John G. Carolin, great-grandson of both Francis and Thaddeus Mott, brothers of Alexander Brown Mott and sons of Valentine Mott, M.D., graciously discussed his own family genealogical research with the author in 1994 and in 2005, but could offer no insights into the history of Osceola's head.

Chapter 8

1. Family genealogical materials held by Mary Weedon Keen of Tallahassee (now deceased). Many of her documents were photoduplications of original materials from the Weedon and Whitehurst Family Papers.

2. Sprague, *Origin, Progress, and Conclusion,* 538, notes, "Weeden [*sic*], John J., Private, Co. B," but gives no other details in the text of the book.

3. Charles H. Bridges to Duncan U. Fletcher, 24 August 1932, Weedon and Whitehurst Family Papers.

4. Weedon and Whitehurst Family Papers; Family tradition says that Mary Marable Weedon did not move with Frederick, although no supporting documents are available; St. Johns County (Florida) Deed Books B and L, 139–40, Office of the Clerk of the Circuit Court, St. Augustine.

5. Thomas M. Owen, *History of Alabama and Dictionary of Alabama Biography* (Chicago: S. J. Clarke Publishing, 1921), 4:1741.

6. William Thompson to Frederick Weedon, 16 March 1830, Howell Family Papers. Also the U.S. Census, 1830, Alabama, Madison County, does not list a Wiley Thompson of an appropriate age.

7. William Garrett, *Reminiscences of Public Men in Alabama for Thirty Years* (Atlanta: Plantation Publishing, 1872), 757.

8. Leon County (Florida) Deed Record Book B, pt. 2, p. 565, T1, R1 S & E, Office of the Clerk of the Circuit Court, Tallahassee.

9. Weedon and Whitehurst Family Papers.

10. St. Johns County (Florida) Deed Books B and L, 139–40.

11. Ibid.

12. Although a street in the southwestern quadrant of peninsular St. Augustine commemorates the Weedon name, the exact location of the Weedon home in the 1830s and 1840s is unknown.

13. On 22 April 1856, Daniel W. Whitehurst and Henrietta M. Whitehurst, daughter and son-in-law of Frederick Weedon, deeded to B. A. Putnam title to "Weedon Grove," signed at Key West, Weedon and Whitehurst Family Papers.

14. Charles H. Bridges to Duncan U. Fletcher, 24 August 1932, Weedon and Whitehurst Family Papers.

15. T. Saunders to Frederick Weedon, 3 April 1836, Frederick Weedon Papers.

16. *St. Augustine Florida Herald,* 5 August 1835 and 25 July 1836; Joseph S. Sanchez to Frederick Weedon, December 1835, in Frederick Weedon Papers. See also "Post Returns from Fort Marion," NARA micro. no. 617, roll 1060.

17. James M. Gray, "The Forts of Florida," Dorothy Dodd Florida History Collection, State Library of Florida, Tallahassee. The location of Fort Lane is given as two miles east of Lake Geneva on the St. Johns River, near Lakes Harney and Jesup, at latitude 28° 45′ and longitude 81° 15′.

18. Charles H. Bridges to Duncan U. Fletcher, 24 August 1932, Weedon and Whitehurst Family Papers.

19. See Joel R. Poinsett to Gen. Thomas S. Jesup, 17 May 1837, cited in Sprague, *Origin, Progress, and Conclusion,* 177–79.

20. *St. Augustine Florida Herald,* 18 November 1829, cited in Jean Parker Waterbury, "Long Neglected, Now Restored: The Ximénez-Fatio House (ca. 1797)," *El Escribano* 22 (1985): 10, 14.

21. *St. Augustine News,* 10 February 1844.

22. See, for example, Grant Foreman, *Indian Removal* (Norman: University of Oklahoma Press, 1953), 328; Cohen, *Notices of Florida,* 235; and Motte, *Journey into Wilderness,* 140–41.

23. T. Saunders to Frederick Weedon, 3 April 1836, Frederick Weedon Papers.

24. *Charleston Courier,* 3 January 1838.

25. Weedon and Whitehurst Family Papers. Capt. Pitcairn Morrison, in charge of the emigrating Indians, signed for the U.S. Army.

26. Dr. Robert Lebby to Dr. Johnson, 21 June 1844, in Ellis, *Nathaniel Lebby,* 317.

27. "Letters of Samuel Forry," 101. Forry's use of the (now) antiquated word "quized' has engendered some misunderstanding of the nature of the relationship between Osceola and Weedon. One researcher interpreted the word to mean "mislead" (Boyd, "Asi-Yaholo or Osceola," 304). In so doing, readers were left with an inference that a condition of mistrust or dislike existed between the two men, which condition would be antithetical to any degree of friendship (itself an ambiguous term). To "quiz," however, meant "to banter, to make sport of . . . to look at inquisitively" (*Webster's Encyclopedic Dictionary* [Chicago: Consolidated Book Publishers, 1944], 592), which carries no sense of the pejorative. Indeed, it implies a comfortable closeness. Compare the fact that Weedon used the same word in his diary, describing the "quisical" nature of Osceola's interaction with his wives. These interpretations would also be more in keeping with Storrow's phrase, "his friend Doctor Weedon" (Storrow, "Osceola," 447) and with Osceola's ability to act and speak on friendly terms with individual white men such as Catlin and Graham.

28. John Inman to Frederick Weedon, St. Augustine, 12 July 1838, Frederick Weedon Papers. John Inman (1805–1850) was a journalist and brother of Henry Inman, the well-known portrait painter, who had copied King's Indian portraits for Thomas McKenney. John had worked for several New York newspapers and, around 1838, was editor of the *Columbian Magazine.* From 1833 until his death, he also was editor of the *Commercial Advertiser.* See *National Cyclopaedia of American Biography,* 9:248.

29. The files of the SAHS yield no information regarding a drugstore owned by Frederick Weedon. Family tradition indicates that Dr. Weedon maintained a drugstore or, more properly for the period, an apothecary shop in the downstairs front

room of the family residence. This custom, also, was typical of the period. Because no separate apothecary shop can be located for the doctor in St. Augustine, this certainly may be accurate. However, the family residence cannot be located either (see above).

30. The Weedon family Bible, in the possession of Mary Leslie Keen Drake, Tallahassee, lists Julia's death as having occurred in November 1839. However, the *St. Augustine News* issue of 4 February 1840, of which Daniel Whitehurst himself was publisher, includes the following obituary: "Also on the 1st inst., Miss E. Julia Weedon, aged 16, daughter of Dr. F. Weedon of this city." Without doubt, this must have been a painful notice for Whitehurst to print. In information regarding the life of Dr. B. B. Strobel of Charleston, South Carolina, mention is made of that doctor's having visited St. Augustine in 1839 in order to study the effects of yellow fever. Consequently, this may be a clue to Julia's cause of death. (Information provided to the author by E. Ashby Hammond, M.D., University of Florida, Gainesville, and obtained from a Strobel descendent.)

31. In the *St. Augustine News*, 2 February 1839, there appears an advertisement for the sale of ninety acres of land on the North River (about five miles north of the city proper), as well as a small lot with dwelling and outbuilding. Interested parties are requested to apply "at the law office of D. W. Whitehurst."

32. St. Augustine, St. Johns County Marriage Records, 1843, p. 26. The couple were married by Father Madeore according to the rites of the Roman Catholic Church, and the civil notation was copied by Mr. Dumas, county court clerk, on 12 May 1843.

33. *St. Augustine News*, 20 August 1842.

34. James Covington, "The Armed Occupation Act of 1842," *FHQ* 40 (July 1961): 47. Weedon filed for land at St. Augustine on 11 October 1842.

35. Daniel Whitehurst to Valentine Mott, 2 October 1843, Weedon and Whitehurst Family Papers.

36. *St. Augustine News*, 10 February 1845.

37. According to Weedon family tradition, Frederick's sons left home following the death of their mother because they had tired of the dominance of Henrietta. Although they may indeed have left at that time, they must have had other reasons, because Henrietta had been out of the city for four years (and possibly out of the house for two years longer) by that time.

38. Weedon and Whitehurst Family Papers.

39. Frederick Weedon to Hamilton Weedon, 9 September 1856, Howell Family Papers.

Chapter 9

1. Dr. Robert Lebby to Dr. Johnson, 21 June 1844, in Ellis, *Nathaniel Lebby,* 316.

2. Document accompanying two artifacts that, at the time of the first writing of this book, were on loan to the Florida State Museum of Natural History, Gainesville, for examination and possible purchase from Sun Dance Galleries, Salt Lake

City, Utah. The epilogue of this book is devoted entirely to the examination of these artifacts.

3. Storrow, "Osceola," 443; *Charleston Courier,* 7 February 1838.

4. Mary Weedon Keen, former owner of this artifact, recalled a discussion with Edith Pope that occurred after Mark Boyd borrowed the artifact in preparation for his article in the Osceola edition of the *FHQ.* Edith Pope commented that the pipe smelled strongly of tobacco. Both women examined the pipe more closely and decided that Boyd had smoked it.

5. Goggin, "Osceola," 189.

6. Giddings, *Exiles of Florida,* 165.

7. Storrow, "Osceola," 442.

8. John M. Goggin, "Silver Work of the Florida Seminoles," *El Palacio* 47 (February 1940): 25, 27, 31.

Chapter 10

1. Boyd, "Asi-Yaholo or Osceola," 249–305; Mary Weedon Keen, interview with the author, 15 October 1985.

2. Clay MacCauley, "Seminole Indians of Florida," in *Bureau of American Ethnology Fifth Annual Report, 1883, 1884* (Washington, D.C.: Smithsonian Institution, 1887), 486.

3. *St. Augustine Florida Herald,* 11 September 1834.

4. John W. Hicks, *Microscopy of Hairs: A Practical Guide and Manual,* issue 2 (Washington, D.C.: U.S. Government Printing Office, 1977). Hairs were identified as belonging to three "racial" types, Caucasoid, Negroid, and Mongoloid, the latter encompassing both Amerindians and Asians.

5. George Catlin to Carey A. Harris, 31 January 1838, cited in Bearss, *Osceola at Fort Moultrie,* 14.

6. For centuries, silk fibers and fabrics were treated with salts of tin and lead to increase "drape," that is, their weight and close texture, as well as to reduce the cost of the manufacture. This type of finishing provided the smoothness, luster, and stiffness that were the source of the "rustle" so popular in women's clothing of the nineteenth century. See *Encyclopaedia Britannica* (Chicago: Benton, 1964), 20:668.

Chapter 11

1. *New York Evening Star,* 28 February 1838, p. 2, col. 2.

2. NARA, RG 94, OAG, Generals' Papers and Books, Gen. T. S. Jesup Papers, box 16, folder Misc. 4/6, C. A. Harris to Capt. P. Morrison, War Department, January 30, 1838.

3. J. Van Horne, Lieut. 3rd Inf., Disburs. Agt. to the Seminoles, to Gen. George Gibson, Comy. Gen. Subt., Choctaw Agency, May 23rd, 1836, NARA, RG 192, CGS, Seminole Emigration File, no. 67.

4. Clay MacCauley, the first U.S. government agent to attempt to enumerate the

Florida Indians more than a generation after the end of the Florida Wars of Removal, told his superiors exactly what the Indians had told him. They "don't want nobody telling them what to do," he reported. See MacCauley, "Seminole Indians of Florida." Episcopal bishop William C. Gray and a few intrepid traders, for example Ted Smallwood and Bill Brown, met the Florida Indians on their own terms, deep inside the Big Cypress and the Everglades, and established interrelations based on mutual respect. For further information on this period, see also Harry Kersey, *Pelts, Plumes and Hides: White Traders among the Seminole Indians, 1870–1930* (Gainesville: University Presses of Florida, 1975).

5. Sturtevant, "Notes on Modern Seminole Traditions," 206–17.

6. For further discussion of this topic, see Wickman, *Tree That Bends*.

7. Minnie Moore Willson, *The Seminoles of Florida,* rev. ed. (New York: Moffat, Yard, 1911), 154–55.

8. See, for example, the article regarding Nancy in the *St. Augustine Evening Record,* 20 November 1899, contributed by a J. Brinton Paine of Jacksonville and reprinted from the *Jacksonville Times Union and Citizen.* Mr. Paine takes exception to Nancy's being characterized as having been the mother of Osceola and clarifies the irrationality of the chronologies being touted in other newspaper articles.

9. This information is taken from the U.S. Census of 1920, enumerator Lucien B. Spencer, U.S. agent to the Seminole Indians, and the published work of Jeff Bowen, *Seminoles of Florida Indian Census, 1930–1940, with Birth and Death Records, 1930–1938* (Signal Mountain, Tenn.: Mountain Press, 1997), passim.

10. Name withheld at the request of the family.

11. See Halbert and Ball, *Creek War*; Mahon, *Second Seminole War*; and Woodward, *Woodward's Reminiscences.*

12. Thomas Donaldson, *The George Catlin Indian Gallery in the U.S. National Museum (Smithsonian Institution), with Memoir and Statistics,* pt. 5, Smithsonian Report, 1885, pt. 2 (Washington, D.C.: Smithsonian Institution, 1885), 216, pl. 62.

13. [Welch], *Narrative of the Early Days,* 217.

14. "A ROMANCE OF THE SEMINOLES. Death of the Nephew of the Great Seminole Chief—A Curious History of Savage and Civilized Life," *New York Times,* 3 August 1877, 8.

15. Ibid. The Powell family records do not mention an Alfreta Powell, but the surname is certainly consistent with that of Osceola's biological father.

16. U.S. Bureau of the Census, *U.S. Census of 1860: New York, New Castle, Westchester,* Family No. 39 (Washington, D.C.: U.S. Government Printing Office, 1864).

17. U.S. Bureau of the Census, *U.S. Census of 1870: New York, Fordham, Township of West Farms, Westchester,* Family No. 11 (Washington, D.C.: U.S. Government Printing Office, 1874).

18. "The Williamsburg Suicide: Another Sensation Exploded," *New York Herald,* 2 August 1870.

19. U.S. Bureau of the Census, *U.S. Census of 1900: Kansas, Brown Co., Horton, District 27,* Family No. 311 (Washington, D.C.: U.S. Government Printing Of-

fice, 1904); and *U.S. Census of 1910: Iowa, Linn Co., Marion Township, First Ward, District 92,* Family No. 2 (Washington, D.C.: U.S. Government Printing Office, 1914).

20. Information provided through the courtesy of Carol York, archivist, New Jersey State Archives, personal communication with the author, July 2004.

21. Sam and Silla are shown together with their elder children, and some of Sam's brothers and sisters, on the 1859 Creek Annuity Lists, NARA, RG 75.

22. In the 1890s, Lucy Larney is listed by the Dawes commissioners on a list titled "List of persons whose names are on the Creek Tribal Rolls in the Possession of the Commission to the Five Civilized Tribes who have not been identified as having made application for enrollment as citizens of the Creek Nation and have not been otherwise accounted for." Her last known place of residence was at Eufala Deep Fork. List among the holdings of NARA, Southwest Region, Ft. Worth, Texas.

23. Current-García, *Papers of W. O. Tuggle,* 88, 90.

24. Dawes Seminole Roll, Family No. 589.

25. Rev. Orson Douglas to Commissioner of Indian Affairs Crawford, 15 August 1843, NARA, RG 75, Office of Indian Affairs, Seminole File D816, cited in Foreman, *Five Civilized Tribes,* 239.

26. W. A. Evans, oral history interview, 23 January 1937, transcript in WPA Indian Oral History Interviews file, vol. 24, Oklahoma Historical Society, Oklahoma City; see also the same story in Carolyn Thomas Foreman, *Indians Abroad* (Norman: University of Oklahoma Press, 1943), 160.

27. Mary A. Lilley, "Autobiography of Mary A. Lilley," Oklahoma Historical Society, MS Collections, typescript, 5.

28. *Van Buren (Arkansas) Intelligencer* of 14 October 1843, in Coe, *Red Patriots,* 119.

29. Foreman, *Indians Abroad,* 160–65.

30. Evans, oral history interview, 40–41.

31. *Van Buren (Arkansas) Intelligencer,* 14 October 1843.

32. Lilley, "Autobiography."

33. *Indian Missionary* 1, no. 4 (December 1884): 1.

34. Lilley, "Autobiography;" and Philip A. Lewis, oral history interview, WPA files, Oklahoma Historical Society. Mr. Lewis's grandfather was one of Kendle Lewis's slaves.

35. N. Sayre Harris, "Journal of a Tour in the Indian Territory [1844]," *Chronicles of Oklahoma* 10 (1932): 235.

Chapter 12

1. Frederick Weedon diary, "31st" [31 January 1838], Howell Family Papers.

2. *Army and Navy Chronicle* 6 (12 April 1838): 234.

3. Francis D. Heitman, *Historical Register and Dictionary of the United States Army, from Its Organization, September 29, 1789, to March 2, 1903* (Washington, D.C.: U.S. Government Printing Office, 1903), 1:729.

4. *The Biennial Register of All Officers and Agents in the Service of the United States with the Names, Force, and Condition, of all Ships and Vessels Belonging to the United States* (Washington, D.C.: Blair and Rives, 1838); Sprague, *Origin, Progress, and Conclusion,* 540–41.

5. Bearss, *Osceola at Fort Moultrie,* 2.

6. Ibid., 5–6.

7. Heitman, *Historical Register and Dictionary,* 511, 1022.

8. Dr. Robert Lebby to Dr. Johnson, 21 June 1844, in Ellis, *Nathaniel Lebby,* 317.

9. NARA, RG 75, Office of Indian Affairs, Florida Emigration, in Bearss, *Osceola at Fort Moultrie,* 34.

10. Dr. Robert Lebby to Dr. Johnson, ibid.

11. Heitman, *Historical Register and Dictionary,* 342; Fremont Rider, ed., *The American Genealogical-Biographical Index to American Genealogical, Biographical, and Local History Materials* (Middletown, Conn.: Godfrey Memorial Library, 1952), 1:137.

12. Robert F. Sumrall, telephone conversation with the author, 7 November 1985.

13. William Brown, telephone conversation with the author, 8 November 1985.

14. James S. Hutchins, telephone conversations with the author, 10, 11 January 1986. See also James S. Hutchins, "Dear Hook: Letters from Bennet Riley, Alphonso Wetmore, and Reuben Holmes, 1822–1833," *Missouri Historical Society Bulletin* 36 (July 1980): 203–20.

15. Reuben Holmes to Maj. J. H. Hook, 1 October 1831, in Hutchins, "Dear Hook," 215.

16. Hutchins, "Dear Hook," 203. Hook's papers appear as the Papers of Major James H. Hook, 1818–1832, NARA, RG 192, CGS.

17. *Army and Navy Chronicle* 6 (12 April 1838): 234.

18. Hutchins, "Dear Hook," 204.

19. *Army and Navy Chronicle* 16 (5 July 1879): 873–74.

20. *New York Times,* 16 July 1836. My thanks to Frank Laumer for bringing this item to my attention.

21. NARA, RG 21, Records of the United States District Court of the District of Columbia, Administration Case 2313, Inventory of Hook Estate.

22. *Daily National Intelligencer,* 1, 8, 25 December 1841, and 27 June 1842.

23. Inventory of Hook Estate, cited in Hutchins, "Dear Hook," 204.

24. James S. Hutchins, letter to the author, 10 January 1986.

25. Hutchins, "Dear Hook," 215.

26. James S. Hutchins, letter to the author, 10 January 1986.

27. Linda Eisenhart, letter to the author, 15 July 1986.

28. Coe, *Red Patriots,* 112–13.

29. F. M. Setzler to Julien C. Yonge, 12 September 1954, in Goggin, "Osceola," 175.

30. Smithsonian Institution, neg. no. 44, 262-H, in Biography files, "Osceola," SAHS.

31. Linda Eisenhart, letter to the author, 15 July 1986.

32. *Charleston Mercury,* 21 March 1838, cited in Goggin, "Osceola," 175.

33. Coe, *Red Patriots*, 3, 192–94, 196; John Gibbon, "Reading Signs," *Journal of the Military Service Institution of the United States* 5 (December 1884): 403.

34. Heitman, *Historical Register and Dictionary*, 206.

35. John C. Casey Papers, acc. no. 4026.3998, Thomas Gilcrease Institute of History and Art, Tulsa.

Chapter 13

1. See, for example, John Mollo, *Uniforms of the American Revolution, 1775–1781*, 2nd ed. (Poole, Dorset, England: Blandford Press, 1985), 159: "The figure wears . . . [the] fringed rifle frock . . . which Washington would have liked to issue to all his army."

2. Frederick P. Todd, *Soldiers of the American Army, 1775–1954* (1941; rev. ed., Chicago: Henry Regnery, 1954), "Thompson's Pennsylvania Rifle Battalion, 1775," n.p.

3. See William C. Sturtevant, "Seminole Men's Clothing," in *Essays on the Verbal and Visual Arts* (Seattle: University of Washington Press, 1967), 171: "The ultimate origins of *men's shirts* . . . were non-Indian garments. I cannot yet pinpoint the time and place of Euro-american influence, but it is significant that the earlier forms of both men's and women's cloth garments among the Seminole can be quite closely paralleled not only elsewhere in the Southeast but also among such groups as the Winnebago and Menomini—they must have copied the same frontier styles at the same period. But once adopted, these garments evolved independently among the Seminole until very recent years. The available types of trade cloth, of which they have always been made, changed over time, but the cut and decoration of the garments have changed without direct outside influence for most of their history."

4. Mollo, *Uniforms of the American Revolution*, pl. 16, p. 169: "[The regiment wore] frontier dress," and pl. 143, p. 197: the Iroquois leader Red Jacket, "celebrated orator and chief of the Seneca," is depicted wearing his "blue cloth hunting shirt." See also Preben Kannick, *Military Uniforms in Color*, ed. W. Y. Carmen (New York: Macmillan, 1968), pl. 126, p. 173: "In 1776 the problem of providing some form of uniform [for the American army] caused Washington to advise the states to equip their troops with 'hunting shirts,' which originated in the type of body garment common in the frontier areas, where they were worn by trappers. His argument was that, besides being cheap and practical, they led the enemy to believe that he was merely up against irregular troops." See also Company of Military Historians, *Military Uniforms in America: The Era of the American Revolution, 1755–1795* (San Rafael, Calif.: Presidio Press, 1974), 104: Mrs. Mary Morgan of Philadelphia described for her sister in Baltimore the uniform of the Ranger Battalion of the Associators of the City and Liberties of Philadelphia, ca. 1775, by saying, "Then their is the Rangers Mr. Frances Capt. Their uniform is tanned shirts with a cape fringed. A belt round their wastes with a Tommy hawk sticking in it. Some of them paint their faces and stick painted feathers in their heads, in short their aim is to resemble Indians as much as possible."

5. Charles Loch Mowat, *East Florida as a British Province, 1763–1784* (Gainesville: University Presses of Florida, 1964), 101.

6. Medical Society of the County of Kings, *Supplement to the Annual Report of the Medical Society of the County of Kings* (n.p.: Medical Society of the County of Kings), 1908, 7.

7. Cecile R. Gantaume, letter to the author, 17 July 1986; Allen Johnson and Dumas Malone, eds., *Dictionary of American Biography* (New York: Charles Scribner's Sons, 1957), 3:406–7.

8. Goggin, "Osceola," 182; and Sturtevant, "Osceola's Coats?" 315–16. Goggin's article wrongly locates the agency in Narbeth, a suburb of Philadelphia.

9. Sturtevant, "Osceola's Coats?" 315–16.

10. Beth Pierce, conversation with the author, 5 September 1986.

11. John Tharpe Lawrence to R. A. Gray, 10 February 1939, photoduplicate in Osceola Biography File, Dorothy Dodd Florida Collection, State Library of Florida, Tallahassee. The whereabouts of the original is unknown.

12. Ibid., 21 February 1939.

13. Sturtevant, "Osceola's Coats?" 327.

14. Helen Adeline Wellington, "Characteristic Periods of Seminole Clothing" (master's thesis, Iowa State College, 1942), 35.

15. For details of regimental activities, see Cohen, *Notices of Florida*; Edwin J. Scott, *Random Recollections of a Long Life, 1806–1876* (Columbia, S.C.: Charles A. Calvo, Jr., 1884), 109, 143.

16. Paul Quattlebaum, "Quattlebaum, a Palatine Family in South Carolina," pt. 2, *South Carolina Historical and Genealogical Magazine* 48 (April 1947): 84; also in Charles E. Beveridge and Charles Capin McLaughlin, eds., *The Papers of Frederick Law Olmstead* (Baltimore: Johns Hopkins University Press, 1981), 2:286–87.

17. Paul Quattlebaum, Jr., telephone conversation with the author, 21 July 1986.

18. Mahon, *History of Second Seminole War*, 156, 158.

19. Prince, *Amidst a Storm of Bullets*, entry for 21 January 1837.

20. Museum keeper Dale Idiens, letter to the author, 11 July 1986.

21. H. E. McGuire to Edward F. Corson, 17 January 1934, Corson Papers, Florida Historical Society Collection, University of South Florida Library, Tampa.

22. Ibid., and letter fragment.

23. For a discussion of Creek and Seminole straps and pouches, see John M. Goggin, "Beaded Shoulder Pouches of the Florida Seminole," *Florida Anthropologist* 4 (May 1951): 2–17.

24. The pieces sold at Sotheby's New York auction house on 4 December 1997. The prices were beyond the means of the museum, but the loss to Florida was incalculable.

25. Richard Rose, curator of anthropology, Rochester Museum and Science Center, personal communication to the author, 26 February 1987.

26. Frederick Weedon, diary (n.d.).

27. Goggin, "Osceola," 175.

28. National Museum of Natural History/Smithsonian Institution, cat. no. 76,181, accession card.

29. Edward Garner, telephone conversation with the author, 17 August 1986.

Epilogue

1. William Hartley and Ellen Hartley, *Osceola: The Unconquered Indian* (New York: Hawthorne Books, 1973), 130.

2. [Smith], *Sketch of the Seminole War,* 5.

3. Catlin lithograph documents, SAHS.

4. Ibid.

5. Frederick Weedon to George Catlin, in Ward, "Disappearance of the Head," 197.

6. [Smith], *Sketch of the Seminole War,* iv.

7. The only work covering this specific topic has been done by M. L. Brown. See his "Notes on U.S. Arsenals, Depots, and Martial Firearms of the Second Seminole War," *FHQ* 61 (April 1983): 445–58; and his *Firearms in Colonial America: The Impact on History and Technology, 1492–1792* (Washington, D.C.: Smithsonian Press, 1980).

8. An example of this attitude is available in a statement by John Rogers Vinton. In a letter to Lt. C. Tompkins, dated 18 July 1840, Vinton said: "You know how plain and vulgar the Seminoles dress in general & the artist must therefore borrow largely from his fancy if he wd. paint their vesture by any wiles of taste. . . . Still I know not whether these are imperative distinctions, or how far the privates are interdicted from indulging their passion for finery. I only recite what has happened to fall under my own observation." For a copy of this letter, see Boyd Collection, Otto G. Richter Library, Special Collections, University of Miami, Florida; and Goggin, "Osceola," 167.

9. Examination was conducted on 31 August and 1–2 September 1983 by laboratory technicians James Levy and Joseph Hutto (Bureau of Archaeological Research, Division of Archives and History, State of Florida, Tallahassee), senior curator P. R. Wickman (Museum of Florida History, Tallahassee), and registrars Deborah Harding (Florida State Museum) and Dennis Pullen (Museum of Florida History).

10. William Jenks produced weapons in the United States from 1839 to 1858. His breech-loading carbine was made under United States government contract by the Remington Company at Herkimer, New York, and by N. P. Ames at Chicopee Falls, Massachusetts. See Arthur Merwyn Carey, *American Firearms Makers: When, Where, and What They Made, from the Colonial Period to the End of the Nineteenth Century* (New York: Crowell, 1953).

11. Harry Hunter, letter to the author, 8 September 1983, and telephone conversations, 8, 19 September 1983.

12. Norman Flayderman, telephone conversation with the author, 21 September 1983.

13. Donald Ball, telephone conversation with the author, 13 February 1984.

14. Mary Weedon Keen, telephone conversation with the author, 24 April 1986; Josephine Stipe, telephone conversation with the author, 25 April 1986; Glenn C. Anderson to Mary Weedon Keen, 3 March 1986; Glenn C. Anderson to Josephine Weedon Stipe, 3 March 1986.

Bibliography

Unpublished Materials

Alabama Census Records. 1830. Alabama Department or Archives and History, Montgomery.

Boyd, Mark F. Collection. Otto G. Richter Library, University of Miami, Coral Gables.

Buswell, James O., III. "Florida Seminole Religious Ritual: Resistance and Change." Ph.D. diss., St. Louis University, 1972.

Casey, John C. Papers. Cat. no. 4026.3998. Thomas Gilcrease Institute of History and Art, Tulsa, Okla.

Catlin, George C. Two lithograph documents, ca. 1838. Osceola File. St. Augustine Historical Society, St. Augustine.

Chaney, Margaret A. "A Tribal History of the Seminole Indians." Master's thesis, University of Oklahoma, 1928.

Corson, Edward F. Papers. Florida Historical Society Collections, University of South Florida Library, Tampa.

Densmore, Frances. "The Collection of Water-Color Drawings of the North American Indians by Seth Eastman in the James Jerome Hill Reference Library, Saint Paul." 1954. James Jerome Hill Reference Library, St. Paul, Minn. Mimeo.

Dickison, Martin F., and Lucy B. Wayne. "Archaeological Mitigation of Two Seminole Sites in Marion County, Florida (8Mr542 and 8Mr543)." 1985. Elkay Properties, Atlanta. Mimeo.

DuVal, William, to John C. Calhoun. 11 February 1825. Manuscript Collection, box 9, P. K. Yonge Library of Florida History, University of Florida Library, Gainesville.

Evans, W. A. Oral History Interview, 23 January 1937. Transcript in WPA Indian Oral History Interviews file, vol. 24, pp. 40–41. Oklahoma Historical Society, Oklahoma City.

Florida Land Register, 1804–1820. MSS796, "Register of the Land Office East of Pearl River." Jefferson Building, Manuscripts, Library of Congress, Washington, D.C.

Goggin, John M. "Source Materials for the Study of the Florida Seminole Indians." 1959. Laboratory Notes No. 3. University of Florida, Department of Anthropology, Gainesville.

Gray, James M. "The Forts of Florida." 1972. Dorothy Dodd Florida Collection. State Library of Florida, Tallahassee. Mimeo.

Griffin, John W. "The Search for Osceola." John W. Griffin personal files, St. Augustine.

Howell Family Papers. Acc. no. 89.184. Alabama Department of Archives and History, Montgomery.

"Indian materials available in 1950 as per 1848 deposit of Dr. Nathan S. Jarvis." Typescript, Native American Collections, Brooklyn Museum, New York.

Lamb, D. S. "A History of the United States Army Medical Museum, 1862 to 1917, Compiled from the Official Records." Manuscript on file at the Otis Historical Archives, National Museum of Health and Medicine, Armed Forces Institute of Pathology (Walter Reed Medical Center), Washington, D.C.

Lawrence, John Tharpe, to Secretary of State. 10 February 1939. Osceola Biography File. Dorothy Dodd Florida Collection. State Library of Florida, Tallahassee.

Leon County (Florida) Deed Book B, pt. 2, p. 565, Tl R1 S&E. Office of the Clerk of the Circuit Court, Tallahassee.

Lilley, Mrs. Mary A. Autobiography. MS Collections. Oklahoma Historical Society, Oklahoma City.

Martini, Don. "Who Was Who among the Southern Indians: A Genealogical Notebook, 1698–1907," 466. Typescript, Collections of the Oklahoma Historical Society, Oklahoma City.

McQueen, James. Christening Record, 18 October 1695. County of Edinburgh, Parish of Edinburgh, Old Parochial Register. General Register Office, Edinburgh, Scotland.

Mott, Valentine. "Last Will and Testament of Valentine Mott." County of New York. Clerk of the Surrogate's Court. Liber 156, p. 228. Proved date 24 May 1865.

National Archives and Records Administration. Record Group (RG) 75. Records of the Department of the Interior, Bureau of Indian Affairs, Washington, D.C.

———. RG 94. Records of the Office of the Adjutant General.

———. RG 192. Office of Commissary General of Subsistence.

———. "Post Returns from Fort Marion." Microfilm no. 617. Roll 1060.

——. Southwest Region, Fort Worth, Texas, "List of Persons Enrolled on Creek Cards Whose Names May Be on the Rolls of the Cherokee, Choctaw, and Chickasaw Nation."

Osceola File. St. Augustine Historical Society, St. Augustine.

Osceola File. Works Progress Administration Files. Florida Historical Society Collection.

Paine, Charles Raymond. "The Seminole War of 1817–18." Master's thesis, University of Oklahoma, 1938.

Powell, Bruce C., Jr., and Evelyne D. Powell. "Osceola, Cousin of the Columbus County, North Carolina, Powells or Not?" 1975. John W. Griffin personal files, St. Augustine.

"Powell Records of Virginia, North Carolina, South Carolina, Georgia." Leon Saxon Powell personal files, Tallahassee. Copy in the personal files of the author.

Reed, Erik K., to T. Dale Stewart. 3 December 1968. John W. Griffin personal files, St. Augustine.

——. 31 December 1968. "Forensic Report." John W. Griffin personal files, St. Augustine. Mimeo.

St. Johns County (Florida) Deed Books B and L, 139–40. Office of the Clerk of the Circuit Court, St. Augustine.

St. Johns County (Florida) Marriage Records, 1843, p. 26. Marriage of Daniel Winchester Whitehurst to Henrietta Weedon. Recorded by County Court Clerk, 12 May 1843. St. Augustine.

Sturtevant, William C. "The Mikasuki Seminole: Medical Beliefs and Practices." Ph.D. diss., Yale University, 1954.

Tarvin [Turvin], Marion Elisha. "The Mascogees or Creek Indians." Typescript, MS Collections. Oklahoma Historical Society, Oklahoma City.

Vinton, John Rogers, to Christopher Tomkins. 18 July 1840. Christopher Tomkins Personal Collection. New Orleans.

Webster, Lucien B. Papers. St. Augustine Historical Society, St. Augustine.

Weedon, Frederick. Papers. SPR 251. Alabama Department of Archives and History, Montgomery.

Weedon and Whitehurst Family Papers. Southern Historical Collection. University of North Carolina, Chapel Hill.

Wellington, Helen Adaline. "Characteristic Periods of Seminole Clothing." Master's thesis, Iowa State College, 1942.

White, David H. "The John Forbes Company, Heir to the Florida Indian Trade, 1801–1819." Master's thesis, University of Alabama, 1973.

Wickman, Patricia, to Nestor A. Moreno, St. Augustine, 2 September 1970. St. Augustine Historical Society, Coppinger File.

Newspapers

Apalachicola (Fla.) Gazette. 1838.
Army and Navy Chronicle. 1836–1838.

Army and Navy Journal. 1879.
Atlanta Journal–Atlanta Constitution. 1983.
Augusta Constitutionalist. N.d.
Chadburn (N.C.) Columbus County News. 1975.
Charleston Courier. 1828, 1836–1838.
Charleston Mercury. 1837–1838.
Charleston News and Courier. 1951.
Charleston Observer. 1827.
Collier County (Fla.) News. 1950.
Columbia (S.C.) Southern Christian Herald. 1836.
Daily National Intelligencer. 1819, 1841–1842.
Fort Lauderdale News. 1984.
Indian Missionary. 1884.
Inverness (Fla.) Chronicle. 1983.
Jacksonville Florida Times-Union. 1950–1951.
Miami Herald. 1948, 1951–1952, 1965.
National Intelligencer. 1819, 1838.
New York Evening Star. 1837, 1838.
New York Times. 1858, 1877, 1947, 1952, 1966.
New York Weekly Herald. 1841.
Niles National Register. 1837.
Okeechobee (Fla.) News. 1950.
Plant City (Fla.) Courier. 1942.
St. Augustine Florida Herald. 1829, 1834–1838.
St. Augustine News. 1839–1840, 1842, 1844.
St. Augustine Tatler. 1896.
St. Petersburg Times. 1939, 1966–1967.
Savannah Georgian. 1837.
Savannah Republican. N.d.
Southern Patriot (Charleston, S.C.). 1838.
Tallahassee Democrat. 1966–1968.
Tallahassee Floridian. 1837.
Tampa Tribune. 1951, 1966.
Van Buren (Ark.) Intelligencer. 1843.

Other Published Materials

Abbott, Henry. *Catalogue of a Collection of Egyptian Antiquities . . . now exhibit-
    ing at the Stuyvesant Institute.* New York: J. W. Watson, 1854.
"A Description of Osceola." *South Carolina Historical Magazine* 65 (April 1964):
    85–86.
American Anti-Slavery Almanac. New York: Webster and Southard, 1839.
American "Orson." "The Seminoles: A Desultory Sketch of the Character of the

Seminole Creek Indians of Florida." *Knickerbocker Magazine* 7 (May 1836): 453–55.

American State Papers: Military Affairs. Washington, D.C.: Gales and Seaton, 1861.

Antle, H. R. "Interpretation of Seminole Clan Relationship Terms." *Chronicles of Oklahoma* 14 (Winter 1936): 343–48.

Backus, Electus. "Diary of a Campaign in Florida in 1837–1838." *Historical Magazine* 10 (September 1866): 279–85.

Badger, Alfred S. *Osceola: An Address Delivered before the St. Augustine Institute of Science and Historical Society.* St. Augustine: Record Press, n.d.

Baker, Henry A. "Archaeological Investigations at Fort Cooper, Inverness, Florida." In *Bureau of Historic Sites and Properties,* Bulletin no. 5. Tallahassee: Tallahassee Division of Archives, History, and Records Management, 1976.

Bartram, William. *Travels through North and South Carolina, Georgia, East and West Florida, the Cherokee Country, the Extensive Territories of the Muscogulges or Creek Confederacy and the Country of the Choctaws.* 1791. Reprint, New Haven: Yale University Press, 1958.

———. "Observations on the Creek and Cherokee Indians, 1789." *Transactions of the American Ethnological Society.* Vol. 3, pt. 1. New York: American Ethnological Society, 1853.

Bearss, Edwin C. *Osceola at Fort Moultrie, Sullivan's Island, South Carolina, Fort Sumter National Monument.* Washington, D.C.: Division of History, Office of Archaeology and Historic Preservation, 1968.

Bell, John H. *Letter from J. H. Bell, acting agent for the Indians of Florida, to Honorable John Floyd of the House of Representatives of the United States relative to Indian settlements in Florida.* Washington, D.C.: Gales, 1822.

Bemrose, John. *Reminiscences of the Second Seminole War.* Edited by John K. Mahon. Gainesville: University Presses of Florida, 1966.

Benton, Thomas Hart. *Thirty Years' View; or, A history of the working of the American government for thirty years, from 1820 to 1850.* New York: D. Appleton, 1854–56.

Beveridge, Charles E., and Charles Capin McLaughlin, eds. *The Papers of Frederick Law Olmstead.* 2 vols. Baltimore: Johns Hopkins University Press, 1981.

Biennial Register of All Officers and Agents in the Service of the United States With the Names, Force, and Condition, of all Ships and Vessels Belonging to the United States. Prepared at the Department of State. In pursuance of resolutions of Congress of April 27, 1816, and July 14, 1832. Washington, D.C.: Blair and Rives, 1838.

Bowen, Jeff. *Seminoles of Florida Indian Census, 1930–1940, with Birth and Death Records, 1930–1938.* Signal Mountain, Tenn.: Mountain Press, 1997.

Boyd, Mark Frederick. "Jacksonville and the Seminole War, 1835, 1836." *Florida Historical Quarterly* 3 (January–April 1925).

———. "Diego Pena's Mission to Apalachee and Apalachicola in 1716." *Florida Historical Quarterly* 28 (July 1949): 1–27.

——. "The Seminole War: Its Background and Onset." *Florida Historical Quarterly* 30 (July 1951): 3–115.

——. "Asi-Yaholo or Osceola." *Florida Historical Quarterly* 33 (January–April 1955): 249–305.

——. "Florida Aflame: Background and Onset of the Seminole War, 1835." *Florida Historical Quarterly* 30 (July 1951).

Brown, Jefferson B. *Key West: The Old and the New.* St. Augustine: Record Company, 1912.

Brown, M. L. *Firearms in Colonial America: The Impact on History and Technology, 1492–1792.* Washington, D.C.: Smithsonian Press, 1980.

——. "Notes on U.S. Arsenals, Depots, and Martial Firearms of the Second Seminole War." *Florida Historical Quarterly* 61 (April 1983): 445–58.

Brownell, Charles DeWolf. *The Indian Races of North and South America: Comprising an account of the principal aboriginal races; a description of their national customs, mythology, and religious ceremonies; the history of their most powerful tribes, and of their most celebrated chiefs and warriors; their intercourse and wars with the European settlers, and a great variety of anecdote and description, illustrative of personal and national character.* Boston: H. Wentworth, 1853.

Buker, George E. *Swamp Sailors: Riverine Warfare in the Everglades, 1835–1842.* Gainesville: University Presses of Florida, 1975.

Burk, Jerry L. "Oklahoma Seminole Indians." *Chronicles of Oklahoma* 51 (Summer 1973): 211–23.

Burt, Jesse, and Robert B. Ferguson. *Indians of the Southeast: Then and Now.* Nashville: Abingdon Press, 1973.

Campbell, J. B. *Campbell's Abstract of Creek Indian Census Cards and Index.* Muscogee, Okla.: Phoenix Job Printing Company, 1915.

——. *Campbell's Abstract of Seminole Indian Census Cards and Index.* Muscogee, Okla.: Oklahoma Printing Company, 1925.

Carey, Arthur Merwyn. *American Firearms Makers: When, Where, and What They Made, from the Colonial Period to the End of the Nineteenth Century.* New York: Crowell, 1953.

Carlisle, Robert J. *An Account of Bellevue Hospital with a Catalogue of the Medical and Surgical Staff from 1736 to 1894.* New York: Society of the Alumni of Bellevue Hospital, 1893.

Carter, Clarence Edward, comp. and ed. *The Territorial Papers of the United States, vol. 23, The Territory of Florida, 1824–1828.* Washington, D.C.: U.S. Government Printing Office, 1958.

Carter, Clarence E., and John P. Bloom, comps. and eds. *The Territorial Papers of the United States.* Washington, D.C.: U.S. Government Printing Office, 1934–. New York: AMS Press, 1972–.

Castelnau, Francis, Comte de. "Essay on Middle Florida, 1837–1838." Translated by Arthur R. Seymour. *Florida Historical Quarterly* 26 (January 1948): 199–255.

Catalog of the Surgical and Pathological Museum of Valentine Mott, MD., LLD.

Bound Pamphlets, no. 68. New York Academy of Medicine Rare Books Collection. New York: n.p., 1858.

Catlin, George. *Letters and Notes on the Manners, Customs, and Conditions of the North American Indians.* 2 vols. London: Published by the Author, 1841.

———. *North American Indians, Being Letters, Notes on Their Manners, Customs, and Conditions during Eight Years' Travel among the Wildest Tribes of Indians in North America, 1832–1839.* 2 vols. 1866. Reprint, Edinburgh: J. Grant, 1926.

Chambers, John Whiteclay II, ed. *Oxford Companion to American Military History.* Oxford: Oxford University Press, 1999.

Clayton, Lawrence A., Vernon James Knight, Jr., and Edward C. Moore, eds. *The De Soto Chronicles: The Expedition of Hernando de Soto to North America in 1539–1543.* 2 vols. Tuscaloosa: University of Alabama Press, 1993.

Cline, Howard Francis. *Notes on Colonial Indians and Communities in Florida, 1700–1821.* New York: Garland Press, 1974. (Originally defendant's exhibits nos. 100, 121, United States Indian Claims Commission, docket no. 280.)

Coe, Charles H. *Red Patriots: The Story of the Seminoles.* 1898. Reprint, Gainesville: University Presses of Florida, 1974.

———. "The Parentage and Birthplace of Osceola." *Florida Historical Quarterly* 17 (April 1939): 304–11.

Cohen, M[yer] M. *Notices of Florida and the Campaigns.* 1836. Reprint, Gainesville: University Presses of Florida, 1964.

———. Sidebar Comments. *Quarterly Anti-Slavery Magazine* 2, no. 4 (July 1837): 419–20.

Company of Military Historians. *Military Uniforms in America: The Era of the American Revolution, 1755–1795.* San Rafael, Calif.: Presidio Press, 1974.

Cooper, Barnsby Blake. *The Life of Sir Astley Cooper, Bart., Interspersed with Sketches from His Note-Books of Distinguished Contemporary Characters.* 2 vols. London: John W. Parker, 1843.

Cory, Charles. *Hunting and Fishing in Florida.* 2nd ed. Boston: Estes and Lauriat, 1896.

Cotterill, R. S. *The Southern Indians: The Story of the Civilized Tribes before Removal.* Norman: University of Oklahoma Press, 1954.

Coulter, Merton E. "A List of the First Shipload of Georgia Settlers." *Georgia Historical Quarterly* 30, no. 4 (December 1947).

Covington, James. "English Gifts to the Indians, 1765–1766." *Florida Anthropologist* 13 (September 1960): 71–75.

———. "The Armed Occupation Act of 1842." *Florida Historical Quarterly* 40 (July 1961): 41–52.

———, collector and annotator. "The British Meet the Seminoles: Negotiations between British Authorities in East Florida and the Indians: 1763–68." In *Contributions of the Florida State Museum,* Social Sciences, no. 7. Gainesville: Florida State Museum, 1961.

Craig, Alan K., and Christopher S. Peebles. "Ethnoecologic Change among the

Seminoles, 1740-1840." In *Man and Cultural Heritage: Papers in Honor of Fred B. Kniffen,* edited by H. J. Walker and W. G. Haag, 83-96. *Geoscience and Man* 5 (10 June 1974).

Croffut, W. A., ed. *Fifty Years in Camp and Field: Diary of Major General Ethan Allen Hitchcock, USA.* New York: Putnam's Sons, 1909.

Cullum, George Washington. *Biographical Register of the Officers and Graduates of the U.S. Military Academy at West Point, N.Y., from Its Establishment, in 1802, to 1890.* 3 vols. Boston: Houghton, Mifflin, 1891.

Current-Garcia, Eugene, ed. *Shem, Ham, and Japheth: The Papers of W. O. Tuggle, Comprising His Indian Diary, Sketches, and Observations, Myths, and Washington Journal in the Territory and at the Capital, 1879-1882.* Athens: University of Georgia Press, 1973.

Davis, T. Frederick. "The Seminole Council, October 23-25, 1834." *Florida Historical Quarterly* 7 (April 1929): 330-56.

Dayton, Abram C. *Last Days of Knickerbocker Life.* New York: G. P. Putnam's Sons, 1897.

Dobson, David. *Directory of Scots Banished to the American Plantations.* Baltimore: Genealogical Publishing, 1983.

———. *The Original Scots Colonists of Early America.* Baltimore: Genealogical Publishing, 1989.

Dockstader, Frederick I. *Great North American Indians: Profiles in Life and Leadership.* New York: Van Nostrand Reinhold, 1977.

Doherty, Herbert J., Jr. "R. K. Call vs. the Federal Government on the Seminole War." *Florida Historical Quarterly* 31 (January 1953): 163-80.

Donaldson, Thomas [Corwin]. *George Catlin's Indian Gallery in the U.S. National Museum (Smithsonian Institution), with Memoir and Statistics.* Part 5. Smithsonian Report for 1885, Part 2. Washington, D.C.: Smithsonian Institution, 1885.

———. *George Catlin's Indian Gallery in the U.S. National Museum (Smithsonian Institution), with Memoir and Statistics.* Author's edition. Washington, D.C.: U.S. Government Printing Office, 1887.

Dowd, John T. "The Investigations of the Vandalized Graves of Two Historic Personages: Osceola, Seminole War Chief, and Colonel William M. Shy, Civil War Hero." *Tennessee Anthropologist* 5 (Spring 1980): 47-72.

Dowling, Daniel J. *The Charleston (SC) Directory; and Register for 1835-6. Containing the Names, Occupations, and Residences of Persons in Business, Heads of Families, &c. Collected by James Smith. And the City Register; Consisting of a Variety of Useful Information, connected with our Trade and Commerce.* Charleston, S.C.: Daniel J. Dowling, 1835.

———. *Sketch of the Seminole War.* Charleston, S.C.: J. P. Beile and W. H. Berrett, 1836.

Elderkin, James D. *Biographical sketches and anecdotes of a solider of three wars, as written by himself: The Florida, the Mexican war, and the great rebellion, together with sketches of travel, also of service in a militia company and a member of the Detroit light guard band for over thirty years.* Detroit: Record Printing, 1899.

Ellis, E. Detreville. *Nathaniel Lebby, Patriot, and Some of His Descendants.* N.p.: privately printed, 1967.

Ellis, Edward Sylvester [Gordon]. *Osceola, Chief of the Seminoles.* New York: Dutton, 1899.

Ellis, Leonora Beck. "Three Dynasties on Tiger-Tail." *Outing Magazine* 3, no. 7 (March 1901): 697–701.

———. "The Seminoles of Florida." *Gunton's Magazine* 25 (December 1903): 495–505.

Elzas, Barnett A. *The Jews of South Carolina from the Earliest Days to the Present Day.* Philadelphia: Lippincott, 1905.

Encyclopaedia Britannica. 14th ed. 23 vols. Chicago: Encyclopaedia Britannica, 1964.

Evans, Hedvig Tetans. "Seminole Folktales." *Florida Historical Quarterly* 56 (April 1978): 473–94.

Ewers, John C. "Charles Bird King, Painter of Indian Visitors to the Nation's Capital." In *Annual Report of the Smithsonian Institution for 1953,* 463–73. Washington, D.C.: U.S. Government Printing Office, 1954.

Fairbanks, Charles H. *Ethnohistorical Report of the Florida Indians.* Indian Claims Commission, Dockets no. 73, 151. 1957. Reprint, New York: Garland Press, 1974.

Fairchild, Henry Le Roy. *A History of the New York Academy of Sciences, Formerly the Lyceum of Natural History by Henry Le Roy Fairchild, Recording Secretary.* New York: Published by the Author, 1887.

Fisher, George Jackson. *Biographical Sketches of the Deceased Physicians of Westchester Co., N.Y.* New York: Hall, Clayton, 1861.

Florida Writers' Project. *The Seminole Indians in Florida.* Tallahassee: Florida State Department of Agriculture, 1940.

Ford, Alice, *John James Audubon.* Norman: University of Oklahoma Press, 1964.

Foreman, Carolyn Thomas. *Indians Abroad.* Norman: University of Oklahoma Press, 1943.

Foreman, Grant. *Indian Removal.* Norman: University of Oklahoma Press, 1953.

———. *The Five Civilized Tribes: Cherokee, Chickasaw, Choctaw, Creek, Seminole.* 5th ed. Norman: University of Oklahoma Press, 1974.

Francis, Samuel W. *Memoir of the Life and Character of Professor Valentine Mott.* New York: W. J. Middleton, 1865.

Francke, Arthur E., Jr. *Fort Mellon, 1837–42: A Microcosm of the Second Seminole War.* Miami: Banyan Books, 1977.

Fundaburke, Emma Lila, ed. *Southeastern Indians Life Portraits: A Catalogue of Pictures, 1564–1860.* Luverne, Ala.: Emma Lila Fundaburke, 1958.

Further Information regarding the Aborigines, together with some particulars relative to the Seminole War. Printed for the Friends Society of Philadelphia. London: Harvey and Darton, 1839.

Garrett, William. *Reminiscences of Public Men in Alabama for Thirty Years.* Atlanta: Plantation Publishing, 1872.

Gibbon, John. "Reading Signs." *Journal of the Military Service Institution of the United States* 5 (December 1884): 396–403.

Giddings, Joshua R. *The Exiles of Florida; or, the Crimes Committed by Our Government against the Maroons, Who Fled from South Carolina and Other Slave States, Seeking Protection under Spanish Law.* 1858. Reprint, Gainesville: University Presses of Florida, 1964.

Gifford, G. E., Jr. "John James Audubon and His Charleston-Physician Friends." *Journal of the South Carolina Medical Association* 75, no. 6 (June 1979): 257–63.

Gluckman, Stephen J., and Christopher S. Peebles. "Oven Hill (Di-15), a Refuge Site in the Suwannee River." *Florida Anthropologist* 27 (March 1974): 21–30.

Goggin, John M. "Silver Work of the Florida Seminole." *El Palacio* 47 (February 1940): 25–32.

———. "A Florida Indian Trading Post, circa 1763–1784." *Southern Indian Studies* 1, no. 3 (1949): 5–38.

———. "Beaded Shoulder Pouches of the Florida Seminole." *Florida Anthropologist* 4 (May 1951): 2–17.

———. "Osceola: Portraits, Features, and Dress." *Florida Historical Quarterly* 33 (January–April 1955): 161–92.

———. "Seminole Pottery." In *Prehistoric Pottery of the Eastern United States,* ed. James B. Griffin. Ann Arbor: University of Michigan Museum of Anthropology, 1958.

———. "Style Areas in Southeastern Indian Art." *Proceedings of the Twenty-ninth International Congress of Americanists.* New York: Cooper Square Publishers, 1967.

Goggin, John M., Mary E. Godwin, Earl Hester, David Prang, and Robert Sprangenberg. "An Historic Indian Burial, Alachua County, Florida." *Florida Anthropologist* 2 (May 1949): 10–25.

Gongaware, George J. *The History of the German Friendly Society of Charleston, South Carolina, 1766–1916.* Richmond, Va.: Garrett and Massie, 1935.

Green, Michael D. *The Creeks: A Critical Bibliography.* Bloomington: Indiana University Press, 1979.

———. *The Politics of Indian Removal: Creek Government and Society in Crisis.* Lincoln: University of Nebraska Press, 1982.

Griffin, John W., ed. *The Florida Indian and His Neighbors.* Winter Park, Fla.: Inter-American Center, 1949.

Groce, George C., and David H. Wallace. *New York Historical Society's Dictionary of Artists in America.* New Haven, Conn.: Yale University Press, 1957.

Gross, S. D. *Memoir of Valentine Mott, M.D. LL.D., professor of surgery in the City of New York; member of the Institute of France.* Philadelphia: Lindsay and Blakiston, 1868.

Halbert, H. S., and T. H. Ball. *The Creek War of 1813 and 1814.* 1895. Reprint, Tuscaloosa: University of Alabama Press, 1995.

Halfern, Albert von. *Der Letzte der Seminolen: Scenen aus den Kämpfen der Indi-*

aner Florida's gegen die Weissen, nebst Ruckblick auf die Zustände der Vereinigten Staaten. Dresden: Arnoldische Buchhandlung, 1846.

Hammer Galleries. *Art Objects and Furnishings from the William Randolph Hearst Collection.* New York: Hammer Galleries, 1941.

Hann, John H., ed. and trans. *Missions to the Calusa.* Gainesville: University Presses of Florida, 1991.

Harmon, Joyce Elizabeth. *Trade and Privateering in Spanish Florida, 1732–1763.* St. Augustine: St. Augustine Historical Society, 1969.

Harris, N. Sayre. "Journal of a Tour in the Indian Country." *Chronicles of Oklahoma* 10 (1932): 219–56.

Hartley, William, and Ellen Hartley. *Osceola, the Unconquered Indian.* New York: Hawthorn Books, 1973.

Hawkins, Benjamin. *Letters of Benjamin Hawkins.* Vol. 9 of *Collections of the Georgia Historical Society,* 1916.

———. *A Sketch of the Creek Country in 1798 and 1799.* Vol. 3, pt. 1 of *Collections of the Georgia Historical Society.* 1848. Reprint, New York: Kraus Reprint, 1971.

———. *The Collected Works of Benjamin Hawkins, 1796–1810,* edited by H. Thomas Foster II. Tuscaloosa: University of Alabama Press, 2003.

Heitman, Francis B. *Historical Register and Dictionary of the United States Army, from Its Organization, September 29, 1789, to March 2, 1903.* 2 vols. Washington, D.C.: U.S. Government Printing Office, 1903.

Hicks, John W. *Microscopy of Hairs: A Practical Guide and Manual.* Issue 2. Washington, D.C.: U.S. Government Printing Office, 1977.

Hodgson, W[illiam] B. "Creek Confederacy." In *Creek Indian History.* Reprint of Georgia Historical Society Publications, vol. 3, pt. 1. Americus, Ga.: Americus Book Company, 1938.

Horan, James D. *The McKenney-Hall Portrait Gallery of American Indians.* New York: Crown Publishers, 1972.

Howard, Oliver Otis. *Autobiography of Oliver Otis Howard, Major General United States Army.* New York: Baker and Taylor, 1907.

———. *My Life and Experiences among Our Hostile Indians: A Record of Personal Observations, Adventures, and Campaigns among the Indians of the Great West, with Some Account of Their Life, Habits, Traits, Religion, Ceremonies, Dress, Savage Instincts, and Customs in Peace and War.* 1907. Reprint, New York: Da Capo Press, 1972.

Hudson, Charles M., ed. *Red, White, and Black.* Athens: University of Georgia Press, 1971.

———. *Four Centuries of Southern Indians.* Athens: University of Georgia Press, 1975.

———. *Black Drink: A Native American Tea.* Athens: University of Georgia Press, 1979.

Hutchins, James S. "'Dear Hook': Letters from Bennet Riley, Alphonso Wetmore, and Reuben Holmes, 1822–1833." *Missouri Historical Society Bulletin* 36 (July 1980): 203–20.

International Art Treasures Exhibition Catalogue, Presented by the British Antique Dealers Association. Bath, England: 1973.

Ivers, Larry. "The Battle of Fort Mose." *Georgia Historical Quarterly* 51, no. 2 (June 1967).

Jackson, J. B. S. *A Descriptive Catalogue of the Anatomical Museum of the Boston Society for Medical Improvement.* Boston: William D. Ticknor, 1847.

———. *A Descriptive Catalogue of the Warren Anatomical Museum.* Boston: A. Williams, 1870.

Jaruco, El Conde de San Juan de. *Historia de Familias Cubanas.* 7 vols. Miami: Ediciones Universal, 1985.

Jarvis, Nathan S. "An Army Surgeon's Notes on Frontier Service, 1833–1848." *Journal of the Military Service Institution of the United States* 39 (September–October 1906): 275–86.

———. *Art of the Eastern Plains Indians: The Nathan Sturges Jarvis Collection.* New York: Brooklyn Institute of Arts and Sciences Museum, n.d.

Jesup, Thomas S. "The Case of Osceola." *Magazine of American History* 5 (1880): 447–50.

Johnson, Allen, and Dumas Malone, eds. *Dictionary of American Biography.* 11 vols. New York: Charles Scribner's Sons, 1957.

Kannick, Preben. *Military Uniforms in Color.* Edited by W. Y. Carmen. New York: Macmillan, 1968.

Kersey, Harry. *Pelts, Plumes and Hides: White Traders among the Seminole Indians, 1870–1930.* Gainesville: University Presses of Florida, 1975.

———. "Private Societies and the Maintenance of Seminole Tribal Integrity, 1899–1957." *Florida Historical Quarterly* 56 (January 1978): 297–316.

King, Moses. *King's Handbook of New York City.* Boston: Moses King, 1893.

King, R. T. "Clan Affiliation and Leadership among the Twentieth Century Florida Indians." *Florida Historical Quarterly* 55 (July 1976): 138–52.

Koonce, James Council Bernard. *The Seminole Indians.* Micanopy, Fla.: n.p., 1870.

Krogman, Wilton Marion. *The Human Skeleton in Forensic Medicine.* 3rd ed. Springfield, Ill.: Charles C. Thomas, 1978.

Laumer, Frank. *Dade's Last Command.* Gainesville: University Presses of Florida, 1995.

"Letters of Samuel Forry, Surgeon U.S. Army, 1837–1838." Parts 1–3. *Florida Historical Quarterly* 6 (January–April 1928): 133–48, 206–19; 7 (July 1928): 88–105.

Logan, John A. *The Volunteer Soldier of America, with Memoir of the Author and Military Reminiscences from General Logan's Private Journal.* Chicago: R. S. Peals, 1887.

Lorant, Stefan, ed. *The New World: The First Pictures of America.* New York: Duell, Sloan and Pearce, 1946.

Lossing, Benson J. *Pictorial Field-Book of the Revolution and the War of 1812.* 2 vols. 1859. Reprint, Rutland, Vt.: C. E. Tuttle, 1972.

Loughridge, R. M. *English and Muskokee Dictionary: Collected from Various Sources and Revised.* 1884. Reprint, Okmulgee, Okla.: B. Frank Belvin, General Missionary to the Creek and Seminole Indians, Baptist Home Mission Board, 1964.

Lumpkin, Wilson. *The Removal of the Cherokee Indians from Georgia.* 2 vols. New York: Dodd, Mead, 1907.

MacCauley, Clay. "Seminole Indians of Florida." In *Bureau of American Ethnology Fifth Annual Report, 1883, 1884.* Washington, D.C.: Smithsonian Institution, 1887.

Mahon, John K. *History of the Second Seminole War, 1835–1842.* Gainesville: University Presses of Florida, 1967.

Marquis's Who Was Who in America, Historical Volume, 1607–1896. Chicago: A. N. Marquis, 1963.

Matthews, Washington. "The Catlin Collection of Indian Paintings." In *Report of the National Museum for 1890.* Washington, D.C.: n.p., 1892.

McCarthy, Joseph Edward. "Portraits of Osceola and the Artists Who Painted Them." *Papers of the Jacksonville Historical Society* 2:23–44.

McKenney, Thomas L. *Catalogue of the One Hundred and Fifteen Indian Portraits, Representing Eighteen Different Tribes, Accompanied by a Few Brief Remarks on the Character etc. of Most of Them.* Philadelphia: [Edward C. Biddle], 1836.

McKenney, Thomas L., and James Hall. *History of the Indian Tribes of North America, with Biographical Sketches and Anecdotes of the Principal Chiefs. Embellished with One Hundred and Twenty Portraits, from the Indian Gallery in the Department of War, at Washington.* Vol. 1. Philadelphia: Edward C. Biddle, 1836.

———. *History of the Indian Tribes of North America, with Biographical Sketches and Anecdotes of the Principal Chiefs. Embellished with One Hundred and Twenty Portraits, from the Indian Gallery in the Department of War, at Washington.* Vol. 2. Philadelphia: Greenough, 1838.

———. *History of the Indian Tribes of North America, with Biographical Sketches and Anecdotes of the Principal Chiefs. Embellished with One Hundred and Twenty Portraits, from the Indian Gallery in the Department of War, at Washington.* 3 vols. Folio. Philadelphia: Daniel Rice and James G. Clark, 1842–44.

———. *History of the Indian Tribes of North America, with Biographical Sketches and Anecdotes of the Principal Chiefs. Embellished with One Hundred and Twenty Portraits, from the Indian Gallery in the Department of War, at Washington.* Vol. 2, 8vo. Philadelphia: Daniel Rice and James G. Clark, 1854.

———. *The Indian Tribes of North America, with Biographical Sketches and Anecdotes of the Principal Chiefs.* Vol. 2. Edited by Frederick Webb Hodge and David I. Bushnell, Jr. Edinburgh: John Grant, 1934.

McNeer, May Yonge. *War Chief of the Seminoles.* New York: Random House, 1954.

McReynolds, Edwin C. *The Seminoles*. Norman: University of Oklahoma Press, 1957.

Medical Society of the County of Kings. *Supplement to the Annual Report of the Medical Society of the County of Kings*. N.p.: Medical Society of the County of Kings, 1908.

Milanich, Jerald, and Samuel Proctor, eds. *Tacachale: Essays on the Indians of Florida and Southeastern Georgia during the Historic Period*. Gainesville: University Presses of Florida, 1978.

Miller, John A. *A Voyage to the Spanish Main*. N.p.: n.p., 1827.

Mollo, John. *Uniforms of the American Revolution, 1775–1781*. 2nd ed. Poole, Dorset, England: Blandford Press, 1985.

Mooney, Michael MacDonald, ed. *George Catlin: Letters and Notes on the North American Indians*. New York: Clarkson N. Potter, 1975.

Morse, Jedidiah. *A Report to the Secretary of War of the United States, on Indian Affairs, Comprising a Narrative of a Tour Performed in the Summer of 1820, under a Commission from the President of the United States, for the Purpose of Ascertaining, for the Use of the Government, the Actual State of the Indian Tribes in Our Country*. Washington, D.C.: Davis and Force, 1822.

Mott, Valentine. *Travels in Europe and the East*. N.p.: Published by the author, 1841.

Motte, Jacob Rhett. *Journey into Wilderness: An Army Surgeon's Account of Life in Camp and Field during the Creek and Seminole Wars, 1836–1838*, edited by James F. Sunderman. 2nd ed. Gainesville: University Presses of Florida, 1963.

Moulton, Gary E., ed. *The Papers of Chief John Ross, Vol. 1: 1807–1839*. Norman: University of Oklahoma Press, 1985.

Mowat, Charles Loch. *East Florida as a British Province, 1763–1784*. Reprint, Gainesville: University Presses of Florida, 1964.

Narrative of a Voyage to the Spanish Main in the Ship "Two Friends"; the occupation of Amelia Island, by M'Gregor etc.,—Sketches of the Province of East Florida, and anecdotes illustrative of the Habits and Manners of the Indians: with an Appendix, containing a Detail of the Seminole war, and the execution of Arbuthnot and Ambrister. 1819. Reprint, Gainesville: University Presses of Florida, 1978.

National Cyclopaedia of American Biography. 11 vols. New York: James T. White, 1900, 1907.

O'Connell, Mrs. Morgan John. *The Coppingers of Ballyvolane and Barryscourt*. Manchester, England: Guardian Letterpress, 1883.

"Original Narratives of Indian Attacks in Florida: An Indian Attack of 1856 on the Home of Willoughby Tillis. Narrative of James Dallas Tillis." *Florida Historical Quarterly* 8 (April 1930): 179–87.

"Osceola and the Charlestonians." *Florida Historical Quarterly* 33 (January–April 1955): 247–48.

Owen, Thomas M. *History of Alabama and Directory of Alabama Biography*. 4 vols. Chicago: S. J. Clarke Publishing, 1921.

Parsons-Abbott Census. *1832 Creek Census*. Transcribed by James L. Douthat. Signal Mountain, Tenn.: Institute of Historic Research, 1995.

Peek, Peter V. *Inklings of adventure in the campaigns of the Florida Indian war; and a sketch of the life of the author.* Schenectady, N.Y.: I. Riggs, 1846.

Peters, Virginia Bergman. *The Florida Wars.* Hamden, Conn.: Archon Books, 1979.

Porter, Kenneth W. "Seminole Flight from Fort Marion." *Florida Historical Quarterly* 22 (January 1944).

———. "The Episode of Osceola's Wife: Fact or Fiction?" *Florida Historical Quarterly* 26 (July 1947): 92–98.

[Potter, Woodburne.] *The War in Florida, Being an Exposition of Its Causes and an Accurate History of the Campaigns of Generals Clinch, Gaines, and Scott By a late staff officer.* 1836. Reprint, N.p.: Readex Microprint, 1966.

Pound, Merritt B. *Benjamin Hawkins—Indian Agent.* Athens: University of Georgia Press, 1951.

Powell, William H. *A History of the Organization and Movements of the Fourth Regiment of Infantry, United States Army, from May 30, 1796, to December 31, 1870; Together with a Record of the Military Services of All Officers Who Have at Any Time Belonged to the Regiment.* Washington, D.C.: n.p., 1871.

Pratt, Theodore. *Seminole, a Drama of the Florida Indian.* 1953. Reprint, New York: Fawcett, 1954.

Prince, Henry. *Amidst a Storm of Bullets: 1836–1842, the Diary of Lt. Henry Prince of Florida.* Edited by Frank Laumer. Seminole Wars Historic Foundation, Inc., Contribution Number One. Tampa: University of Tampa Press, 1998.

Prucha, Francis Paul. *The Sword of the Republic: The United States Army on the Frontier, 1783–1846.* New York: Macmillan, 1969.

———. *A Bibliographical Guide to the History of Indian-White Relations in the United States.* Chicago: University of Chicago Press, 1977.

Quattlebaum, Paul. "Quattlebaum, a Palatine Family in South Carolina." Pt. 2. *South Carolina Historical and Genealogical Magazine* 48 (April 1947): 84–94.

Ransom, James Birchett. *Osceola; or, Fact and fiction: a tale of the Seminole War, by a Southerner.* New York: Harper and Brothers, 1838.

Read, William A. *Florida Place Names of Indian Origin and Seminole Personal Names.* 1934. Reprint, Tuscaloosa: University of Alabama Press, 2004.

Remini, Robert V. *Andrew Jackson and the Course of American Empire, 1767–1821.* Vol. 1. New York: Harper and Row, 1977.

———. *Andrew Jackson and His Indian Wars.* New York: Viking Penguin Books, 2001.

Rhees, William H. *An Account of the Smithsonian Institution, its Founder, Building, Operations, etc., prepared from the Reports of Prof Henry to the Regents, and other Authentic Sources.* Washington, D.C.: Smithsonian Institution, 1859.

Rider, Fremont, ed. *The American Genealogical-Biographical Index to American Genealogical, Biographical, and Local History Materials.* 2 vols. Middletown, Conn.: Godfrey Memorial Library, 1952.

Robertson, Fred L. *Soldiers of Florida in the Seminole Indian, Civil, and Spanish American War.* [Tallahassee]: Florida Board of State Institutions, 1903.

Ross, John. "Report of the Cherokee Deputation into Florida, Washington City (D. C.), Feby. 17th, 1838." *Chronicles of Oklahoma* 9, no. 4 (December 1931).

Rutledge, Anna Wells. *Artists in the Life of Charleston: Through Colony and State from Restoration to Reconstruction.* 1949. Reprint, Columbia: University of South Carolina Press, 1980.

Salwen, Peter. *Upper West Side Story: A History and Guide.* New York: Abbeville Press, 1989.

Sarkesian, Sam C. *America's Forgotten Wars: The Counterrevolutionary Past and Lessons for the Future.* Westport, Conn.: Greenwood Press, 1984.

Schene, Michael G. "The Georgia Volunteers and Fort Cooper." In *Bureau of Historic Sites and Properties,* Bulletin no. 5. Tallahassee: Tallahassee Division of Archives, History, and Records Management, 1976.

Schlereth, Thomas J. *Artifacts and the American Past.* Nashville: American Association for State and Local History, 1980.

Scott, Edwin J. *Random Recollections of a Long Life, 1806–1876.* Columbia, S.C.: Charles A. Calvo, Jr., 1884.

Sellers, Charles Coleman. *Mr. Peale's Museum: Charles Willson Peale and the First Popular Museum of Natural Science and Art.* New York: W. W. Norton, 1980.

Seminole Saga: The Jesup Report. Fort Myers Beach, Fla.: Island Press, 1973.

Simmons, William H. *Notices of East Florida, with an Account of the Seminole Nation of Indians.* 1822. Reprint, Gainesville: University Presses of Florida, 1973.

"A Sketch of the Indian Tribes known under the Appellation of Muskogees (Seminoles) Etc., by an Officer of the Medical Staff U.S. Army." *Monthly Magazine of Religion and Literature* 1 (January 1840): 137–47.

[Smith, W. W.] *Sketch of the Seminole War and Sketches during a Campaign. By a Lieutenant of the Left Wing.* Charleston, S.C.: Dan J. Dowling, 1836.

Spoehr, Alexander. *The Florida Seminole Camp.* Anthropological Series, vol. 33, no. 3. Chicago: Field Museum of Natural History, 1944.

Sprague, John T. *The Origin, Progress, and Conclusion of the Florida War; to which is appended a record of Officers, Non-Commissioned Officers, Musicians, and Privates of the U.S. Army, Navy, and Marine Corps, who were killed in battle or died of disease. As also the names of Officers Who Were Distinguished by Brevets, and the Names of Others Recommended. Together with the order for collecting the remains of the dead in Florida, and the ceremony of interest at St. Augustine, East Florida, on the fourteenth day of August, 1842.* 1848. Reprint, Gainesville: University Presses of Florida, 1964.

Stern, Robert A. M., Thomas Mellins, and David Fishman. *New York 1880: Architecture and Urbanism in the Gilded Age.* New York: Monacelli Press, 1999.

Stiggins, George. *Creek Indian History: A Historical Narrative of the Genealogy, Traditions, and Downfall of the Ispocoga or Creek Indian Tribe of Indians by One of the Tribe.* Tuscaloosa: University of Alabama Press, 1989.

Stokes, Phelps. *The Iconography of Manhattan Island, 1498–1909.* New York: Robert H. Dodd, 1928.

Storrow, Thomas W. "Osceola, the Seminole War-Chief." *Knickerbocker Magazine* 24 (November 1844): 427–48.

Stovall, Bates M. "Frontier Painter." *Natural History* 63 (November 1954): 408-13.

Sturtevant, William C. "Notes on Modern Seminole Traditions of Osceola." *Florida Historical Quarterly* 33 (January–April 1955): 206-17.

———. "Osceola's Coats?" *Florida Historical Quarterly* 34 (April 1956): 315-28.

———. "A Seminole Medicine Maker." In *In the Company of Man*, edited by Joseph B. Casagrande. New York: Harper and Brothers, 1960.

———. "Seminole Men's Clothing." In *Essays on the Verbal and Visual Arts: Proceedings of the 1966 Annual Spring Meeting of the American Ethnological Society*. Seattle: University of Washington Press, 1967.

———. "Creek into Seminole." In *North American Indians in Historical Perspective*, edited by Eleanor Burke Leacock and Nancy Oestreich Lurie. New York: Random House, 1971.

Swanton, John R. "Early History of the Creek Indians and Their Neighbors." In *Bureau of American Ethnology*, Bulletin 73. Washington, D.C.: U.S. Government Printing Office, 1922.

———. "Social Organization and Social Uses of the Indians of the Creek Confederacy." In *Forty-second Annual Report of the Bureau of American Ethnology*, 23-358. Washington, D.C.: U.S. Government Printing Office, 1928.

———. "The Indians of Southeastern United States." In *Bureau of American Ethnology*, Bulletin 137. Washington, D.C.: U.S. Government Printing Office, 1946.

———. "The Indian Tribes of North America." In *Bureau of American Ethnology*, Bulletin 145. Washington, D.C.: U.S. Government Printing Office, 1952.

Tebbel, John [W.], and Keith Jennison. *The American Indian Wars*. New York: Harper and Brothers, 1960.

Todd, Frederick P. *Soldiers of the American Army, 1775-1954*. 1941. Rev. ed., Chicago: Henry Regnery, 1954.

Truettner, William H. *The Natural Man Observed: A Study of Catlin's Indian Gallery*. Washington, D.C.: Smithsonian Institution Press, 1979.

Trumbull, Henry. *History of the Indian Wars*. Boston: N. C. Barton, 1846.

United States of America. *Passenger Arrivals, 1819-1820*. Washington, D.C.: Gales and Seaton, 1821.

U.S. Bureau of the Census. *U.S. Census of 1860: New York*. Washington, D.C.: U.S. Government Printing Office, 1864.

———. *U.S. Census of 1870: New York*. Washington, D.C.: U.S. Government Printing Office, 1874.

———. *U.S. Census of 1900: Kansas*. Washington, D.C.: U.S. Government Printing Office, 1904.

———. *U.S. Census of 1910: Iowa*. Washington, D.C.: U.S. Government Printing Office, 1914.

U.S. Congress. House. *Trial of Scott and Gaines*. 25th Cong., 2nd Sess., 1838. H. Doc. 78.

———. *Jesup's Conduct of the War*. 25th Cong., 2nd Sess., 12 March 1838. H. Doc. 219.

———. *Indian Prisoners of War.* 25th Cong., 2nd Sess., 1838. H. Doc. 327.

———. Senate. *General Jesup's Report of His Command.* 25th Cong., 2nd Sess., 7 July 1838. S. Doc. 507.

Vail, R. W. G. *Knickerbocker Birthday: A Sesqui-Centennial History of the New York Historical Society.* New York: New York Historical Society, 1954.

Van Arsdol, Ted. *Frontier Soldier: The Letters of Maj. John S. Hatheway, 1833–1853.* Vancouver, Wash.: Vancouver National Historic Reserve Trust, 1999.

Viola, Herman J. *The Indian Legacy of Charles Bird King.* Athens: Ohio University Press, 1976.

Ward, May McNeer. "The Disappearance of the Head of Osceola." *Florida Historical Quarterly* 33 (January–April 1955): 193–201.

Waring, Joseph I. *A History of Medicine in South Carolina, 1825–1900.* Columbia: South Carolina Medical Association, 1967.

Waterbury, Jean Parker. "'. . . Really an Amiable Looking Indian . . . ,' John Rogers Vinton's Portrait of Osceola." *El Escribano* 19 (1982): 29–36.

———. "'Long Neglected, Now Restored': The Ximénez-Fatio House (ca. 1797)." *El Escribano* 22 (1985): 1–29.

Weedon, Hamilton M. "OSCEOLA: Stories of the Seminole War Heard as a Youth." *Montgomery (Ala.) Advertiser,* 17 December 1905.

Weisman, Brent Richards. *Like Beads on a String: A Culture History of the Seminole Indians in Northern Peninsular Florida.* Tuscaloosa: University of Alabama Press, 1989.

[Welch, Andrew.] *A Narrative of the Early Days and Remembrances of Oceola Nikkanochee, Prince of Econchatti, a Young Seminole Indian; Son of Econchatti-Mico, King of the Red Hills, in Florida; with a Brief History of His Nation, and His Renowned Uncle, Oceola, and His Parents, Written by His Guardian.* 1841. Reprint, Gainesville: University Presses of Florida, 1977.

White, Frank F., Jr. "A Journal of Lt. Robert C. Buchanan during the Seminole War: The Battle of Lake Okeechobee." *Florida Historical Quarterly* 29 (October 1950): 132–51.

———. "A Scouting Expedition along Lake Panasofkee." *Florida Historical Quarterly* 31 (January 1953): 282–89.

Wickman, Patricia R. *The Tree That Bends: Discourse, Power, and the Survival of the Maskókî People.* Tuscaloosa: University of Alabama Press, 1999.

Williams, John Lee. *The Territory of Florida; or, Sketches of the Topography, Civil, and Natural History, of the Country, the Climate, and the Indian Tribes, from the First Discovery to the Present Time.* 1837. Reprint, Gainesville: University Presses of Florida, 1962.

Williams, Walter L., ed. *Southeastern Indians since the Removal Era.* Athens: University of Georgia Press, 1979.

Willson, Minnie Moore. *The Seminoles of Florida.* Rev. ed. New York: Moffat, Yard, and Co., 1911.

Wisconsin Historical Society. *Second Annual Report and Collections of the State*

Historical Society of Wisconsin for the Year 1855. Madison: Wisconsin Historical Society, 1856.

Woodhouse, James H. *Autobiography. Compiled between Dec. 3rd, 1896, and Dec. 10th, 1896, principally from memory, but with facts and dates verified by reference to the author's journals and ship logs.* New Haven, Conn.: W. H. Hale, typewriter and mimeographer, 1897.

Woodward, Arthur. "Indian Use of the Silver Gorget." *Indian Notes* (Museum of the American Indian, Heye Foundation) 3, no. 4 (October 1926).

Woodward, Thomas S. *Woodward's Reminiscences of the Creek, or Muscogee Indians, Contained in Letters to Friends in Georgia and Alabama.* 1859. Reprint, Tuscaloosa, Ala.: Weatherford Printing, 1939.

Young, Rogers W. "Fort Marion during the Seminole War." *Florida Historical Quarterly* 13 (April 1935): 193–223.

Zubillaga, Felix, ed. *Monumenta Antiquae Floridae.* Rome: Monumenta Missionum Socieatus Iesu, 1946.

Index

Familial designations in parentheses after an entry identify the person's relationship to Osceola unless otherwise indicated. Page numbers for figures are given in boldface type. Indian names are not inverted (see, for example, Coe hadjo).

"A," rebuttal by, of Mr. Wise, 88–91

Abbot, Henry, collection of Egyptian artifacts, 197

Abéca. *See* Abiákî (Sam Jones)

Abiákî (Sam Jones): antiremoval activist, 22, 24, 65; and Cherokee ambassadors, 26; clan of, 74; at Fort King council, 14; meaning of name, 9–10; nickname acquired by, 13; Osceola's mentor, 9–10, 13, 65, 74, 76; status of, 71; variant spellings of, 10, 307n9

Abraham (black spy), 13–14, 25, 65, 71, 74, 94–95

Abram. *See* Abraham (black spy)

accoutrements, Osceola's, 212–13, 222, 272, 292; alleged, 282–89; spurs, 121, 124, 144, 149, 272, 292. See also *names of specific items*

adornments, personal, Osceola's. *See under* artifacts, Osceola's; Weedon family, Osceola's artifacts in

Albums Unique (Catlin), 59, 133, 303

alcohol: consumption of, 142; as preservative, 182, 184–85, 199

Alibamos Indians, 316n88

Alligator (Creek war leader), 18; on Osceola's wound, 93–94, 136, 308n22

Amathla, Charley. *See* Emathla, Charley

American Anti-Slavery Almanac (Giddings), 58, 133

American Revolutionary War, 38

anatomical specimens, preservation techniques for, 179–85, 199

Anderson, Glenn C., and Osceola's artifacts, 288–89

Ansel ("a negro"), on rumor about Osceola, 20

antiremoval activists, 15–20, 87, 95–101; Abiákî, 22, 24, 65; capture (capitulation) of, 24–25, 95–101, 97–101; escape of, from Fort Marion, 27, 101–6, 137, 259; P. McQueen,

7-8, 11, 48-51, 53; Prophet Francis, 50, 53. *See also* First Battle of the Withlacoochee; Osceola, antiremoval activist; Wars of Removal
apocryphal stories. *See* Osceola, rumors about
Arbuthnot, Alexander (British agent), 53
archaeologists, and Osceola's grave site, 157-62, 164, 178, 270
Army and Navy Chronicle: on knifing of treaty, 94-95; on Osceola's artifacts, 257-58, 262; on Thompson and Osceola, 91
artifacts, Osceola's
    alleged, 282-89
    described, at his death, 147-51, 212, 279
    as gifts from Osceola, 86, 137, 215, 269, 273-74, 277-78
    not found with his body, 153, 158-59, 163
    removed from his body, 90, 150-51, 174-75, 178, 186-87, 196-97
    sold at auction, 277, 340n24
    types of: accoutrements, 272, 292; clothing, 267-71, 291-92, 339nn3, 4; headgear, 271-72, 292; listed, 265-67; personal adornments, 273-78, 278, 292-94; personal possessions, 279, 294; physical remains, 42, 159-61, 279-81, 294
    See also death cast, Osceola's; head, Osceola's; Hook, James Harvey; Osceola, hair; Weedon family, Osceola's artifacts in
artists. *See under* images of Osceola
Asse yahola. *See* Osceola
attire, Osceola's. *See* artifacts, Osceola's; images of Osceola; Osceola, attire of, described
auction, artifacts sold at, 277, 340n24
Audubon, John James, 169-71

ball game, Indian, 15, 22, 96
Barnum, P. T., 183
battles: Black Point, 16; Camp Izard, 84, 96; "spotted lake," 20; Wahoo

Swamp, 19; Welika Pond, 19; Withlacoochee (First), 17-18, 84-85, 87, 93-94, 136
Bearss, Edwin C., 147, 151, 157-58
Beebe, William S., and Osceola's artifacts, 264, 274
belts, Osceola's, 277-78, 278, 293
Bemeau, Jean, Bemo abducted by, 60, 252
Bemo, John Douglas (nephew), 248, 253; family of, 255-56; ministry of, 59-60, 252, 254-55; visit of, to Osceola, 149, 254
Bemo line, and Osceola's descendents, 252-56
Bemrose, John, on: C. Emathla's execution, 91; Graham and Osceola, 83-84, 86; Indian observers, 87; knifing of treaty, 94; Thompson and Osceola, 88, 90
Bernard, Timothy (Hawkins's assistant), 306n3
Big Town Clan, 92, 317n26
Billie, Susie Jim, recollections of, 307nn9, 11
Bird Clan (Osceola's clan), 72-74, 143, 235-37, 273
black cook, at site of Thompson's murder, 79, 93
Black Drink, The (Catlin), 120, 298
Black Drink Singer. *See* Osceola
blacks, 24, 98; Abraham, 13-14, 25, 65, 71, 74, 94-95; at First Battle of the Withlacoochee, 94; Pompey, 150, 177; possibly in Osceola's family, 6, 39, 42, 58, 160-61; resistance fighters, 25, 103; slaves, in Florida, 10-11, 79, 93
Blue Snake, capture of, 24, 97
Bob Cat. *See* Coacoochee (Wildcat)
bones, Osceola's. *See* Osceola, bones
Bowen, A. M., image of Osceola by, 131, 302
Bowlegs, Billy. *See* Bowlegs family
Bowlegs family, 24, 231, 237, 264; wife of Billy (II), 237, 238
British, relations of, with Indians, 8, 10, 53, 314n61
Brown, Harvey, 104-5, 187-88
Brown, Isaac, P. McQueen pursued by, 53-54

Brownell, Charles de Wolf, image of Osceola in book by, 132–33

Bufford, J[ohn] H., and images of Osceola, 123, 222, 300

buildings, in Tallassee, 36

bullet pouch, Osceola's, 276–77, 292

Caballo, Juan (black resistance fighter), 25, 103

cane, small whalebone, Osceola's, 279, 294

capitulation, treaty of (1814) (Treaty of Fort Jackson), 7–8, 51, 53

capture (capitulation) of: Blue Snake, 24, 97; Coacoochee (Wildcat), 24, 97–100; Coe hadjo, 24–25; Micanopy, 28, 96; Philip, 24, 28, 85, 97–101. *See also* Osceola, capture (capitulation)

Carter, William, and Osceola's artifacts, 275

Casey, John C.: and Osceola's artifacts, 90–91, 262, 264, 274; relationship of, with Indians, 264; and Rindisbacher paintings, 262; on Spaniards, 82, 317n26

Catalogue of One Hundred and Fifteen Indian Portraits (McKenney), 125–29

Catlin, George, 107, 112, 130, 177, 240
at Fort Moultrie, 114–15, 126
gift to, from Osceola, 277
images of Osceola by, 59, 116–19, 118, 120, 121–22, 127–28, 130–33, 132, 180–81, 298–99, 302–3
Osceola's artifacts depicted by: accoutrements, 272, 282–83, 285; clothing, 270–71; headgear, 272; personal adornments, 220, 274–78
Osceola's family sketched by, 59, 131–32, 132, 302
during Osceola's illness, 140, 147–48
on Osceola's linguistic ability, 78
relationship of, with Osceola, 28, 86, 142, 143
work of, compared to Curtis, 119
works of, in Smithsonian Institution, 185–86

Catsa Bogah, meaning of name, 36, 73

census: Dawes Rolls, 46, 313n48; Parsons Abbott (1832), 46–47, 248

Charleston, S.C. *See* Fort Moultrie

Che-cho-ter (the Morning Dew), possible wife of Osceola, 58

Checote (Chicola), Sam (H. Homarty's brother-in-law), 45–47, 249

Cherokee Indians, 26, 31, 106, 137, 310n7

chicken thief (at Fort Moultrie), 143

Chicola (Checote), Sam (H. Homarty's brother-in-law), 45–47, 249

chief, Indian. *See* Osceola, leadership qualities; power hierarchy, Indian

children, and clan kinship, 5–6, 47–48, 52, 306n3

Chufi hadjo (mad or drunk rabbit). *See* Powell, William (father)

citizenship standards, Indian, present-day, 6

civil war. *See* Creek War of 1813–1814

clans: Big Town, 92, 317n26; Osceola's, 72–74, 143, 235–37, 273; Panther, 74, 231, 237; role of warriors in, 12, 55; Wind, 73. *See also* kinship system, Indian

Clarke, Ransome, 261

climate, Florida, 9, 102, 206, 258–59

clothing, Osceola's, 267–71, 291–92, 339nn3, 4

Coacoochee (Wildcat), 237; capture of, 24, 97–101; escape of, from prison, 27, 102–6, 137, 259; leadership qualities of, 144, 307n11

Coahajo. *See* Coe hadjo

Coça people, Cherokee term for Maskókî, 31

Coe, Charles, on: Beebe, 264; death cast, 262–63; Osceola's head, 164, 180–81

Coe hadjo: capture of, 24–25, 135; and capture of Osceola, 89, 100–101; and death cast, 150, 177; proemigrationist, 21–22, 68, 89

Cohen, Myer, 18, 58; on anatomical interest in Indian bodies, 181; on Graham and Osceola, 83–86; images of Osceola in book by, 108, 109; on Osceola's linguistic ability, 78

Colin, Achille, bust of Osceola made by, 280
Colin Bust (from death cast), 280
collections
    Abbot's Egyptian artifacts, 197
    Armed Forces Institute of Pathology (Walter Reed), 198
    Bellevue Hospital, 198
    Fisher's, presented to Heye Foundation, 268
    Hook's Indian curiosities, 257–58, 260–64
    images of Osceola in, 122–23; American Museum of Natural History, New York City, 120, 122; Boyd Collection, University of Miami, 130; Charleston Museum, Charleston, S.C., 117, 119; Chrysler Museum, Norfolk, Va., 115; Museum of the American Indian, New York City, 110, 111–12; New York Historical Society, 133; Smithsonian American Art Museum, 118, 122; South Caroliniana Library, University of South Carolina, Columbia, 120–21
    Jarvis's Indian artifacts, 197–98
    NMHM, 184–85, 330n59
    Office of the Chief Medical Examiner (NYC), 198
    Osceola's artifacts, 267–70, 274–76, 278, 278–79; physical remains, 279–81; from Weedon family, 213–14, 216, 217, 218, 219, 220, 221
    U.S. Military Academy (West Point), 262
    See also Mott, Valentine
Cooper, Astly, 183
Cooper, Sarah, suicide of, 245–46
Cooper, Simon, and Osceola's descendents, 240, 242–47
Cooper family, and Osceola's descendents, 240, 242–47, 251
Copinger, Ann (Nancy). See Copinger, Nancy (maternal grandmother)
Copinger, Nancy (maternal grandmother), 38, 42, 52, 73
Copinger, Polly (mother), 32, 38, 59, 73,

236; children of, 44, 59, 61, 72–73, 235, 243, 248; emigration of, 8–9, 46–48, 52–53, 312n40
Copinger (Coppinger) families: described, 39–42, 311n31. See also names of individual relatives
Copinger (maternal grandfather), possible identification of, 39–42, 161
Coppinger families. See Copinger (Coppinger) families
Corson, Edward F., and Osceola's artifacts, 275
Cowácuchî(t). See Coacoochee (Wildcat)
Coweta, Ga., Powell family at, 46–47, 52
Creek Indians. See Maskókî (Creek)
Creek War of 1813–1814, 7–8, 11, 36, 48–51
Creek War of 1836, 36, 46
Cuba, 82; Coppinger family in, 41–42
culture, Indian, changes in, 7–8, 10, 13, 16, 36, 58, 61–62, 69–70, 76, 314n61; kinship system, 48, 56–57, 232–34. See also Maskókî (Creek), traditions
Currier, N[athaniel], lithographic company of, 123–24, 127, 222, 300
Curtis, Robert John: images of Osceola by, 116–17, 117, 119–22, 124, 127, 298–300; Osceola's artifacts depicted by, 272, 274, 277; work of, compared to Catlin, 119

Dawes Commission, 46
Dawes Rolls, 46, 313n48
Day and Haghe, lithographic company of, 130, 301
death cast, Osceola's, 176, 186; copies from, 204, 279–81; displayed, 178, 279; making of, 150, 174–78; in museum, 262–63, 279–81
descendents, Osceola's. See Osceola, descendents
diary entries, Weedon's, 145
    on Indians' reaction to news of transfer, 138–39
    on Osceola: burial, 150–51, 157, 257; last days, 144, 146–49, 161–62; temperament, 115, 139–41

disease, 19–20, 27, 65, 97, 102, 135–37, 140, 208, 226, 258–59; Strobel's study of, 171–72, 334n30. *See also* Osceola, health

"dog people" *(if'athi)*, 73

Douglas, Orson, letter by, about Bemo, 59–60

"drunk or crazy/mad wolf." *See* Yaha hadjo (brother-in-law)

Durant, Benjamin (Betsy's father), 49, 73, 313n50

Durant, Betsy (P. McQueen's wife), 8, 240; emigration of, 52, 247; family of, 37–38, 48–49, 52–54, 56, 73, 247, 313n50; and Osceola's descendents, 247

Durant, John (Betsy's brother), 53–54

Durant, Sandy (Betsy's brother), 53–54

DuVal, William P., 124–25

Econchatti Micco (brother-in-law), 61–64

Econchatti (town), 61–62, 316n88

Ecunhutkee (town), 40, 312n36

El Castillo de San Marcos. *See* Fort Marion

El Escribano, portrait of Osceola reproduced in, 129

Emathla, Charley, 89, 146; execution of, 15–16, 62, 87, 90–92, 144; family of, 92

Emathla *(emathli)*, meaning of name, 46

emigration: of Osceola's family, 8–9, 46–48, 52–54, 247–49, 312n40; reports on Indians' desire for, 20–21, 23. *See also* antiremoval activists; forced emigration; proemigration faction

escape from Fort Marion, 27, 101–6, 137, 259; list of escapees, 103; Osceola's refusal to participate in, 103–6, 137

Euchee Billy. *See* Uchee Billy (John Hicks)

family, Osceola's
blacks as possible members of, 6, 39, 42, 58, 160–61
brother, 72–74
children, 58–59, 103–4, 132, 149, 156, 161

clan of, 72–74, 143, 235–37, 273
Copinger branch, 39–42
emigration of, 8–9, 46–48, 52–54, 247–49, 312n40; forced, 28, 65–66, 153, 208, 231, 247
at Fort Marion, 103–4
at Fort Mellon, 26–27, 58–59, 101, 135, 242
images of, 58–59, 131–32, *132*, 302
McQueen branch, 31–35, 37–39, 313n50
nephews: Bemo, 59–60, 149, 248, 252, **253**, 254–56; Nikkanochee, 61–64, 86, 130, 240, **241**, 248
nieces, 64–65, 84, 86–87
and Osceola's relationship with Graham, 83–86
Powell branch, 42–48, 313n43
sisters, 45–47, 52, 59–65, 73, 104, 248–49, 313n48
Spaniards as possible members of, 39–42, 81, 311n31, 312n35, 312n40
wives, 58–59, 103–4, *132*, 139–40, 148–49, 256, 325n26
See also Osceola, descendents

feathers, Osceola's, 273, 292–93

First Battle of the Withlacoochee, 17–18, 84–85, 87, 93–94, 136

First Seminole War, 36

Fisher, George Jackson, and Osceola's artifacts, 268

Fixico hadjo chupco (Long Jack), 237, **239**

Florida: climate, 9, 102, 206, 258–59; immigration to, by Osceola's family, 8–9, 53, 247, 312n40; Indians' knowledge of, 12–13; and "ownership" of Osceola's grave, 154–55; slaves in, 10–11, 79, 93. *See also* Seminole Indians

forced emigration: official sanction of, 11, 13, 16, 20; of Osceola's family, 28, 65–66, 153, 208, 231, 247; public sentiment for, 10, 18; Trail of Tears, 8, 231. *See also* antiremoval activists; Indian Territory (Oklahoma)

Foreman, Grant, on Bemo, 59–60

Forry, Samuel, 208, 333n27

Fort Gaines, 53

Fort Gibson, 61, 70

Fort Hawkins, 53

Fort Jackson (treaty of capitulation, 1814), 7–8, 51, 53

Fort King, council at (1834), 13–15, 94–95

Fort Marion: artists at, 111–12; described, 102, 105–6; escape from, 27, 101–6, 137, 259; Osceola's refusal to escape from, 103–6, 137; prisoners at, 26–28, 59, 63, 65, 101–6, 137–39, 325n26

Fort Mellon, 22, 96, 112; Osceola's family at, 26–27, 58–59, 101, 135, 242

Fort Mims, slaughter at, 50–51

Fort Moultrie: artists at, 113–19, 121, 126, 143, 146–47; prisoners at, 27–28, 113–14, 141–43, 226. See also grave site, Osceola's

Fort Pierce (abandoned), Weedon's residence at, 209–10

Fort Toulouse. See Fort Jackson (treaty of capitulation, 1814)

Fos'yaholi. See Osceola, Charlie (Fos'yaholi) (brother)

Fourth Seminole War, 234

Fowler, L. N., offer by, to purchase Osceola's head, 188–89

Francis, Josiah (Prophet Francis), anti-removal activist, 50, 53

friendlies (Indians), 242; attacked by whites, 61–62; betrayed by Jackson, 51, 53; P. McQueen pursued by, 53–54. See also proemigration faction

garters, Osceola's, 220, 221, 222, 263–64, 278

Giddings, Joshua, 58, 215; image of Osceola in book by, 133; on Osceola's linguistic ability, 78–79

Goggin, John, 215, 217–18, 263, 269, 280

Gould, James M. (Herald publisher), and image of Osceola, 112–13

Graham, John, 63; gifts to, from Osceola, 86, 269, 273–74; military

career of, 85–86; relationship of, with Osceola, 64–65, 75, 78, 83–86

graphic representations. See images of Osceola

grave site, Osceola's, 151–54, 152; archaeological examination of, 157–62, 164, 178, 270; neonatal infant buried at, 161–62; vandalism of, 155–58

gravestone, Osceola's, 154, 157

Green Corn Ceremony, 23, 74–75

guns, Osceola's, 212, 272; alleged, 282–89

hair, Osceola's. See Osceola, hair

hairbrush, Osceola's, 279, 294

Hall, James (writer), 125–26

Hamerton, R. J., image of Osceola by, 130

Hanson, [I. M.], and authentication of Osceola's head, 188

Harney, William, 137; on Indian emigration, 20–21, 23; and Osceola, 21, 86, 96

Harrison, Joseph, Catlin's works acquired by, 186

Hatheway, John Samuel, 141, 259

Hawkins, Benjamin (Indian agent), 306n3; influence of, on tribes, 7, 50–51, 54; on P. McQueen, 32–33, 38, 43; Tallassee described by, 36–37; on W. Powell, 32, 42–43, 52

head

Osceola's, 195–96, 279, 294; acquired by Mott, 165, 189–93, 209, 225; authenticated, 187–88; investigations concerning whereabouts of, 196–99; missing, 150–51, 159–61, 199; possible exhibition of, 179–84, 187, 199, 211; preservation of, 179–81, 199; role of doctors in removing, 167–68, 172–78, 192, 199; rumors about, 163–68, 187, 196–99, 328n24, 329n37; treatment of, not unique, 179–85, 192, 199

Uchee Billy's, 181–82, 188–89

headgear, Osceola's, 271–72, 292

head lice, 27, 136, 226–28

"he goes ahead, he goes out in front" (Abiákî), 9–10

Hernández, Joseph M.: and Osceola's capture, 25, 82, 85, 97–101, 207; Osceola's image authenticated by, 111; and Weedon, 206

Hicks, John. See Uchee Billy (John Hicks)

Hilis' hadjo. See Prophet Francis

hilíswa haya. See medicine people

Hitchiti (language), 6, 10, 17, 57, 307n9

Homarty, Hepsy (sister), 45–47, 52, 248–49, 313n48

Homarty, meaning of name, 46

Hook, James Harvey
  biographical information, 260–62
  Indian curiosities of, 257–58, 260–64
  and Osceola's artifacts: blue "guard" (garter), 263–64, 278; bust (bas relief), 262–63; dispersed, after Hook's death, 262–64; feathers, 273; obtained by, 90–91, 186–87, 257–58, 260, 262, 271–73

Horne, J. Van, on journey to Indian Territory, 232

Hossa yaholo, sometimes confused with Osceola, 52

Hubbard, Richard William, possibly "young Mr. Hubard," 129, 322n46

Hubbard, William James, possibly "young Mr. Hubard," 129, 322n46

Humphreys, Gad (Indian agent), 70, 142

if'athî ("dog people"), 73

"I give it to you; you give it to me" (Micco), 54–55

images of Osceola
  artists', 132–33, 300–301; A. M. Bowen, 131, 302; at Fort Marion, 111–12; at Fort Moultrie, 113–19, 121, 126, 143, 146–47; Hamerton, 130; Keenan, 108, 109, 119–21, 124, 127, 297, 299; Laning, 115–16; Neagle, 122–23, 300; Pierce, 123–24, 127, 300
  authenticated by Hernández, 111
  in book by: Brownell, 132–33; Cohen, 108, 109; Giddings, 133; Ransom, 123–24; Sprague, 112, 131; Williams, 112–13, 214
  divided into two categories, 107–8
  family, 58–59, 131–32, 132, 302
  McKenney-Hall portrait, 124–28, 130, 268; text accompanying, 128–29
  mentioned in Herald, 112–13
  See also Catlin, George; Curtis, Robert John; death cast, Osceola's; Osceola, attire of, described; Vinton, John Rogers

Indian Removal Act (1830), 11, 13

Indian Territory (Oklahoma), 6, 22–23, 61, 92, 149, 229–34. See also forced emigration; Muscogee (Creek) Nation of Oklahoma

infant, neonatal, buried at Osceola's grave site, 161–62

Inman, Henry (artist), 125–26, 333n28

Inman, John (journalist), 208, 333n28

internecine conflict. See Creek War of 1813–1814

Jackson, Andrew, 7–9, 54; and McKenney, 124–25; as president, 11, 70, 124–25; and treaty of capitulation (1814), 7, 8, 51, 53

Jackson, J. W., and Osceola's artifacts, 212, 284, 286

Jarvis, Nathan S.: collection of Indian artifacts, 197–98; and Osceola's capture, 85, 135

Jenks, William (weapons manufacturer), 288, 341n10

Jesup, Thomas S.: attempts of, to remove Indians, 19–23; peace talks sabotaged by, 26; white flag violated by, 24–25, 96–101, 134–35, 153

Jewett, William, lithographic company of, 132–33, 302–3

Jimmie family, and Osceola's descendents, 237, 240

John Horse (Juan Caballo) (black resistance fighter), 25, 103

Johns, Jane (Welch's patient), 323n51

Jones, Sam. See Abiákî (Sam Jones)

Jumper (Creek war leader), 18, 71; family of, 231, 237, 255

Keen, Mary Blanche Weedon (F. Weedon's great-granddaughter), 165, 213–14, 216, 223
Keenan, William, images of Osceola by, 108, 109, 119–21, 124, 127, 297, 299
"keepers of the light." See medicine people
King, Charles Bird (artist), 124, 126
King Philip. See Philip (Micanopy's brother-in-law)
kinship system, Indian, 235, 323n5; children in, 5–6, 47–48, 52, 306n3. See also under culture, Indian, changes in
knives, Osceola's, 213, 222, 272, 292

languages, 54–55; Hitchiti, 6, 10, 17, 57, 307n9; Maskókî (Creek), 6, 17, 31, 57, 82–83, 310nn7, 8. See also linguistic ability, Osceola's; names
Laning, W. M., images of Osceola by, 115–16
Lawrence, Elizabeth Graham (J. Lawrence's grandmother), 86
Lawrence, John Tharpe (J. Graham's great-nephew), 86, 269
leadership. See Osceola, leadership qualities; power hierarchy, Indian
Lebby, Robert, 96, 140, 208; on C. Emathla's execution, 92; on Osceola and Catlin, 119; on Osceola and Coe hadjo, 100–101; on Osceola's burial, 151, 211, 259; on Osceola's influence, 143; on Osceola's linguistic ability, 77–78
Leeder, Hepsy. See Homarty, Hepsy (sister)
legends, about Osceola. See Osceola, rumors about
leggings, Osceola's, 271, 291
Lendrum, Thomas W., as possible identity of "A," 91
Lewis, Harriet (Bemo's wife), 255
Lewis, John Otto (artist), 124
Lilley, John, work of, with Bemo, 254–55

Lilley, Mary A., work of, with Bemo, 254–55
linguistic ability, Osceola's, 6, 76–83, 140, 312n40
lithographers: Bowen, A. M., 131, 302; Bowen, J. T., 300–301; Currier, 123–24, 127, 222, 300; Day and Haghe, 130, 301; Jewett, 132–33, 302–3; N. Orr and Richardson, 131, 302–3; Waldo, 132–33, 302–3
Long Jack (Fixico hadjo chupco), 237, 239
looking glass, Osceola's, 279

mad or drunk rabbit (Chufi hadjo). See Powell, William (father)
malaria, 19, 65, 97, 136
Marchand, Sehoy,(I) (S. McGillivray's mother), 49, 313n50
Marchand, Sehoy, (II) (S. McGillivray's grandmother), 49, 313n50
Maskókî (Creek) Indians: amalgamation of, 56–57; and British, 8, 10, 53, 314n61; and Cherokee, 26, 31, 106, 137, 310n7; language, 6, 17, 31, 57, 82–83, 310nn7, 8; "mother" towns of, 9; origin of names, 31, 309n4; traditions, 54–55, 154, 158–59, 173–78, 211; use of names, 306n2; warfare, style of, 12, 16–17, 144. See also culture, Indian, changes in; kinship system, Indian; Muscogee (Creek) Nation of Oklahoma; Wars of Removal
matrilineal society. See kinship system, Indian
McGillivray, Alexander (Betsy Durant's maternal uncle), 49, 73
McGillivray, Lachlan (S. McGillivray's father), 49, 313n50
McGillivray, Sophia (Betsy Durant's mother), 49, 52, 56, 73, 313n50
McIntosh, John, 249–50
McIntosh, William, 250; fight between, and Indians, 53–54
McKenney, Thomas Loraine, 37; and Indian portraits, 124–29
McKenney-Hall portrait. See under images of Osceola

McPherson, Malcolm (S. Marchand [II]'s husband), 313n50

McQueen, Ann (Nancy). *See* Copinger, Nancy (maternal grandmother)

McQueen, Betsy. *See* Durant, Betsy (P. McQueen's wife)

McQueen, Bob (James's son), 37–38

McQueen, Fullunny (James's son), 37–39

McQueen, James (maternal great-grandfather), 6; background, 31–35; death of, 7, 38; family, 37–39, 48; on Hawkins, 32–33

McQueen, Muscogee (Betsy Durant's daughter), 48

McQueen, Peter (clan grandfather), 73, 240, 313n50; antiremoval activist, 7–8, 11, 48–51, 53; children of, 37, 48, 247; death of, 8, 55–56, 240; described, 37; emigration of, 8, 52–54; and Osceola's descendents, 247; white woman kidnapped by, 53–54

McQueen, Sophia (Betsy Durant's daughter), 48, 56, 247

McQueen, Willy (Peter's nephew), 37–38, 48, 247, 313n50

McQueen line, and Osceola's descendents, 247

measles, 27, 102, 137, 140, 259

medicine, Indian. *See* medicine people

medicine people, 11, 75; and escape from Fort Marion, 105–6; during Osceola's last days, 140, 146–49, 173–78; Susie Jim Billie, 307n9; tobacco used by, 142, 216. *See also* Abiákî (Sam Jones)

mementos, Morrison's. *See* Hook, James Harvey, and Osceola's artifacts

Menawa (Big Warrior), 37, 48

Miami, Lucy, and Jimmie family, 240

Micanopy, 138, 237, 271; capture of, 28, 96; family of, 132, 302; at Fort King council, 13, 94–95; image of, 132, 132, 302; proemigrationist, 13, 22–23, 25, 65, 96, 230; status of, 68, 71, 143

Micanopy (town), 18–19

Miccosukee (language). *See* Hitchiti (language)

Micco (title), 54–55

Mik-e-no-pa. *See* Micanopy

Mikísuúkî (language). *See* Hitchiti (language)

mikkó anópî(t). *See* Micanopy

moccasins, Osceola's, 271, 291–92

Moniac, William, 35

Morrison, Pitcairn, 135, 137, 207, 229–30; illness of, 141, 144, 146–47, 175, 259; military career, 258–59; Osceola's artifacts removed on orders of, 90, 150–51, 174–75, 178, 186–87, 257; prisoners escorted by, to South Carolina, 27, 138, 259. *See also* Hook, James Harvey, and Osceola's artifacts

Mott, Alexander Brown (V. Mott's son), 195–96, 198

Mott, Valentine, **191**
background, 168, 190, 193, 208
family of, 195–96
homes of, 193–95, **194**
Memorial Library, 195–96
Museum, 195
and Osceola's head: acquisition of, 165, 189–93, 209, 225; deposited in collection, 190–95; not mentioned in will, 195–96
specimen collection, 189–90, 192–93, 195; disposition of, 195–96

Motte, Jacob Rhett, 71; in defense of Jesup, 134–35; on Osceola, 130, 137; and Osceola's artifacts, 267–68, 278

Muscogee (Creek) Nation of Oklahoma: names from, on Dawes Rolls, 46, 313n48; present-day, 6, 22–23, 233. *See also* Maskókî (Creek)

museums. *See* collections

N. Orr and Richardson, lithographic company of, 131, 302–3

names, 17, 31, 36, 47, 306n1, 2, 309n4
in census (1832), 46–47, 248
on Dawes Rolls, 46, 313n48
"dog people," 73
"free people," 57
"keepers of the light" (medicine people), 11
meaning of: Abiákî, 9–10; Catsa

Bogah, 36, 73; Emathla (emathlî), 46; Fullunny, 38–39; Homarty, 46; Micco, 54–55; nicknames, 13, 47–48, 51; Tallassee, 310n8; tastenákî thlocco, 10, 76
Osceola: ceremonial names of, 9, 74–76; as surname, 72, 234
See also languages
Natchez (Netches) Indians, 35, 38
Nathleocee (niece), 64–65, 84, 86
National Intelligencer, on Thompson and Osceola, 88–91
Native revivalist movement. See antiremoval activists
natural sciences, interest in, and Indian specimens, 182–87
Neagle, John, image of Osceola by, 122–23, 300
Neamathla (hinéja emathlî, respected warrior), 56, 61
Netches (Natchez) Indians, 35, 38
New York City, and Osceola's head, 196–99
Nikkanochee (nephew), 61–64, 86, 130, 240, 241, 248

O'Brien family, possible connection of, to Osceola, 39
Oceola Nikkanochee. See Nikkanochee (nephew)
Oceola (Vinton), 110, 297
Oconee and Ogeechee Creeks, 31
Oklahoma. See Indian Territory (Oklahoma)
Old Jumper. See Jumper (Creek war leader)
Old Mad Jackson. See Jackson, Andrew
Old Nancy. See Osceola, Nancy (Charlie's wife)
Old Tommie Tiger, family of, and Osceola's descendents, 236–37
Omathily, Charly. See Emathla, Charley
Open Door (Tensquátowah) (Tecumseh's brother), 7, 49–51
Orr, N., and Richardson, lithographic company of, 131, 302–3
Osceola
Abiákî's apprentice, 9–10, 13, 65, 74, 76

antiremoval activist, 11, 13–16, 21–23, 91–92, 95–101, 203, 230
attire of, described, 114–17, 119, 121, 123, 127, 129–31, 218, 285; in poem, 142
birth, 311n23
birthplace, 5, 36–37, 73
bones: allegedly stolen, 156–58; casts made from, 280–81, 294; controversy over return to Florida, 154–56; examined, 42, 159–61
burial, 149–51, 157–59, 211, 257, 259
C. Emathla executed by, 16, 87, 90–92, 144
capture (capitulation), 14–15, 24–26, 54, 82, 85, 88–90, 95–101, 137, 207
ceremonial names of, 9, 74–76
clan of, 72–74, 143, 235–37, 273
death, 121, 144, 146–49, 161–62, 259, 279; interval between, and burial, 172–79
descendents, 234; Bemo line, 252–56; Charlie Osceola's family, 234–36; Cooper family, 240, 242–47; Jimmie family, 237, 240; McQueen line, 247; Nikkanochee, 240, 241; Old Tommie Tiger's family, 236–37; Powell line, 247–52
early years (as Billy Powell), 5–9, 52, 56–58
at First Battle of the Withlacoochee, 17–18, 87, 93–94
at Fort King council, 13–15, 94–95
genetic makeup of, 6, 42, 160–61, 226
hair, 177, 212, 214–15, 279, 294; analysis of, 223–28; fabric covering of, 225, 227, 335n6; head lice egg cases in, 136, 226–28
and Harney, 21, 86, 96
health, 19–20, 25, 27, 65, 113–15, 135–37, 140, 142–44, 146–49, 172, 226
imprisonment, 26–28, 60, 63, 101–6, 136–49, 226
last days, 140, 144, 146–49, 161–62, 173–78
last wishes, 146–49, 153–54, 163

leadership qualities, 11–12, 16–20, 38, 67–72, 106, 142–43, 307n11

linguistic ability, 6, 76–83, 140, 312n40

physical characteristics, 12, 113–15, 220

relationship of, with: Catlin, 28, 86, 142, 143; Graham, 64–65, 75, 78, 83–86

rumors about, 18–20, 308n22, 311n23, 31; knifing of treaty, 14, 94–95

as surname, 72, 234

temperament, 28–29, 29, 96, 115, 139–43, 207, 216, 333n27

and Thompson: altercation between, 14–15, 87–91; Osceola's capture, 14–15, 88–90; Thompson killed by Osceola, 16–17, 67, 69, 87, 90, 92–93, 146, 166–67

wounded in battle, 18, 93–94, 136, 160, 308n22

See also artifacts, Osceola's; death cast, Osceola's; family, Osceola's; grave site, Osceola's; head, Osceola's; images of Osceola

Osceola, Charlie (Fos'yaholi) (brother), 72–74; and Osceola's descendents, 234–36

Osceola, Jimmie O'Toole, 152

Osceola, Joe Dan, and controversy over Osceola's bones, 156

Osceola, Mike, and controversy over Osceola's bones, 154–55

Osceola, Nancy (Charlie's wife), 72–73; and Osceola's descendents, 234–36

Osceola; or, Fact and Fiction (Ransom), 123–24

Osceola, the Black Drink (Catlin), 118, 298

Osceola (Curtis), 117, 298

Panther Clan, 74, 231, 237

Peale, Charles Willson (artist), 182–84

Pediculus humanus capitis (head louse), 27, 136, 226–28

pencil, mechanical, Osceola's, 275, 279, 294

Peyton, R. H., 24; and authentication of

Osceola's head, 187–88; on Osceola's antiremoval stance, 91–92

Phagan, John (Indian agent), 70, 128

Philip (Micanopy's brother-in-law), 65, 74, 237, 309n44; capture of, 24, 28, 85, 97–101

phrenology, 181–82, 199, 240

physical remains, Osceola's. *See* death cast, Osceola's; head, Osceola's; Osceola, bones; Osceola, hair

Pickell, John, on Osceola's family, 101

Pierce, F., image of Osceola by, 123–24, 127, 300

pipe, Osceola's, 142, 174, 212, 215–17, 216, 279, 294, 335n4

poem, about Osceola, 142

Poinsett, passengers onboard, 27–28

Pompey (black interpreter), and death cast, 150, 177

Pond, Samuel, and Osceola's artifacts, 284, 286

Pope, Edith (Tugby), and story about Osceola's head, 164–65

possessions, personal, Osceola's. *See* artifacts, Osceola's; Weedon family, Osceola's artifacts in

Potter, Woodburne, 70–71, 75–77, 79

"Pound," William. *See* Powell, William (father)

powder horn, 212, 272, 292; alleged, 282–86

Powell, Alfreta, 243, 246, 336n15

Powell, Billy. *See* Osceola

Powell, Hepsy. *See* Homarty, Hepsy (sister)

Powell, John (Lucy's adopted son), 250–52

Powell, Lucy (William's daughter), 47, 248–51

Powell, Martha (William's daughter), 47, 248–49

Powell, Polly Copinger. *See* Copinger, Polly (mother)

Powell, Priscilla (Silla) (S. Checote's wife), 45–47, 248–49

Powell, William (father): in 1832 census, 46–47, 248; emigration of, 8, 46–48, 52–53, 247–49, 312n40; family of, 5–6, 32, 42–48, 52, 59, 247–50; mis-

identified as "Pound," 32, 43; nick-
named Chufî hadjo (mad or drunk rabbit), 47–48
Powell line, and Osceola's descendents,
247–52
Powell's people. *See* family, Osceola's
Powell's town (Osceola's secret camp),
18–19, 21, 63
power hierarchy, Indian, 49, 54–55, 67–
72, 93. *See also* Osceola, leadership
qualities
preservation techniques, for anatomical
specimens, 179–85, 199
Primus ("the negro"), 20, 96, 136
Prince, Henry, 20, 94, 96, 272, 308n22
proemigration faction: C. Emathla, 16,
89; Coe hadjo, 21–22, 68, 89; J. Ross
(Cherokee), 26; Micanopy, 13, 22–23,
25, 65, 96, 230. *See also* friendlies
(Indians)
Prophet Francis, antiremoval activist,
50, 53
prophets. *See* medicine people

Quattlebaum, Paul, and Osceola's artifacts, 270–71
quinsy (tonsillitis with abscess), cause of
Osceola's death, 144, 146–49

Ransom, James Birchett: images
of Osceola in book by, 123–24;
Osceola's artifacts described by,
271–72, 277; poem by, 142
Recli, Carlo, and Osceola's death cast,
262–63
"Red Sticks," 7, 11, 51
Reed, Erik, 42, 159–60
Reid, Robert Raymond, 63, 84, 86
removal of Indians. *See* antiremoval activ-
ists; forced emigration; Wars of Re-
moval
Rindisbacher, Peter (artist), 262
River in the Wind (Pope), story of
Osceola's head in, 165
Roberts, J. Milnor, and Osceola's arti-
facts, 276–77
Rogers, Erastus, killed in Indian raid, 92
Ross, John (Cherokee), 26

rumors, about Osceola. *See* head,
Osceola's, rumors about; Osceola,
rumors about

Sánchez, Vanancio, on Osceola's linguistic ability, 82
sashes, Osceola's, 276–78, 294
scarves, Osceola's, 273, 292
Second Seminole War, 12, 17, 36, 52, 285
Seminolee, Wife and Child of the Chief
(Catlin), 132, 302
Seminole Indians, 335n4; amalgamation of, 56–57; and controversy over
Osceola's bones, 154–56; present-day,
6, 22–23, 233–34; structures (buildings) of, 36. *See also* culture, Indian,
changes in; Wars of Removal
Sharp Knife. *See* Jackson, Andrew
Shawanóe (Shawnee) Indians, 7, 31
shirts, Osceola's. *See* clothing, Osceola's
Shiver, Otis W., and alleged theft of
Osceola's bones, 156
silver items, Osceola's, 212, 217, 217–18,
273–75, 293
slaves, in Florida, 10–11, 79, 93
Smith, W. W., on: anatomical interest in
Indian bodies, 181; Osceola's weapons, 282, 285; Osceola's wound,
93–94
South Carolina, and "ownership" of
Osceola's grave, 154–55
Souvenir of the North American Indians
(Catlin), 131–32, 302
Spaniards: Indian wives of, 82, 317n26;
as possible members of Osceola's
family, 39–42, 81, 311n31, 312n35,
312n40
spies, U.S., 13–14, 25, 65, 98
Sprague, John T.: on breakup Powell's
family, 52; on C. Emathla's execution, 91; on Fort King council, 13–
14, 95; image of Osceola in book
by, 112, 131; on Osceola's wife,
58; on Osceola's wound, 93, 136,
308n22
spurs, Osceola's, 121, 124, 144, 149,
272, 292
St. Augustine. *See* Fort Marion

St. Augustine Florida Herald, and image of Osceola, 112–13

St. Augustine Historical Society, Vinton painting of Osceola reproduced by, 129

Stewart, Robert W. (S. McQueen's husband), 48, 247

Stewart, T. Dale, 42, 159–61

Stipe, Josephine Weedon (F. Weedon's great-granddaughter), and Osceola's artifacts, 213, 222, 288–89

Storrow, Thomas W., on Osceola: with artists, 114–15; death of, 149; decapitation of, 164; and Graham, 84; knifing of treaty by, 95; spurs of, 121, 144, 272, 292; temperament of, 29, 141–43, 216

Strobel, Benjamin Beard (B. B.): background, 168–72, 334n30; consulting physician at Fort Moultrie, 144, 147–49; and Osceola's death cast, 150, 174–78; and Osceola's head, 167–68, 172–78, 199; on Osceola's linguistic ability, 78

structures (buildings), in Tallassee, 36

Stuart, (Mrs.), kidnapped by Indians, 53–54

Sturtevant, William, 72–74, 85, 234–36, 269

Sully, Robert Matthew (artist), 126–27

Tallassee (people): mixed blood of, 6, 38–39; P. McQueen's influence with, 34–35, 38

Tallassee (town): birthplace of Osceola, 5, 36–37; early history of, 34–36

Tallassee (word), meaning of, 310n8

Tarvin, Marion Elisha (S. Marchand [II]'s descendent), 313n50

tastenákî thlocco (title), 10, 76

Tchlokî(t) (Maskókî term for Cherokees), 31, 310n7

Tecumseh, 7, 11, 49–51

Tensquátowah (the Open Door) (Tecumseh's brother), 7, 49–51

theater performance, Osceola's attendance at, 142

Third Seminole War, 36, 231

Thompson, Wiley (Indian agent), 58, 128, 272; altercation between, and Osceola, 14–15, 87–91; at Fort King council, 13–15; killed by Osceola, 16–17, 67, 69, 87, 90, 92–93, 146, 166–67; negotiations with Indians, 70–71; no familial link to Weedons, 201–2; Osceola's capture by, 14–15, 88–90

tobacco, 142, 215–16

tomahawk, Osceola's, 272, 292

Tompkins, Christopher, and portrait of Osceola, 129

tonsillitis with abscess (quinsy), cause of Osceola's death, 144, 146–49

traders, description of, 37

Trail of Tears, 8; Seminole, 231

trappings, Osceola's, 270–71, 291

treachery, Jesup's. *See* white flag, violation of

treaties, effect of, on Indians. *See* culture, Indian, changes in

treaty, knifing of, by Osceola, 14, 94–95

Treaty of: Fort Gibson, 61, 70; Fort Jackson (treaty of capitulation, 1814), 7–8, 51, 53; Ghent (Article Nine), 8, 314n61; Moultrie Creek, 10, 61–62, 70; Payne's Landing, 13, 16, 60–61; Utrecht (1713), 34

treaty of capitulation (1814) (Treaty of Fort Jackson), 7–8, 51, 53

truce, violation of. *See* white flag, violation of

Tuggle, William Orrie, on Powell family, 45–47, 249–51

turban, Osceola's, 271–72, 292

Uchee Billy (John Hicks), 137–39; head of, 181–82, 188–89

U.S. Commission to the Five Civilized Tribes (Dawes Commission), 46

Uscin-Yahola. *See* Osceola

Ussa yaholo. *See* Osceola

vandalism, of Osceola's grave site, 155–58

"Viator," on knifing of treaty, 94–95

Vinton, John Rogers, 341n8; artifacts of Osceola depicted by, 222, 271, 274; images of Osceola by, 108, 110, 111–13, 123, 129–31, 133, 212, 214, 297, 301; Osceola's status described by, 68

Waldo, Samuel Lovett, lithographic company of, 132–33, 302–3
war council, plans of (1835), 15–16
Ward, May McNeer (F. Weedon's granddaughter), on Osceola's head, 196
warfare, Creek style, 12, 16–17, 144
War of 1812, 8, 36, 314n61
Warren, John, and Nikkanochee, 62
warriors, role of, in clan, 12, 55
Wars of Removal, 9, 12, 36; Creek War of 1813–1814, 7–8, 11, 36, 48–51; Creek War of 1836, 36, 46; First Seminole War, 36; Second Seminole War, 12, 17, 36, 52, 285; Third Seminole War, 36, 231. See also antiremoval activists; forced emigration; Indian Territory (Oklahoma)
"Wartula," on Thompson and Osceola, 91
Weatherford, William (Red Eagle), 313n50
Webster, Lucien B., gift to, from Osceola, 277–78
Weedon, Frederick, 27, 86, 204, 259, 284, 286, 329n30, 333n27
    background, 200–201
    comments of, on: Osceola's antiremoval stance, 92; Osceola's artifacts, 272; Osceola's linguistic ability, 79; Thompson's death, 93
    family, 201–2, 208–10, 332n4, 334nn30, 37
    homes of, 179–80, 202–3, 209–10, 329n30, 332n12, 333n29
    military affiliation, 203, 206–7
    and Osceola's head: authentication of, 187–88; preservation of, 179–81, 199; removal of, 167–68, 172–78, 199; rumors about, 165–68, 187, 328n24, 329n37

    and Uchee Billy's head, 181–82, 188–89
    writing Osceola's history planned by, 208
    See also death cast, Osceola's; diary entries, Weedon's; Weedon family, Osceola's artifacts in
Weedon, Hamilton M. (F. Weedon's son), 166–67; and Osceola's artifacts, 212–14
Weedon, Mary Wells Thompson (F. Weedon's wife), 201–3, 205, 210
Weedon, William Henry Harrison (F. Weedon's son), and Osceola's artifacts, 213
Weedon family, Osceola's artifacts in, 288–89
    accoutrements, 212; sheath knife, 213, 222, 272
    listed, 211–12
    pencil sketch, 212, 214–15
    personal adornments: earrings, 212–13, 218, 219; garter, 220, 221, 222, 263–64, 278; silver concho (bangle), 212, 217, 217–18, 273–74, 293
    provenance, 213–14
    See also death cast, Osceola's; head, Osceola's; Osceola, hair; pipe, Osceola's
Welch, James Andrew, 323n51; on Graham and Osceola, 64–65, 83–84; on knifing of treaty, 95; on Nikkanochee, 61–64, 130, 240; on Osceola's head, 180, 189
West Point, Ga., Powell family at, 45–46
white flag, violation of, 24–25, 96–101, 134–35, 153
Whitehurst, Daniel Winchester (F. Weedon's son-in-law), 164, 167, 171; family, 206–10; and Osceola's head, 189–93, 209, 212, 225
Whitehurst, Henrietta Weedon (F. Weedon's daughter), 177, 209–10, 212–14, 225, 227, 334n37
Wildcat. See Coacoochee (Wildcat)

Williams, John Lee, image of Osceola in book by, 112–13, 214

Wind Clan, 73

Wise, (Mr.), "A's" rebuttal of, 88–91

Withlacoochee, First Battle of the, 17–18, 84–85, 87, 93–94, 136

Woodward, Thomas (Tom) Simpson: on McQueen family, 31–35, 48, 51, 247; on Osceola's status, 67–69; P. McQueen pursued by, 53–54; on Seminole amalgamation, 57; Tallassee described by, 36

Yaha hadjo (brother-in-law), 60–61, 63, 73, 181, 248

Yargee (Menawa's son), wives of, 37, 48, 247

yellow fever, 171, 208, 334n30

"young Mr. Hubard," possible identity of, 129, 322n46